The Making of Modern Baseball

To my former baseball teammates and field managers

THE MAKING OF MODERN Baseball

Over 100 Years of Change That Formed America's Favorite Pastime

FRANK P. JOZSA, JR.

MEYER & MEYER SPORT

British Library Cataloguing in Publication Data

A catalogue record for this book is available from the British Library

The Making of Modern Baseball

Maidenhead: Meyer & Meyer Sport (UK) Ltd., 2020

ISBN: 978-1-78255-189-8

Aachen, Auckland, Beirut, Cairo, Cape Town, Dubai, Hägendorf, Hong Kong, Indianapolis, Maidenhead, Manila, New Delhi, Singapore, Sydney, Tehran, Vienna

Member of the World Sports Publishers' Association (WSPA), www.w-s-p-a.org

Printed by: C-M Books, Ann Arbor, MI, USA

ISBN: 978-1-78255-189-8

Email: info@m-m-sports.com

www.thesportspublisher.com

CONTENTS

FOREWORD

A former classmate and teammate of mine during the 1950s in Terre Haute, Indiana, Pfeiffer University professor emeritus of economics and business administration Frank P. Jozsa Jr. is the author of several books about the history, operation, and success of teams in the American League and National League of Major League Baseball. In his effort to write *The Making of Modern Baseball*, he thoroughly researched and then identified and analyzed the essential elements–activities, events, organizations, people, policies, and other matters–that undoubtedly changed the sport of professional baseball between 1876 and 2019.

Jozsa's book, for example, includes chapters that discuss the significance and impact of various baseball stats, the Major League Baseball Players Association, team relocations, league expansions, franchise business, and differences in small, midsized, and large sports markets. In chapter 10, for example, he highlights and explains the surgery that extended my and other baseball pitchers' careers and improved their performances for years while playing on teams in the big leagues.

Based on its contents and Jozsa's knowledge and research of the game, I recommend *The Making of Modern Baseball* to owners and executives of major league clubs, researchers of baseball and especially professional baseball, college and university professors who teach sports business, history, management and marketing, and also avid fans of such teams as the Chicago White Sox, Cleveland Indians, and New York Yankees in the American League, and Los Angeles Dodgers, San Francisco Giants, and St. Louis Cardinals in the National League. In my opinion, this is one of Jozsa's most important books and a major contribution to the literature.

–Tommy John Jr.
Professional Major League Baseball Pitcher, 1963-1974/1976-1989
Four-time MLB All-Star.

ACKNOWLEDGMENTS

While researching, writing, and reviewing the manuscript for this book during 2017, 2018, and early 2019, a few individuals provided assistance, concepts, and information for it. Most important to my project, Pfeiffer University's library director and assistant professor of library science Lara Little found numerous readings about the history of Major League Baseball, its teams, and different things that transformed the sport, which she then promptly forwarded to me.

I appreciate Lara's professionalism and her commitment to spend time and obtain articles, reports, and studies for me regarding topics in the book. Certainly, Lara is a valuable employee and a superstar librarian for the university's administration, faculty, and staff, and especially for the school's undergraduate and graduate students.

Individuals who contributed to my research included, in no specific order, Winthrop University Professor of Economics and Director of the Center for Economics Education, Dr. Gary Stone; University of Michigan Professor of Sport Management, Dr. Rodney D. Fort; Loras College Professor Emeritus of Economics, Laddie Sula; and *Forbes* sportswriter Kurt Badenhausen.

University of Wisconsin–Oshkosh Professor of Economics Lee Van Scyoc mailed me his article on competitive balance to research such questions as: what is competitive balance, why is it important, how do you measure it, what have the major leagues done to bring about competitive balance, and have they been successful? Special thanks to Lee, Gary, Rodney, Laddie, and Kurt for their insightful remarks with respect to topics in *The Making of Modern Baseball.*

My fiancée and best friend Maureen Fogle allowed me to use her computer to organize and write a manuscript for this book. She understood how important it was for me to complete this project and then submit a professional copy of it to my publisher, Meyer & Meyer Sport, on or before the due date of my contract. Once again, thanks to Maureen for her cooperation, patience, and support, particularly since my retirement as an economics/business administration/finance/statistics professor from Pfeiffer University in 2007.

ABBREVIATIONS

AA	American Association
ABA	American Basketball Association
ABC	American Broadcasting Corporation
ABG	American Baseball Guild
AFL	American Federation of Labor
AL	American League
ALCS	American League Championship Series
ALDS	American League Division Series
AOL	America Online
A's	Athletics
BA	Batting average
BABIP	Batting average on balls in play
BALCO	Bay Area Laboratory Co-Operative
BPBBP	Brotherhood of Professional Base Ball Players
BIS	Baseball info solutions
BB/K	Walk to strikeout rate
BB%	Walk rate
BB/9	Walks per nine innings
BHOF	Baseball Hall of Fame
BJ	Blue Jays
BWAA	Baseball Writers Association of America
CBA	Collective bargaining agreement
CBS	Columbia Broadcasting System
CD	Central Division
CDT	Comprehensive drug testing
CEO	Chief executive officer
CFL	Canadian Football League
CL	Continental League
CT	Connecticut
DC	District of Columbia
dERA	Defense-Independent ERA

DH	Designated hitter
DRS	Defensive runs saved
EBITDA	Earnings before interest, taxes, depreciation, and amortization
ED	East Division
ERA	Earned run average
ESPN	Entertainment Sports Programming Network
FB%	Fly ball percentage
FIP	Fielding independent pitching
FL	Federal League
FPBPA	Fraternity of Professional Baseball Players of America
FSR	Scouting report
GB%	Ground ball percentage
GG	Gold Glove
GTA	Greater Toronto Area
HD	High definition
HGH	Human growth hormone
HHI	Herfindahl-Hirschman Index
IFFB%	Infield fly ball percentage
IPA	Independent program administrator
ISO	Isolated power
ISD	Idealized standard deviation
JSC	Joint study committee
K%	Strikeout rate
K/9	Strikeouts per nine innings
KU	Kansas University
LA	Los Angeles
LAAA	Los Angeles Angels of Anaheim
LCS	League Championship Series
LD%	Line drive percentage
LI	Leverage index
LOB%	Left on base percentage
MA	Massachusetts
MD	Maryland
MLB	Major League Baseball
MLBPA	Major League Baseball Players Association
MLS	Major League Soccer

MO	Missouri
MOY	Manager of the Year
MRP	Marginal revenue product
MVP	Most Valuable Player
MXL	Mexican League
NA	Not applicable
NB	Nebraska
NBA	National Basketball Association
NBC	National Broadcasting Corporation
NC	North Carolina
NFL	National Football League
NHL	National Hockey League
NJ	New Jersey
NL	National League
NLCS	National League Championship Series
NLDS	National League Division Series
NLRA	National labor relations act
NLRB	National labor relations board
NNL	Negro National League
NPR	National Public Radio
NY	New York
OBP	On-base percentage
OOPS	On-base plus slugging
OPS	On-base plus slugging percentage
PA	Pennsylvania
PAs	Plate appearances
%	Percent
PCL	Pacific Coast League
PCTCH	Percentage change
PECOTA	Player empirical comparison and optimization test algorithm
PED	Performance enhancing drug
PPA	Players' Protective Association
Pub	Public
RBI	Runs batted in
RC	Runs created
RFK	Robert F. Kennedy

ROY	Rookie of the Year
RR	Rolaids Relief
SABR	Society for American Baseball Research
SE	Southeast
SLG	Slugging percentage
SLG-BA	Slugging percentage minus batting average
SMSA	Standard Metropolitan Statistical Area
SS	Silver Slugger
TBN	The Baseball Network
THG	Tetrahydrogestrinone
TSN	Turner Sports Network
TZ	Total zone
TZL	Total zone with location data
UBR	Ultimate base running
UCL	Ulnar collateral ligament reconstruction
US	United States
WAR	Wins above replacement
WD	West Division
WHIP	Walks plus hits per innings pitched
Win%	Winning percentage
WL	Western League
wOBA	Weighted on-base average
WPA	Win probability added
wRAA	Weighted runs above average
wRC	Weighted runs created
wRC+	Weighted runs created plus
WWW	World Wide Web
xFIP	Expected fielding independent pitching

CHAPTER 1

Introduction

Once the American League and National League joined together and merged to officially form Major League Baseball in 1901, the sport gradually changed over the next 118 years because of different—but also new and complex—business, cultural, financial, and social reasons. Based, in part, on the experience, participation, and skill of big-league coaches, managers, players, and their teams, the two leagues and their regular seasons and postseasons continued to operate each year though they occasionally struggled due to domestic and international economic depressions and recessions, military conflicts, political problems, and other challenges. Nevertheless, baseball was America's most popular and perhaps its richest professional sport for most of the twentieth and early twenty-first centuries.

PURPOSE

To appreciate and better understand the sport and learn facts and gain more knowledge about the development, progress, and success of Major League Baseball and when, how, and why it changed during this 118-year period, this book reveals how such things as circumstances, data, dates, events, institutions, teams, champions, other historical internal and external matters, and different problems of the sport really transformed it. A few of these things, for example, have been the recruitment, entry, and performance of ballplayers from foreign countries, the extent to which competitive balance or parity exists among teams within and between the American and National Leagues, and the expansion of new franchises located in cities within metropolitan areas of the United States and two provinces of Canada.

The book's audience includes baseball fans, sports scholars, researchers, American and National league officials, those in the minor leagues, and big-league team owners, executives, managers, and players. Other audiences are members of the Society for American Baseball Research and college and university faculty who currently teach sports business, economics, history, and management to undergraduate and graduate students. The book is also a valuable reference text in these academic disciplines and also as a volume in public libraries. Consequently, it is appropriate and useful for anyone who reads articles, reports, and studies in such publications as *Baseball America*, *Baseball Digest*, *ESPN the Magazine*, *Journal of Sports Economics*, *Journal of Sport Management*, *Sport*, *Sporting News*, *Sports Illustrated*, and *Sports Weekly*.

Some key aspects of *The Making of Modern Baseball* for readers are, first, that it identifies the primary things that transformed and improved (or not) this sport; second, that it appeals to several types of audiences; third, that its author is aware of and very knowledgeable about baseball and historical growth of the sports industry; and fourth, that the author has written six books on various topics in professional baseball, including *Baseball, Inc.: The National Pastime As Big Business* (2006), *Baseball in Crisis: Spiraling Costs, Bad Behavior, Uncertain Future* (2008), and *Major League Baseball Expansions and Team Relocations: A History, 1876–2008* (2010).[1]

LITERATURE REVIEW

Originally published as a first edition in 1950 and then reprinted and redistributed in 2014, *100 Years of Baseball: The Intimate and Dramatic Story of Modern Baseball* looks into the past at stories that made the headlines. Through the years as baseball

1 *Frank P. Jozsa Jr., Baseball, Inc.: The National Pastime As Big Business (Jefferson, NC: McFarland, 2006); Baseball in Crisis: Spiraling Costs, Bad Behavior, Uncertain Future (Jefferson, NC: McFarland, 2008); Major League Baseball Expansions and Team Relocations: A History, 1876–2008 (Jefferson, NC: McFarland, 2010).*

grew more popular, Lee Allen and coauthor Andy Gondle trace the development of such things as the New York Knickerbockers; Jackie Robinson; the dark days of 1919; the shenanigans of Leo Durocher and Lee MacPhail; and the New York Yankees' World Series monopoly.

The story of America's pastime is rooted in the country's life. Furthermore, the most commonly told stories of baseball are not a mystery. For a full-fledged history of professional baseball with all its crises, climaxes, and heroes, *100 Years of Baseball* is a book that excites readers particularly because of its stories and their focus on incidents and people involved in the sport.[2]

G. Scott Thomas's *The Best (and Worst) of Baseball's Modern Era* offers lists of the top and bottom teams and their players from 1961 through 2016, accompanied by a detailed breakdown of fifty-six Major League Baseball seasons. Which team was the best during the modern era? Who was the most difficult batter to strike out? Who was the period's best second baseman? Who enjoyed the greatest single game at the plate? Which game featured the worst pitching? The rankings come in relentless order, page after page, all backed with cutting-edge statistical analysis.[3]

The Best (and Worst) of Baseball's Modern Era is appropriate for any fan with an interest in looking at baseball from a historical perspective and with a wonderful, eye-opening delight. Thomas skillfully distilled the modern game into a series of lists and narratives which provide many hours of provocative reading. He introduces an intriguing and sophisticated approach to quantifying player and team performances. Indeed, stat heads will especially enjoy reading it.

In *Baseball: A History of America's Favorite Game*, author George Vecsey casts a fresh eye on the game, illuminates its foibles and triumphs, and makes a classic story refreshingly new. The book is a narrative of America's can-do spirit, in which stalwart immigrants such as Henry Chadwick transplant cricket and rounders into the fertile American culture and in which die-hard unionist baseballers such as Charles

---

2 *See a description of 100 Years of Baseball: The Intimate and Dramatic Story of Modern Baseball on www.amazon.com.*

3 *For a customer review and more details about The Best (and Worst) of Baseball's Modern Era, see them on www.amazon.com.*

Comiskey and Connie Mack eventually become the tightfisted avatars of the game's big-money establishment.

In his seamless and succinct popular history, former *New York Times* sports columnist Vecsey brings together landmark events and personalities. His account of the game's early days is especially strong. For example, in debunking Abner Doubleday's role as the founder of baseball, Vecsey argues that the only verifiable association is a request Doubleday, as a US army commander, made for baseball equipment for his troops in 1871. Recommended for small sports collections in need of a general history of America's pastime, Vecsey's book covers the game for more than forty years.[4]

Most of all, *Baseball: A History of America's Favorite Game* is a testament to the unbreakable bond between our nation's pastime and its fans, who remained loyal through the fifty-year-long interdict on black athletes, the Black Sox scandal, franchise relocation, and the use of performance-enhancing drugs by some major league stars. Reverent and playful, the book begs to be read in the span of a rain-delayed doubleheader of a game, and so enjoyable that, like a favorite team's championship run, one hopes it never ends.

The Making of Modern Baseball, however, differs from these and other publications because they do not cover or include the same or similar group of topics in their chapters. Although interesting and well-written, their purpose, scope, and theme are simply different than writing about things that specifically transformed the characteristics, image, operations, and popularity of Major League Baseball between 1876 and 2019.

BOOK OVERVIEW

Besides an appendix that includes tables of baseball data, a bibliography, and an index, the book consists of acknowledgements, a foreword written by former pitcher Tommy John, abbreviations, an introduction, and nine core chapters. As an overview

---

4 *Alan Moores, "Recreation and Sports," The Booklist (August 2006): 26 and "Baseball: A History of America's Favorite Game," Publishers Weekly (12 June 2006): 46.*

for readers of *The Making of Modern Baseball*, the following is a summary of chapters 2 through 10.

Besides historical players' statistics like batting average, earned run average, hits, home runs, and on-base percentage, different but more unique and complex types of analytics have emerged to represent and report the performances of batters, fielders, and pitchers and their teams. Titled "Baseball Stats," chapter 2 defines and clarifies the role of sabermetrics and its use in measuring the contributions of players in games and in analyzing teams in divisions of the American and National League.

For several years, there has been above-average but stable and even growth of the percentage of international players on the majority of teams in the big leagues and also on those in the minor leagues. Chapter 3, "Immigrant Ballplayers," explains why and when this occurred and how it affected teams and influenced the progress and success of the sport. A current and useful source of historical information is my book *Baseball Beyond Borders: From Distant Lands to the Major Leagues*, published in 2013.[5]

Other than big-leaguers' performances in regular seasons and postseasons, several other factors influenced changes in their numbers and compensation including the sport's history of a union and free agency, labor strikes, lockouts, and franchise owner-union collective bargaining agreements. Titled "Players Association," chapter 4 discusses these topics and provides historical data in tables about players' salaries and growth in them during various seasons and periods.

To establish a local, regional, national, and even international fan base and to generate plenty of revenue, particularly from their home games, American and National League teams sometimes struggled individually to be consistent, popular, and competitive in their division each big-league season. Chapter 5, "Market Effects," denotes the extent of parity and relevant demographic, economic, and financial data that exists among teams in Major League Baseball as of 2018 and whether the results are bad, good, or neither for the future of the sport.

5 *Frank P. Jozsa Jr., Baseball Beyond Borders: From Distant Lands to the Major Leagues (Lanham, MD: Scarecrow Press, 2013).*

Since the early 1900s, various big-league teams have moved from a site (ballpark or sports complex) in a city or metropolitan area to another site in order to survive and become more competitive and also to prosper economically as a franchise. Based on data in the literature and information in my and other authors' baseball books, chapter 6 reveals why, when, and where Major League Baseball clubs relocated somewhere else. Readers learn and realize, for example, how much teams' attendances changed as a result of shifting to another place and its impact on the sport.

To penetrate and exploit new and former sports markets primarily in the United States (along with two in Canada), Major League Baseball officials approved applications from investors or investment groups to allow the entry of professional teams into both the American and National Leagues. Some teams thrived while others eventually moved to another site, merged, or simply dissolved. Chapter 7 identifies these expansion franchises and why they have been significant in contributing to the development of the sport and its audiences.

Since the mid-to-late 1990s, sportswriters at *Forbes* and other magazines have estimated the market value of franchises in each professional sport. Besides providing recent amounts of these values, chapter 8, for example, gives reasons for why baseball's New York Yankees ranked highest and Tampa Bay Devils lowest among thirty-two teams in value in specific but recent years. In addition, the chapter includes their revenues and other financial data from operations and why these amounts are important from an economics perspective. This information is not only interesting but also relevant to the current and future growth and success of the sport.

To attract fans to their home games while earning more income from operations, a majority of Major League Baseball teams have built and financed or partially financed the construction of a new ballpark or renovated an existing facility. It has become increasingly controversial, however, as to whether public (taxpayer) money should be, was, or will be spent on subsidizing ballpark projects. Among other topics, chapter 9 highlights these conflicts and any decisions by government and non-government officials to erect a new facility or renovate a current one.

Chapter 10 contains other things that transformed this professional sport but to a lesser extent than those in previous chapters. Some of them are the effects and results of steroids and other illegal drugs and substances in the sport, such rule changes as the designated hitter and other reforms, and Tommy John surgery. A former high school teammate and lifelong friend of mine, John's medical operation extended his and the career of other pitchers who damaged their arm while throwing fastballs and other types of pitches to batters in games.

CHAPTER 2

Baseball Stats

Twenty-five years after becoming a professional sports organization, the National League (NL) joined with the American League (AL) to form Major League Baseball (MLB) in 1901. That year, the NL consisted of eight teams located within metropolitan areas of such populated cities as Brooklyn, Cincinnati, and St. Louis, while three of eight clubs in the AL had home sites in Boston, Milwaukee, and Washington.

While action and drama occur on the playing field during MLB games, quantitative information based on statistics and other mathematical data is also generated. Besides counting runs in teams' games of a regular season and postseason, there are such different but important and well-known measurements as averages of and hits by batters, number of strikeouts and walks by pitchers, and individual and total errors and putouts by catchers, infielders, and outfielders. Although expressed numerically, these results provide baseball clubs, fans, players, statisticians, and other groups with ways to better evaluate players and their performances.

As this professional sport matured and became increasingly popular in America during the twentieth and early twenty-first centuries, newspaper columnists, editors, journalists, reporters, fans, scholars, and executives in front offices of AL and NL teams demanded more analytical and detailed information about aspects of the game and those who played it.

To that end, this chapter reveals the history of how baseball began to identify, record, and use quantifiable data and to evolve and be successful domestically and in some other countries as a major professional sport. From that perspective, chapter 2 also explains the role of statistics and the application of different types of basic and advanced equations and formulas for fans and others to learn and better understand and appreciate the game and its complexities. Although the focus is on both ordinary and advanced baseball data and measuring the performances and career achievements of players on teams in these two longstanding but interdependent big leagues, the timeline of documenting and maintaining stats actually began approximately forty years before the NL organized and began to operate in the mid-1870s.[1]

HISTORICAL TIMELINE

1830s–1860s

In 1837, the Constitution of the Olympic Ball Club of Philadelphia—who played an early ancestor of baseball called town ball—mandated that a scorebook be kept to record runs scored by all players on all teams. Eight years later, the first box score of a game appeared in the *New York Morning News* with batters' columns including only their number of runs and outs. In 1858, baseball box scores continued to expand, adding nine more columns per player. These consisted of each player's total foul outs and his times catching a ball on one bounce (which then counted as an out). To recognize batters who hit their way on base but did not score, in 1867, New York writer Henry Chadwick began awarding them a base hit. His other innovations included defining and measuring total bases and unearned runs.[2]

1 *See Richard Schell, "SABR, Baseball Statistics, and Computing: The Last Forty Years" at http://www.sabr.org cited 4 August 2017; Alan Schwartz, "A Numbers Revolution," www.espn.com cited 27 July 2017; "Grunk Very Good: A History of Baseball Statistics," www.blessyouboys.com cited 4 August 2017; Michael Lewis, Moneyball: The Art of Winning an Unfair Game (New York, NY: W.W. Norton & Company, 2004).*

2 *Idem, Alan Schwartz, "A Numbers Revolution" and "Baseball Statistics and Analysis," www.fangraphs.com cited 4 August 2017.*

1870s–1890s

With hits per game and total bases per game being the preferred ways of rating batters' achievements, a baseball fan named H.A. Dobson wrote to Henry Chadwick in 1872 and argued that this unfairly favored leadoff hitters, who bat more often each game. As a result, Dobson proposed a new system and called it hits per times at bat. This became increasingly popular and eventually known as a player's batting average. A Philadelphia Athletics baseball scorekeeper rated fielders not by errors they committed but by plays successfully made per game. This metric didn't catch on until Bill James resurrected it more than 100 years later and titled it the range factor.

In 1879, baseball's NL designated reached first base as an official statistic but discarded it after one year and then tried bases touched but also scrapped it. During the 1880s to 1890s, the professional American Association (AA) awarded a pitching championship to New York Metropolitans' Tim Keefe because of his league low .0362 earned-run-per-at-bat ratio and the NL and AA decided that batting average should count walks as full-fledged hits. However, after St. Louis ballplayer Tip O'Neill hit .492, the one-year experiment ended and pitchers were moved back approximately 5–6 feet to their present 60 feet and 6 inches distance from home plate.

1900s–1910s

In 1912, few starting pitchers completed their baseball games. Consequently, NL president John Heydler scraped earned runs per game and replaced it with earned runs per nine innings pitched which is now known as the earned run average. During the next four years, *Who's Who in Baseball* debuted and included the first-ever seasonal register of active players' batting and fielding averages. It was baseball's first attempt at a comprehensive record book and was titled *Balldom*, published by stat freak George Moreland; *Baseball Magazine's* F.C. Lane—perhaps the sport's first authentic sabermetrician—began an all-out assault on the worthlessness of BA and assigned higher weights to doubles, triples, and home runs while also proposing new respect for walks. The NL hired AL Munro and Walter Elias to keep official numbers, and eventually, this duo founded and organized the Elias Sports Bureau.

1920s–1950s

After runs batted in (RBIs) became an official statistic during 1919–1921, fans started focusing more on players' statistics rather than simply scores of games, in part, because the New York Yankees' outfielder Babe Ruth shattered former Chicago White Stockings player Ned Williamson's 1884 home run record of twenty-seven with twenty-nine (1919) and then he hit fifty-four (1920) and fifty-nine (1921). In the 1940s, former major leaguer Ethan Allen invented All-Star Baseball—a tabletop game that allowed kids to stage games with a spinner atop circular discs whose circumference was sectioned off according to players' real-life statistics.

Besides those highlights, Brooklyn Dodgers owner Branch Rickey hired Allan Roth as his team statistician in 1947. Roth proceeded to adopt and keep various new statistics to rate players' performances including early types of on-base percentage, batting average with runners in scoring position, results in different ball-strike counts, and more. Harold Richman, an 11-year-old kid from Long Island, invented a new tabletop statistics game using dice in 1948 and thirteen years later, he named it Strat-O-Matic and published it commercially.

In 1951, *New York Daily News* sportswriter Hy Turkin and Broadway musician and statistics fan Cy Thompson published *Official Encyclopedia of Baseball*, the game's first historical register. Because baseball data was difficult to find, the only statistics included were games played, batting averages for hitters, and won-lost records for pitchers. One year later, the Topps company added full statistics lines on the back of their annual baseball cards and then from 1953 to 1963, Canadian military officer George Lindsey collected and applied sophisticated statistical analysis to baseball's numbers. In fact, he published two seminal articles in military journal *Operations Research* that examined the benefits and costs of such strategies in baseball games as steals, sacrifices, and intentional walks through his unique base-out matrix.

1960s–1970s

During the 1960s, Harvard University professor William Gamson began a new baseball pool called Baseball Seminar, a forerunner of modern fantasy baseball; retired metallurgist and consultant in the development of the atom bomb Earnshaw Cook authored the first full-length sabermetric book in 1964, *Percentage Baseball*;

and five years later the sport's first comprehensive historical register–*The Baseball Encyclopedia*–debuted and contained more than 2,300 pages that included at least seventeen statistics for each big-league player each year dating to 1876. Being a massive technological undertaking, it was the first trade book in the United States entirely typeset by computers.

In the 1970s, software engineer Harlan Mills and his brother Eldon invented a new statistic called player win average, which was based on everything a hitter, pitcher, or fielder did and how they affected the probability of their team eventually winning a game. The Mills released their method in an obscure book titled *Player Win Averages* in 1970. One year later, the Society for American Baseball Research (SABR) formed in Cooperstown, New York, and Bill James self-published his first *Baseball Abstract*. Then in 1979, Houston Astros president and statistics buff Tal Smith hired Steve Mann to be the first modern stat analyst for an MLB club.

1980s

During this ten-year period, a company named STATS Inc. developed the Edge 1.000 computer system to help big-league clubs keep specialized statistics and *Sporting News* reported that Detroit Tigers' Ty Cobb was awarded two too many hits in 1910 and therefore had actually but not officially lost the AL batting race to Cleveland's Nap Lajoie by .001 percentage points. In addition to those news items, a profile of Bill James in *Sports Illustrated* introduced sabermetrics to the public and Ballantine won a bidding war to nationally publish James' *Baseball Abstract*, which became an annual bestseller.

During 1982, San Francisco National Public Radio (NPR) announcer Eric Walker published *The Sinister First Baseman*, a collection of baseball essays with many of them building a new statistical philosophy based on power and on-base percentage. As a result, Oakland Athletics executive Sandy Alderson hired Walker as a consultant to establish the club's philosophy and for team manager Steve Boros to use computer data to make strategic decisions.

Prompted by Pete Palmer and John Thorn's *The Hidden Game of Baseball*– a comprehensive analysis of new statistics in 1984–the *New York Times* started publishing a weekly box with a new statistic: on-base plus slugging percentage and, facing bankruptcy, STATS Inc. shifted its focus from developing software for teams to maintaining and distributing statistics for the public. Then in 1989, *Total Baseball* was published as a rival to *The Baseball Encyclopedia* and *Retrosheet* began a massive compilation and online publishing of old box scores and play-by-plays. This allowed droves of historical research never before possible.

1990s–2000s

In the 1990s, *USA Today* joined with STATS Inc. to overhaul box scores that included batters' walks, number of strikeouts, players left on base, an updated BA, pitch counts, and a new statistic called holds. STATS Inc., meanwhile, revolutionized statistics delivery by updating its American Online (AOL) box scores and statistics during games, in fact, pitch-by-pitch. Ultimately, this caused a lawsuit filed by the National Basketball Association (NBA) and other professional sports leagues, who claimed a violation of broadcast licenses.

Between 1995 and 2000, *Baseball Prospectus* began publishing an annual book and website, and introduced the statistics community to such things as value over replacement level, player empirical comparison and optimization test algorithm, pitcher abuse points, and more. After losing a decision in US District Court, STATS Inc. won its appeal of the NBA lawsuit and also secured the right to disseminate statistics in real time. After twenty-two years of fighting among SABR members, Major League Baseball (MLB), and the Elias Sports Bureau, MLB Commissioner Bud Selig announced that Chicago Cubs' Hack Wilson's record RBI total from 1930 would officially change from 190 to 191.

In 2000, John Dewan sold STATS Inc. to News Corporation for $45 million and one year later, Voros McCracken published his Defense Independent Pitching Stats system in which pitchers have little influence over whether batted balls fall in for hits or are turned into outs by the team's defense. He then was hired as a statistical analyst for the Boston Red Sox. In 2001, Bill James unveiled his Win Shares system and one year later, joined the Red Sox as a baseball-operations advisor. During 2003, MLB.com decided to outfit ballparks with sophisticated camera systems to capture pitch and throw velocities, runner speeds, batted-ball trajectories and more data, in part, to build an entire new set of fielding statistics.

CORE BASEBALL STATISTICS

One notable aspect of the sport of baseball is the wealth of interesting, memorable, and useful information recorded about the game. The effectiveness of former and current players—including batters, catchers, infielders, and pitchers—is typically assessed by particular numerical measures. For example, the usual measure of hitting effectiveness of a ballplayer is batting average, which is accurately computed by dividing the number of hits by number of at-bats in games. This statistic gives the proportion of opportunities (at-bats) in which the batter succeeds (gets a hit). The batter with the highest batting average during an MLB season is typically called the best hitter for that period.

Besides their average number of hits per opportunity, batters are also evaluated on their ability to reach one, two, three, or four bases on a single hit. These, respectively, are called singles, doubles, triples, and home runs. In addition, another way to measure batters' effectiveness is their slugging average in games. This stat is computed by dividing the total number of bases by the number of opportunities. Since it weights hits by the number of bases reached, this measure reflects the ability of a batter to successfully hit a baseball for distance. The most-valued hit in baseball, of course, is the home run where a player advances four bases on one hit. After the number of home runs is recorded for all players, those batters with the largest number of them at the end of a season are given special recognition.

While AL and NL teams' scouts, general managers, and staff analysts study numerical data in order to evaluate and make decisions about ability and the actual and potential contribution of players, their coaches and especially on-the-field catchers and pitchers use statistics of batters on opposing teams to determine how best to pitch to them and thus strategically position players during innings of a game. Coaches and team batters, alternatively, study opposing pitchers to figure out how best to hit against them and often make adjustments to their decisions during a game based on statistics such as choosing who to put in the lineup and which relief pitcher to bring in during an inning.

Throughout most of professional baseball history, several core stats have been traditionally used for various reasons. A player's batting average and his runs batted in and home runs, for example, are popular and the most commonly referenced hitting statistics. Any players that lead the AL and NL in these three statistics are each a Triple Crown winner and a likely candidate to be their league's Most Valuable Player (MVP). For pitchers, the most often-cited and traditional statistics are earned run average and the number of wins and strikeouts. A pitcher that leads his league in these stats is also referred to as a Triple Crown winner and a potential winner of the league's prestigious Cy Young Award.

To identify these and other measurements and better interpret and comprehend their meaning in the sport of baseball, a number of them are listed and defined here in no specific order for batters (offense), pitchers (defense), and different types. Besides definitions, the following are one or more of their characteristics including problems in what they actually represent.[3]

Batting average (BA), as defined, has two primary flaws. First, the stat ignores a segment of offensive actions just because they are not hits, and 100 years ago, someone decided a hit and a walk were fundamentally different. In reality, the difference is among players with similar BAs but much different walk rates to get on base. The second major flaw is that BA treats every hit equally even though some are more valuable than others. In other words, the stat treats a single, double, triple, and home run as the same thing, even though a hitter who only hit doubles would, for example, help his team score a lot more runs than a hitter who only hit singles. If you treat everything equally, you are not getting a very accurate measure of players' contribution to run-scoring for their team.

A defensive statistic of pitchers, **earned run average (ERA)**, is popular as a measurement because it seems to answer a very important question. That is, it reveals how many runs a pitcher gave up that were actually his fault, but unfortunately, despite its name, ERA does not properly answer that question. Simply put, the distinction between unearned and earned runs is not an accurate demarcation between runs that were and were not a pitcher's fault. There are two primary reasons for this difference. First, the official scorer of games determines if something was an error or not and official scorers do not necessarily record errors consistently. This means that the same botched play might be scored an error one day and a hit in

3 *One reference is Rob Lazlo, "How to Understand Baseball Stats in a Game," www.guysgirls.com cited 27 July 2017.*

another. Second and more importantly, bad defense occurs in forms beyond rule book errors. While most of them are obvious, others can be judgmental.

Left on base percentage (LOB%) for most pitchers is about the league average—which is approximately 70–72% depending upon the season—and pitchers that deviate from that average tend to see their numbers regress towards average in the future. In other words, if you see pitchers with a sixty LOB%, they are letting lots of runners score so their ERA will likely be high. But according to the odds, they will strand more runners on base in the future and therefore lower their ERA.

Not all pitchers regress toward the league average because those with relatively high strikeouts have some control over their LOB% in games. Pitchers that record a high number of strikeouts, for example, can pitch their way out of jams more easily than pitchers who rely on their team's defense, so they are able to maintain an LOB% that is higher than the league average. Also, if a pitcher is not a major-league caliber starter or a borderline case, it is likely that their true-talent LOB% is below the league average.

Several years ago, **on-base percentage (OBP)** was a big leap forward because it gave credit to hitters who reached base via a walk or hit-by-a-pitch during games when their BA ignored those things. Anytime a player does not make an out, he is contributing positively to the run-scoring process and OBP captures that better than BA because it incorporates a big slice of offensive activity that BA does not consider. Getting on base via a walk does not help a team quite as much as getting a hit, but it is certainly valuable enough to warrant inclusion in even the most simplistic metrics. Certainly, OBP has become synonymous with the book *Moneyball* because in the early 2000s, teams were not properly valuing players with high OBPs. As a result, the AL's Oakland Athletics swiped talented players for cheap because they were one of the few teams that paid attention to walk rates and thus OBP.[4]

According to some experts, **on-base plus slugging percentage (OPS)** is not a perfect measurement because it treats OBP as equal in value with slugging percentage (SLG), while OBP is roughly twice as important as SLG in terms of its effect on run scoring. However, OPS has value as a metric because it is accepted and used more widely than other more accurate statistics while also being a relatively accurate representation

4 *Idem, Michael Lewis, Moneyball: The Art of Winning an Unfair Game.*

of offense. Because you can find OPS on baseball cards and hear about it in broadcasts of games, it is a simple statistic that has made its way into the mainstream of baseball data.

Runs batted in (RBIs) is one of the most famous baseball statistics and it measures the number of runners who score due to a hit, walk, sacrifice, or fielder's choice. Generally speaking, a 100 RBI season is considered worthy of admiration and the notion of driving in runs or being an RBI guy is highly valued. There are essentially, however, two ways to approach the problem with using RBI as a statistic. First, there is very little evidence that timely or clutch hitting is a skill separate from regular hitting. Second, even if those are real skills, RBI is a very crude way to measure them. Thus, officials who maintain records should consider using something else.

While there isn't really evidence that hitting with men on base is a skill independent of a player's regular abilities, the more important reason why RBI is not a good measure of offensive performance in any way is that it doesn't even capture the performance it means to. Batters do not have equal opportunities to collect RBIs. In fact, in some cases, hitters could rack up plenty of RBIs despite performing quite poorly, simply because they were given very favorable circumstances and opportunities in games.

Saves by pitchers are a monster as evidenced by the furious closer run in pitching. Players with little other value find themselves highly coveted simply for being the one tabbed by the manager with finishing out the ninth inning of a game on a regular basis. With approximately thirty such jobs available on all MLB teams, identifying those players prepared to move into that role can determine the balance of power in a league. At the beginning of a season, there is little that helps to project saves more than meticulously poring through depth charts and determining who will win each individual job. But in any baseball league, this knowledge will be required to simply stay level with the competition. The real gains to be made, however, are found by figuring out which closers are most likely to tank or fail and, in turn, which relievers are most likely to move up and take their spots.

In baseball games, **slugging percentage (SLG)** is the number of total bases divided by the number of at-bats of a hitter. Its basic formula is the sum of singles, doubles times two, triples times three, and home runs times four divided by at-bats, which are different than plate appearances. An equivalent formula is the total number of hits plus doubles, triples times two, and home runs times three divided by at-bats. The latter formula is not as intuitive but more convenient to use because singles are often not given although they can easily be determined. In fact, singles can be derived from a formula because they are simply hits not for extra bases or number of hits minus the sum of doubles, triples, and home runs. Also, total bases equal the sum of singles, two times doubles, three times triples, and four times home runs.

Walks plus hits per innings pitched (WHIP) is essentially a measurement of how many base runners a pitcher allows per inning in a game. Given that preventing base runners is the fundamental role of pitchers, a rate statistic designed to tell you how many they allow definitely points you in the right direction. In other words, WHIP is more of a quick reference stat rather than something you should use for a full-fledged analysis of a pitcher. If you want to determine base runners allowed using a rate stat, weighted on-base average (wOBA) is preferable because batters faced is a better denominator than innings.

WHIP is also deficient since it treats all times on base equally, for example, equating a walk with a home run. A statistic like wOBA is more useful in that regard since it combines all the different aspects of hitting into one metric, and weights each of them in proportion to their actual run value. While BA, OBP, and SLG each fall short in accuracy and scope, wOBA measures and captures a player's offensive value more accurately and comprehensively. Thus, WHIP is no longer at the forefront of statistical analysis although it is easy to calculate and correlates relatively well with more accurate statistics. Think of WHIP as something like OPS. It is a little rough around the edges but generally provides a good starting point.

ALL-TIME PLAYER PERFORMANCES

Except for players' LOB% and wOBA—which is not always available in the literature—table 2.1 contains the all-time AL and NL leaders in hitting and pitching among MLB's core statistics as of August 2018. Being remarkable and truly historic as a group, the table includes players on teams during the so-called dead ball era. Are any of these results threatened to be exceeded by one or more current players on MLB teams? According to the following data, most of these records will remain intact for several years—or more likely decades.

From *first to tenth* in the AL statistically for current and all-time players, respectively, as of August 2018—Fernando Rodney ranked eighth to Mariano Rivera with 754 games pitched and ninth with 261 saves, CC Sabathia fifth to Roger Clemens with 2,832 strikeouts, and Miguel Cabrera tenth to Babe Ruth with a .954 OPS; *eleventh to twentieth*, Miguel Cabrera eleventh to Babe Ruth with a .556 SLG and twentieth to Ty Cobb with a .318 BA, CC Sabathia seventeen to Walter Johnson with 233 wins, and Justin Verlander thirteenth to Addie Josh with a 1.17 WHIP; *twenty-first to thirtieth*, Miguel Cabrera twenty-first to Ted Williams with a .398 OBP and CC Sabathia twenty-seventh to Walter Johnson in innings pitched; *greater than thirty*, Ichiro Suzuki thirty-ninth to Ty Cobb with 1,308 runs and forty-seventh to Carl Yastremski with 2,219 games, Felix Hernandez fifty-third to Ed Walsh with 3.32 ERA, and Robinson Cano fifty-fifth to Babe Ruth with 1,210 RBIs.

From *first to tenth* in the NL by statistic for current and all-time leaders, respectively—Joey Votto fifth to Billy Hamilton with a .428 OBP and eighth to Barry Bonds with a .951 OPS, Clayton Kershaw first with a 1.00 WHIP and seventh to Mordecai with a 2.36 ERA, and Kenley Jansen eighth to Trevor Hoffman with 262 saves; *eleventh to twentieth*, Ryan Braun fifteenth to Barry Bonds with a .536 SLG, and Clayton Kershaw seventeenth to Steve Carlton with 2,244 strikeouts and ninety-seventh to Alexander/Mathewson with 150 wins; *twenty-first to thirtieth*, Jonathan Broxton twenty-seventh to John Franco with 659 games pitched; *greater than thirty*, Joey Votto thirty-sixth to Willie Keeler with a .311 BA, Ryan Howard fifty-third to Hank Aaron with 1,194 RBIs, Chase Utley ninety-sixth to Barry Bonds with 1,102 runs and one-hundredth to Pete Rose with 1,919 games, and Matt Cain one-hundred forty-sixth to Warren Spahn with 2,085 innings pitched.

ADVANCED METRICS

Sabermetrics research began in middle years of the twentieth century. A member of the Princeton University class of 1921, Earnshaw Cook was an engineer who specialized in metallurgy. He spent most of his working life at the American Brake Shoe Company in Mahwah, New Jersey, and later served as a consult on the Manhattan Project before retiring from the industry in 1945. During the 1950s and 1960s, Cook worked as

Table 2.1 All-Time Career Leaders, Major League Baseball, by League, as of August 2018

Statistic	Player	AL	Player	NL
Hitting				
BA	Ty Cobb	.367	Willie Keeler	.371
Games	Carl Yastremski	3,308	Pete Rose	3,562
OBP	Ted Williams	.482	Billy Hamilton	.462
OPS	Babe Ruth	1.167	Barry Bonds	1.051
RBIs	Babe Ruth	2,201	Hank Aaron	2,202
Runs	Ty Cobb	2,246	Barry Bonds	2,227
SLG	Babe Ruth	.692	Barry Bonds	.607
Pitching				
ERA	Ed Walsh	1.81	Mordecai Brown	1.93
Games	Mariano Rivera	1,115	John Franco	1,119
Innings Pitched	Walter Johnson	5,914	Warren Spahn	5,243
Saves	Mariano Rivera	652	Trevor Hoffman	601
Strikeouts	Roger Clemens	4,167	Steve Carlton	4,000
WHIP	Addie Joss	.97	Clayton Kershaw	1.00
Wins	Walter Johnson	417	Alexander/Mathewson	373

Note: Major League Baseball consists of the American League (AL) and National League (NL). Abbreviated is batting average (BA), on-base percentage (OBP), on-base plus slugging percentage (OPS), runs batted in (RBIs), slugging percentage (SLG), earned run average (ERA), and walks plus hits per innings pitched (WHIP). In the NL, pitchers Grover Alexander and Christy Mathewson tied each other in number of wins.

Source: "All-Time Leaders," www.mlb.com cited 1 August 2018.

a mechanical engineering professor at Johns Hopkins University, where he authored several academic papers.

Cook was one of the earliest researchers who contributed to statistically analyzing baseball data. He reported the majority of his research in his 1964 book, *Percentage*

Baseball. It was the first of its kind to gain national media attention although widely criticized and not accepted by most baseball organizations.[5]

Following Cook's research, the idea of advanced or more complicated baseball statistics did not become prominent in the baseball community until Bill James began writing his annual *Baseball Abstracts* in 1977. Born in Holton, Kansas, James never knew his mother who died in 1954. His father was a janitor at a high school. After four years at Kansas University (KU), he joined the Army in 1971. He was the last person in Kansas to be sent to fight in the Vietnam War although he never saw action there. Instead, James spent two years stationed in South Korea, during which time he wrote to KU about taking his final class. Told he had met all his graduation requirements, James returned to Lawrence, Kansas in 1973 with degrees in English and economics. Two years later he also finished an education degree from the same school.[6]

Being an aspiring writer and obsessive sports fan, James began writing baseball articles after leaving the United States Army during his mid-twenties. Many of his first baseball writings came while he was doing night shifts as a security guard at Stokely-Van Camp's pork and beans cannery. Unlike most writers, his pieces did not recount games in epic terms or offer insights gleaned from interviews with players. A typical James piece posed a question, for example, which pitchers and catchers allowed

---

5 *Cook first set about his statistical baseball studies with the goal of proving that Ty Cobb—holder of the highest career batting average at .366—was better than Babe Ruth, the premier power hitter of the first half of the twentieth century. Additionally Cook sought to understand strategical issues such as batting order and relief pitching rather than accept the traditional strategies of baseball. Sports Illustrated writer Frank Deford learned of Cook's work and interviewed him for the lead story of a 1964 issue with the title "Baseball is Played All Wrong." Using tools of the time, such as a slide rule and a Friden STW mechanical calculator, Earnshaw Cook published the culmination of his work, Percentage Baseball in 1964. This was the first book of baseball statistics studies to gain national media attention. Though Cook received some support from Los Angeles Dodgers manager Walter Alston and Chicago White Sox owner Bill Veeck, most baseball executives and managers rejected Cook's mathematical approach and academic language. He was also criticized for lax mathematical models and inadequate numerical evidence by statisticians, such as George Lindsey (himself a baseball statistician), who advised that it be "kept out of the sight of students of the theory of probability." Modern author Michael Lewis describes Cook's prose as "crafted to alienate [baseball statistics] converts." See Earnshaw Cook, Percentage Baseball (Boston, MA: MIT Press, 1964).*

6 *Scott Gray, The Mind of Bill James: How a Complete Outsider Changed Baseball (New York, NY: Three Rivers Press, 2006). This is the first book to chronicle the life and ideas of "the serious baseball fan's high priest," the impact of his brilliant and entertaining writings, and how someone who never pitched a ball, held a bat, or managed a team fundamentally changed the way baseball is interpreted, analyzed, and even played.*

runners to steal the most bases? Then, he presented data and an analysis written in a lively, insightful, and witty style that provided an answer. In other words, James believed that most people misunderstood how the game of baseball was played, claiming that it is actually defined by the conditions and circumstances under which the sport existed.

Before James was able to bring the concept of sabermetrics to a major sport, MLB player Davey Johnson used an IBM System/360 at team owner Jerold Hoffberger's brewery to write a FORTRAN baseball computer simulation while playing for the Baltimore Orioles in the early 1970s. Although unsuccessful, Johnson used his results and proposed to his manager Earl Weaver to bat second in the lineup. He also wrote IBM BASIC programs to help him manage the minor league Tidewater Tides and then, after becoming manager of the New York Mets in 1984, Johnson arranged for a team employee to write a dBASE II application to compile and store advanced metrics on team statistics.

Craig R. Wright was another employee in MLB and worked for the Texas Rangers in the early 1980s. During his time with the club, he became known as the first front office employee in big-league history to work with the title *sabermetrician*. In 1989, Wright coauthored a book named *The Diamond Appraised* whose aim was to approach the game from both theoretical and practical standpoints and also answer such questions as: what constitutes excellence in a catcher? Was Ty Cobb or Pete Rose a more valuable player? Should some pitchers be trained to become knuckleball specialists? Does baseball need a system like pro football's instant replay?[7]

Sabermetricians—considered baseball statisticians—began their study of the sport by trying to replace the longtime favorite batters' statistic known as batting average. Some claimed that it provided a relatively poor fit for actual runs scored. According to sabermetric reasoning, runs win ballgames and a good measure of a player's worth is his ability to help his team score more runs than the opponent.

A number of traditional statistics are used by sabermetricians in the evaluation of other positions. For a specific pitcher, they count the number of games in which he was declared the winner or loser and number of runs allowed. Pitchers, in fact, are

---

7 *Carl R. Wright and Tom House, The Diamond Appraised (New York, NY: Simon & Schuster, 1989).*

usually rated in terms of the average number of earned runs allowed for a nine-inning game. Other data, meanwhile, is useful in understanding pitching ability. A pitcher records a strikeout when the batter fails to hit the ball in the field and records a walk when he throws four inaccurate pitches to the batter. A pitcher who can throw the ball very fast can record a high number of strikeouts while another one with poor control who is erratic or relatively inaccurate will record a large number of walks.

Some sabermetric stats have entered the mainstream baseball world. Among those that measure a batter's overall performance is on-base plus slugging percentage (OPS). It adds a hitter's on-base percentage—number of times he reached base by any means divided by total plate appearances—to his slugging percentage or total bases divided by at-bats. Some baseball historians argue, however, that the OPS formula is flawed and that more weight should be shifted towards on-base percentage (OPB).

In pitching, opponent on-base plus slugging (OOPS) has become a popular way to better and more accurately measure a pitcher's actual performance. When analyzing statistics of that on-the-field position, some other useful categories to consider include strikeouts per nine innings pitched (K/IP), strikeouts per walk (K/BB), and home runs per nine innings (HR/9).

Since 2001, sabermetrics has increasingly put more emphasis on defense-independent pitching statistics. These stats, such as defense-independent ERA (dERA), attempt to evaluate a pitcher according to those events governed solely by the pitcher's performance, regardless of the strength of the defensive players with him in games.

Also important in evaluating players' performances are statistics in certain in-game situations. For example, a certain batter's ability to hit left-handed pitchers might sway a manager to give him more chances to face lefties. In addition, other batters may have a history of success against a given pitcher or vice versa, and a manager could use this information to organize a favorable match-up.

To inform and educate readers regarding current metrics in the sport, the following is a summary of some advanced baseball stats. As a result, the most rudimentary fans and others can become aware and more knowledgeable about the mysterious world of baseball analytics, or sabermetrics as referred to in the industry. Because there are many different types that exist, these are several relative to players' hitting, pitching, and total performance.[8]

A slash line typically looks like three different numbers rounded to the thousandth decimal place and separated by forward slashes. The first of those numbers represents batting average, the second *on-base percentage,* and the third *slugging percentage*. Former Boston Red Sox slugger Ted Williams, for example, had one of the most impressive all-time slash lines in his 1941 MLB season at .406/.526/.735. In addition, he led the AL with 135 runs scored and 37 home runs, and ranked fourth with 120 RBIs.

Isolated power (ISO) is a statistic that goes hand-in-hand with slugging percentage. It is calculated by subtracting batting average from slugging percentage (SLG–BA) to reveal how many extra bases a player averaged per at-bat. ISO is important because it removes singles from the equation and gives a better idea of a player's true power capability. For example, four singles and zero home runs in ten at-bats are both a .400 batting average and slugging percentage. In comparison, one home run and zero singles in ten at bats are a .100 batting average and a .400 slugging percentage. While the first player's ISO is .000, the second's is .300. This difference in percentages denotes that the second player hit for extra bases more often than the first. For example, on August 7, 2017, the Los Angeles Dodgers' Cody Bellinger had MLB's highest ISO at .344 while the Miami Marlins' Dee Gordon ranked one-hundred sixth at .065.

Zone% is the percentage of pitches a player sees inside of the strike zone. A low zone% usually means a batter has a high swing percent. Pitchers, however, typically refuse to throw many strikes to batters who are known to swing at a lot of very high, low or outside pitches. The definition of strike zone varies by source, year, and umpire, which means small differences in zone% should be expected among hitters even if they behave the same way.

F-strike% represents the percentage of first pitches a batter sees that end up being strikes. It usually characterizes a fear factor for pitchers and shows how willing or

---

8 *Zach Pincince, "Understanding Advanced Baseball Stats: Hitting," www.baseballessential.com cited 27 July 2017.*

unwilling they are on average to attack this particular hitter right out of the gate. While batters prefer a low and pitchers a high f-strike%, the MLB average for all players from 2005 to 2008 was 59 percent. In fact, there is very little variation in the average of this stat from year to year.

SwStr% is the percentage of pitches at which a batter swings and misses. It is common sense that swinging and missing means a bad result for hitters. To be accurate about this stat, get results from players who had a qualifying season, that is, at least 3.1 plate appearances per team game or roughly 500 total plate appearances. Indeed, swStr% is most effective given a large sample size of data to work with but beware of stats skewed by small sample sizes. In addition, the stat should not be confused with batters' whiff rate or swinging strikes per swing.

PLATE DISCIPLINE

Plate discipline stats are very important for hitters and pitchers because they reveal a hitter's approach or approaches against a particular pitcher or pitchers. To be accurate, it is important to know some of the underlying factors at play. Is this hitter especially aggressive? Are we looking at a swing and miss starting pitcher? Does the hitter have trouble making contact with one or more types of pitches?

This type of data includes strikeout rate (K%) and walk rate (BB%). These are essentially the same thing as strikeouts and walks, but applied as a rate-based stat by dividing each of them by the player's total number of plate appearances. They show how often, on average, a player strikes out and walks. The application of these stats is pretty straightforward since a player with a high BB% and low K% would typically have good batting discipline while a player with opposite-type numbers would probably have poor batting discipline. If a player has a lot of Ks and limited BBs, he is labelled a hacker. If there are numerous BBs, a batter is patient during his plate appearances. It is important to understand, therefore, that while a given BB% might be considered poor, it is possible to have success with that poor rate given other valuable skills. In early August 2017, the Cincinnati Reds' Joey Votto ranked first in MLB with a BB% of 17.3 while the Texas Rangers' Joey Gallo had the highest K% at 38.1.

Another common stat used to measure plate discipline is a player's walk-to-strikeout rate (BB/K) in games. This is a straightforward stat and measured simply by dividing a player's walks by their total strikeouts. The result gives the average number of times a player walks between each strikeout. With a BB/K of 1.00, it means a player walks as often as striking out—which is exceptionally good plate discipline.

There are actually other advanced stats that can be used to get a much deeper and more comprehensive look into a player's approach at the plate. While it is not necessary to get very in-depth with these stats, a simple description and league context are enough to apply them.

An O-swing%, for example, represents the percentage of pitches a player swings at, which are outside of the strikeout zone. It makes sense that the more batters swing at bad pitches, the less likely they will get a hit, thus, the lower the percentage the better for them. Pitchers, meanwhile, prefer a high O-swing%. From 2002 to 2008 in MLB, this stat varied between 16 percent in 2004 to 25 percent in 2008.

Z-swing% is the percentage of pitches a player swings at that are inside the strikeout zone. Although it is not really a good or bad stat, a low Z-swing% typically denotes that the particular player has a very patient approach or discipline at the plate. Swing% represents the percentage of total pitches a player swings at in a game. Similar to the Z-swing%, a low percentage usually signifies more patience while at bat. But if a pitcher has a great change-up, curve, or slider that few batters can consistently hit, it does not really matter where he throws it. The same is true if he has a tremendous fastball that hitters have trouble making contact with while at the plate.

O-contact% is the percentage of pitches a player makes contact with that are outside the strikeout zone. Obviously, the more contact made, the better off is a batter. So, players with a relatively high O-contact% are better at putting the barrel of their bat on the ball. In comparison, contact% represents the percentage of total pitches with which a player makes contact. A 95% contact rate, however, means a very different thing if the player does or does not have much power in swinging at a pitch.

Good contact on pitches outside the strike zone might be good, but if a player is swinging at lots of bad pitches and grounding out weakly to an infielder, this is not a very useful result. Additionally, not all pitches inside the zone are created equal. Ideally, a batter should only swing at pitches for which he can make solid contact, but that set of pitches is not easily defined by in and out of the strike zone.

BATTED BALL DATA

The most common batted ball stat in baseball is batting average on balls in play (BABIP). While a typical batting average reflects how often a player gets a hit, the BABIP determines how often a player ends up getting a base hit when his batted ball falls in only fair territory or within the field of play.

BABIP is calculated by subtracting home runs from total hits and dividing that by at-bats minus strikeouts and home runs plus sacrifice flies. Overall, it is a statistic largely out of the batters' control, which makes sense because as a hitter, once you hit the ball onto the field, you can not affect what happens to it next. For pitchers, they typically want to adjust their expectations toward that player's career average rather than the league average.

Batters have much more control over their BABIP than pitchers do, which is another way of saying that a higher percentage of batter BABIPs is controlled by actual talent. It is certainly possible for hitters to improve their offensive game and raise their BABIP, but dramatic spikes are usually due to luck. If a hitter, for example, has a career .320 BABIP and suddenly it falls to .260 during the first month of his baseball season, you should not expect him to regress to .300 or remain at .260. In fact, he is more likely to have a .320 BABIP going forward in games. Hitters who consistently hit above or below .300 for their BABIP are not simply getting lucky. They are actually leveraging a skill which needs to be accounted for when analyzing their performance. Besides BABIP, the following are some other batted ball data.

To illustrate, **LD%** stands for line drive percentage or percentage of balls a player hits that end up as line drives. As you know, line drives are harder to field than any other type of batted ball, so you can expect them to fall for hits much more often than others. Typically, a line drive produces 1.26 runs per out, fly balls 0.13 runs per out, and ground balls 0.05 runs per out. In other words, batters want to hit lots of line drives and fly balls in games while pitchers generally try to get batters to hit ground balls especially at their infielders.

The MLB average on liners recently was .690, which means that a line drive fell for a hit roughly 69 percent of the time. It makes perfect sense, then, that the more line drives players hit, the higher you can expect their BABIP. This result is supported when you compare the BABIP of players with an LD% above-league average to their counterparts with an average or below-league average mark.

Ground ball percentage (GB%) represents the percentage of balls a batter hits that end up as ground balls in the infield or outfield. During a recent season, the MLB average on grounders was just .239, which means that approximately 24 percent of ground balls ended up as hits. Based on that, you would expect players who hit a lot of grounders to have a lower BABIP; this, however, is not necessarily true because most ground ball hitters end up being speedsters who are more likely to beat out grounders than the average player. In general, you can expect players with a high GB% to have a slightly higher BABIP, but you definitely need to consider their speed before making that assumption. In the 2016 MLB season, for example, the Philadelphia Phillies' Howie Kendrick had the highest GB% at 61 percent while the New York Yankees' Jacoby Ellsbury ranked forty-ninth at 46.6 percent.

FB% stands for fly ball percentage, which is the percentage of balls a player hits that end up as fly balls. Flies are the type of batted ball least likely to end up as a hit, and the MLB average has been only .212 or a 21 percent success rate. Also, because a fraction of fly balls end up as home runs, the league average BABIP for flies is even lower at .126. This indicates that fly balls which stay in the field end up as hits approximately 13 percent of the time. It's no secret that players who hit lots of flies will experience a lower BABIP than others, and a quick comparison of players with an above-league average FB% or .297 to their counterparts' .318 drive home or prove that argument. During a particular season, for example, the Chicago White Sox's Todd Frazier had the highest FB% in MLB at 45.5 percent while the Chicago Cubs' Addison Russell placed forty-eighth at 34.9 percent.

IFFB% is the infield fly ball percentage or the proportion of fly balls a player hits that end up as infield popups and usually caught by the other team in a game. Since lazy flies to the infield are relatively easy to field, they are considered essentially automatic outs. Because of that result, it would be fair to predict that a player who hits a lot of infield flies is not likely to have a very good BABIP relative to others. However, the player with the worst IFFB% in a recent season of MLB was only 17.3 percent. Thus, hitting a lot of automatic outs is not going to make a huge difference between batted balls but definitely a noticeable one. Batters who avoid these easy outs—those with better than league-average IFFB%—had a slightly higher BABIP (.312) than their counterparts (.298) in a recent season.

HR/FB% represents a hitter's home run to fly ball rate. This is the percentage of fly balls a player hits that end up as home runs. While this stat does not play much of a role in BABIP since home runs are factored out of the BABIP equation, it is definitely a key component of a player's batted ball profile. Although HR/FB% is largely skill based, it typically does not fluctuate by much from year-to-year. Thus, a ballplayer who posts a HR/FB% much lower than his career norm is very likely to bounce back the following season and vice versa. In MLB's 2016 season, this stat exceeded 30 percent for only Milwaukee Brewer's Ryan Braun, Miami Marlin's (Milwaukee Brewers as of 2018) Christian Yelich, Arizona Diamondback's Yasmany Tomas, and Oakland Athletics' Khris Davis.

IFH% stands for infield hit percentage, which is the percentage of ground balls a player hits that end up being infield hits. Because it relates to the fact that speedy players can often beat out grounders, IFH% is the stat that actually measures that skill. MLB players with a GB% and IFH% that were both above the league average had a .315 BABIP in a recent year as opposed to their counterparts whose BABIP was lower at .300.

Besides those stats being helpful to evaluate individuals, using them to establish a batted ball profile helps fans and others get a better idea of a player's actual hitting skill set. For the most part, a player with a solid LD% and IFH% expects to achieve an above-average BABIP while a player with a relatively high FB% and IFFB% expects to post a below-average mark.

Weighted on-base average (wOBA) combines all the different aspects of hitting into one metric, weighting each of them in proportion to their actual run value. While batting average, on-base percentage, and slugging percentage fall short in accuracy and scope, the wOBA measures and also captures offensive value more accurately and comprehensively. This statistic, based on linear weights, is designed to measure a player's overall offensive contributions per plate appearance.

It is determined by taking the observed run values of various offensive events– single, double, triple, or home run—and dividing that sum by a player's plate appearances, and then revising the result to be on the same scale as on-base percentage. Unlike a statistic like OPS, wOBA attempts to assign the proper value for each type of hitting event. As of mid-August 2017, twelve MLB players had wOBAs that exceeded .400 including the Arizona Diamondbacks' Paul Goldschmidt and Houston Astros' Jose Altuve.

Weighted runs created plus (wRC+) is a stat that uniquely analyzes an MLB player's overall effectiveness as a hitter, while adjusting for the effects of ballparks and his league. This stat originated from the weighted runs created (wRC) statistic, which is a more refined version of Bill James' runs created (RC) stat that attempted to weigh a player's total offensive value and measure it by runs. Since wRC+ is ballpark and league-adjusted, it allows anyone to compare two or more players who performed in different years, leagues, and ballparks.

For those not familiar with the scale, 100 is average for this stat. Any number higher is above average while anything below 100 is below average. In the 2016 MLB season, the Los Angeles Angels' Mike Trout had the highest in MLB followed by the Boston Red Sox's David Ortiz, Cincinnati Reds' Joey Votto, Washington National's Daniel Murphy, and Toronto Blue Jays' Josh Donaldson.

Both wRC and wRC+ are easy to use once you learn their scales. Since wRC is a counting stat, be aware of the current number of plate appearances (PAs) of the batter in question. A player with a 10 wRC in 50 PAs is very good but not one with a 10 wRC in 200 PAs. Similarly, 50 RBIs in 100 PAs is considered excellent, but 50 RBIs in 700 PAs would be inferior. Thus, wRC is a measure of raw production and should be used as such. But remember, it is not ballpark, league, or position adjusted.

Using wRC+ is even easier to interpret than wRC because the league average for position players is always 100. If a player has a 110 wRC+, his score is ten percentage points better than the league average offensively. This is a great tool for comparing the at-bat-by-at bat offensive performance of any two players in the league. However, understand that wRC+ does not control for position in a team's batting order.

PITCHING STATS

Besides the core or basic statistics about this position, Fielding Independent Pitching (FIP) measures what a pitcher's ERA would be over a given period of time if he experienced league-average results on balls in play and also in timing. In other words, FIP denotes a pitcher's performance that strips out the role of defense, luck, and sequencing. This makes it a more stable indicator of how a pitcher actually performed than a runs-allowed-based stat, which is highly dependent on the quality of defense played to support him in the field. Certain pitchers have the ability to consistently post lower ERAs than their FIP suggests, but overall, FIP captures most pitchers' true performances very well.

If you had to bet on a pitcher's ERA or FIP for accuracy, FIP is better. Nevertheless, while FIP tells you about a subset of a pitcher's results, it can possibly miss something important about the pitcher's profile which, in turn, allows his batters to have consistently high or low BABIPs. FIP is a terrific stat, but as always, looking into the components of it and other measures of pitching will help anyone understand how a particular pitcher is truly performing. MLB pitchers' FIPs varied from 6.18 to 2.07 in mid-August 2017.

Developed by Dave Studeman and published on website *The Hardball Times*, the expected fielding independent pitching (xFIP) is a regressed version of FIP. It is calculated in the same way as FIP, except it replaces a pitcher's home run total with an estimate of how many home runs he should have allowed given the number of fly balls surrendered while assuming a league-average home run-to-fly ball percentage of between 9 percent and 10 percent.[9]

As a stat, xFIP removes some of the fluctuation in type of hits and gives a better idea of how well a pitcher performed over a given period of time while controlling

---

9 *The Hardball Times is a bunch of people who like to write about baseball. The site was founded in the early spring of 2004 by Aaron Gleeman and Matthew Namee (Bill James' research assistant at the time). Aaron and Matthew also recruited Baseball Graphs' Dave Studeman to help create and maintain the site. The fundamental idea was for The Hardball Times or THT to be a robust baseball website, featuring outstanding commentary, analysis, and research. It was not conceived as a blog but an edited online magazine with in-depth articles each day. Aaron, Matthew, and Dave were among the ten founding writers. See "What is the Hardball Times?" www.hardballtimes.com cited 7 August 2017.*

for defense, batted ball luck and sequencing, and HR/FB%. In other words, xFIP denotes how a pitcher might be expected to perform given an average HR/FB% because we do not expect pitchers to have much control over the statistic. They can somewhat control how many fly balls to allow, but only a limited set of pitchers can truly influence their HR/FB%. This makes xFIP a very useful statistic if used properly. As of mid-August 2017, Chicago White Sox's Derek Holland had the highest xFIP at 5.40 while the Cleveland Indians' Corey Kluber's was lowest at 2.38.

Strikeouts per 9 innings (K/9) and walks per 9 innings (BB/9) are rate statistics that measure, respectively, how many strikeouts and walks a pitcher averages over nine innings. Even though not many pitchers throw nine innings in a game anymore, this is a way of standardizing the statistic to be on an easy-to-understand scale like many other pitching stats scaled to twenty-seven outs. Alternatively, use K% and BB% if you prefer other statistics that measure strikeouts and then walks per batter faced. For pitchers, more strikeouts and fewer walks are goals in their performances.

Baseball teams care about K/9 and BB/9 for two important reasons. First, pitchers have some, if not a lot of control over their strikeout and walk rates. This means these stats are a decent measure of pitchers' performances and skills. While strikeouts and walks are not the only aspects of pitching, they are two which are mostly attributable to the pitcher rather than to him and his team combined. Second, strikeouts and walks are useful because they are stable predictors of success. You do not need more than a few dozen batters faced in a game to get a sense of how effective or ineffective a pitcher is when it comes to strikeouts and walks. Obviously, talent changes and opponents matter. However, pitchers who collect strikeouts routinely prevent runs while those who allow walks typically permit relatively more runs. Thus, you get a sense of how a pitcher performs rather quickly when using these two statistics.

DEFENSIVE STATS

As many baseball statisticians know, UZR primer is an advanced defensive metric that uses play-by-play data recorded by baseball info solutions (BIS) to estimate each fielder's defensive contribution in theoretical runs above or below an average fielder at his position during that player's league and season. Thus, a shortstop with a UZR primer of zero is exactly average as compared to others in the same league and season. However, if this stat is a plus, the fielder is above average, and if it is a minus, the fielder is below average. At 19.6, the Red Sox's Mookie Betts had the highest UZR primer in MLB in mid-August 2017 while the Orioles' Adam Jones' ranked among the worst at −10.8.

Defensive runs saved (DRS) is a defensive statistic calculated by *The Fielding Bible*, an organization operated by John Dewan that rates individual players as being above or below average on defense. Much like UZR primer, players are measured in runs above or below average, and thus, BIS data is used as an input. Since DRS is measured in number of runs, it can be compared easily with a player's offensive contributions such as weighted runs above average (wRAA) and similar statistics. In MLB as of mid-August 2017, the DRS of Betts was 30 but −21 for the Giants' Denard Spahn.[10]

A yearly project conducted by statistician Tom Tango, the Scouting Report (FSR) rates players on their defensive ability based on fan observations and voting. Fans are asked to rate players on a 0-100 scale—with 0 being worst and 100 best—in a number of different categories such as instinct, speed, hands, arm strength, accuracy, and first step. These raw ratings are presented on leaderboards and player pages of the website fangraphs.com.

While UZR primer and DRS are based from data collected by BIS, total zone (TZ) is the only defensive statistic calculated exclusively by using play-by-play data available from non-profit organization, Retrosheet. Invented by Sean Smith, this statistic is calculated in a variety of ways depending upon how much data is available in that specific year. But since it only requires play-by-play data, TZ scores can be calculated for any player in baseball history.

As a result, TZ was used in historical scores on such sites as baseball-reference.com and fangraphs.com prior to 2002. The TZ with location data (TZL) is an improved

---

10 *Weighted runs above average (wRAA) measures the number of offensive runs a player contributes to his team compared to the average player. A wRAA of zero is the league average. So a positive wRAA value denotes above-average performance and a negative wRAA denotes below-average performance. This is also a counting statistic like RBIs, so players accrue more or fewer runs as they play. For more details, see "wRAA," www.fangraphs.com cited 7 August 2017.*

version of TZ that Smith developed in 2010 because it uses game-day hit location data to make calculations more accurate.

OTHER METRICS

Frequently cited in the literature, wins above replacement or WAR is an attempt by the sabermetric baseball community to summarize a player's total contributions to their team in one statistic. Because analysts and fans should always use more than one metric at a time when evaluating players, WAR is all-inclusive and provides a useful reference point for comparing them. WAR offers an estimate to answer the question: If a player got injured and his team had to replace him with a freely available minor leaguer or an AAA player from the bench, how much value would the team lose? Since value is expressed in wins, someone could say that player X is worth +6.3 wins to his team while player Y is only worth +3.5 wins. For this example, this means that player X is much be more valuable than player Y. As of August 2017, the Yankees' Aaron Judge and Astros' Jose Altuve had high WARs but not the Angels' Albert Pujols or the Rockies' Carlos Gonzalez.

UBR primer ultimate base running (UBR) is a stat used to account for the value a player adds to his team via base running on non-stolen base plays. Much like UZR and wRAA, run value is determined using linear weights with each individual base running event receiving a specific run value. Although base running is not an extremely huge part of the game, stealing an extra base and avoiding outs on the bases can add a few runs during games of a season. In MLB's 2014 season, for example, the Washington Nationals were the best base running team in the sport.

Win probability added (WPA) captures the change in win expectancy from one plate appearance to the next and credits or debits a player based on how much his action increased a team's odds of winning. Most sabermetric statistics are context neutral—they do not consider the situation of a particular event or how some plays are more crucial to a win than others. While wOBA rates all home runs equally, intuitively a home run in the third inning of a blowout is less important to a win than a home run in the bottom of the ninth inning of a close game. Consequently, WPA captures the difference between them. The Nationals' Bryce Harper and Angels' Mike Trout each had WPAs exceeding 4.2 in their 2017 season.

The leverage index (LI) attempts to quantify pressure in games to determine if a player has been used primarily in high- or low-leverage situations. There are different iterations of LI including the following types: **pLI or** a player's average LI for all game events; **phLI or a** batter's average LI in only pinch-hit events; **gmLI or a** pitcher's average LI when he enters the game; **inLI or a** pitcher's average LI at the start of each inning; and **exLI or a** pitcher's average LI when exiting a game. Estimated low, average, or high, these stats show the effects of pressure on a player in a given situation.[11]

The clutch statistic measures how well a player performed in high leverage situations. In the words of FanGraphs' creator David Appelman, this calculation measures how much better or worse a player does in high leverage situations than he would have accomplished in a context neutral environment. It also compares a player against himself. For example, a player who hits .300 in high-leverage situations—when overall a .300 hitter—is not a clutch hitter.

Based on the majority of players on teams in MLB, they end up with clutch scores between 1 and -1 with zero being neutral, positive scores being clutch, and negative scores being a choke. Only a few players each year are lucky enough—or unlucky enough—to have extreme clutch scores. In MLB's 2015 season, for example, the Tigers' Miguel Cabrera and Angels' Mike Trout had very high clutch scores.

As a stat, clutch does a good job of describing the past, but it does very little to predict the future. Simply because a player was clutch at one point does not mean he will continue to perform well in high-leverage situations, and vice versa. Very few

---

11 *To calculate the LI, take the current base-out state, inning, and score and find the possible changes in win expectancy (WE) that could occur during a particular plate appearance. Then multiple those potential changes by the odds of that potential change occurring, add them up, and divide by the average potential swing in WE to get the LI. For clarity, imagine the home team has a WE of 0.60 and then assume that there are only two possible outcomes of this play, a single or strikeout. Imagine each occurs 50% of the time on average. Also, assume the WE after a single is 0.7 and after a strikeout 0.4, and the average swing is 0.04. To get the LI of this fictional situation, find (0.1 x 0.5 + 0.2 x 0.5)/0.04. The solution is 3.75, which is extremely high. For more details and measurement, see "LI," www.fangraphs.com cited 7 August 2017.*

players have the ability to be consistently clutch in performances throughout their careers. Furthermore, choking in one season does not beget the same in the future.

To conclude this chapter, undoubtedly statistical analysis and particularly sabermetric concepts have truly changed baseball as a sport for fans, the general public, and the media, and especially for MLB teams and the decisions of their field managers and players at various positions. By collecting both historical and game-day data and using simple and complex equations and formulas, statisticians are able to pinpoint and more thoroughly evaluate the performances of catchers, infielders, outfielders, and pitchers and also the effectiveness of hitters or batters given their plate appearances. Based on readings in the literature and other sources, this has improved the game now and likely in the future and perhaps made it more fun, interesting, and successful.[12]

12 *For various readings on different but interesting and specific topics in this chapter, see Thomas Brady, "Do Sabermetrics Suggest a Baseball Hall of Fame Revision?" IIE Annual Conference Proceedings (2012): 1–4; Ronny Coleman, "Stats Are More Than Inside Baseball," Fire Chief (October 2008): 30, 32–33; Lee Van Scyoc and Kevin McGee, "Testing for Competitive Balance," Empirical Economics (May 2016): 1029–1043; Stephen Gross, "With MacPhail, Phils Finally Go to Sabermetrics," Morning Call (1 July 2015): C.1; Brendan Kennedy, "Newest Jay Ready to Go to WAR," Toronto Star (2 April 2015): M.4; "Sabermetrics Are Revolutionizing Baseball," University Wire (14 May 2014): 1; Joseph Abisaid, "Traditional Baseball Statistics Still Dominate News Stories," Newspaper Research Journal (June 2017): 158–173; Bruce Miles, "In Sabermetrics Value, Cubs Annihilate Mets," Daily Herald (17 October 2015): 3; Heather O'Neill, "Do Major League Baseball Hitters Engage in Opportunistic Behavior?" International Advances in Economic Research (August 2013): 215–232; Tom Verducci, "Welcome to the New Age of Information," Sports Illustrated (5 April 2004): 50–54; David Waldstein, "Where Analytics Don't Add Up," New York Times (11 January 2018): 1,9; Brian Costa and Jared Diamond, "Baseball Learns Data's Downside," Wall Street Journal (4 October 2017): A1, A10; Jared Diamond, "How Players Use New Data Analytics," Wall Street Journal (21 September 2017): A16.*

CHAPTER 3

Immigrant Ballplayers

For various cultural, economic, social, and sport-specific reasons, since the late 1950s there has been steady growth in the number of foreign-born players on teams in Major League Baseball (MLB). On rosters of teams in the American League (AL) and National League (NL), they represented approximately 3.6 percent in 1958, 6.9 percent in 1968, 8.8 percent in 1978, and 19.8 percent in 1998. Then, in three years of the early 2000s, the percentages of these athletes were 28.1 percent in 2008, 29.8 percent in 2017, and approximately 27 percent on opening day in 2018. In addition, the proportion of international ballplayers in the minor leagues and on teams affiliated with MLB clubs varied between 45 and 50 percent during the 2000s. If trends continue into the future, there will be a larger proportion of these players from minor A, AA, and AAA teams on those in the big leagues after 2017.[1]

At the beginning of MLB's 2017 season, the 259 players born outside the United States came from a pool of 868 and represented a record-high nineteen countries and territories beyond the US border. Previously, there were eighteen countries and territories represented on opening day rosters in 1998 and 2016. The 259 foreign-born players and the percentage of 29.8 are both the highest figures in history,

1 *For more specific historical information about foreign and international players on teams in Major League Baseball, see chapter 13 in Frank P. Jozsa Jr.'s two books: Baseball, Inc.: The National Pastime as Big Business (Jefferson, NC: McFarland, 2006) and Baseball Beyond Borders: From Distant Lands to the Major Leagues (Lanham, MD: Scarecrow Press, 2013).*

eclipsing the previous record totals of 246 players on 2007 opening day rosters and 29.2 percent on 2005 opening day rosters.[2]

As it has each year since MLB began releasing this type of annual data in 1995, the Dominican Republic again led the major leagues in 2017 with ninety-three players while Venezuela ranked second with seventy-six—the country's highest total in history and far eclipsing its previous high of sixty-six in 2012. Matching its record total in 2016, Cuba placed third with twenty-three players.

Rounding out the total number of players per country on April 3, 2017 were Puerto Rico with sixteen; Mexico with nine; Japan with eight; Canada with six; South Korea with five; and Curacao and Nicaragua with four each. Other nations included Panama with four; Australia, Brazil, and Columbia each with two; and Germany, Netherlands, Taiwan, and the US Virgin Islands each with one. Interestingly, the Minnesota Twins' Max Kepler, a native of Berlin, is the first German-born product of MLB's European Elite Camp to appear on an opening day roster in MLB history. Also, the New York Yankees' Didi Gregorius became the first player from the Netherlands to appear on three consecutive opening day rosters.

On April 3, 2017, the Texas Rangers had the most foreign-born players with a total of fourteen on its roster, who spanned six different countries and territories outside the US. Following the Rangers in numbers of these players were the San Diego Padres and Seattle Mariners each with twelve and then the Chicago White Sox, Cleveland Indians, Los Angeles Angels, and Philadelphia Phillies each with eleven. The Kansas City Royals' and Seattle Mariners' international players came from eight different countries and territories outside the US, marking the most of all teams in MLB. The Los Angeles Dodgers had seven foreign-born players on their roster. The Pittsburgh Pirates had six players from the Dominican Republic while opening day rosters' of the Colorado Rockies, Detroit Tigers, Phillies, and Padres consisted of six players each from Venezuela.

Besides rosters on opening day, table 3.1 lists the number of non-US players on AL and NL teams' active rosters as of August 8, 2018. The table reveals three interesting distributions. First, the largest proportions of players were from the Dominican Republic at 36 percent and Venezuela at 31 percent and the fewest with less than 1

2 *See, for example, "Opening Day Rosters Feature Record 259 Players Born Outside the US," www.mlb.com cited 9 August 2017, and Stuart Anderson, "27 Percent of Major League Baseball Players Are Foreign-Born," www.forbes.com cited 21 November 2018.*

percent each were from Aruba, Canada, Nicaragua, Saudi Arabia, and Taiwan. Second, pitchers were primarily from the Dominican Republic, catchers and infielders from Venezuela, outfielders from Venezuela and the Dominican Republic, and designated hitters from the Dominican Republic followed by Cuba and Venezuela. Third, for non-US players at each position, 41 percent were pitchers, 32 percent infielders, 15 percent outfielders, 10 percent catchers; and 2 percent designated hitters. Especially as pitchers and infielders, these countries' ballplayers were special and talented, and thus they contributed in some way to their MLB team's performances.

Table 3.1 Number of Non-US Players, Major League Baseball by Country, as of August 2018

Country	Pitchers	Catchers	Infielders	Outfielders	DH	Total
Aruba	0	0	1	0	0	1
Brazil	1	1	0	0	0	2
Canada	0	0	0	1	0	1
Columbia	3	1	1	0	0	5
Cuba	3	1	9	4	1	18
Dominican Republic	41	2	27	12	2	84
Germany	1	0	0	1	0	2
Japan	3	0	0	0	0	3
Mexico	8	0	0	0	0	8
Netherlands	1	0	6	0	0	7
Nicaragua	1	0	0	0	0	1
Panama	2	0	2	0	0	4
Puerto Rico	6	6	3	2	0	17
Saudi Arabia	1	0	0	0	0	1
South Korea	2	0	1	1	0	4
Taiwan	1	0	0	0	0	1
Venezuela	21	12	26	13	1	73

Note: DH is designated hitter. The numbers in columns exclude players on the disabled list and in the minor leagues. As of August 8, 2018, there were no players from Australia, Dhahran, or the US Virgin Islands on the active rosters of MLB teams.

Source: "Major League Baseball Team Rosters," www.espn.com cited 8 August 2017.

Based on baseball's history and a thorough research of the literature, the next sections of this chapter feature similar but relevant facts, perspectives, and viewpoints about the role, significance, and success of non-US-born ballplayers while on AL and then NL teams in MLB and their qualifications for being inducted into the Baseball Hall of Fame (BHOF). Besides data in the tables, there are articles, books, and Internet sources in the bibliography for readers to further research and learn how these athletes greatly influenced the sport, particularly in big-league seasons of the 1990s and early 2000s.

AMERICAN LEAGUE

Historical Performances: Award Winners

After each MLB regular season and following the World Series, a few players on teams in the AL and NL receive awards for their outstanding performances. For the highest hitting average during a regular season, there is a batting champion while the most outstanding pitcher in each league wins a Cy Young award. In addition, there is Most Valuable Player (MVP), Rookie of the Year (ROY), and Rolaids Relief (RR) awards to players in the AL and NL. This section discusses those won by non-US-born players in the AL and highlights those who were on the league's all-star team and others who were elected into the BHOF.[3]

Batting Champion

To be eligible and win a batting title in the AL, a player must have at least 3.1 appearances at bat or 502 in total for his team during a 162-game MLB season and achieve the highest batting average (BA) or number of hits per appearance. In 1901, Philadelphia Athletics' Nap Lajoie hit .426 and became the AL's first official batting champion. In later seasons, Detroit Tigers' outfielder Ty Cobb won twelve batting

3 *Three Internet sources that have information about awards and their winners are "Batting Average Year-by-Year Leaders," www.baseball-almanac.com cited 24 November 2012, "MLB Most Valuable Player MVP Awards & Cy Young Awards Winners," www.baseball-reference.com cited 11 August 2017, and "MLB Rookie of the Year Awards," www.baseball-reference.com cited 11 August 2017.*

titles during his career and finished with a lifetime .366 BA, which is the highest in MLB history.

Regarding non-US-born players on teams in the AL, five infielders and five outfielders were batting champions (table 3.2). Within the group, Minnesota Twins' Rod Carew from Panama won seven titles and had the highest single-season average at .388 in 1977. Although Carew hit few home runs, he rarely struck out while at bat. Given these ten champions—but excluding those currently on active rosters of teams—Carew had the highest lifetime BA at .328. In 1972, however, he hit only .318 but nonetheless won a title.

Table 3.2 Non-US Players, American League Award Winners, by Country, Team, and Year

Name	Country	Team	Year
Batting Champion			
Bobby Avila	Mexico	Cleveland Indians	1954
Tony Oliva	Cuba	Minnesota Twins	1964–1965, 1971
Rod Carew	Panama	Minnesota Twins	1969, 1972–1975, 1977–1978
Julio Franco	Dominican Republic	Texas Rangers	1991
Bernie Williams	Puerto Rico	New York Yankees	1998
Ichiro Suzuki	Japan	Seattle Mariners	2001, 2004
Manny Ramirez	Dominican Republic	Boston Red Sox	2002
Magglio Ordonez	Venezuela	Detroit Tigers	2007
Miguel Cabrera	Venezuela	Detroit Tigers	2011–2013, 2015
Jose Altuve	Venezuela	Houston Astros	2014, 2016–2017
Cy Young			
Mike Cuellar	Cuba	Baltimore Orioles	1969
Willie Hernandez	Puerto Rico	Detroit Tigers	1984
Pedro Martinez	Dominican Republic	Boston Red Sox	1999, 2000
Johan Santana	Venezuela	Minnesota Twins	2004, 2006

Name	Country	Team	Year
Bartolo Colon	Dominican Republic	Los Angeles Angels	2005
Felix Hernandez	Venezuela	Seattle Mariners	2010
Most Valuable Player			
Zoilo Versalles	Cuba	Minnesota Twins	1965
Rod Carew	Panama	Minnesota Twins	1977
Willie Hernandez	Puerto Rico	Detroit Tigers	1984
George Bell	Dominican Republic	Toronto Blue Jays	1987
Jose Canseco	Cuba	Oakland Athletics	1988
Juan Gonzalez	Puerto Rico	Texas Rangers	1996, 1998
Ivan Rodriguez	Puerto Rico	Texas Rangers	1999
Ichiro Suzuki	Japan	Seattle Mariners	2001
Miguel Tejada	Dominican Republic	Oakland Athletics	2002
Vladimir Guerrero	Dominican Republic	Anaheim Angels	2004
Justin Morneau	Canada	Minnesota Twins	2006
Miguel Cabrera	Venezuela	Detroit Tigers	2012–2013
Jose Altuve	Venezuela	Houston Astros	2017
Rookie of the Year			
Luis Aparicio	Venezuela	Chicago White Sox	1956
Tony Oliva	Cuba	Minnesota Twins	1964
Rod Carew	Panama	Minnesota Twins	1967
Alfredo Griffin	Dominican Republic	Toronto Blue Jays	1979
Ozzie Guillen	Venezuela	Chicago White Sox	1985
Jose Canseco	Cuba	Oakland Athletics	1986
Sandy Alomar Jr.	Puerto Rico	Cleveland Indians	1990
Carlos Beltran	Puerto Rico	Kansas City Royals	1999
Kazuhiro Sasaki	Japan	Seattle Mariners	2000
Ichiro Suzuki	Japan	Seattle Mariners	2001
Angel Berroa	Dominican Republic	Kansas City Royals	2003

(continued)

Table 3.2 continued

Name	Country	Team	Year
Neftali Feliz	Dominican Republic	Texas Rangers	2010
Jose Abreu	Cuba	Chicago White Sox	2014
Carlos Correa	Puerto Rico	Houston Astros	2015
Shohei Ohtani	Japan	Los Angeles Angels	2018
Rolaids Relief Award			
Jose Mesa	Dominican Republic	Cleveland Indians	1995
Mariano Rivera	Panama	New York Yankees	1999, 2001, 2004–2005, 2009
Francisco Rodriguez	Venezuela	Los Angeles Angels	2006, 2008
Rafael Soriano	Dominican Republic	Tampa Bay Rays	2010
Jose Valverde	Dominican Republic	Detroit Tigers	2011

Note: Name, Country, Team, and Year are self-explanatory. Although born in another country, players from Puerto Rico are US citizens.

Source: Frank P. Jozsa Jr., Baseball Beyond Borders: From Distant Lands to the Major Leagues (Lanham, MD: Scarecrow Press, 2013); George Vass, "The Wide World of Baseball," Baseball Digest (February 2003): 11–16; "Batting Average Year-by-Year Leaders," www.baseball-almanac.com cited 11 August 2017; "MLB Most Valuable Player MVP Awards & Cy Young Awards Winners," www.baseball-reference.com cited 11 August 2017; "MLB Rookie of the Year Awards," www.baseball-reference.com cited 11 August 2017; "2012 American League All-Star Roster," www.espn.go.com cited 11 August 2017; "Rolaids Relief Award," www.baseball-reference.com cited 21 November 2018.

Other popular batting champions in the AL were the Tigers' Miguel Cabrera from Venezuela with four titles, Twins' Tony Oliva from Cuba with three, and then with two each, Jose Altuve from Venezuela and the former Seattle Mariners' Ichiro Suzuki from Japan. In contrast to such line-drive, single-base hitters as Carew, Oliva, Suzuki, and the former Cleveland Indians' shortstop Bobby Avila from Mexico, the other batting champions had power while hitting baseballs and most of them frequently slugged doubles, triples, and home runs during games in their careers. For other information about these excellent batters, Rod Carew was an all-star in eighteen AL seasons, Manny Ramirez in twelve, and Suzuki in ten. In short, these champions were among the greatest hitters of all players in MLB history.

Cy Young

From 1956 to 1966, a Denton True "Cy" Young award was given to the most outstanding pitcher on a team in MLB. The first recipient was Brooklyn Dodgers' Don Newcombe because he won twenty-seven games in 1956. Beginning in 1967, however, there were pitchers from both the AL and NL who won a Cy Young. That year, they were the Boston Red Sox's Jim Lonborg and San Francisco Giants' Mike McCormick.

Since 2010, members of the Baseball Writers Association of America (BWAA) and one representative from each MLB team have voted for the first, second, third, fourth, and fifth most outstanding starting or relief pitcher in the AL and NL. Mathematically, the formula to determine the Cy Young winner is a weighted sum of votes. The AL and NL pitchers who receive the highest scores win the award.

As of 2012, six different non-US-born pitchers won a Cy Young in the AL. During 2000– 2012, Venezuela's Johan Santana won two of them and so did Dominican Pedro Martinez in 1999–2000. In addition, Martinez played eighteen seasons in MLB and among the group of pitchers has the highest number of victories at 219 and eight appearances on all-star teams. Although Puerto Rico's Willie Hernandez and Venezuela's Felix Hernandez were not necessarily starting pitchers in their team's games, they entered them sometime during the mid-to-late innings to stop rallies and prevent the rival team from scoring any runs. Interestingly, each of them had won fewer than one hundred games in the AL as of 2012.

Cuba's Mike Cuellar pitched for AL pennant winners and World Series teams with the Baltimore Orioles, while Dominican Bartolo Colon's record was 21–8 in 2005. That season, he had a very low earned run average (ERA) for the league's Los Angeles Angels. Truly, these six athletes were outstanding players because of their ability to control pitches and consistently throw them in or near the strike zone, and thus win many games for their team.

Most Valuable Player

Each MLB season since 1931, someone from the AL and NL won a Most Valuable Player (MVP) award. All active players are eligible to receive this honor based on their performance as a hitter or either a pitcher, catcher, infielder, or outfielder.

Currently, members of the BWAA vote to select the leagues' MVPs. When baseball's first commissioner died of a heart attack in November 1944, the MVP official title became the Kennesaw Mountain Landis Memorial Baseball Award. That year, the winners of it were two native Americans—Detroit Tigers' pitcher Hal Newhouser in the AL and St. Louis Cardinals' shortstop Marty Marion in the NL.

As indicated in the third part of table 3.2, thirteen different non-US-born players were successful enough during a MLB season for them to win an MVP award in the AL. Puerto Rico's Juan Gonzalez, who played seventeen years including thirteen with the Texas Rangers, had a .316 BA and earned his award in two seasons. Besides being an outstanding hitter, he was a three-time all-star and had 1,404 runs batted in (RBIs) during his career.

Regarding achievements of two other MVPs, Cuba's Zoilo Versalles played shortstop for the Minnesota Twins and in 1965, he scored 126 runs, hit forty-five doubles, and had 308 total bases. Equally impressive, Japan's Ichiro Suzuki batted .350 for the Seattle Mariners in 2001. Moreover, he stole fifty-six bases and had 242 hits in 157 games.

Except for Versalles, batting champions Carew and Suzuki, and Cy Young winner Willie Hernandez, the other MVPs in the group were sluggers in the AL. Indeed, they hit numerous home runs, batted in at least one hundred runs during some MLB regular seasons, and occasionally had a .300 or higher BA. For example, their BAs and RBIs during MVP years were, respectively, .332 and 113 for Puerto Rico's Ivan Rodriguez in 1999, .308 and 131 for Dominican Miguel Tejada in 2002, .337 and 126 for Dominican Vladimir Guerrero in 2004, .321 and 130 for Canadian Justin Morneau in 2006, .330 and 139 for Dominican Miguel Cabrera in 2012 and .348 and 137 in 2013, and .346 and 81 for Venezuelan Jose Altuve in 2017.

In addition to them, Dominican George Bell and Cuban Jose Canseco were valuable players and had more than one excellent season for their respective team. While at bat during games, they swung with power and frequently hit baseballs for long distances into the outfield and over the wall for home runs. In 1987, Toronto Blue Jays' Bell had 369 total bases, hit forty-seven home runs, and led the AL with 134 RBIs. One year later, the Oakland Athletics' Canseco led the league with forty-two home runs and 124 RBIs. During their careers in MLB, Bell played on five and Canseco six AL all-star teams. Since they are still active players on teams' rosters, the Mariners' and Miami Marlins' Suzuki and Tigers' Cabrera may win another MVP before they retire from the sport.

Rookie of the Year

To qualify for rookie of the year (ROY), a MLB player must have at least 130 at bats or fifty innings played in games during a season, and be available for forty-five days on a team's active roster before September 1. In 1947, ROY became a national award in MLB and on April 15, Jackie Robinson became the first African American to perform in a game of the big leagues. He played in the infield for the Brooklyn Dodgers and won ROY, which in 1947 was a single but combined award for the AL and NL.

From 1956 to 2018, fifteen different non-US-born players were ROY winners in the AL. The first was Venezuela's Luis Aparicio. In 1956, he played shortstop for the Chicago White Sox, averaged .266 while at bat, and had 143 hits and 215 total bases in 152 games. Then, during their ROY season in the 1960s, Cuba's Oliva and Panama's Carew each had a BA of at least .292 and 150 hits. In addition to them, Dominican Alfredo Griffin won his award in 1979 because of his .281 BA, 179 hits, and eighty-one runs while in the 1980s, Venezuelan Ozzie Guillen and Cuban Jose Canseco had special years for teams because of their above-average number of hits, RBIs, and total bases in games.

Sandy Alomar Jr. and Carlos Beltran, both from Puerto Rico, won a ROY award in the AL during the 1990s. In fact, they excelled while at bat, scored many runs, and made few errors for their teams in regular season games. During their respective ROY seasons in the 2000s, Japanese pitcher Kazuhiro Sasaki had thirty-seven saves, seventy-eight strikeouts, and a 3.16 ERA for the Seattle Mariners; Japanese outfielder Ichiro Suzuki batted .350, had 242 hits, and stole fifty-six bases for the Seattle Mariners; Dominican infielder Angel Berroa had 163 hits and scored ninety-two runs for the Kansas City Royals; Dominican pitcher Neftali Feliz finished fifty-nine games with a 2.73 ERA for the Texas Rangers; Cuban infielder Jose Abreu had a .581 slugging percentage (SLG) for the White Sox; and Puerto Rican infielder Carlos Correa's on-base plus slugging percentage (OPS) was .857 for the Houston Astros in 2015.

Signed to a $2.315 million bonus and former player for the Nippon Ham Fighters, right-handed pitcher Shohei Ohtani was 4–2 with a 3.31 ERA and sixty-three strikeouts over fifty-one innings for the Angels. As a designated hitter, he batted .285 with twenty-two homeruns and sixty-one RBIs and also achieved a .925 on base plus slugging percentage (OPS) in 367 plate appearances. Ohtani was the first MLB player with fifteen homeruns and fifty strikeouts in the same season. In comparison to other rookies in the AL, these fifteen non-US-born professional athletes had performed well enough on their teams during a MLB season to win ROY and become heroes among fans in their local communities and also home countries.[4]

Rolaids Relief Award

Since 1976, five non-US-born pitchers have won a Rolaids Relief (RR) award in the AL as of 2018 (the RR was discontinued in 2012). Rather than win it according to the number of votes cast from members of the BWAA, MLB players earned the award based on their statistical performance in a regular season. That is, the result depended on a relative but explicit point system. Specifically, there were five points given for saving a game and two for a win, negative two for a loss, one for a tough save, and negative two for a blown save. The AL and NL relief pitchers that received the most points won the award. Rolaids sponsored the event, in part, because the company's historic slogan R-O-L-A-I-D-S represents relief from indigestion.[5]

After saving forty-six games for the Cleveland Indians with an ERA of 1.13 and fifty-eight strikeouts, Dominican pitcher Jose Mesa won an RR in 1995. Four years later and again in 2001, 2004, 2005 and 2009, Panama's Mariano Rivera had enough saves, low ERAs, and numbers of strikeouts for the New York Yankees to be the best relief pitcher during these five seasons in the AL. Technically, he won these awards primarily because his cut fastball moved downward or simply dropped as it approached batters, and he threw it consistently somewhere in or near the strike zone. After Mariano retired in 2013, eventually he will receive enough votes and unanimous approval for his entry into the BHOF.

Another great relief pitcher, especially in 2006 and 2008, was Venezuelan Francisco Rodriguez of the Los Angeles Angels. During each of these MLB seasons, he saved

---

4 *See Ronald Blum, "Ohtani, Acuna Named Rookies of the Year," Charlotte Observer (13 November 2018): 2B.*

5 *Discontinued after MLB's 2012 season, the AL's Rolaids Relief Award was renamed Mariano Rivera Award in 2014. See "Mariano Rivera Award," www.baseball-reference.com cited 13 November 2018.*

more than forty-five games, had a low ERA, and struck out more than seventy-five batters. Besides Rodriguez, Dominican pitchers Rafael Soriano in 2010 and Jose Valverde in 2011 kept their team competitive in its respective division. While in relief of their teams' starting pitchers, they were effective at fooling or tricking batters with their pitches and getting them to hit baseballs in the air or on the ground for an out. Soriano, for example, had a 1.73 ERA for the Tampa Bay Rays while Valverde saved forty-nine games for the Detroit Tigers. In other words, they deserved to win an RR award for their outstanding performances on AL teams.

Other Awards

Awarded to players in MLB for the 1957 season, AL and NL players at nine positions each won a Gold Glove (GG) for their superior fielding performances. The Rawlings Group—a company with headquarters in St. Louis, Missouri—manufacture's gold lame-tanned leather gloves, affixes them to a walnut base, and then presents the gloves to AL and NL players who each receive the most votes from teams' coaches and managers.[6]

From 1958 to 2018 in the AL, non-US-born players with the most GGs by position included pitcher Johan Santana of Venezuela, catcher Ivan Rodriguez of Puerto Rico, first baseman Rafael Palmeiro of Cuba, second baseman Roberto Alomar of Puerto Rico, and third baseman Adrian Beltre of the Dominican Republic. Besides them, there were shortstops Luis Aparicio of Venezuela and Omar Visquel of Columbia, outfielders Ichiro Suzuki of Japan, Minnie Minosa of Cuba, and Sixto Lezcano of Puerto Rico, and catcher Salvador Perez of Venezuela. Indeed, each of these players made few errors, if any, while fielding baseballs hit by batters on the ground and then throwing them to a teammate at a base in the infield or home plate. In addition, they caught baseballs hit in the air to them by batters including fast and slow line drives and tricky grounders.[7]

---

6 *The recipients of this fifty-six-year-old award, including players from the US by name, year, and position are in "American League Gold Glove Award Winners," www.baseball-reference.com cited 17 December 2012.*

7 *In MLB's 2018 season, AL gold glove winners were Royals' catcher Salvador Perez of Venezuela and Angels' shortstop Andrelton of Curacao. The reference is "American League Gold Glove Winners."*

From 1980 to 2018, MLB teams' coaches and managers have voted for and then awarded a Silver Slugger (SS) to the best offensive player at each position in the AL and NL. To win a SS, each player must excel in such categories as their BA, slugging and on-base percentages, number of RBIs, and a general impression of their overall value and leadership to their team on offense. Manufactured by Hillerich & Bradbsy, who also makes Louisville Slugger bats, the award is a three-foot (ninety-one centimeter) bat-shaped trophy engraved with the name of a winner at a position including a DH in each league.[8]

Of the many SSs awarded thus far in the AL, the non-US-born players with most of them by position are catcher Ivan Rodriguez, first baseman Carlos Delgado, and second baseman Roberto Alomar each of Puerto Rico, and shortstop Miguel Tejada and third baseman Adrian Beltre each of the Dominican Republic. There are also outfielders Manny Ramirez and Vladimir Guerrero of the Dominican Republic, Juan Gonzalez of Puerto Rico, and designated hitter David Ortiz of the Dominican Republic. Because of their strong wrists and arms, and coordination to swing bats with speed and power generated from their hips and legs, Rodriguez and the other SS winners made contact and hit baseballs for singles and extra bases. Thus, these athletes were important to their teams in winning games during regular MLB seasons and perhaps in playoffs and World Series.[9]

Based on their primary positions in games, table 3.3 denotes that the rosters of fifteen AL teams contained a total of 118 non-US ballplayers as of August 8, 2018. While forty-four—or 37 percent of the group—were on clubs in the Central Division (CD), forty-eight or 41 percent played in the West Division (WD) and another twenty-six or 22 percent in the East Division (ED).

By division, the ED had the least number of non-US players at each position. Also, the CD's teams ranked first in catchers, infielders, and outfielders while those in the WD

---

8 *Besides foreigners, many players born in the US have won this award including Carlton Fisk at catcher, Don Mattingly at first base, Lou Whitaker at second base, Wade Boggs at third base, Derek Jeter at shortstop, David Winfield in the outfield, and Don Baylor at designated hitter. See "Silver Slugger Award Winners—American League," www.baseball-reference.com cited 17 December 2012.*

9 *In MLB's 2018 season, AL silver slugger awardees included Royals catcher Salvador Perez of Venezuela, White Sox first baseman Jose Abreu of Cuba, Astros second baseman Jose Altuve of Venezuela, Indians third baseman Jose Ramirez of the Dominican Republic, and Indians shortstop Francisco Lindor of Puerto Rico. The reference is "Silver Slugger Award Winners—American League."*

were first in pitchers and tied for first in designated hitters (DHs). These results occurred, in part, because of only four or less on rosters of the ED's Baltimore Orioles and Boston Red Sox but eleven each on those of the CD's Chicago White Sox and Cleveland Indians and sixteen on the WD's Texas Rangers and eleven on the Los Angeles Angels.

Table 3.3 Non-US Players, American League by Division, Team, and Position, 2018 Season

Team	Pitchers	Catchers	Infielders	Outfielders	DH	Total
East Division						
Baltimore Orioles	2	0	2	0	0	4
Boston Red Sox	1	1	2	0	0	4
New York Yankees	2	0	3	0	0	5
Tampa Bay Rays	3	2	2	1	0	8
Toronto Blue Jays	1	0	2	1	1	5
Central Division						
Chicago White Sox	5	2	3	1	0	11
Cleveland Indians	2	2	5	1	1	11
Detroit Tigers	4	0	2	1	1	8
Kansas City Royals	2	1	2	1	0	6
Minnesota Twins	2	1	3	2	0	8
West Division						
Houston Astros	3	1	3	1	0	8
Los Angeles Angels	5	2	3	0	1	11
Oakland Athletics	4	0	0	0	0	4
Seattle Mariners	5	0	2	1	1	9
Texas Rangers	5	2	6	3	0	16

Note: DH is designated hitter. The numbers in columns exclude players on the disabled list and in the minor leagues.

Source: "Major League Baseball Team Rosters," www.espn.com cited 8 August 2018.

Based on these players' positions in games, pitchers were ranked first with forty-six or 39 percent of the total; infielders second with forty or 34 percent; catchers third with fourteen or 12 percent; outfielders fourth with thirteen or 11 percent; and DHs fifth with five or 4 percent. In other words, given their experience, interest, and skill in the sport, the most talented players from non-US countries excelled in pitching but not as outfielders. As a group, they were also productive as infielders but not very competitive or useful on teams as DHs.

Except for the Orioles, Red Sox, and Athletics with four in addition to the Yankees and Blue Jays each with five, the allocation of players across the other ten AL teams was between six and sixteen and normally distributed except for the number that performed for the Rangers. Furthermore, the roster of the Indians included at least one player at each position while Americans dominated those of all teams except the Rangers.

Baseball Hall of Fame

Since 1936, the most prestigious honor for retired professional ballplayers and baseball managers, umpires, pioneers, franchise executives and owners, and organizers is their induction into the Baseball Hall of Fame (BHOF). For players to be eligible, there are requirements. They must have been retired for five years, had at least ten years of experience in MLB or the former Negro Leagues, and received a preliminary review and approval by a screening committee. Qualified members of the BWAA or a Veterans Committee vote and may submit ballots to admit up to ten players in each election. Any player who receives seventy-five percent or more of all ballots wins an election and thus admission into the BHOF. If voted for in less than five percent of all ballots, these individuals will not appear on ballots as candidates in future BHOF elections. However, under special circumstances such as illness or death, a player and other candidates may be eligible for induction without meeting all of these requirements.[10]

As of 2018, there were seven non-US-born players from AL teams in the BHOF. The first of them was former Chicago White Sox infielder Luis Aparicio from Venezuela.

---

10 *For data and historical information about the careers of former and current MLB players from the US and foreign countries and the Baseball Hall of Fame, see such readings as Teddy Mitrosilis, "Foreign-Born Players in Baseball's Hall of Fame," www.thepostgame.com cited 5 November 2012, "Deep List of Candidates Rounds Out Hall's List," www.losangeles.dodgers.mlb.com cited 30 November 2012, "National Baseball Hall of Fame and Museum," www.wikipedia.org cited 30 November 2012, "Biography by Baseball Almanac," www.baseball-almanac.com cited 30 November 2012, "Sports Biographies," www.hickoksports.com cited 1 December 2012, and "Baseball Hall of Fame," www.baseballhall.org cited 3 December 2017.*

During his eighteen years in MLB, he never played a single inning in games at any other position than shortstop. Admired, popular, and also respected for his slick fielding and his ability to steal bases and score runs, Aparicio led all AL shortstops in fielding percentage for eight consecutive seasons. He won nine GG awards, once held White Sox all-time records for games played and assists, and AL records for putouts and total chances. Although his lifetime BA was mediocre at .262, Aparicio had 2,677 hits and 506 stolen bases in 2,599 games. He won a ROY award in 1956 and played on ten AL all-star teams. Being a team leader, Luis Aparicio contributed outstanding defense, played solid but fundamental offense, and did intangible things that never appeared in a game's box score. Undoubtedly, he belongs in the BHOF.

Seven years after Aparicio's induction, Rod Carew from Panama joined him and other members in the BHOF. Carew used a variety of crouched batting stances to hit over .300 in fifteen consecutive seasons, nine of them with the AL's Minnesota Twins and six with the California Angels. Besides his ROY award in 1967 and MVP in 1977, Carew won seven batting titles and had 3,053 career hits. He played on eighteen AL all-star teams and in 1969 successfully stole home base seven times. With respect to MLB records, he ranks second all-time in stealing home behind the Detroit Tigers' Ty Cobb. Another big league player said this about Carew as a hitter: "He has an uncanny ability to move the ball around as if the bat were some kind of magic wand." Given his achievements in the AL, Rod Carew was an outstanding player who deserves to be in the BHOF.

Bert Blyleven was the first non-US-born pitcher from the AL in baseball's hall of fame. A native of Zeist, Netherlands, he played on five different teams (four in the AL) for a total of twenty-two MLB seasons. His results were remarkable from pitching in games. Blyleven had outstanding control, a wicked curveball, and fluid motion on the mound. Nicknamed the "Dutch Master," he had 287 wins and 3,701 strikeouts or 6.7 per nine-inning game, 60 shutouts, 242 complete games, and pitched 4,970 innings to 20,491 batters. Blyleven was a key cog in contributing to World Series victories for the 1979 Pittsburg Pirates and again for the 1987 Minnesota Twins. In fact, he started a game and won another for the Pirates against the Baltimore Orioles, and won a game but lost another for the Twins despite pitching a shutout against the St. Louis Cardinals for five innings. In short, Bert Blyleven was a competitive and durable pitcher. Undoubtedly, he is a great addition to the BHOF.

Elected into the BHOF on January 5, 2011, Puerto Rican Roberto Alomar was a twelve-time all-star and ten-time GG winner who performed as an infielder for seventeen MLB seasons with seven different teams. During his career, he had 2,724 hits, 210 home runs, and averaged .300 as a batter. In 1996, Alomar had a heated exchange with umpire John Hirschbeck during a Baltimore Orioles game. Because of the argument, he spit in Hirschbeck's face and then said that personal stress caused the umpire to make mistakes while calling balls and strikes thrown from the pitcher to hitters. After the game, Hirschbeck tried to start a fight with Alomar in the Orioles' locker room. Incredibly, the two of them eventually became friends. As a player on MLB teams, Alomar earned $76 million. Despite his inexcusable behavior, dispute, and poor relations with an umpire, Roberto Alomar was a marvelous player who accomplished enough while on teams in the AL for admission into the BHOF.

Inducted in 2015, Dominican pitcher Pedro Martinez was an eight-time all-star who finished his career with a record of 219–100 and a winning percentage of .687 that is sixth all-time, and trails only Whitey Ford's .690 among modern-era pitchers with at least 150 victories. Martinez won five ERA titles en route to a career mark of 2.93, captured six walks plus hits per innings pitched (WHIP) titles—in fact his career WHIP of 1.054 ranks fifth all-time and is the best of any modern-era starter—and he averaged 10.04 strikeouts per nine innings—third all-time behind Randy Johnson and Kerry Wood. His 3,154 strikeouts rank thirteenth all-time, and his strikeout-to-walk ratio of 4.15-to-1 ranks third all-time.

Puerto Rican catcher Ivan Rodriguez entered the BHOF in 2017 after a 21-year career in which he was a 14-time all-star and winner of thirteen GG awards for his defensive excellence. He was the 1999 AL MVP winner and finished with a career batting average of .296 with 311 home runs. He is one of six major leaguers with a minimum batting average, 2,800 hits, 550 doubles, 300 home runs, and 1,300 RBIs. His GG's are the most by a catcher and fourth most at any position. He had quick feet that allowed him to block balls in the dirt, was excellent at running down and catching foul balls, was fearless on plays at the plate, and had an incredible throwing arm.

Born in 1975 in the Dominican Republic, Vladimir Guerrero was signed by the Montreal Expos at age 18 where he quickly established himself as one of baseball's top prospects. In his seven full seasons with the Expos, Guerrero averaged 33 home runs, 100 RBI and 173 hits, coming within one home run in 2002 of reaching the 40/40 mark in home runs and stolen bases. He signed with the Los Angeles Angels as a free agent following the 2003 season, and in 2004 won the AL MVP Award after hitting 39 home runs, driving in 126 runs, and leading the AL in runs scored (124) and total bases (366).

Guerrero played six seasons with the Angels before finishing his career with stints in Texas and Baltimore. He retired following the 2011 MLB season with a .318 career batting average, 449 home runs, 1,496 RBIs and 2,590 hits, nine All-Star Games, and eight SS awards, and led his league in assists twice as an outfielder. His 31-game hitting streak in 1999 remains tied for twenty-fifth on the all-time list.

Four other non-US-born players are in baseball's hall of fame besides those who played on teams in MLB. These athletes are Cubans Cristobal Torriente, Martin Dihigo, and Jose Mendez of the Negro National League (NNL) and Germany's Barney Dreyfuss, a sports pioneer and executive. Left-handed power hitter Torriente, who performed for several Negro teams, led the Chicago American Giants to consecutive titles from 1920 to 1922. In addition, he was a key player on one of the best all-time defensive outfields in the NNL. During the winter of 1920, while a member of a Cuban club named Almendares, Torriente outplayed former New York Yankees' legend Babe Ruth in a nine-game exhibition series.

Martin Dihigo was perhaps the most versatile player in baseball history. Known as "El Maestro," he skillfully played all nine positions. Dihigo became a national institution in his native Cuba but also starred in many other countries including Mexico, Puerto Rico, and Venezuela, and also spent twelve seasons in the Negro leagues. Playing in the Mexican League (MXL) in 1938, he went 18–2 and led the league with a 0.90 ERA, while also winning the batting crown with a .387 BA.

A long-time player for the Kansas City Monarchs, Jose Mendez was a right-handed pitcher of the Cuban Stars from 1908 to 1926. Nicknamed "Black Diamond," he had a blazing fastball, sharp curve, and in 1909 pitched a perfect ten-inning game. As a player-manager of the Monarchs, Mendez led the NNL team to consecutive pennants during 1923–1925. A Negro league committee inducted Dihigo into the BHOF in 1977, and twenty-nine years later, Mendez and Torriente.

An innovative baseball team owner and policy maker, Barney Dreyfuss merged his NL Louisville Colonels franchise with the Pittsburgh Pirates in 1900. From then to 1932, the Pirates won six NL pennants, two World Series, and finished no lower than third place in twenty-one MLB seasons. Furthermore, he was an original advocate for a commissioner's office in MLB and served as the NL's first vice president. A Veterans Committee elected Dreyfuss to the BHOF in 2008.

Other former Cuban players on AL teams, such as the White Sox's Minnie Minoso, Twins' Tony Oliva, and Red Sox's Luis Tiant, had memorable careers in MLB. Minoso has been hampered by arcane rules established by the BHOF's board of directors and the BWWA's missteps in considering his case decades ago. Although he ranks as one of the definitive stars of baseball's integration era, Minoso repeatedly fell short of election. Oliva was a three-time batting champion, accumulated 1,917 hits and an eight-time all-star, while in nineteen seasons, pitcher Tiant had a .571 winning percentage, 3.30 ERA, and struck out 2,416 batters.

NATIONAL LEAGUE

Historical Performances: Award Winners

Similar to the type of results in the AL, this section identifies and discusses awards earned by non-US-born players who competed most, if not all, of their years for teams in the NL and those with exceptional careers in the league who received enough votes on ballots for their induction into the BHOF.[11]

Batting Champion

To be eligible to win a batting title in the NL, a player must make at least 3.1 appearances at bat or 502 for his team during games in a regular season of MLB and have the highest average or number of hits per appearance. Born in the US, the Chicago White Stockings' infielder Ross Barnes won the NL's first

11 *The most accessible, accurate, and useful information including details about such MLB awards as Batting Champion, Most Valuable Player, Rookie of the Year, and Rolaids Relief pitcher is the website www.baseball-reference.com. For biographies of players and others in the Baseball Hall of Fame, see them and their performances in www.baseballhall.org, www.baseball-almanac.com, www.mlb.com, and the sources in table 3.2.*

award when he hit .403 on average in 1876 and led all batters in runs, hits, and total bases. He specialized in fair-foul hits, which were squib bunts that landed fair, rolled across the foul line, but remained in play under the rules of that year. After his retirement, Barnes became an umpire in 1890 for baseball's Players League.

For the highest BA in a career among NL players, American infielder Roger Hornsby—who played thirteen seasons with the St. Louis Cardinals and four with the Chicago Cubs in the NL but also a few with the American League (AL) St. Louis Browns—hit .358. He led the NL in BA seven times and ranks fourth in MLB history. In addition, Hornsby led the league nine times in on-base and slugging percentages, five times in runs scored, four times in doubles and runs batted in (RBIs), and twice in triples and home runs. According to BHOF standards, he ranks as the third greatest of all-time among MLB players. Meanwhile, the former San Diego Padres outfielder Tony Gwynn and Louisville Colonels and Pittsburgh Pirates infielder and outfielder Honus Wagner each led the NL eight times in BA during respectively their twenty and twenty-one years in the league.

As denoted in table 3.4, ten non-US-born men had the highest BA of all players in different seasons of the NL. Among these great hitters, the most successful of them was outfielder Roberto Clemente from the city of Carolina in Puerto Rico and then infielder and outfielder Larry Walker from Maple Ridge in British Columbia, Canada. While playing eighteen years in 2,433 games for the Pittsburgh Pirates, Clemente had a .317 BA and won four batting titles. He appeared in twelve all-star games, won the league's MVP award in 1966, and seven years later, elected into the BHOF.

Clemente was, of course, a dark-skinned Hispanic at a time when American society had not yet fully accepted minorities in baseball's major leagues. This prejudice—or at least provincialism plus insensitivity—was reflected in his Topps baseball cards. For much of his career, these cards referred to him as "Bob Clemente," as did the persistent practice of even some highly sympathetic sportswriters who quoted Clemente's heavily accented English utterances phonetically.

Table 3.4 Non-US Players, National League Award Winners, by Country, Team, and Year

Name	Country	Team	Year
Batting Champion			
Roberto Clemente	Puerto Rico	Pittsburgh Pirates	1961, 1964–1965, 1967
Matty Alou	Dominican Republic	Pittsburgh Pirates	1966
Rico Carty	Dominican Republic	Atlanta Braves	1970
Andres Galarraga	Venezuela	Colorado Rockies	1993
Larry Walker	Canada	Colorado Rockies	1998–1999, 2001
Albert Pujols	Dominican Republic	St. Louis Cardinals	2003
Hanley Ramirez	Dominican Republic	Florida Marlins	2009
Carlos Gonzalez	Venezuela	Colorado Rockies	2010
Jose Reyes	Dominican Republic	New York Mets	2011
Justin Morneau	Canada	Colorado Rockies	2014
Cy Young			
Ferguson Jenkins	Canada	Chicago Cubs	1971
Fernando Valenzuela	Mexico	Los Angeles Dodgers	1981
Pedro Martinez	Dominican Republic	Montreal Expos	1997, 1999–2000
Eric Gagne	Canada	Los Angeles Dodgers	2003
Most Valuable Player			
Roberto Clemente	Puerto Rico	Pittsburgh Pirates	1966
Orlando Cepeda	Puerto Rico	St. Louis Cardinals	1967
Larry Walker	Canada	Colorado Rockies	1997
Sammy Sosa	Dominican Republic	Chicago Cubs	1998
Albert Pujols	Dominican Republic	St. Louis Cardinals	2005, 2008–2009
Joey Votto	Canada	Cincinnati Reds	2010
Rookie of the Year			
Orlando Cepeda	Puerto Rico	San Francisco Giants	1958

Name	Country	Team	Year
Fernando Valenzuela	Mexico	Los Angeles Dodgers	1981
Benito Santiago	Puerto Rico	San Diego Padres	1987
Raul Mondesi	Dominican Republic	Los Angeles Dodgers	1994
Hideo Nomo	Japan	Los Angeles Dodgers	1995
Rafael Furcal	Dominican Republic	Atlanta Braves	2000
Albert Pujols	Dominican Republic	St. Louis Cardinals	2001
Hanley Ramirez	Dominican Republic	Florida Marlins	2006
Geovany Soto	Puerto Rico	Chicago Cubs	2008
Jose Fernandez	Cuba	Miami Marlins	2013
Ronald Acuna Jr.	Venezuela	Atlanta Braves	2018
Rolaids Relief Award			
Antonio Alfonseca	Dominican Republic	Florida Marlins	2000
Armando Benitez	Dominican Republic	New York Mets	2001
Eric Gagne	Canada	Los Angeles Dodgers	2003–2004
Jose Valverde	Dominican Republic	Arizona Diamondbacks	2007
John Axford	Canada	Milwaukee Brewers	2011
Trevor Hoffman Award			
Kenley Jansen	Curacao	Los Angeles Dodgers	2016

Note: Name, Country, Team, and Year are self-explanatory. The table excludes Hall of Fame players from the Negro Leagues in America.

Source: Frank P. Jozsa Jr., Baseball Beyond Borders: From Distant Lands to the Major Leagues (Lanham, MD: Scarecrow Press, 2013); George Vass, "The Wide World of Baseball," Baseball Digest (February 2003), 11–16; "Batting Average Year-by-Year Leaders," www.baseball-almanac.com cited 11 August 2017; "MLB Most Valuable Player MVP Awards & Cy Young Awards Winners," www.baseball-reference.com cited 11 August 2017; "MLB Rookie of the Year Awards," www.baseball-reference.com cited 11 August 2017; "2012 National League All-Star Roster," www.espn.go.com cited 11 August 2017; "Rolaids Relief Award," www.baseball-reference.com cited 21 November 2018; "Trevor Hoffman Award," www.baseball-reference.com cited 13 November 2018.

Although not a member of the BHOF as of 2018, Walker won three batting titles in seventeen years including six seasons with the Colorado Rockies and others with the former Montreal Expos. He was a five-time all-star and the league's MVP in 1997. Twelve years later, Walker became a member of the Canadian BHOF and Museum. He was a nine-time winner of the Tip O'Neill Award for being the top Canadian baseball player of the year and a member of Canada's Sports Hall of Fame in 2007 and the British Columbia Sports Hall of Fame in 2009. Truly, Roberto Clemente and Larry Walker were two of the greatest ballplayers in the NL's 143-year history.[12]

Besides Clemente and Walker, three hitters ranked from highest to lowest during years each of them won a title. They were .370 for Venezuelan Andres Galarraga in 1993, .366 for Dominican Rico Carty in 1970, and .359 for Dominican Albert Pujols in 2003. Following Pujols, other players and their BAs were .337 for Dominican Jose Reyes in 2011, .336 for Venezuelan Carlos Gonzalez in 2010, .342 each for Dominicans' Matty Alou in 1966 and Hanley Ramirez in 2009, and .319 for Canadian Justin Morneau in 2014. Except for Gonzalez and Alou, the other players were on multiple NL all-star teams while Pujols won three MVP awards between 2001 and 2012 as an infielder and slugger for the St. Louis Cardinals.

Based on their lifetime BAs as of 2016, Pujols is among the highest of the group at .306 in seventeen seasons and Moreau the lowest at .281 in fourteen seasons. Clemente, Walker, and the other eight players are heroes among sports fans across the world and especially for kids and teenagers who play on baseball teams in their home countries.

Cy Young

From 1956 through 1966, the most outstanding pitcher in MLB won a Cy Young award each season. The first recipient was Brooklyn Dodgers' Don Newcombe and in 1966, the Los Angeles Dodgers' Sandy Koufax won the eleventh award. Then in MLB seasons from 1967 through 2018, a pitcher on a team in each league won a Cy Young.

---

12 *The Canadian Baseball Hall of Fame gives the Tip O'Neill Award to the Canadian baseball player judged to have excelled in individual achievement and team contribution while adhering to the highest ideals of the game of baseball. Former MLB player Larry Walker won it in 1987, 1990, 1992, 1994–95, and 1997–98. See "Tip O'Neill Award," www.baseball-reference.com cited 1 March 2013.*

In these fifty-one years of the NL, four foreign players received enough votes from groups, including the BWWA as of 2018, to win an award for their performances on the pitcher's mound. In order, by years, these men were right-hander Ferguson "Fergie" Jenkins of Canada in 1971, left-hander Fernando Valenzuela of Mexico in 1981, and right-handers Pedro Martinez of the Dominican Republic in 1997, 1999, and 2000, and Eric Gagne of Canada in 2003.

During the year he pitched and won a Cy Young, the Chicago Cubs' Jenkins had a 2.77 ERA and won twenty-four games. Although batters frequently hit home runs off his pitches, he gave up so few hits and almost no walks that home runs did not diminish his team's performances very much in games. Jenkins was also a good hitter, slugging three homers in 1970 and another six in 1971.

To earn their Cy Young awards, the ERAs and number of wins were 2.48 and thirteen for the Los Angeles Dodgers' Valenzuela; 2.93, 2.07, 1.74 seventeen, twenty-three, eighteen for the Montreal Expos' Martinez; and 1.20 and two for the Dodgers' Gagne. Similar to the majority of NL batting champions, these four pitchers played on three or more all-star teams. Except for Gagne, they each pitched at least eleven years in the league and won more than 170 games during their careers. In short, Jenkins and the other three foreign-born players earned Cy Young awards because of their outstanding pitching performances in NL seasons.

Most Valuable Player

Except during 1901–1910, 1915–1921 and 1930, a ballplayer from a team had won an MVP award in an MLB season. Based on their performance as a batter or at a specific position on the infield or outfield or as a catcher, all active players are eligible to be an MVP. As of 2010, BWAA members vote to determine who will receive the award. From 1911 to 1914 and then for forty-two years, American-born players won an MVP in the NL. At different positions, four of them were St. Louis Cardinals infielder Frank Frisch in 1931, Philadelphia Phillies pitcher Jim Konstanty in 1950, Brooklyn Dodgers catcher Roy Campanella in 1955, and Cincinnati Reds outfielder Frank Robinson in 1961.

In the NL, the first non-US-born MVP was Pittsburgh Pirates outfielder Roberto Clemente. Although he did not lead the league statistically in any categories as a hitter during 1966, Clemente had a .317 BA, twenty-nine home runs, a .536 slugging percentage, and 119 RBIs in 154 games. Additionally, he made few errors or mental mistakes while catching baseballs hit in the air or on the ground to him in the outfield. Runners that tried to move forward while on base did not challenge Clemente because of his ability to throw any baseball he caught with velocity and accuracy to teammates near first, second, or third base on the infield, and at home plate. Arguably, Roberto Clemente is the greatest Latino player in the history of MLB.

St. Louis Cardinals' first baseman Orlando Cepeda was the second non-US-born player to win an MVP award in the NL. In 1967, he was successful in contributing runs to the Cardinals' NL pennant and World Series championship. That season, Cepeda led the league with 111 RBIs, hit twenty-five home runs, and had a .325 BA in 151 games. He was also one of the best defensive infielders in the league and a natural leader at his position. Orlando Cepeda won an MVP primarily because of his tremendous power as a hitter and flexible skills while playing in the Cardinals' infield. Because Cepeda lived and played in years when America was at a crossroads of social change and racial intolerance, he was often the target of racial slurs from fans and the media. Nevertheless, Cepeda always managed to remain a proud and dignified man, and a pioneer, role model, and spokesperson for Hispanic players everywhere.

One year before he became an NL batting champion in 1998, Colorado Rockies outfielder Larry Walker of Canada won an MVP award. Besides his amazing .720 slugging and .452 on-base percentages, he had 130 RBIs and led the league with 409 total bases and forty-nine home runs. Although the Rockies finished seven games behind the San Francisco Giants and in third place of the league's WD, Walker's .366 BA ranked in the top five among all players. In 1997, Larry Walker was an MVP and ranked ahead of all active ballplayers in the NL.

Following awards to Clemente, Cepeda and Walker, Chicago Cubs' outfielder Sammy Sosa was the second foreign-born player to win an MVP in the NL. In 1998, Sosa was awesome on offense for his team because he scored 134 runs, hit sixty-six home runs, contributed 158 RBIs, accounted for 416 total bases, and had a .308 BA and .647 slugging percentage. Sosa and the Cardinals' Mark McGwire competed for MLB's home run title, which caused attendances to soar for their teams when they played in games especially against each other in Chicago and St. Louis. After playing eighteen seasons with four different teams in MLB, Sosa retired after the 2007 season.

Dominican Albert Pujols won MVP awards in 2005, 2008, and 2009 while playing infield for the St. Louis Cardinals in the NL. During those three MLB seasons, his highest and lowest performances as a hitter on his teams were .357 and .327 in BAs, forty-seven and thirty-seven in home runs, 135 and 116 in RBIs, .658 and .609 in slugging percentages, and 161 and 148 in number of regular season games. If he avoids seriously injuring himself, Albert Pujols will challenge Roberto Clemente to become the greatest Latino player in MLB history and then five years after retirement, unanimously inducted into the BHOF on the first ballot.

The NL's MVP in 2010 was Cincinnati Reds infielder Joey Votto of Canada. Besides being an all-star player, he had a .324 BA and hit thirty-one home runs and achieved 113 RBIs in 150 games. Remarkably, Votto led the league in on-base, slugging, and on-base-plus-slugging percentages. While playing at first base, he committed only five errors and achieved a fielding percent of .996 in 1,283 innings. Indeed, Joey Votto was an MVP for the Reds that year and among all players on teams in the NL.

Rookie of the Year

To qualify for rookie of the year (ROY), an NL (and AL) player must have a minimum of 130 at bats or fifty innings in games per season and be available for forty-five days on a team's active roster before September 1. During 1947 and 1948, only one player each year received a ROY award for both leagues. In 1947, it was Brooklyn Dodgers first baseman Jackie Robinson and one year later, Boston Braves shortstop Alvin Dark. Then, from 1949 through 2018, a player in the AL and NL each won ROY.

Between 1958 and 2018, eleven non-US-born players won ROY awards in the NL. Seven of them retired before 2018 while the other four continue to perform on teams in MLB. The first group includes Orlando Cepeda, Benito Santiago, and Geovany Soto of Puerto Rico, Fernando Valenzuela of Mexico, Raul Mondesi of the Dominican Republic, Hideo Nomo of Japan, and Rafael Furcal of the Dominican Republic.

To highlight their performances when they won their ROYs, first baseman Cepeda had a .312 BA and hit twenty-five home runs and ninety-six RBIs for the third-place San Francisco Giants in 1958. Twenty-three years later, Los Angeles Dodgers southpaw pitcher Valenzuela won thirteen and also completed eleven games, struck out 180 batters, and had a 2.48 ERA in 192 innings. Then in 1987, San Diego Padres' catcher

Santiago batted .300 and hit eighteen home runs and seventy-nine RBIs in 146 games. Additionally, he won an SS award for being an effective and very powerful hitter.[13]

Retired in 2005 after playing thirteen years in MLB, Dodgers' outfielder Mondesi was ROY in 1994 because in 112 games of the regular season he hit .306 on average with sixteen home runs and fifty-six RBIs. Since he was productive and had a .516 slugging percentage, the Dodgers won the league's WD. However, because of disputes between team owners and the MLB Players Association (MLBPA) about the leagues' revenue-sharing plan and other economic issues, the union began its strike on August 12, 1994. Consequently, MLB teams participated in fewer regular season games that year and the league cancelled the playoffs and World Series.

For his performance while pitching, Los Angeles Dodgers' Hideo Nomo won a ROY award in 1995. He played in twenty-eight games, pitched 191 innings, and had thirteen victories, led the league in striking out 236 batters, and established a 2.54 ERA. In the NL Division Series (NLDS), Nomo pitched five innings in game three against the Cincinnati Reds, but the Dodgers lost it 10–1. Even so, Hideo Nomo was the most productive rookie in the league. As such, he became the fifth foreign-born player to receive a ROY award in the NL.

As a batter, Atlanta Braves shortstop Rafael Furcal was mediocre since he hit only four home runs and fifty-six RBIs in 2000. Nevertheless, he had 134 hits, 174 total bases, and a .382 slugging percentage in 131 games. As a clever, quick, and reliable fielder on defense, Furcal was spectacular in that he participated in 289 assists and committed just twenty-three errors. Additionally, the Braves won the league's ED that season but were later defeated in three games by the St. Louis Cardinals in the NLDS.

After playing in only thirty games during the 2005–2007 MLB seasons, catcher Geovany Sota excelled in 2008 for the Cubs. As a hitter, he had a .285 BA, twenty-three home runs, eighty-six RBIs, and a .504 slugging percentage. While catching for his team that season, Soto had 762 put-outs and made only four errors in 847

---

13 *The Silver Slugger Award, formally called the Hillerich & Bradsby Silver Slugger Award, goes to the best hitter at each position in both the National and American League. Makers of the Louisville Slugger bat, Hillerich & Bradsby, started it in 1980. Teams' coaches and manager vote for the award but cannot vote for a player on their team. For its history, see "The Silver Slugger Award," www.baseball-reference.com cited 1 March 2013.*

innings of 104 games. Consequently, Soto was outstanding at his position and in hitting to win an ROY award in 2008

Since they are on the current rosters of teams in MLB, the second group of foreign-born ROY winners still has an opportunity to contribute their talents in games and win additional awards in the sport. These athletes include Albert Pujols and Hanley Ramirez of the Dominican Republic, and Jose Fernandez of Cuba.

When they won their ROY award in a MLB season, each of them performed above expectations for their club and in comparison to other rookies in the NL. Being an NL all-star, infielder and outfielder Albert Pujols won ROY in 2001 because he had a .329 BA and slugging percentage of .610, and hit thirty-seven home runs and 130 RBIs in 161 regular season games for the St. Louis Cardinals. Despite his outstanding performance during the regular season, the Cardinals lost three games to the Arizona Diamondbacks in the NLDS.

The Florida Marlins' Hanley Ramirez won an ROY award in 2006 for several reasons. During 1,323 innings of 158 games, he had seventeen home runs and fifty-nine RBIs but also 185 hits and 304 total bases. While playing at shortstop and third base in games for the Marlins, Dominican Ramirez made 410 assists and only twenty-six errors. Given his .292 BA, Hanley Ramirez outperformed other rookies to become ROY in the NL.

Cuban pitcher Jose Fernandez is the most recent foreign player to win ROY in the NL. As a unanimous selection in the 2013 MLB season, he won two-thirds of his games, posted a 2.19 ERA in 172 innings, struck out 187 batters, and had a WHIP of .979. In addition, he was an all-star and placed third for the league's CY Young award.

Making his debut with the Atlanta Braves while only 20 years old, Venezuelan outfielder Ronald Acuna Jr. hit .293 with twenty-six home runs and sixty-four RBIs, and stole sixteen bases with an .917 OPS. He established a Braves record with eight leadoff homers in 2018 and tied a franchise mark by homering in five consecutive games.[14]

---

14 *Idem. See Ronald Blum, "Ohtani, Acuna Named Rookies of the Year."*

The next category of award winners is foreign players who replaced other pitchers on their team, usually in the middle or late innings of games. While playing, these relief pitchers' primary goal was to confuse batters and get them out by throwing different combinations of pitches in the strike zone including cut fastballs, curves, sliders, and change-ups. Most relief pitchers have pinpoint control, walk few hitters, and generally receive little publicity from the media for their efforts during games of MLB seasons.

Rolaids Relief Award

Rather than receiving the most votes from members of the BWAA, a big-league pitcher wins a Rolaids Relief (RR) award based on his performance in games during an MLB season (RR discontinued in 2012). More specifically, he earns five points for a save and two for a win, negative two each for a loss and blown save, and one for a tough save. Since its first year in 1976, five foreign-born pitchers have won an RR award while on a team in the NL. To identify them, next is an overview of their accomplishments.[15]

In order by MLB seasons, the winners of an RR award while on teams in the NL as of 2018 include the Dominican Republic's Antonio Alfonseca in 2000 and Armando Benitez in 2001, Canada's Eric Gagne in 2003 and 2004, the Dominican Republic's Jose Valverde in 2007, and Canada's John Axford in 2011. In other years, mostly US-born pitchers won the award in the NL.

These five athletes, indeed, were outstanding relief pitchers for their teams during the MLB regular season. Alfonseca had forty-five saves and finished sixty-two games in relief for the Florida Marlins in 2000. One year later, Benitez won six and saved forty-three games for the New York Mets. For Dodgers games in Los Angeles and elsewhere, in 2003 and 2004, respectively, Gagne had fifty-five and forty-five saves, 1.20 and 2.19 ERAs, and 137 and 114 strikeouts. Then Valverde had forty-seven saves and a 2.66 ERA for the Arizona Diamondbacks in 2007 and four years later, Axford finished sixty-three and saved forty-six games for the Milwaukee Brewers. According to their performances, each of these players was the best relief pitcher in the NL during at least one MLB season of the 2000s.

---

15 *Adopted by MLB, the RR Award was renamed Trevor Hoffman Award in the NL in 2014. See "Trevor Hoffman Award," www.baseball-reference.com cited 13 November 2018.*

While he was a relief pitcher for the Detroit Tigers in the AL, Jose Valverde also received a RR award in 2011. He won only two games but saved forty-nine of them, struck out sixty-nine batters, and had a 2.24 ERA. During his ten-year career on teams in MLB, Valverde was a three-time all-star, finished 489 games and won twenty-six of them, and had 277 saves in 590 innings.

Trevor Hoffman Award

The RR Award was renamed the Trevor Hoffman Award after MLB's 2012 season. Curacao's Kenly Jansen won it in 2016. Jansen saved forty-seven games and had a 1.83 ERA and struck out 104 batters in 68 innings. He led MLB with a 0.67 WHIP, had the best strikeout-to-walk ratio in the NL, topped all relievers with a .150 batting-average against, and helped the Dodgers to a fourth consecutive West title. Also, Jansen anchored a bullpen that combined to set a franchise record with 590 2/3 innings pitched and 607 total appearances, both of which led MLB.

Based on their performances while pitching and the number of RR awards they have won since 1976, the most successful in each group of teams has been the Dodgers' Eric Gagne of Canada in the NL and the Yankees' Mariano Rivera of Panama in the AL.

Other Awards

Since 1958, many players in the NL and AL have won a Rawlings Gold Glove (GG) award for their superior performances at specific fielding positions in games during a MLB season. Teams' coaches and managers vote for players who, because of their outstanding performances, receive a gold lame-tanned leather glove affixed to a walnut base. For the 1957 MLB season, AL Chicago White Sox' outfielder Minnie Minoso of Cuba won a GG. In fact, there was only one award given to players at each position in the infield and outfield on AL and NL teams combined.[16]

16 *Historical data about MLB's Gold Glove and Silver Slugger awards were in "Rawlings Gold Glove Award," www.wikipedia.org cited 23 December 2012, "National League Gold Glove Award Winners," www.baseball-reference.com cited 23 December 2012, "Silver Slugger Award," www.wikipedia.org cited 23 December 2012, and "Silver Slugger Award Winners–National League," www.baseball-reference.com cited 23 December 2012.*

Some non-US-born players have won multiple GG awards at a position during their careers on teams in the NL as of 2018. These individuals and their number of GGs—in parentheses—include catchers Tony Pena (three) of the Dominican Republic and Yadier Molina (eight) and Benito Santiago (three) of Puerto Rico; first baseman Andres Galarraga (two) of Venezuela, and second basemen Vinny Castillo (three) of the Dominican Republic, Manny Trillo (three) of Venezuela, and Felix Millan (two) of Puerto Rico.[17]

Others who won multiple GGs in the NL were shortstops Omar Vizquel (eleven) of Venezuela, Edgar Renteria (two) of Columbia, Rey Ordonez (three) of Cuba, and Dave Concepcion (five) of Venezuela, and outfielders Larry Walker (seven) of Canada, Andruw Jones (ten) of Curacao, Cesar Geronimo (four) and Cesar Cedeno (five) of the Dominican Republic, and Roberto Clemente (twelve) of Puerto Rico. Besides these players, several other foreigners won only one GG award in the NL including pitchers Fernando Valenzuela of Mexico and Joaquin Andujar of the Dominican Republic.

Since 1980, players in each league of MLB have won a Silver Slugger (SS) award for being the best hitter at their position on a team during a MLB season. Given to players annually by US manufacturer Hillerich & Bradsby and based on votes from teams' coaches and managers, the award is a ninety-one-centimeter, sterling silver-plated, bat-shaped trophy engraved with the winner's name.

A few non-US-born players at each position on a baseball field have won multiple SS awards in the NL. These individuals and their number of awards, in parentheses, include pitchers Carlos Zambrano (three) of Venezuela and Fernando Valenzuela (two) of Mexico, catcher Benito Santiago (four) of Puerto Rico, first basemen Albert Pujols (four) of the Dominican Republic and Andres Galarraga (two) of Venezuela, and second baseman Manny Trillo (two) of Venezuela.

Others who won at their position were third baseman Vinny Castilla (three) of Mexico, and shortstops Hanley Ramirez (two) of the Dominican Republic, Edgar Renteria (three) of Columbia, and Dave Concepcion (two) of Venezuela. The outfielders with multiple SS awards were Larry Walker (three) of Canada, Sammy Sosa (six) and

17 *In MLB's 2018 season, NL gold glove winners were Cardinals' catcher Yadier Molina of Puerto Rico and Braves' centerfielder Ender Inciarte of Venezuela. The reference is "National League Gold Glove Award Winners."*

Vladimir Guerrero (three) of the Dominican Republic, and Carlos Beltran (two) and Jose Cruz (two) of Puerto Rico. Additionally, several Puerto Rican and foreign players won one SS award at their position on teams in the NL between 1980 and 2012. For details about their performances, see the data on websites baseball-reference.com and mlb.com.[18]

For other events in MLB, several foreign players on NL teams won awards for being the MVP on all-star, championship series, and World Series teams. Some of these MVPs, for example, were infielder Tony Perez of Cuba, outfielder Melky Cabrera, and pitcher Juan Marichal of the Dominican Republic in an all-star game, outfielder Marco Scutaro and infielder Manny Trillo of Venezuela in a championship series, and pitcher Jose Rijo and infielder and outfielder Pedro Guerrero of the Dominican Republic in a World Series. In short, these players won MVP awards because they outperformed others during games and series of games of these events.

With his impressive performance in 1877, Boston Red Stockings pitcher Tommy Bond of Ireland became the NL's first and only Triple Crown champion born in a foreign country. He led the league by winning forty games and having a 2.11 ERA and 170 strikeouts. Besides these statistics, Bond pitched fifty-eight complete games in 521 innings that year and won forty or more games in three consecutive MLB seasons. After seven years in the big leagues, he retired in 1884 and four years later, coached baseball at Harvard University in Boston. Tommy Bond was a baseball umpire in 1883 and 1885, and then worked in the city's assessor office for thirty-five years. He died in 1941.

Baseball Hall of Fame

Established in 1936 at a site in Cooperstown, New York, the Baseball Hall of Fame (BHOF) honors former professional players and others for their exemplary contribution to the game. For anyone to be eligible for the BHOF and then elected to it by active and honorary members of the Baseball Writers Association of America (BWWA) or a Veterans Committee, there are specific requirements regarding their career in and retirement from MLB or the Negro Leagues. Each year, a BWWA screening committee prepares ballots that list candidates who are eligible for the first time (at least five

18 *In MLB's 2018 season, NL silver slugger awardees included Rockies' pitcher German Marquez of Puerto Rico, Cubs' second baseman Javier Baez of Puerto Rico, and Diamondbacks' outfielder David Peralta of Venezuela. The reference is "Silver Slugger Award Winners—National League."*

years after retirement) and nominated by any two of six members of the committee, or who had received a vote on a minimum of five percent of the ballots cast in the preceding election. For admission into the BHOF, an eligible candidate must get at least seventy-five percent of votes on a ballot.[19]

As of 2016, five non-US-born players, who performed primarily for clubs in the NL and then retired, are in the BHOF. In chronological order of their induction, they are Roberto Clemente of Puerto Rico in 1973, Juan Marichal of the Dominican Republic in 1983, Ferguson Jenkins of Canada in 1991, Orlando Cepeda of Puerto Rico in 1999, and Tony Perez of Cuba in 2000.

During his eighteen seasons with the Pittsburgh Pirates, Roberto Clemente played in 2,433 games and won an MVP award and four batting championships. He hit 240 home runs and 1,305 RBIs, and had 3,000 hits while at bat and 4,492 total bases. Clemente was equally brilliant in right field, where he displayed a precise and powerful arm when throwing a baseball for distance. Besides being on twelve all-star teams, most sports fans remember him for his generosity, humility, and efforts to help others. At thirty-eight-years-old, he died in a plane crash while transporting relief supplies to earthquake victims in Nicaragua. Roberto Clemente was the first non-US-born player inducted into the BHOF.

Juan Marichal pitched the majority of his sixteen-year career with the San Francisco Giants. In 471 total games, he won 243 of them and had a 2.89 ERA with 2,303 strikeouts He hurled a no-hitter in 1963 and played on nine NL all-star teams. As a right-handed pitcher, he had a smooth motion but lifted his left leg very high in the air when throwing a baseball from the pitcher's mound to batters. After retiring from baseball in 1975, Juan Marichal became a minister of sports in the Dominican Republic.

During his nineteen years in MLB, Ferguson Jenkins pitched for four different teams including ten seasons with the Chicago Cubs. In 664 career games, he won 284 of them and had 3,192 strikeouts and a 3.34 ERA in 4,500 innings. Jenkins was an all-star three times and won a Cy Young award in 1971. While pitching, he was a diligent

19 See "2012 Hall of Fame Voting," www.baseball-reference.com cited 19 December 2012, "2013 Official Hall of Fame Ballot," www.baseball-reference.com cited 19 December 2012, Teddy Mitrosilis, "Foreign-Born Players in Baseball's Hall of Fame," www.thepostgame.com cited 5 November 2012, and each player's profile at www.baseballhall.org.

workhorse, had pinpoint control with an easy, uncomplicated motion, and effectively changed speeds to keep batters off balance especially in such hitter's ballparks as Wrigley Field in Chicago. Interestingly, Ferguson Jenkins is the only member of the BHOF who struck out more than 3,000 batters during his career but walked fewer than 1,000 of them.

While playing on teams for seventeen years in MLB, Orlando Cepeda had a .297 BA, .499 slugging percentage, 379 home runs, and 1,365 RBIs in 2,124 games. He was ROY in 1958 with the San Francisco Giants, MVP in 1967 with the St. Louis Cardinals, and selected to seven all-star teams. Despite a series of knee injuries, Orlando Cepeda was a powerful hitter and competent infielder whose father, Pedro Cepeda, was also a professional ballplayer and known as the Babe Ruth of the Caribbean.

As a member of four different MLB teams during his twenty-three-year career, including Cincinnati's Big Red Machine clubs of the early-to-mid-1970s, Tony Perez had 2,732 hits, 379 home runs, and 1,652 RBIs in 2,777 games. Besides playing on seven all-star and two world-championship teams, he was an MVP candidate in several MLB seasons. Respected for his ability to get hits yet control his swing while at bat, Perez belted three home runs in the 1975 World Series won by the Reds in seven games. On July 11, 1967, his fifteenth-inning home run off Oakland Athletics and future Hall of Fame pitcher Catfish Hunter propelled the NL to victory in the longest all-star game in MLB history.

According to the distribution of votes in 2017 for the BHOF, there were a few foreign-born players with one or more years of experience on teams in the NL who appeared somewhere on the ballot and received between 10 percent and 75 percent of the vote. Their names and approximate percentages were Vladimir Guerrero at 71 percent, Mannie Ramirez at 23 percent, and Larry Walker at 21 percent. With less than 10 percent, the list included Sammy Sosa at 8 percent and Edgar Renteria at 0.5 percent. In addition to them, Orlando Cabrera received a few votes. Besides Guerrero, Ramirez, and Walker, Venezuelan Omar Vizquel each received more than 21 percent of votes in 2018 but not Sosa. Renteria, however, did not appear on the ballot because of his very low percentage in 2017.

According to the data in table 3.5, there were 110 non-US-born players on rosters of thirty teams in the NL as of August 8, 2018. Forty-one or 37 percent of them performed on clubs in the Philadelphia Phillies and then Miami Marlins had the most players, only four each played for the New York Mets, Arizona Diamondbacks, and San Francisco Giants.

By position from most to least, pitchers ranked first with fifty or 46 percent of the group followed by infielders with thirty or 27 percent, outfielders with twenty or 18 percent, and catchers with ten or 9 percent. In contrast to the AL, the distribution of positions in the NL was very similar except the latter league does not include DHs as a position.

Table 3.5 Non-US Players, National League by Division, Team, and Position, 2018 Season

Team	Pitchers	Catchers	Infielders	Outfielders	Total
East Division					
Atlanta Braves	2	0	2	2	6
Miami Marlins	6	0	3	2	11
New York Mets	1	0	3	0	4
Philadelphia Phillies	6	2	4	2	14
Washington Nationals	4	0	1	1	6
Central Division					
Chicago Cubs	4	2	1	0	7
Cincinnati Reds	3	0	3	0	6
Milwaukee Brewers	4	1	3	1	9
Pittsburgh Pirates	4	2	1	2	9
St. Louis Cardinals	1	2	2	1	6
West Division					
Arizona Diamondbacks	1	0	2	1	4
Colorado Rockies	4	0	0	2	6
Los Angeles Dodgers	6	1	0	2	9
San Diego Padres	2	0	4	3	9
San Francisco Giants	2	0	1	1	4

Note: There is no designated hitter on teams in the National League. The numbers in columns exclude players on the disabled list and in the minor leagues.

Source: "Major League Baseball Team Rosters," www.espn.com cited 8 August 2017.

Across three divisions in the NL, the ED had the most pitchers and infielders and WD a majority of the outfielders. Furthermore, the CD had four catchers and WD only one of them because of zero whom caught for the Arizona Diamondbacks, Colorado Rockies, and Giants.

In comparing leagues, there was a more unequal distribution of players across teams in the AL than NL. The variation in total number of players—AL's 118 and NL's 110 and also significant differences in the population of players between respective divisions in each league—fifteen in the ED, six in the CD, and sixteen in the WD—plus the AL's DH position and teams' international recruitment polices were each factors in the allocation of non-US-born players in MLB during early August 2018.

This chapter revealed the effects of non-US-born ballplayers on former and current teams in MLB's AL and NL and how they influenced the sport and its history in different ways. While some of them excelled and won awards as batters, others performed in regular season and postseason games as pitchers, catchers, and fielders.

On MLB's opening day in late March 2018, immigrant players were approximately 27 percent of all teams' rosters. If trends continue, players from such countries as the Dominican Republic and Venezuela will win more AL and NL batting, fielding and pitching titles, and also greatly contribute to their teams' records in regular season games and postseason championships.[20]

---

20 *For different but interesting articles involving the import and employment of ballplayers from non-US nations, see for example, Ben Strauss, "Major League Baseball to Let Cuban Players Sign Directly With Teams," New York Times (2 March 2016): 1; Ira Boudway, "Major League Baseball Might Miss a Closed-Off Cuba," Business Week (22 December 2014): 1; "Major League Baseball: Around the Horn," Deseret News (2 May 2010): D.10; Jim Morton, "Major Baseball Mission," Herald Sun (2 July 2009): 75; Andrew Linker, "International Players Continue to Influence Game Greatly," The Patriot (16 July 2007): T16; Joe Bushika, "America's Game no Longer," North Adams Transcript (26 April 2007): 1; Margaret Coker, "Baseball Goes to Bat to Ease Rules on Foreign Players," The Atlanta Journal (3 May 2006): A.1; Frank Fitzpatrick, "As International Players Arrive, Big 4 Tapping Into Global Markets," Knight Ridder Tribune News Service (2 November 2005): 1; "Foreign Players on the Rise in MLB," Niagara Falls Review (3 April 2003): B4; Carl Fleming, "Foreigners Breaking Down the Barriers," Infomart (5 April 2001): 48.*

CHAPTER 4

Players Association

EARLY HISTORY

Opposed to the reserve clause and a growing movement led by Chicago White Stockings president Albert Spalding to cap Major League Baseball (MLB) players' salaries, lawyer and National League (NL) New York Giants pitcher John Montgomery Ward and eight other players in 1885 formed the first players' union in the sport. They named it the Brotherhood of Professional Base Ball Players (BPBBP). Besides raising player salaries in recognition of the sport's growing popularity and growth in revenue generated by the game, the players' organization also aimed to combat the reserve clause which restricted their movements and also helped to suppress salaries.[1]

The Brotherhood gained official recognition when NL franchise owners met with the group's representatives during November 1887. However, relations between them became increasingly difficult because, in part, the owners were unwilling to make significant concessions on the reserve clause and salaries. This, in turn, led to the development of the Players League in 1890. It folded, however, after completing one season even though the Boston Reds defeated the Brooklyn Ward's Wonders by more than six games to win the pennant.

1 *For more about baseball's first union, see the "Brotherhood of Professional Baseball Players," www.baseball-reference.com cited 16 August 2017.*

The BPBBP had little chance of success because team owners had no economic incentive to negotiate with it. It was not until 1935 that the National Labor Relations Act (NLRA) guaranteed the right to union representation and collective bargaining for employees. Without any of the twentieth century advancements won by unions and labor activists and with no marketplace competition for their services even after organizing, professional baseball players had little power and no recourse to the owners who simply ignored their efforts.

Legally, players proved the reserve clause could not be enforced in big-league baseball, but short of the courts breaking up the collusion between owners that perpetuated the clause anyway, there was little progress to be made. While this type of collusion certainly could be seen as a violation of antitrust laws, this did not help the Brotherhood since the Sherman Antitrust Act was not passed until 1890, and thus, after the BPBBP and major league owners had broken off negotiations.

Other attempts to organize players in the sport before the 1960s included the creation of the Players' Protective Association (PPA) in 1900; Fraternity of Professional Baseball Players of America (FPBPA) in 1912; and American Baseball Guild (ABG) in 1946. The PPA primarily demanded elimination of the reserve clause. The development of the American League (AL) in 1901 meant that dissatisfied NL players could, for a while, ignore their contracts and seek better terms with teams in the new circuit. A number of prominent stars actually did that such as future Hall of Famers Cy Young, Jimmy Collins, and Napoleon Lajoie. Sometimes this led to lawsuits until the AL and NL made peace in 1903 and agreed to honor the reserve clause and thereby respect each other's contracts. As a result, the PPA's power waned significantly after these leagues' agreement.[2]

Led by Columbia law graduate and former major leaguer Dave Fultz, the FPBPA sought to repeal the reserve clause and also wanted such basic rights as players being given copies of their contracts, which was still not a standard practice done by teams. Among the union's requests was that teams paint the center field fence of ballparks a dark green to improve visibility of pitches and reduce the risk of injury.[3]

---

2 *"Players Protective Association," www.baseball-reference.com cited 16 August 2017.*

3 *See Adam Dorhauer, "The Unionization of Baseball," www.hardballtimes.com cited 16 August 2017.*

Before the FPBPA organized, players had to pay for their own uniforms and did not have to be notified by team owners when placed on waivers. The union nominally had the right to appeal disputes to the National Commission—the equivalent of today's MLB Commissioner's Office—but the National Commission did not always respond and was not required to give written explanations for fines or suspensions.

Like the AL and NL, baseball's 1914–1915 Federal League (FL) attempted to gain favor with players by acknowledging the FPBPA. While it did not abolish the reserve clause, the FL agreed to certain rights such as requiring an increase in players' salaries on renewed contracts and conceded to most of the union's demands.

In response to the FL, AL and NL officials agreed to meet with the FPBPA and implement some of its demands. AL and NL teams, for example, increased players' salaries to counter the offers coming from those in the FL. To illustrate, Detroit Tigers' all-star Ty Cobb's salary rose from under $12,000 in 1913 to $20,000 in 1915, which adjusted for inflation, is still a bit below the league minimum in 2015. The AL and NL managed to appease the union just enough to hold onto most of their talented players, leaving the FL unable to catch up. After two seasons, the FL folded, and the AL and NL returned to their usual positions against players.

Following the collapse of the FL in late 1915, the FPBPA considered going on strike and also attempted to strengthen its organization by affiliating with the American Federation of Labor (AFL). However, the AFL's vaudeville-performing union claimed jurisdiction over baseball as a form of entertainment and therefore blocked the FPBPA's admission. Without the AFL's backing, however, the strike threat fell apart and the union dissolved shortly thereafter.

Though short-lived, the ABG existed during two events that threatened to upset team owners' stranglehold on labor negotiations in the sport. First was a near-strike by the NL's Pittsburgh Pirates. In fact, Pittsburgh players voted 20–16 in favor of going on strike during the 1946 season, but they fell short of the two-thirds supermajority they had agreed to in order to approve the action.[4]

---

4 *Idem, "The Unionization of Baseball."*

The other event involved Jorge Pasquel, the newly appointed president of the Mexican League (MXL). As a team owner, Pasquel had greatly improved the star power of his professional baseball league by signing American Negro League stars. Some of the era's best players, including pitcher Satchel Paige and slugger Josh Gibson for example, had both played for Pasquel in Mexico at some point during the 1930s and 1940s. When Pasquel took over as league president in 1946, he started extending attractive offers to MLB's biggest stars.

Although reports on exact figures differ, he offered the St. Louis Cardinals' Stan Musial something in the range of $175,000 over a few years. He also approached Boston Red Sox's Ted Williams, New York Yankees' Joe DiMaggio, and Cleveland Indians' Bob Feller with salary offers at six digits per year. While each player turned him down, Pasquel did manage to sign roughly two dozen major leaguers, including a handful of all-stars. The biggest of the names Pasquel bought was St. Louis Browns' Vern Stephens, who signed for something similar to the amount offered Musial. Unfortunately for Pasquel, his biggest signing was also his shortest lived. Within a week, Stephens left Mexico to return to the AL.

Part of the problem was that, while Pasquel personally had the wealth to pay players large salaries, his league was not capable of sustaining that kind of spending. In fact, Mexican players received a small fraction of what was being offered to American stars. Furthermore, the ballfields and clubhouses in Mexico were well below major league standards—one field even had an active railroad line running across the outfield and goats grazing on it before a game.

Mexican teams also had trouble getting equipment from established American manufacturers and often had to make do with much lower quality. In addition, travel to the more remote cities in the league could be treacherous with airplanes landing in unpaved cow pastures and buses navigating narrow mountain roads. Some players were alarmed by the constant presence of Pasquel's armed bodyguards. Because of culture shock and the language barrier many of the American ballplayers experienced, the MXL no longer seemed like an alternative to others on teams in the AL and NL.

Even the added security of Pasquel's multiyear contracts was not that attractive as players questioned whether the league would actually have the money to pay them throughout the life of their contracts. Within a year, nearly all the major leaguers that Pasquel had signed left the league and joined teams in MLB.

Before disbanding, the ABG managed to negotiate a few concessions from management, most significantly a pension plan for players with at least five years of experience in the majors. The players who switched to the Mexican League played a significant role in giving the Guild enough leverage it needed to achieve a signature victory, but those advantages were largely abandoned in negotiations. In fact, MLB Commissioner Happy Chandler banned AL and NL players who had jumped—save for Stephens who returned almost immediately—not only from the majors but from the minors as well, and even threatened amateur and college players that they could be blackballed if they played with or against those players in semiprofessional games.

As a result, the banned players sued MLB for antitrust violations, challenging the ruling in the *Federal Baseball Ruling case*. A lower court, however, ruled the exemption no longer held—expansions in the court's understanding of commerce as well as baseball's invasion of television and radio broadcast markets meant the Supreme Court's decision that baseball was not participating in interstate commerce had no longer applied.[5]

Because the decision came from a lower court, however, it did not erase the precedent set by *Federal Baseball Ruling*. Rather than appeal to the Supreme Court and risk losing the exemption altogether, Commissioner Chandler reached a settlement with the players and reinstated them. Even after regaining their jobs, however, most of these players had missed roughly three years from the ban and were therefore removed from the new pension plan.

5 *Federal Baseball Club v. National League—full case name: Federal Base Ball Club of Baltimore, Inc. v. National League of Professional Base Ball Clubs et al., 259 US 200—often called the Federal Baseball Ruling—was a case in which the US Supreme Court ruled that Major League Baseball was exempt from the provisions of the Sherman Antitrust Act. The case was argued on April 19, 1922 and decided on May 29, 1922 with Justice Oliver Wendell Holmes, Jr. delivering the unanimous majority opinion. See "Federal Baseball Club v. National League," www.baseball-reference.com cited 16 August 2017.*

MAJOR LEAGUE BASEBALL PLAYERS ASSOCIATION

Though it took a while to become what it is now, the current MLBPA actually originated during the 1950s. Its first legal representative, J. Norman Lewis, refused to call the organization a union because most players favored a conservative approach and feared that pushing management for further gains would cause MLB team owners to rescind any improvements won by the ABG.[6]

In 1959, Philadelphia Phillies' representative Robin Roberts encouraged the MLBPA to hire full-time staff from outside the game and expand its role as a union—which meant negotiating endorsements and other off-the-field contracts but not negotiating with teams on behalf of the players. During the spring, baseball agent Frank Scott was hired as the organization's first executive director, and the union established a permanent office in New York.

To increase his staff, Scott hired Robert Cannon to serve as the union's legal counsel. Cannon was a Wisconsin judge and son of Raymond Cannon, a minor league pitcher and congressman who represented some of the Chicago Black Sox players after their ban and also headed an attempt at unionization in 1922. Although neither of them was a full-time employee of the union—Scott continued working as an agent and Cannon as a judge during their time with the MLBPA. Nonetheless, their hiring was a significant step toward Roberts' vision for the union.

While employed, Scott and Cannon favored a conservative approach to labor negotiations. They worked within the team owners' system for modest, incremental change and relied largely on the benevolence and trust of the owners to bring about improvements. As such, they sought to maintain goodwill with owners at all times, avoided making public statements on behalf of the players, and generally were much more pro-management than later MLBPA leaders.

---

6 *For specific information about baseball unions, see "Major League Baseball Players Association: Our History," www.mlbplayers.com cited 21 August2017; "Major League Baseball Players Association," www.mlbpa.org cited 21 August 2017; Peter Dreier, "The Fascinating Story of Major League Baseball's Players Union Stimulated by the Death of Jim Bunning," www.salon.com cited 21 August 2017; "A Celebration of Baseball Unionism," www.nyujlpp.org cited 21 August 2017.*

Before hiring Cannon, Scott had considered Happy Chandler—retired from the Commissioner's Office—as a candidate for the job of union legal counsel. In fact, Cannon himself would later be considered for the role of MLB Commissioner, and during his time with the union, explicitly told players and owners that he considered the interests of players as secondary to the interests of baseball.

1960s

In 1965, the players union decided to expand the role of its leadership from part-time to full-time. Cannon initially was offered the job but was hesitant to leave his judicial position in Wisconsin. He attempted to relocate the union's office to Milwaukee or Chicago to better accommodate his schedule, but the union wished to remain headquartered in New York. Personal clashes with Roberts, whom Cannon later labeled an anti-owner radical, and his disputes with other union leaders—including future Senator Jim Bunning—over the direction of the MLBPA cast Cannon's role into doubt.

While Cannon seemed to be the MLBPA's heir apparent, Roberts was pushing for another, more pro-labor candidate. That was top economic advisor of the United Steelworkers union, Marvin Miller. When Cannon officially left the union in 1966, Miller was hired as its first full-time director and quickly transformed the MLBPA. Miller immediately began to mold the players into a bona fide labor union. His first steps were to shore up the union's finances by beginning a group licensing program and also educating players about the fundamentals and benefits of organizing and solidarity.

During late 1966, Miller signed a deal with MLB owners eliminating the players' pension contribution of $2 per day—up to $344 per year—which had gone directly into the pension fund, and replaced it with voluntary dues check-off of the same amount as union dues. This new arrangement, interestingly, covered the MLBPA's $150,000 annual budget. In addition, owners agreed to funnel $4.1 million into the players' pension plan each year, thereby replacing the previous agreement that was strictly tied to World Series and all-star game money. This, in turn, amounted to a 100 percent increase in benefits for all players, coaches, managers, and trainers who had been active since 1957. Miller also negotiated increases in life and health insurance and also widow's benefits.

As of 1966, the MLBPA started its group licensing program and allowed companies to use players' names and pictures to sell products. With assistance from agent Scott, Miller signed a business deal with Coca-Cola to use player photos on the underside of Coke bottle caps, which netted $60,000 per year for two years. This agreement helped the union survive before dues were technically activated in mid-1967. Because baseball owners demanded money from Coca-Cola to use the team logos, Coke had to airbrush the logos off the players' hats.

Players and their representatives from four major North American sports met to discuss common issues in April 1967. Two months later, Marvin Miller, general counsel Dick Moss, and player Tim McCarver met with the owners' negotiating team before the all-star game in Anaheim, California. Miller told AL president Joe Cronin that the union intended to negotiate not just a minimum salary, but also a large set of issues such as scheduling, length of season, grievances, and travel time and expenses.

In late 1967, players sent a statement of policy to team owners outlining their desired changes. These included such things as no double-headers after night games, no split double-headers, guidelines for temperature and wind that force postponements of games, revisions to the reserve clause, an increase in the minimum salary, a reduction in the length of the season, and an impartial arbitrator for grievances. At baseball's winter meetings, owners refused to meet with the union's executive board about these matters.

During 1968, Miller helped players negotiate the first-ever collective bargaining agreement (CBA) in professional sports. It raised the minimum salary in baseball from $6,000—the level at which it had been stuck for two decades—to $10,000 and set the tone for future advances. Besides a higher minimum salary, the CBA contained an improved and standardized contract form; increases in cash allowances for incidentals such as meals and spring training; a formalized procedure for grievances; and new scheduling rules. Two years later, Miller helped players negotiate the right to arbitration to resolve grievances—an achievement he considered the most significant of the union's early years because the process paved the way for further gains.[7]

7 *Some players' grievances were as follows: First, outfielder Curt Blefary was fined by the Orioles for participating in an off-season basketball game with players on the Senators, in violation of an Orioles rule. Blefary lost his case. Second, Cincinnati's player rep Milt Pappas protested that Reds players had been bumped out of first class in lieu of the press. First class accommodations (if available) were*

At its winter meetings at the Palace Hotel in San Francisco in December 1968, the union's executive board once again heard that team owners were too busy to see them about problems. After their own meeting, the board called players around the country looking for commitments to not sign contracts without a pension agreement. A total of 450 players agreed, and Miller held a press conference to read off their names.

As a result, the owners' first pension offer was a $5.1 million annual contribution, an increase of $1 million than previously. Miller logically countered that there were four new owners and teams worthy of players and beneficiaries, so the proposed increase was only from $205,000 per team to $212,500 and also did not reflect baseball's massive new television deal.

In early 1969, more than 100 players attended a meeting at New York's Hotel Biltmore. While there, Miller gave a detailed report of the past four months of pension negotiations, supplemented by two league reps. As such, the MLBPA proposed a three-man arbitration panel to settle the current pension dispute. Although owners refused it, they increased their pension offer from $5.1 to $5.3 million.

The players' reps voted the new offer down but then met with the owners group to reach a compromise over the pension dispute. The owners' annual contribution was raised to $5.45 million and the agreement increased benefits, lowered pension eligibility from five years to four and retroactive to 1959, and also lowered the earliest age a player could begin collecting his pension from 50 to 45.

During spring training in 1969, Miller toured teams' spring camps and encouraged players to unite and close ranks. He explained what had been gained thus far in negotiations and urged players to stick together. Then, players and owners held

---

required for the players under the CBA. Miller met with Reds president Bob Howsam, who relented. Third, a group of AL players filed a grievance in protest of staying at the Lord Baltimore hotel in Baltimore. Commissioner Eckert upheld the grievance, but John Gaherin had to pressure manager Eddie Stanky to get the White Sox to comply. September 1968. *To gain leverage, Miller advised players not to sign their 1969 contracts until a new pension agreement was negotiated. See Marc Nomandin, "50 Years Ago, Marvin Miller and the MLBPA Changed Sports Forever," www.sbnation.com cited 21 August 2018, Mark Armour, "Collective Bargaining Agreement (1968)," www.pursuitofpennants.wordpress.com cited 21 August 2018, and Mark Armour and Dan Levitt, "A History of the MLBPA's Collective Bargaining Agreement: Part 1," www.fangraphs.com cited 21 August 2018.*

their first meeting of the Joint Study Committee (JSC) on the reserve clause, which had been created by the CBA a year earlier. In their opening statement, the owners claimed that chaos would ensue if any changes were made to the reserve clause.

At another meeting of the JSC, owners claimed that the reserve clause only protected the rank-and-file players. In October, Curt Flood was traded from the St. Louis Cardinals to the Philadelphia Phillies. A month later, Flood met with Miller and told him he wanted to sue the baseball commissioner, AL and NL presidents, and twenty-four teams regarding free agency. Miller then invited Flood to the upcoming player meetings to speak to the executive board.

After being rebuffed at the owners' winter meetings the previous two years, the players made their own plans in 1969 and met in San Juan, Puerto Rico. Commissioner Bowie Kuhn came and told the players he was their commissioner too and hoped the new CBA negotiations would speed up since the current one expired on December 31. Several players voiced complaints regarding the use of AstroTurf, stadium design, the new all-star voting by fans, and CBA negotiations and also repeatedly stressed the fact that they had no input in issues that involved them.

Curt Flood appeared at the executive board meeting and told players of his plans. After being asked tough questions about his motivation to sue, Flood firmly stated that his profession was unjust. The players unanimously voted to support Flood's legal case financially and thus former Supreme Court justice Arthur Goldberg—who had earlier worked with Miller at the Steelworkers union—was hired as Flood's attorney.

In December 1969, Flood wrote a letter to Kuhn and claimed he should be a free agent. Kuhn denied his request. The letter was made public by Boston Red Sox player Carl Yastrzemski and many players indicated their support for Flood. Importantly, the CBA expired and needed replacement by April 5, the day before MLB's 1970 season started.

In retrospect, among the many milestones achieved under Miller was the right to free agency for players. Indeed, Flood's unsuccessful challenge of the reserve clause got the ball rolling toward that goal. Funded by his fellow players, Flood sued MLB privately but eventually lost his case in the US Supreme Court. Nevertheless, the battle educated countless players and millions of Americans about the fundamental inequity of the reserve system, which in effect, perpetually renewed a player's contract and essentially linked him to one club for life, or until the club decided to get rid of him.[8]

1970s

After the CBA deadline passed without a new agreement in April 1970, club owners submitted a final offer to Miller, who wrote a summary of the proposal and sent it to the players without a recommendation. The players voted it down 503–89 despite the previous thirty-five negotiating sessions. In May, Miller agreed to a new CBA, subject to a vote of the players, who subsequently approved it on June 8. It was a three year-deal covering 1970–1972. Some noteworthy gains in it included an increase in the minimum salary to $12,000, $12,500, and $13,500 over the three years of the agreement; increases in players' share of the playoff pool, severance pay for those cut in the spring or during the season, and in their spring training allowance; additional travel guidelines; recognition of the MLBPA as the sole representative of players in all matters except salaries; and an acknowledgement that players may use agents. Most importantly, however, an outside arbitrator could be used for all players' grievances not involving integrity of the game.

At his annual spring training meetings with each team during early 1971, Miller read section 10-A covering the reserve clause of the standard contract. He believed players could play a year with a renewed contract and then become free agents. Then in June, players filed an unfair labor practice charge with the NLRB after owners refused to share details of their new national television deal. The union argued that pension benefits were traditionally tied to television contract proceeds, but owners wanted to sever that link. Subsequently, the NLRB ruled for the union.

---

8 *From May to June 1970, the trial of Flood v. Kuhn took before Judge Irving Ben Cooper of the US District Court in New York. Testifying for baseball were Bowie Kuhn, Joe Cronin, Chub Feeney, John McHale (Expos), Francis Dale (Reds), Bob Reynolds (Angels), Bing Devine (Cardinals), Ewing Kauffman (Royals), and Joe Garagiola (broadcaster). Testifying for Flood were former players' Jackie Robinson, Hank Greenberg and Jim Brosnan, former owner Bill Veeck, and Flood himself. In August, Judge Cooper ruled for baseball citing earlier Supreme Court rulings that antitrust laws do not apply to baseball. During April 1971, the US Court of Appeals for the Second Circuit upheld Judge Cooper in the Flood ruling. See "Curt Flood Case Decided," www.history.com cited 22 August 2018, Rene Rismondo, "May 19, 1970: Flood v. Kuhn Begins in Federal Court," www.mlbplayers.com cited 22 August 2018, and "June 19, 1972: Flood v. Kuhn is Decided," www.blackthen.com cited 22 August 2018.*

With the pension agreement expiring on March 31, 1972, negotiations ramped up for a new deal. The underwriters of the pension and benefit plan notified both parties that their premiums were going up and that it would cost an additional $372,000 per year to maintain the existing medical portion of plan. The owners told Miller they would cover this increase. The players asked for a $1.2 million increase per year in owner pension contributions. Then in June, the US Supreme Court upheld the lower court ruling in *Flood v. Kuhn*, reaffirming baseball's antitrust exemption. The decision acknowledged that baseball is interstate commerce, but says that Congress, not the courts, should be the party to address the issue.

During early 1973, Miller and team owners agreed to a new CBA covering 1973 to 1975. Key gains included neutral binding salary arbitration for players with at least two years' service time; ten-five players—ten years in the majors, five with the current team—could veto trades; five-year players could not be sent to the minors without consent; minimum salary increased to $15,000 for 1973–1974 and $16,000 in 1975; and an increase in spring training allowance. In addition, clubs and players agreed to a new three-year pension agreement, aligning the timing of the two agreements for the first time.

In late 1974, Oakland Athletics pitcher Jim Hunter charged club owner Charlie Finley with breach of contract. MLBPA's general counsel Dick Moss filed two grievances on behalf of Hunter, one against MLB asking that Hunter be declared a free agent and a second against the club for remuneration of the $50,000. Arbitrator Peter Seitz found for Hunter in the first grievance, declaring that Finley had not met the terms of the contract triggering Section 7-A and that Hunter is therefore a free agent. In the second grievance, he ruled that Finley must pay Hunter $50,000 plus interest. Finley sued to overturn Seitz's ruling and also filed for a preliminary injunction to stop Hunter's free agency. Hunter signed with the New York Yankees for $3.2 million over five years, which was three times larger than the largest annual contract previously issued.

Two pitchers—Andy Messersmith and Dave McNally—refused to sign their renewed contracts in 1975. The idea was simple: A team could legally renew a player's contract because the player had signed a contract saying it could be renewed. Messersmith's contract with the Los Angeles Dodgers in 1974, for example, gave the team the right to renew that contract for 1975, even without Messersmith's signature. However,

Messersmith never signed away the right to renew the contract again in 1976. Because the clause only allowed for one-year renewals, the Dodgers could not renew Messersmith again without his approval and the same for McNally, who planned to retire after the 1975 season and only joined the effort on principle. After the Dodgers and Expos attempted to renew Messersmith's and McNally's contracts for 1976, the union filed a grievance. Arbitrator Seitz ruled in favor of the players and declared Messersmith and McNally free agents.

This, however, did not fully abolish the reserve clause. Following the ruling, the owners realized any player could become a free agent by simply refusing to sign his contract. Thus, they quickly agreed to a new CBA that placed restrictions on the reserve clause and allowed for free agency in exchange for guaranteeing teams control over a player for a certain number of years.

The 1976 free agents set a new market, and teams scrambled to sign their best players to keep them from testing free agency. Meanwhile, Don Fehr replaced Dick Moss who resigned as general counsel in 1977 and one year later, the owner's chief negotiator John Gaherin quit and former General Electric negotiator Ray Grebey replaced him. This indicated that owners were getting ready for a fight at the expiration of the CBA in December 1979.

During mid-1979, negotiations began on the new CBA to replace one that would expire on December 31. The owners, meanwhile, voted to put 2 percent of their 1980 gate receipts into a mutual assistance fund to prepare for a strike. After the CBA expired, the owners' first proposal included that in a player's first six years he would receive a defined salary based on experience and performance thereby ending salary arbitration, and that teams that lose premier free agents would receive a player from the signing team. Alternatively, the players proposed free agency at four rather than six years and an end to the current requirement that a free agent must wait five years before becoming a free agent again.

1980s

After negotiating with owners for five months, the union set a strike date of May 22, 1980. However, after an all-night session at the Doral Inn in New York, the two sides announced a new four-year agreement for 1980 to 1983. The breakthrough came when management agreed to Miller's proposal to form a one-year JSC on free agent compensation. In August, the JSC held its first meeting.

During February 1981, Grebey announced that the JSC was unable to reach an agreement and that owners would unilaterally put their compensation proposal into effect. After the MLBPA voted to set a May 29 strike date, federal mediator Ken Moffett engaged to help negotiations. Miller filed an unfair labor practice charge with the National Labor Relations Board (NLRB) and petitioned that owners turn over financial data to prove their claims of huge losses. The NLRB issued a complaint in support of the union and asked owners to supply the data requested by Miller. Then in May, representatives for both players and owners met with NLRB officials.

One month later, the MLBPA offered a new compensation proposal in which clubs would create a pool of MLB players from which teams losing free agents could choose. Judge Werker rejected the NLRB's petition for an injunction, further ruling that players must go on strike within the next 24 to 48 hours or forfeit their right to do so. In June, Miller announced the strike and removed himself from further negotiations. After missing seven sessions, Miller rejoined the negotiations.

During the first forty-eight days of the strike, seventeen negotiating sessions were held. After several postponements, the NLRB hearing over the players' claim of unfair labor practices against the owners took place in New York. On July 10, the union agreed but owners rejected the proposal. Negotiations move to Washington at Secretary Donovan's request. In late July, a settlement was announced whereby a free agent is defined as being in the top 20 percent at his position based on a statistical formula and required teams losing free agents to receive a major league player. Players and owners unanimously ratified the agreement.

In November 1983, ten months after the former director of the Federal Mediation and Conciliation Service Ken Moffett replaced retiring Marvin Miller and became executive director of the MLBPA, the union's executive board fired him. Miller, who served as interim chief, was temporarily replaced by Don Fehr and Gene Orza joined the union as associate general counsel.

After months of work and negotiation, team owners approved the Joint Drug Committee's drug treatment program, which players had accepted on May 23,

1984. In general, if a club suspected a problem but the player declined treatment, a three-person board of professionals reviewed the case. If the board recommended treatment and the player declined, the commissioner could impose penalties.

During late 1984, negotiations started for a new CBA with Fehr leading the talks for players and Lee MacPhail for the owners. When the CBA expired in December, the two major issues to be negotiated for the next agreement were players' share of the new television deal for their pension and benefit plan and owners' desire to slow the rise in salaries. In negotiations, MacPhail claimed clubs were struggling financially and provided the union with financial data for the previous thirteen years, which showed an industry profit only in 1978. According to the data, the clubs lost $92 million in 1982, $66 million in 1983, and projected large losses into the future.

After examining the books, Stanford economics professor Roger Noll contended baseball actually made $24 million in 1984 and that the so-called losses were caused by bookkeeping artifices such as charging sister companies below market rates for television, radio, concession, and parking revenue, mixing in real estate properties, and large executive salaries. As a result, owners proposed that teams with higher-than-average payrolls could not sign free agents unless they were for less-than-average salaries; trades for players who would put team above the average payroll would be prohibited; all clubs must be under the 1985 payroll level by 1988; and salary arbitration awards would be capped at double the player's previous salary.

Unhappy with the owners offer, the union's executive board authorized a strike on August 6, 1985. Commissioner Peter Ueberroth, who had replaced Kuhn, entered the negotiations and recommended that owners drop their salary cap proposals and that the players agree to three years of service time for salary arbitration rather than two. He suggested the strike deadline be extended while talks continued on the pension contribution.

In renewed negotiations, Fehr offered to accept less than one-third of the television revenue for the pension plan if owners agreed to use the difference to help poorer clubs. Shortly after the strike began on August 6, the parties reached an agreement on the new CBA. Then Ueberroth spoke at a general managers meeting, advising attendees that long-term deals are not smart business and that if they wanted to sign a free agent, they must first justify the deal economically to him.

After becoming executive director, Fehr led the players during a period of unprecedented growth in baseball as industry revenues climbed to $6.5 billion while players' salaries increased from an average of $413,000 in 1986 to nearly $3 million in 2009. However, despite industry growth, owners repeatedly tried to find ways to thwart free-agency rights won by players. None of those efforts was more cynical than when owners collectively decided not to pursue free agents in the player markets following the 1985–1987 MLB seasons.

The MLBPA filed grievances alleging ownership collusion in early 1986 and again in February 1987. In September, arbitrator Tom Roberts ruled that team owners violated the basic agreement in the first collusion case, and later, in January 1988, determined damages of $10.5 million. In October 1989, arbitrator George Nicolau ruled that owners again violated the basic agreement in the second collusion case, awarding damages of $38 million. Then in January 1988, the MLBPA filed a third collusion grievance due to an off-season players market for which the owners created an information bank to share information and restrain salaries.

1990s

After successful negotiations in early 1990, MLB Commissioner Vincent announced a new four-year (1990–1993) CBA. The agreement could be reopened by either the players or owners after three years; the minimum salary was raised to $100,000 from $68,000; the pension and benefit plan contribution by the owners was increased to an average of $55 million over four years; and salary arbitration eligibility remained at three years but the top 17 percent of two-year players by service time became eligible. Known as Super-2s, this represented about fifteen players per year. Later, arbitrator George Nicolau decided for players in collusion III (1987 group) and ruled the information bank to be illegal.

Nicolau also awarded collusion II players $102.5 million, bringing the total for the first two cases to $113 million. With the status of damages for collusion III undecided, players and the union agreed to settle the three cases for $280 million, essentially calculated as the $115 million already awarded plus collusion III and any other remaining damages to be settled plus interest.

During the mid-1990s, the players went on strike, feeling they needed to act well before the end of the season to give the two sides time to negotiate before the profitable postseason. Owners voted to open the 1995 season with replacement players and US Federal Justice Sonya Sotomayor upheld the NLRB request for an injunction, returning players' labor situation to the pre-strike system and calling off their strike. After camps opened, there was a 144-game schedule.

In December 1996, the union formally approved contracts covering the years 1995 to 2000. The terms of the new CBA included: a new luxury tax on team payrolls—1997: 35% over $51 million; 1998: 35% over $55 million; 1999: 34% over $58.9 million; 2000-2001: no tax. The MLBPA established the Players Trust, a 501 (c)(3) charitable foundation administered by the players, whose purpose was to give back to local communities through time, money, and celebrity. The organization is the first charitable foundation in professional sports overseen by the players.

From 1997 to 1999, MLBPA executive director Fehr criticized owners for not including players in their ongoing realignment discussions and proposals, some of which were fairly sweeping; Congress passed the Curt Flood Act of 1998, legislatively reversing the Supreme Court's exemption of baseball from the antitrust laws, at least as they applied to labor relations; and MLB owners established the Blue Ribbon Panel on baseball economics to examine the payroll disparity among teams and make recommendations on how to redress it. Twelve of its sixteen members owned or operated MLB teams while the other four, including former US Senator George Mitchell, had strong ties to teams. There were no MLBPA representatives.

During November 1999, negotiations began on a new CBA since the current one expired on December 31. In mid-December, owners proposed dedicating 48 percent of network television, radio, and gate receipts for player salaries in conjunction with a team payroll cap and floor. According to their scheme, if a team reached the payroll cap it could not sign any free agents other than their own. In addition, the owners wanted a pay-for-performance system for pre-free agency players to replace the current arbitration system. Fehr responded that this system would affect the mobility of free agents and the pay-for-performance plan would eliminate multiyear contracts, guaranteed salaries, and the maximum 20 percent cut rule. He further contended there is no known economic problem in baseball. Thus, the CBA expired in December.

2000s

During August 2002, players and owners reached preliminary agreement on a new labor contract hours before the scheduled strike date. The agreement was baseball's first labor deal reached without a work stoppage and the first to include random testing for steroids. The next round of bargaining, in 2002, brought a contract without a strike or lockout and the same was true for the agreement reached in 2006. That year was Fehr's final contract negotiation as executive director and it ensured sixteen years of labor peace in baseball.

Fehr also played an important part in spreading the popularity of baseball beyond North America. That included efforts to help create and develop the World Baseball Classic, the sport's first World Cup-styled international tournament featuring active major leaguers. Then in June 2009, he announced his impending retirement and because of his recommendation, the players named Michael Weiner, a longtime counsel with the MLBPA, as their new executive director in December 2009. As such, he inherited a union that was united, powerful, and effective.[9]

Weiner was the lead negotiator when the sides reached agreement on their 2006 CBA, which extended through the 2011 season. However, as executive director, he negotiated his first CBA in 2011 by steering an unprecedented level of player involvement to reach perhaps the most comprehensive agreement in the union's history. More than 230 different players attended at least one bargaining session to negotiate a deal that addressed, among many issues, such things as league realignment, expansion of postseason play, numerous health and safety issues, and benefit plan increases for current and former players. This latest agreement was settled more than a month before the previous agreement expired, and ensured uninterrupted play through 2016.

---

9 *A sample of articles on globalization of baseball and/or international players include: Michael Parsons, "Opening Day Far Too Global for True Fans," Florida Today (12 February 2014): 2; Gene Budig, "Baseball on the Up and Up," Charleston Gazette (19 March 2013): A4; Ezra Fieser, "Red Sox-Yankees Series Highlights Globalization of Baseball," Christian Science Monitor (8 April 2011): 2; David Waldstein, "How an M.L.B. Tour of Cuba Went From a Dream to Reality," New York Times (15 December 2015): 1; Scott Tainsky and Jason Winfree, "Discrimination and Demand: The Effect of International Players on Attendance in Major League Baseball," Social Science Quarterly (March 2010): 117; Andrew Linker, "International Players Continue to Influence Game Greatly," The Patriot (16 July 2007): T16.*

Director Weiner's tenure was cut short, unfortunately, when he died in November 2013 after a courageous and inspiring fifteen month battle with brain cancer. Only 51-years-old, Weiner left the baseball community with a lasting impression of his warmth, compassion, sense of fairness, and fierce intellect. His brief tenure as executive director was a period in which players strengthened their involvement in union affairs and collective bargaining, yielding significant improvement in the basic agreement and the game.

During December 2013, the union's board voted unanimously to appoint Tony Clark as its next executive director. Clark, who joined the MLBPA staff in March 2010 as director of player relations and was promoted to deputy executive director in July 2013, was the first former player to lead the organization. He played for six clubs over a productive fifteen-year career as a switch hitter, first baseman, and designated hitter. From Miller to Clark, one constant remained: each generation of players passed along a legacy of equality, fair play, and loyalty to the next generation.

Besides the careers of Miller, Fehr and Weiner, other things in MLB involved both franchise owners and the MLBPA from 2000 to 2017. First, Commissioner Bud Selig proposed a complicated realignment scheme in mid-2000. It resulted in a 16-team NL with four four-team divisions, no wild card, and a 14-team AL with two four-team divisions, one six-team division, and one wild card. The MLBPA countered with a much simpler realignment proposal: shift the Houston Astros to the AL West, creating two 15-team leagues each with three five-team divisions. After the owners tabled realignment until at least 2002, MLB released a report of the Blue Ribbon Panel on baseball economics. The study contended that a competitive imbalance existed between high and low payroll teams and that baseball needed drastic remedies to address the disparities among the franchises.

Second, sometime in 2001, owners and players jointly contributed $5 million to an MLB-MLBPA Disaster Relief Fund and after the 9/11 disaster, baseball's chief executive officer (CEO) Paul Beeston told Fehr that owners would no longer seek contraction in number of teams. But after the CBA expired in October and before game seven of the World Series, Beeston told Fehr that, in fact, contraction would be a point of discussion between them in the upcoming labor negotiations. Then in November, Commissioner Selig announced that MLB voted 28–2 to contract two franchises—widely believed to be the Minnesota Twins and Montreal Expos—for

2002. According to Fehr, "over the last season and especially the last several weeks, we have been reminded, vividly, of the special place baseball holds in America. This makes it all the more unfortunate that the clubs would choose this moment to dash the hopes of so many of its fans."[10]

During late 2001, the union filed a grievance and maintained that contraction needed to be collectively bargained because, in part, the Expos and Twins were believed to be the two franchises targeted for contraction, with the Florida Marlins and Tampa Bay Rays as possible backups. Consequently, Judge Harry Crump issued a temporary restraining order in Minnesota's Hennepin County District Court requiring the Twins to play in the Metrodome in 2002. This, in turn, temporarily halted the contraction of the team. Nevertheless, Selig and Beeston met with Don Fehr and his son Steve to jump-start negotiations. Although Selig proposed the 50 percent sharing of local revenue and a 50 percent competitive balance tax on payrolls above $98 million, the Fehrs rejected Selig's offer.

During December 2001, arbitration hearings on the contraction grievance began before arbitrator Shyam Das. In addition, Congressional hearings were held to consider the contraction proposal, and both Selig and Steve Fehr testified. In response to the contraction plan, the legislators considered removing baseball's antitrust exemption as it relates to teams moving or contracting. Likewise, MLB and the MLBPA began negotiations over contraction, temporarily tabling the grievance hearing but then later called off negotiations over contraction and the grievance hearings. If the arbitrator ruled for the union, damages could include monetary compensation for an impaired free agent market.

Third, during August 2002, team owners and players agreed to a new four-year CBA without a work stoppage. Its terms included an increase in revenue sharing to 34 percent of net local revenue calculated on a straight pool approach; a sliding-scale competitive balance tax with a threshold starting in 2003 at $117 million and increasing over the life of the agreement with the first time over the threshold resulting in a tax of 17.5 percent; a minimum salary of $200,000 in 2002 that increased to $300,000 in 2003; and confidential performance enhancing drug (PED)

---

10 *See David Sheinin and Mark Asher, "Baseball Owners Vote to Eliminate Two Teams," www.washingtonpost.com cited 22 August 2017.*

testing to begin in 2003. If more than five percent of players tested positive, then mandatory random testing would kick in the next year. In September, the owners unanimously ratified the agreement with only the New York Yankees–who would pay most of the competitive balance tax–in opposition. One month later, the players signed the agreement.

Fourth, regarding its actions in 2003, the MLBPA researched for possible collusion relative to the most recent free agent market and confidential, survey-purpose drug testing began in the fall. As a result, MLB and the union learned that 104 or approximately 7 percent of the players anonymously tested positive for anabolic steroids, which was above the five percent threshold that would trigger mandatory random testing in 2004. Thus in late 2003, MLB and the MLBPA agreed to add tetrahydrogestrinone (THG) to their list of prohibited performance enhancing substances. Later, MLB announced results of PED testing and also penalties for random tests. For the first positive test, a player would get treatment and counseling; for the second, a 15-day suspension or a $10,000 fine; and up to a fifth positive test, a one-year suspension or $100,000 fine.

Fifth, the Senate again held hearings on performance enhancing substances in baseball, and in early 2004, Selig and Fehr testified. Senator John McCain told them if baseball does not do more on the issue very soon, they risk motivating Congress to undertake a search for legislative remedies. A few months after Fehr appeared before the Senate Commerce Committee on PED use in baseball, the government received a warrant to seize the confidential drug testing records of the eleven players linked to the Bay Area Laboratory Co-operative (BALCO) case.

In their raid of Comprehensive Drug Testing Inc. (CDT), federal agents collected the results for all players tested plus some on athletes in other sports. The MLBPA and CDT immediately asked for return of the data not related to the eleven players. The government, however, fought to get a search warrant for the remainder of the information. Thus, the random testing program was put on hiatus until July 2004 as MLB and the union put additional confidentiality safeguards in place.

During September, MLBPA lawyers' Michael Weiner, Steve Fehr, and Gene Orza informed each of the 104 players who failed their 2003 drug tests that the government now had their results although Fehr and Selig elected not to know who was on the list. Then, a third judge ordered the government to return the confidential list of positive tests to MLB and the union because the information seized went beyond the scope of the search warrant. The government appealed the judge's decision

Sixth, in the fall of 2005, executive director Fehr offered a proposal in response to Selig's demand for increased PED penalties. He proposed a twenty-game suspension for first time offenders with the commissioner authorized to increase it to thirty games or an arbitrator authorized to reduce it to ten, seventy-five games for a second offense, again with the commissioner able to increase it and an arbitrator able to reduce it, and a penalty at the commissioner's discretion–subject also to an arbitrator appeal–for a third offense. Fehr also agreed to random testing for amphetamines. After Fehr once again appeared before a Senate committee hearing on PED use in baseball, owners and players agreed on a new PED policy. In it, a first offense resulted in a fifty-day suspension, a second offense in a one hundred-day suspension, and a third offense in a lifetime ban of a player but with the right to appeal for reinstatement after two years.

Seventh, during the 2006 World Series in St. Louis, MLB team owners and players announced a new four-year CBA. The new agreement was settled, for the first time, before the expiration of the existing one. Among its key provisions were increases in the competitive balance tax over the term of the agreement and also increases in the minimum salary to $380,000 in 2007, $390,000 in 2008, and $400,000 in 2009. One year later, Maine Senator George Mitchell released the results of his investigation. Most of the eighty-plus players named in the report were either previously suspected or admitted users of performance enhancing substances including Yankees pitchers' Roger Clemens and Andy Pettitte. While Pettitte admits he took PEDs temporarily to help recover from an injury, Clemens vehemently denied it and assailed Mitchell's uncorroborated source, Clemens' long-time personal trainer Brian McNamee.

Eighth, in the aftermath of Mitchell's report, Fehr and Selig appeared once again before Congress in 2008 to answer questions on the use of PEDs in baseball. Meanwhile, Clemens and McNamee testified before Congress where McNamee claimed he regularly injected Clemens with PEDs but Clemens denied it. So, owners and the MLBPA once again revised the Joint Drug Agreement, principally in response to recommendations from the Mitchell Report. Two provisions included administration of the program by an Independent Program Administrator who will issue an annual report summarizing the results of the tests, and adding 600 tests per year, bringing the total to 3,600 for an average of roughly three per player per year.

During mid-to-late 2008, team owners and players agreed to *(a)* use instant replay for home runs for the remainder of the season including the postseason and *(b)* implement nine recommendations proposed by the Safety and Health Advisory Committee to reduce bats breaking into multiple pieces. Thus, bat manufacturers would be certified and held to specific physical standards, and models would be tracked to monitor breakage rates.

Ninth, the MLBPA, Florida Marlins, and MLB announced an agreement regarding the Marlins compliance with revenue sharing provisions of the basic CBA. Also, in 2009, Fehr announced his intention to step down as executive director and Michael Weiner received preliminary endorsement from the executive board to become the next executive director. Although not using the term *collusion,* Weiner expressed his concern over the operation of the current free agent market: "I don't think it's an accident that in recent weeks, management officials, without attribution, have been making predictions about what's going to happen in this year's free agent market." A short time after Fehr's final day, Weiner was formally voted executive director by the Executive Board.

Tenth, under pressure from the MLBPA in 2010, the Marlins committed to using revenue sharing receipts for player-related expenses. Furthermore, the team's finances were also subject to review by MLB and the union for a three-year period. In September of the year, team owners and players agreed to modify free agency rules for the 2010–2011 and 2011–2012 off seasons in response to the MLBPA's suspicions that the recent free-agent markets were unduly inactive. Among provisions were shorter time periods and deadlines, elimination of the requirement that players have to formally file to become free agents, and stricter rules against collusion.

From the fall to winter of 2013, the Ninth Circuit Court of Appeals decided in favor of the MLBPA and against the government, ruling that they had to return the anonymous CDT test results from 2003. Moreover, owners and players released the annual public report from the drug program's independent administrator. Of 3,747 tests, less than 1 percent of them were of an adverse nature with two for performance enhancing substances and fifteen for stimulants. Following a long appellate process, the US Justice Department announced it will not appeal the Ninth Circuit's ruling that the government illegally seized the records from baseball's 2003 anonymous and confidential drug testing for survey purposes. The government had initially taken them in 2004 under a more limited search warrant.

Eleventh, in late 2011, owners and players agreed to a new CBA through December 1, 2016. Important changes were adding a second wild card team to each league's playoffs; moving the Houston Astros from the NL East Division to the AL West Division; elimination of type A and type B player rankings for free agent compensation; revised draft pick compensation system for teams signing or losing free agents; and large-market teams disqualified from receiving revenue sharing funds.

Twelfth, during 2012, arbitrator Shyam Das reversed player Ryan Braun's drug-related suspension, making Braun the first player to successfully challenge such a suspension. Braun appealed his suspension on grounds that his urine sample was improperly handled by the tester. In May, baseball removed Das as an arbitrator. Then one month later, additional revisions are announced to the Joint Drug Prevention and Treatment Program. Some changes were human growth hormone (HGH) blood testing during the off-season, spring training, or for cause, and modifications to the test collection procedure and appeals process.

Thirteenth, starting in the 2013 regular season, owners and players agreed to nutritional in-season testing for HGH. Also, for the first time since 1977 when salary arbitration was under a one-year suspension, no player went to salary arbitration. After Michael Weiner passed away from a brain tumor, the MLBPA's executive board named Tony Clark executive director and former player Dave Winfield a special assistant to Clark.

Fourteenth, during early 2014, team owners and the MLBPA announced the most significant revisions to the Joint Drug Prevention and Treatment Program since 2006. Key elements of it included an increase in random urine collections and blood collections to test for HGH and an eighty-game suspension for a first offense, a 162-game suspension for a second offense, and a permanent suspension for a third. In December, the union and owners released the annual public report from the drug program's independent administrator. The report denoted that of 6,394 urine tests and 1,535 blood tests, twelve in the group were of an adverse nature with two of them for performance enhancing substances and the other ten for stimulants.

Fifteenth, in 2015, the MLBPA and team owners announced new rules to speed up the pace of the game and revisions to the instant replay system. Two key components were that hitters must keep one foot in the batter's box between pitches for called balls and strikes, and that umpires must enforce time limits between innings and during pitching changes. In the summer, MLBPA named Kevin Slowey a special assistant, and the union and owners adopted the Joint Domestic Violence, Sexual Assault, and Child Abuse Policy.

Players' Salaries

For players on teams in MLB, their compensation and the growth in it depends on several variables besides how they performed in games during regular seasons and union negotiations. These include, for example, their club's success in number of wins and qualifying for a postseason, home-site attendance, size of the fan base, extent of media coverage, type and popularity of other professional sports teams in the local and regional markets, wage inflation, and revenue from broadcasting games on television.

Table 4.1 shows the distribution, in five-year increments, amounts, and percentage changes in the minimum and average salary of MLB players from 1965 to 2015. According to the data, the largest increases in players' minimum and average salaries were, respectively, $116,000 in 2000–2015 and $938,000 in 2010–2015, and in percentages, 100 percent in both 1965–1970 and 1980–1985 for the minimum and 222 percent in 1975–1980 for the average. Most likely, players' strikes in 1972, 1980, 1981, 1985, and 1994–1995 boosted salaries in future years and had a greater impact on them than owners' lockouts in 1973, 1976, and 1990 since no regular season games were cancelled then. Furthermore, the average dollar amounts increased proportionately faster than the minimum salary from 1970 to 1985 but not necessarily during 1990–2015. After being awarded free agency in the mid-1970s, the union became increasingly powerful for several years, but beginning in the mid-1980s, it also focused on negotiating improvements in minimum salaries for new players especially in the 2000s.

Table 4.1 MLB Players' Minimum and Average Salaries, 5-Year Increments, 1965–2015

Year	Minimum	PCTCH	Average	PCTCH
1965	6	–	19.0	–
1970	12	100	29.3	54
1975	16	33	44.6	52
1980	30	87	143.7	222
1985	60	100	371.5	158
1990	100	66	578.9	55
1995	109	9	1,071.0	85
2000	200	83	1,988.0	85
2005	316	58	2,589.6	30
2010	400	26	3,014.5	16
2015	502	26	3,952.2	31

Note: MLB is Major League Baseball. Players' minimum and average salaries are in thousands. The PCTCH is five-year percentage change of, respectively, minimum and average salaries. The dash (–) means that percentage changes in 1965 are not applicable.

Source: "2015 Average Salaries in Major League Baseball," www.mlbplayers.com cited 22 August 2017 and Frank P. Jozsa Jr., Baseball, Inc.: National Pastime as Big Business (Jefferson, NC: McFarland, 2006).

Besides such specific labor-market factors as competition for American and international players and their freedom, power of the MLBPA, owners' lockouts, and actual strikes and the threat of them, there were business, cultural, demographic, economic, and social conditions, events, and trends that explained, in part, the amounts and percentage changes in MLB players' salaries as reflected in table 4.1. Listed in no specific order, the following are a few reasons that contributed in some way to variations in the minimum and average salaries of players since the 1990s.

One, teams typically increased their operating revenues from commercial deals with domestic and international television networks, cable channels, satellite radio, and other types of broadcasting companies. These, in turn, provided franchise owners with additional cash flows to competitively recruit, bid for, and sign free agents and also reward their most valuable players whose contracts had expired with long-term, multimillion-dollar contracts.

Two, the renovation of current ballparks and construction of new baseball stadiums at sites of many AL and NL teams resulted in more income for them to spend on players' salaries. Because of additional revenue from sports facilities in such metropolitan areas as Chicago, Cleveland, Detroit and New York, and Cincinnati, Philadelphia, Pittsburgh, San Diego and San Francisco, the AL's White Sox, Indians, Tigers and Yankees, and NL's Reds, Phillies, Pirates, Padres, and Giants respectively could afford to pay more and also trade for and retain all-stars plus those with potential to win games in the future.

Three, after consecutive low-performance seasons, some low-to-high revenue clubs had pressure from their fan base to become competitive again within three years. This affected, at one time or another, the Astros, Mariners, and Red Sox in the AL, and Cubs, Nationals, and Dodgers in the NL. These and other teams spent millions to acquire talented catchers, infielders, outfielders, and pitchers. Even so, many of these deals did not make a tremendous difference in teams' winning division titles, league championships, and World Series because of players' injuries, inferior managers, and retirements.

Four, partly because of sports agents and their skill at being experienced, knowledgeable, and well-prepared when negotiating with teams' general managers and other officials, the majority of MLB players financially prospered for years when they signed contracts and earned millions in salaries and other benefits. Some prominent baseball agents besides Scott Boras—who successfully represented players since the early 2000s—include Arn Tellem, Fernando Cuza, Leigh Steinberg, Sam and Seth Levinson, Doug Reinhardt, Jeff Moorad, and Don Nomura.

Five, the demand and supply for athletes in the labor market combined with the local, regional, national, and international popularity of professional sports reveal why baseball players' annual salaries are relatively high. Compared to others there are an extremely small number of athletes who can consistently pitch 95-mile-per-hour fastballs, have the strength and timing to hit a baseball more than 400 feet, and can accurately catch batters' ground balls in the infield and outfield and throw them to their teammates.

Six, to improve their current and future performances and thus actual and potential salaries, MLB players are able to physically train and practice harder and smarter than in previous years, eat more healthy and nutritious types of food, and recover faster from injuries to arms and other parts of their bodies. Based on teams' resources, abundance of facilities, and plenty of cash, players entertain fans individually and as a group which, in turn, results in higher attendances at home games and more operating revenue and perhaps bigger budgets for expenses including salaries.

Team Payrolls

Since the introduction of free agency in 1976, the MLBPA has opposed a salary cap and ensured that owners remain free to spend as much as they wanted on player salaries. Because some owners signed players to reckless contracts—gains that trickle down to the entire union membership through the salary arbitration process—players' salaries increased, often exponentially, throughout the 1980s, 1990s, and 2000s. Nevertheless, as a share of team revenues, their salaries have declined for more than a decade.[11]

Rather than any one thing, this occurred as a result of different factors. Perhaps first and foremost, MLB teams have simply gotten smarter and more efficient particularly since the late 1990s. Gone are years when a substantial number of MLB teams in either league paid huge amounts of cash on free agent players whose ages exceeded thirty and over. Now, teams are increasingly signing their cornerstone players to team-friendly extensions before they hit the free agent market, while at the same time relying to a greater extent on cheaper, cost-controlled players to replace unfilled holes on the roster. As a result, although the cost of winning games continues to climb, that price is rising more slowly than expected given the hundreds of millions of dollars in additional television revenue flowing into the sport in recent years.

In addition to teams' being less generous and more conscientious, frugal and responsible, factors such as revenue sharing and the luxury tax have further reduced

---

11 *Nathaniel Grow, "The MLBPA Has a Problem," www.fangraphs.com cited 21 August 2017.*

the incentive for them to spend large amounts on payroll. The drop in players' share of league revenues directly correlates, for example, with MLB's fine-tuning of its revenue sharing formula in the 2002 CBA. Unlike the days before revenue sharing, when a team would keep every dollar of extra revenue it generated locally, clubs share approximately 30–35 percent of their local revenues with each other.

In economic terms, this means that revenue sharing has caused teams' marginal revenue product (MRP)—the expected additional revenue generated from each additional dollar spent on payroll—to steadily decline. Or, in plain English, revenue sharing has predictably caused large market teams to become less willing to invest in their on-field product since they now retain a smaller portion of any additional in-stadium revenues that they generate. Add in the luxury tax—which requires clubs to pay a penalty of as much as 50 cents for every dollar spent on player payroll over $190 million—the large market teams that the MLBPA has historically relied on to help drive the free agent market have now become more financially prudent.

Of course, if revenue sharing reduced large market teams' incentive to spend on payroll, this would mostly balance out with increased spending at the lower end of the payroll spectrum, as the additional revenue flowing to smaller market clubs would presumably allow these to spend more on player salaries. Unfortunately for players, this has not proven to be true. Indeed, MLB's payroll disparity has not changed appreciably in the revenue-sharing era, meaning that smaller and some midsized market teams are still spending roughly as little compared to the large market teams as they did before revenue sharing. As a result, revenue sharing and the luxury tax have combined to reduce the incentive for large market clubs to increase their payrolls, without offsetting these decreases through increased spending by smaller market teams.

A third but somewhat surprising factor contributing to the players' declining share of overall league revenues is the recent explosion in MLB's television revenues. With the league's television profits from games tripling in recent years, many assumed that they would, in turn, spend extra revenue on player salaries. In reality, though, teams have little motivation to use their television windfall to increase payroll.

Unlike ticket sales—which generally rise as a team improves against its opponents on the field—television revenue is fixed via long-term broadcasting agreements. As such, while baseball franchises can increase their in-stadium profits to some degree by spending more on payroll—thereby improving the quality of their team—the same is generally not true for television revenue.

As a result, teams have little incentive to spend any added broadcasting profits on payroll, because in economic terms, the added television revenue has not adjusted the team's MRP. So even though MLB's television revenues have increased substantially in recent years, relatively little of this extra money is flowing to the players. Instead, teams are largely pocketing these additional revenues as extra profits, thereby raising the league's overall revenue without a corresponding increase in player payroll. Consequently, the new television money is actually lowering players' share of overall league revenue on a percentage basis.[12]

In August 2018, the MLBPA hired longtime sports law attorney and litigator Bruce Meyer as senior director of collective bargaining and legal. Meyer will focus on negotiation and enforcement of the collective bargaining agreement and report to executive director Tony Clark. Meyer has advised players' unions in basketball, football and hockey, most recently working the past two years under former executive director Don Fehr with the NHL Players' Association. Clark says Meyer's decades of protecting and advancing player rights makes him uniquely qualified for the role.[13]

---

12 *To research topics involving players' salaries in MLB, see such readings as "MLBPA Chief Blasts Yanks' Levine for Betances Remarks," Buffalo News (23 February 2017): C.34; Ronald Blum, "Major League Baseball," Charleston Gazette (24 December 2016): B.3; Noam Schieber, "A Baseball Prodigy, the Players' Union and a Lesson For Labor," International New York Times (8 April 2015): 17; Ron Cook, "Cubs Make Right Call, by Rule, of Course," Pittsburgh Post (3 April 2015): E.1; Ian Gordon, "In the Strike Zone," Mother Jones (July/August 2014): 10, 12; David Wharton, "Union Chief Sets Baseball Players Free," Baltimore Sun (28 November 2012): D.4; David Murphy, "MLB Players Union Boss 'Optimistic' About Deal," Tribune Business News (1 March 2011): 1. In addition to these readings, the author's books contain data and other information on the business, economics, and finance of professional baseball and their teams and players. See, for example, Frank P. Jozsa's American League Franchises: Team Performances and Business Success (New York, NY: Springer, 2015); Baseball in Crisis: Spiraling Costs, Bad Behavior, Uncertain Future (Jefferson, NC: McFarland, 2008); Baseball, Inc.: The National Pastime as Big Business (Jefferson, NC: McFarland, 2006); Major League Baseball Organizations: Team Performances and Financial Consequences (Lanham, MD: Lexington Books, 2016); National League Franchises: Team Performances and Business Success (New York, NY: Springer, 2015).*

13 *"MLB Players Association Hires Sports Litigation Expert Meyer." www.foxsports.com cited 21 November 2018.*

CHAPTER 5

Market Effects

Since free agency began in the mid-1970s, Major League Baseball (MLB) has implemented policies, regulations, and rules to increase competition and thereby establish parity among teams within the American League (AL) and National League (NL). As such, MLB's primary purposes were to boost teams' ability to compete and therefore consistently win games in regular seasons and then qualify for postseasons, attract more fans to home games from their local and regional markets, and generate additional cash flow, revenue, and profit from operations.[1]

During 2002, for example, a competitive balance tax—commonly known as a luxury tax—was introduced in the sport. It placed a financial penalty on teams that exceeded a certain payroll threshold in hopes that these penalties would limit spending for players by the richest franchises. Besides the competitive balance or luxury tax, revenue sharing and the players' draft pick system were also actions taken by MLB to improve competitiveness among clubs and give each of them an equal opportunity to win one or more division titles, league championships, and World Series.

---

1 *For references on topics in this chapter, see Frank P. Jozsa Jr., Major League Baseball Organizations: Team Performances and Financial Consequences (Lanham, MD: Lexington Books, 2016), American League Franchises: Team Performances and Business Success (New York, NY: Springer, 2015), and National League Franchises: Team Performances and Business Success (New York, NY: Springer, 2015).*

A number of complex and less sophisticated methods and mathematical formulas have been used by sports economists and other researchers to statistically measure competitive balance among baseball teams in a group and for various periods of MLB seasons or years. These studies include, in general, quantitative measures of dispersion, inequality, and concentration applied to end-of-season league outcomes such as wins or points percentages. More specifically, some useful types of measurements are the actual standard deviation, actual and idealized standard deviations, Gini coefficient, Herfindahl–Hirschman Index (HHI), Lorenz curves, analysis of variance statistics, concentration ratios, and relative entropy.[2]

Because of differences in applying data, results of the analyses varied and so do their interpretation of whether competitive balance actually exists now or previously in the sport and why. However, each study contributed in some way to the literature on baseball history and also revealed questions, problems, and topics for further research.

To provide more information and especially knowledge and insight about this subject with respect to its significance in baseball during the late twentieth and early twenty-first century, this chapter focuses on identifying and relating a few variables involving AL and then NL teams and the extent of financial parity among and between these organizations. To that end, this is a relatively unique, practical, and straightforward way to understand and realize how the sport and small, midsized, and large market teams within the two leagues were affected comparatively and competitively, from an economic perspective, since the early 1990s.[3]

---

2 *The most common measure of dispersion in random variables, such as batting averages, is the standard deviation. A team with a high (low) standard deviation in individual batting averages has less (more) consistent hitting up and down the lineup. The Gini coefficient, for example, can measure inequality with one indicating maximum inequality–one person having all the salary–and zero indicating salaries are equal among all players. The Herfindahl-Hirschman Index (HHI) is a measure of inequality or concentration from the income distribution and industrial organization literatures and frequently used to measure competitive balance within a baseball league. A Lorenz curve is an analytic tool widely used to represent the distribution of some variable of interest (e.g., fielding averages) among members of teams arrayed on the vertical axis and percentiles on the horizontal axis. One-way analysis of variance tests are used to determine whether all group means are equal to each other. For example, you might compare all ballparks to the one with the lowest park factor. Concentration ratios are a way to measure the relative wins or losses of a baseball team to all those in MLB. To explore the changing competitive balance in MLB, the relative-entropy measure of information theory can be applied. For more details about these types of stats and those of players, see such websites as www.fangraphs.com, www.baseball-reference.com, www.mlb.com, www.sabr.org, and www.espn.com.*

3 *See tables A5.1 and A5.2 in the appendix for the historical performances of respectively AL and NL teams which occurred, in part, because of differences in their financial status and wealth.*

FRANCHISE REVENUES

American League

In the 1991 MLB season, each AL team had an average revenue of $60 million. According to table 5.1, the amounts ranged from $90 million for the New York Yankees to $39 million for the Milwaukee Brewers. Six—or approximately 43 percent—of the clubs exceeded the league's average while revenues of the other eight were each below $60 million. Consequently, the amounts of big market teams like the Yankees, Red Sox, and White Sox were much greater than those who played their home games in ballparks within midsized markets including the Baltimore Orioles, Detroit Tigers, and Texas Rangers, and in smaller markets containing the Minneapolis Twins, Cleveland Indians, and Kansas City Athletics. Furthermore, the standard deviation in revenues—which measures their variation or spread—was $17 million. In other words, substantial inequality existed economically among teams in the AL during early years of the 1990s.

Regarding various teams' results in the postseason, the Twins won the West Division (WD), defeated the East Division (ED) Toronto Blue Jays in the AL Championship Series (ALCS), and in seven games, won the World Series by beating the Atlanta Braves. Interestingly, the Yankees finished fifth, Red Sox third, and White Sox second in their respective division.

To combat the growing revenue disparity among major league teams, MLB first instituted a revenue sharing program in 1996. The plan was slowly phased in over a few years, and then simplified and improved during the 2002 collective bargaining agreement (CBA) negotiations. The current revenue sharing program has not changed much since then, with minor tweaks along the way. Although the plan is not perfect, it gives small-market teams a much needed boost in order to keep them on a somewhat-competitive footing with large market teams.[4]

---

4 *"Revenue Sharing," www.fangraphs.com cited 29 August 2017.*

Table 5.1 Gross Revenues, American League by Team, Selected Years

Team	*Year (Revenue Rank)*					
	1991	1996	2001	2006	2011	2016
Baltimore Orioles	51 (10)	105 (2)	133 (6)	158 (8)	179 (10)	253 (11)
Boston Red Sox	82 (3)	88 (4)	152 (3)	234 (2)	310 (2)	434 (2)
Chicago White Sox	78 (4)	71 (6)	101 (9)	173 (5)	214 (6)	269 (10)
Cleveland Indians	42 (13)	95 (3)	151 (4)	159 (7)	178 (11)	271 (9)
Detroit Tigers	52 (9)	44 (10)	115 (7)	170 (6)	217 (5)	275 (8)
Houston Astros	NA	NA	NA	NA	NA	299 (4)
Kansas City Royals	53 (8)	43 (11)	85 (13)	12 (14)	161 (13)	246 (13)
LA Angels of Anaheim	54 (7)	42 (12)	103 (8)	187 (3)	226 (4)	350 (3)
Milwaukee Brewers	39 (14)	41 (13)	NA	NA	NA	NA
Minnesota Twins	44 (12)	40 (14)	75 (14)	131(13)	213 (7)	249 (12)
New York Yankees	90 (1)	133 (1)	215 (1)	302 (1)	439 (1)	526 (1)
Oakland Athletics	64 (5)	49 (9)	93 (10)	146 (11)	160 (14)	216 (14)
Seattle Mariners	45 (11)	58 (8)	162 (2)	182 (4)	10 (8)	289 (6)
Tampa Bay Rays	NA	NA	92 (11)	134 (12)	162 (12)	205 (15)
Texas Rangers	62 (6)	87 (5)	134 (5)	155 (10)	233 (3)	298 (5)
Toronto Blue Jays	89 (2)	70 (7)	91 (12)	157 (9)	188 (9)	278 (7)

Note: Gross Revenues are rounded to the nearest dollar in millions. Abbreviated is Los Angeles (LA) and Not Applicable (NA). Prior team names include California Angels (1965–1996), Anaheim Angels (1997–2004), and Tampa Bay Devil Rays (1998–2007). Houston Astros shifted from the NL to AL West in 2013 and Milwaukee Brewers from the AL to NL Central in 1998.

Source: "MLB Franchises Revenues and Expenses," www.baseballchronology.com cited 23 August 2017; "The Business of Baseball," www.forbes.com cited 24 August 2017; "Rodney Fort Sports Business Data," www.umich.app.box.com cited 30 April 2018.

In MLB's revenue sharing program, every team contributes approximately 31 percent of their net local revenue which is divided up and equally distributed to every team. Since those in large markets have much greater local revenues than any small-market teams, this places the last group in the black. Additionally, a large amount of MLB's central fund—money acquired through things like national broadcasts—is set aside and then allocated to teams based on their revenues.[5]

To determine differences in amounts among AL clubs in a sample of years as of 1991 and before 2017, table 5.1 denotes their distribution in five-year increments. In 1996, for example, the Orioles and Indians were allocated enough revenue from the league and also from their ticket sales and other sources to rank second and third, respectively, following the Yankees while the Angels and then Brewers and Twins each had the lowest amounts. The revenues of seven—or 50 percent—of the teams were below the league's average of $69 million.[6]

In MLB's 1996 season, the ED's wild-card Orioles defeated the Central Division (CD) Indians but then lost to the Yankees in the ALCS. For those with least amounts, the Brewers finished third and Twins fourth in the CD and Angels fourth in the WD. Thus, the Orioles and Indians benefited most from their share of revenue but not small-market teams including the Royals and Athletics.

While the Yankees and then Mariners and Red Sox had the most revenue of fourteen AL clubs in 2001, the Blue Jays, Royals, and Twins were at the bottom. Since 1996,

5 *After recognizing inherent inequality in the system, MLB officials attempted to implement changes to improve the competitive balance in the game in the early 1990s. Although the sport does not have a salary cap, the revenue sharing structure and competitive balance tax—commonly known as the luxury tax—seek to ensure that team revenues are relatively equal.*
The current structure is designed to financially punish teams that spend excessively in the market for players since teams pay a certain proportion of their net local income—all baseball-related income apart from revenue sharing income—and certain clubs pay an extra portion based on their performance in order to ensure that the most profitable clubs pay more and the least profitable clubs receive more. This plan allows clubs with lower gross revenues to compete in the market for players with those who have higher gross revenues, thus providing a more level playing field. See Evan Zepfel, "Have MLB's Efforts to Preserve Competitive Balance Done Enough?" www.harvardsportsanalysis.org cited 29 August 2017.

6 *For MLB's 2017 season among AL teams, gross revenues ranged from the Yankees' $619 million to the Athletics' $210 million. The average was $309 million or 4 percent more than in 2016. As of early 2019, Forbes had not published teams' revenue for their 2018 season. Besides the sources in table 5.1, see "Rodney Fort Sports Business Data," www.umich.app.box.com cited 6 October 2017.*

however, the average amount per team increased by $58 million—or 84 percent—because of higher attendances, more income from television, and other factors. As a result, the Yankees, Indians, and Mariners each won their division and in the playoffs, the Yankees defeated the wild-card Athletics and also the Mariners and the Indians. Then in the five-game ALCS, New York won, but then lost to the NL Arizona Diamondbacks in the World Series. Although the league's Red Sox ranked third, Rangers fifth and Orioles sixth in revenue, they failed to qualify for the postseason.

From 2001 to 2006, the league's total revenue increased $45 million or by $3.2 million per team. This was significant especially for such small-market clubs as the Twins and Athletics. For the first time, however, the Yankees' amount exceeded $300 million and Red Sox's $200 million. Nevertheless, in the AL Division Series (ALDS), the Yankees lost to the Tigers and Twins to the Athletics and in the ALCS, the Tigers won, but then lost to the NL St. Louis Cardinals in the World Series. Although temporary, revenue sharing improved parity for a few teams in the AL.

Partially because of shifting funds from large to small-market teams through 2011, revenues expanded by above-average amounts for the small-market Royals and Twins but not Indians and Rays. While the league's income increased by $48 million—or 27 percent—the Yankees' revenue exceeded $400 million and Red Sox's $300 million, which in effect opened a wider gap between the two richest clubs and the other twelve. In retrospect, the AL needed to share more revenue among the group to achieve more parity.

During the 2011 postseason, the midsized Rangers and Tigers defeated the Rays and Yankees, respectively, in the ALDS. Meanwhile, three of the four smallest market teams were not able to advance beyond the regular season nor did the wealthy Red Sox. Apparently, not enough revenue was transferred that season to some inferior clubs who simply lacked the talent to effectively compete and win games against rivals in their division. Based on trends, a $93 million revenue gap in 1996 between top and bottom teams in the AL had increased to $279 in 2011.

As of 2016, the difference in revenue between the Yankees and Rays was $321 million. Furthermore, only five—or 33 percent—teams had amounts that exceeded the league average of $297 million with the Astros' and Rangers' revenues each above-average by less than $3 million. This suggests that clubs like the Twins, Royals,

Athletics, and Rays lacked enough revenue to be consistently competitive and thus had fallen further behind the richest teams in the AL.

Despite ranking only ninth with $271 million in revenue in 2016, the midsized-to-small-market Indians succeeded to win ALDS and ALCS titles and almost won the World Series championship in seven games. Because of pitcher Corey Kluber and such sluggers as Mike Napoli, Carlos Santana and Jason Kipnis, Cleveland challenged their competitors and won many games, scoring one or two runs in late innings.

A number of articles and studies critique the effects of revenue sharing and its purpose to reduce inequalities and increase competitiveness and parity of teams in MLB. From 2012 to 2015, for example, three of the five top recipients have been the AL's Rays ($138 million), Royals ($135 million), and Athletics ($114 million) with the two largest payors being the Yankees ($377 million) and Red Sox ($325 million). If the former group of franchise owners invested the money to improve rosters, their teams' payroll should have increased above others at least in the bottom one-fourth of the league. Since this did not happen, fans should know why.[7]

TEAM PAYROLLS

At the beginning of each MLB season, several publications report the payrolls of AL and NL teams based on their rosters as of opening day. Obtained and compiled by baseball's commissioner's office, these amounts typically include such things as

---

7 *Mike Ozanian, "Are MLB Fans Getting a Raw Deal From Revenue Sharing?" www.forbes.com cited 29 August 2017. According to the players' 2012-16 Collective Bargaining Agreement, MLB was essentially divided in two as part of something called market rank disqualification. The top fifteen markets gradually lost their revenue sharing (aside from the Oakland Athletics, who were exempt for a time) and bottom fifteen did not. Market rank disqualification still exists in the new CBA, but how it's calculated changed. The formula is based on something called market score, which is essentially the relationship of the market to the average MLB market based on population, income, and cable households. For example, the Yankees have a market score of 235 which is more than twice as large as the average market. Any market scoring above 100 is above average, and considered disqualified. In the new system, two teams that were previously market rank disqualified—Houston Astros and Atlanta Braves—are no longer disqualified. That means these clubs keep revenue sharing where they previously would have lost it, which is good news for them. But it might not matter too much. Because of the current state of those two franchises, both should end up being payors into the revenue sharing system by 2018 rather than payees. The Astros struck a new television deal going into 2015 and one year later, the Braves a new stadium. See Evan Drellich, "MLB Changes Market Rank Formula in Revenue Sharing," www.bostonherald.com cited 29 August 2017.*

players' termination pay, prorated shares of signing bonuses and earned incentive payments, and buyouts of options and cash transactions.

This data is important for fans because it reflects the commitment of teams to invest in various players, impacts each club's performance in regular and postseason games, and affects the competitive balance of a league during a season. Usually, but not always, prosperous and wealthy teams that exist in large metropolitan areas such as Chicago, Los Angeles, and New York have higher payrolls than those located in midsized and small markets.

In this section, table 5.2 contains the payrolls of AL clubs on opening day as of six equally-spaced MLB seasons. To compare and analyze them, these amounts are ranked from highest to lowest each year depending on the number of teams within the league. Although payrolls were rounded into millions of dollars and appear in the table, there are no ties in rank among teams given the original amounts.

Regarding the AL's 1991 season, the three highest payroll clubs—Oakland Athletics, Boston Red Sox, and California Angels—failed to qualify for the postseason. Ranked sixth and ninth in amounts, respectively, the Blue Jays and Twins each won their division by more than six games and later, the Twins defeated the NL champion Atlanta Braves in seven games to win the World Series. Interestingly, both the Twins and Braves had finished last in their division in the 1990 season.

Based on games behind the leader, the two worst in the group were the Baltimore Orioles and Cleveland Indians. These two teams' payrolls ranked in the bottom one-third of the league along with those of the Chicago White Sox and Seattle Mariners. Also, their amounts were significantly below the league's average payroll of approximately $24 million. In other words, seven clubs had payrolls at or above average indicating a competitive—but not perfect—balance.

Between 1991 and 1996, the league's average payroll increased by $8 million or 33 percent. More specifically, the New York Yankees increased in rank from fifth to first, Orioles from fourteenth to second, and Indians from eleventh to third. Alternatively, the average payrolls of the Brewers declined from seventh to twelfth, Athletics from first to thirteenth, and Royals from fourth to fourteenth. These changes occurred during the period, in part, because revenues greatly expanded for the three former teams but increased by only $2 million or 5 percent for the Brewers and decreased for the Athletics and Royals.

Table 5.2 Payrolls, American League by Team, Selected Years

Team	*Year (Payroll Rank)*					
	1991	1996	2001	2006	2011	2016
Baltimore Orioles	14 (14)	48 (2)	74 (7)	72 (7)	85 (9)	151 (5)
Boston Red Sox	32 (2)	39 (5)	109 (2)	120 (2)	161 (2)	160 (4)
Chicago White Sox	16 (12)	41 (4)	65 (8)	102 (4)	127 (4)	108 (10)
Cleveland Indians	18 (11)	5 (3)	92 (3)	56 (12)	49 (12)	74 (14)
Detroit Tigers	23 (8)	21 (10)	49 (10)	82 (6)	105 (6)	181 (2)
Houston Astros	NA	NA	NA	NA	NA	91 (12)
Kansas City Royals	28 (4)	18 (14)	35 (12)	47 (13)	36 (14)	111 (9)
LA Angels of Anaheim	31 (3)	26 (9)	47 (11)	103 (3)	138 (3)	137 (6)
Milwaukee Brewers	24 (7)	20 (12)	NA	NA	NA	NA
Minnesota Twins	22 (9)	21 (11)	24 (14)	63 (10)	112 (5)	102 (11)
New York Yankees	27 (5)	52 (1)	112 (1)	194 (1)	202 (1)	201 (1)
Oakland Athletics	33 (1)	19 (13)	33 (13)	62 (11)	66 (10)	75 (13)
Seattle Mariners	16 (13)	39 (6)	74 (6)	87 (5)	86 (8)	134 (7)
Tampa Bay Rays	NA	NA	56 (9)	35 (14)	41 (13)	57 (15)
Texas Rangers	22 (10)	35 (7)	88 (4)	68 (9)	92 (7)	128 (8)
Toronto Blue Jays	27 (6)	28 (8)	76 (5)	71 (8)	62 (11)	160 (3)

Note: Payrolls are in millions. Based on actual amounts each year, there were no ties in rank among teams' payrolls. Abbreviated is Los Angeles (LA) and Not Applicable (NA). Prior team names include California Angels (1965–1996), Anaheim Angels (1997–2004), and Tampa Bay Devil Rays (1998–2007). Houston Astros shifted from the NL to AL West in 2013 and Milwaukee Brewers from the AL to NL Central in 1998.

Source: "MLB Payrolls," www.umich.app.box.com cited 31 August 2017; "The Business of Baseball," www.forbes.com cited 24 August 2017; "2016 Total Payroll," www.usatoday.com cited 31 August 2017.

With respect to the final standings in 1996, the Yankees, Indians, and Texas Rangers won their respective division and in the ALDS, the wild card Orioles defeated the Indians and Yankees the Rangers. After that series, the Yankees won the ALCS and then the World Series. Thus, AL teams with the highest payrolls were successful and, from a competitive perspective, dominated others in the group.

Given data in the table, AL teams' average payroll had more than doubled from 1996 to 2001 and so did its deviation—$11 million to $27 million. While the Yankees remained first in rank and Indians third, the Red Sox improved from fifth to second. At the lower end of the distribution were the small-market Royals at twelfth, Athletics at thirteenth, and Twins at fourteenth. Others with a worse ranking than in 1996 included the Orioles, White Sox, and Angels while the Tigers remained tenth and the Mariners sixth. Besides the Red Sox, the Rangers and Blue Jays also placed higher than five years earlier.

In postseason performances of 2001, the Yankees, Indians, and Mariners won their divisions and Athletics the wild card with 102 victories. After the ALDS, the Yankees defeated the Mariners in the ALCS but lost to the NL Arizona Diamondbacks in the World Series. To some extent, these results indicate the lack of parity among big, midsized, and small-market teams.

From 2001 to 2006, the AL's payroll per team rose from $67 to $83 million or 23 percent. The large market Yankees, Red Sox, and Angels ranked highest, and at the bottom of the distribution were the Indians, Royals, and Rays. While amounts dramatically changed upward for the White Sox, Tigers, and Twins, payrolls of the Indians, Rays, and Rangers significantly declined. Besides the Yankees and Red Sox, the Orioles ranked the same as in 2001.

Regarding the 2006 season, the Tigers won an ALDS game and the ALCS but not the World Series while the low-payroll Athletics and Twins competed against each other in the other ALDS game. Thus, two mediocre, small-market teams were in the league's postseason. Otherwise, the Devil Rays and Royals finished last in their divisions with at least 100 losses each. This, in turn, denotes the competitive imbalances among teams in markets of different sizes.

Between 2006 and 2011, the average payroll of teams in the AL increased by $14 million or 16 percent and their deviation by $8 million or 20 percent. Once again, amounts of the Yankees, Red Sox, and Angels ranked first to third in comparison to the Indians at twelfth, Rays at thirteenth and Royals at fourteenth. Due to poor performances and budget constraints, payrolls had declined for the Indians, Royals, Mariners, and Blue Jays. This also happened to the Indians and Blue Jays five years earlier.

After winning ninety-one games in MLB's 2011 season, the low-payroll Rays were a wild card but lost to the Rangers in the ALDS while the Tigers defeated the Yankees in the other game. Based, in part, on their amount and rank in payroll, the trend thus far has been that one small-market team usually qualifies for the postseason but fails to advance and compete in the league's championship series. In comparison, the large market Red Sox won only two pennants and Angels one from 1991 to 2011. In other words, their payrolls were not justified given these teams' performances.

As of 2016, the AL's average payroll was $125 million—an increase of 28 percent since 2011—while its deviation declined by $6 million or 12 percent. The high-low amounts ranged from the Yankees at $201 million to the Rays at $57 million. While the Red Sox fell to fourth and Angels sixth, they were replaced respectively by the Tigers and Blue Jays. Besides the Rays, others below $80 million in payroll included the Indians and Athletics. Interestingly, the Indians and Rays—but not the Athletics or Royals—have been the only clubs consistently at or near the bottom of the distribution since 2006.[8]

By defeating the Red Sox in the ALDS and Blue Jays in the ALCS, and then challenging but losing to the NL Chicago Cubs 4–3 in games of the World Series, the Indians overperformed relative to their payroll. Meanwhile, the small-market Rays, Twins, and Athletics each finished below .500 in the regular season as did the large market White Sox and Angels. Simply put, most teams with below-average payrolls and also revenues have not been competitive in their division since the early 1990s because

8 *For MLB's 2017 season in the AL, the Tigers and Yankees had the highest payrolls at approximately $199 million and Athletics lowest at $81 million. The league average was $141 million or 12 percent more than in 2016. While the league's average increased by $16 million from 2016 to 2017, the deviation in amounts declined from $41 million to $39 million. This suggests more parity in the distribution of payroll among the fifteen teams. In 2018, however, AL teams' average payrolls fell to approximately $134 million. This change was especially apparent for the Orioles, Royals, Tigers, Yankees, and Rangers. Alternatively, most players for the Red Sox, Indians, and Astros received higher salaries.*

their players struggled as a group to score runs to win enough games to qualify for the postseason.

HOME ATTENDANCES

Each MLB season, several factors determine in different ways the actual attendances of teams at their home games. These include such things as the growth, population, and per capita or disposable income of households in the local market and the team's competitiveness and win-loss record in its and other divisions during the regular season, age and location of the ballpark and its amenities, number and popularity of star players who play on a team, average ticket prices for seats at their home games, and whether other professional clubs exist within or near the metropolitan area.

With respect to this topic, table 5.3 contains the distribution of home attendances of AL clubs and how they compared to each other in six specific seasons. This and such data in other tables of the chapter as their revenues and payrolls, and also their performances as reported in table A5.1 of the appendix, denotes the extent of parity or competitive balance among them while located at respective home sites during a period of years.[9]

In MLB's 1991 season, the league's average attendance was 28,300 per team. The Blue Jays ranked first, White Sox second, and Athletics third while at the bottom of the AL were the Tigers at twelfth, Brewers at thirteenth and Indians at fourteenth. Furthermore, seven clubs had attendances greater than average that year, including the large market Red Sox and White Sox, but not the Yankees or midsized Tigers and Mariners. Despite a gap of 36 million between these teams' highest and lowest home attendances, relatively few differences existed among those within small and midsized markets.

9 *Table A5.1 in the appendix shows the performances of AL teams in winning their division, a league pennant, or a World Series during several of their seasons. Based on data in the table, the most successful of them in consecutive five-year periods were the Blue Jays, Yankees twice, Rangers/Yankees, and lastly the Red Sox/Tigers/Royals. Others with some success were the Indians, Angels, and Athletics. Least impressive in performances included the Orioles, Mariners, and Rays.*

Table 5.3 Average Home Attendances, American League by Team, Selected Years

Team	*Year (Attendance Rank)*					
	1991	1996	2001	2006	2011	2016
Baltimore Orioles	31.5 (5)	44.4 (1)	38.6 (4)	26.5 (10)	21.9 (11)	26.8 (10)
Boston Red Sox	31.6 (4)	28.5 (6)	32.4 (6)	36.1 (4)	37.7 (4)	36.4 (4)
Chicago White Sox	36.2 (2)	20.6 (9)	22.0 (12)	36.5 (3)	24.7 (7)	21.8 (12)
Cleveland Indians	12.8 (14)	41.4 (2)	39.6 (3)	24.6 (11)	22.7 (9)	19.6 (13)
Detroit Tigers	20.2 (12)	14.4 (13)	24.0 (9)	32.0 (5)	32.6 (6)	31.1 (7)
Houston Astros	NA	NA	NA	NA	NA	28.4 (8)
Kansas City Royals	26.6 (9)	17.9 (10)	18.9 (13)	17.1 (13)	21.2 (12)	31.5 (6)
LA Angels of Anaheim	29.8 (6)	22.4 (8)	24.7 (8)	42.0 (2)	39.0 (3)	37.2 (3)
Milwaukee Brewers	18.4 (13)	16.3 (12)	NA	NA	NA	NA
Minnesota Twins	28.3 (8)	17.5 (11)	22.2 (11)	28.2 (9)	39.1 (2)	24.2 (11)
New York Yankees	23.0 (11)	28.1 (7)	40.8 (2)	52.3 (1)	45.1 (1)	37.8 (2)
Oakland Athletics	33.5 (3)	14.1 (14)	26.3 (7)	24.4 (12)	18.2 (14)	18.7 (14)
Seattle Mariners	26.5 (10)	33.6 (4)	43.3 (1)	30.6 (6)	23.4 (8)	27.9 (9)
Tampa Bay Rays	NA	NA	16.0 (14)	16.9 (14)	18.8 (13)	15.8 (15)
Texas Rangers	28.4 (7)	35.6 (3)	34.9 (5)	29.4 (7)	36.3 (5)	33.4 (5)
Toronto Blue Jays	49.4 (1)	31.6 (5)	23.6 (10)	28.4 (8)	22.4 (10)	41.8 (1)

Note: Average attendances are in thousands. Abbreviated is Los Angeles (LA) and Not Applicable (NA). Prior team names include California Angels (1965–1996), Anaheim Angels (1997–2004), and Tampa Bay Devil Rays (1998–2007). Houston Astros shifted from the NL to AL West in 2013 and Milwaukee Brewers from the AL to NL Central in 1998.

Source: "MLB Team Attendances," www.baseballpilgramages.com cited 28 August 2017.

Because the Blue Jays were competitive and won the World Series in 1991, they had the AL's second highest revenues at $89 million and also the sixth largest payroll at $27 million. In contrast, the Indians finished seventh in their division, placed thirteenth in revenue, and their payroll was ranked fourteenth at approximately $12 million.

In 1996, the AL's average attendance declined to 26,100 or by 9 percent. Despite losing to the Yankees in the ALCS, the Orioles ranked first in attendance followed by the Indians and Rangers. Alternatively, home games of the Brewers, Tigers, and Athletics attracted the fewest fans since they finished third or worse in their division. The Yankees, meanwhile, improved in rank to seventh, but the Blue Jays, White Sox, and Tigers each declined from five years earlier.

Besides having more people at their home games and winning eighty-eight games in 1996, the Orioles ranked second in both team revenue and players' payroll. The club was popular, in part because of its attractive ballpark, and also because they challenged the Yankees for the ED title. Alternatively, after five seasons, the Blue Jays became a mediocre club while the Orioles and Indians had a larger fan base and substantially higher attendances at games in Baltimore and Cleveland.

In 2001, the AL's average attendance increased by three million or 11 percent. The Mariners, Yankees, and Indians had the three highest numbers of fans at their ballparks in contrast to the White Sox at twelfth place, Royals at thirteenth, and Rays at fourteenth. In addition, the other clubs' attendances at home games in 2001 ranged from the Orioles at Camden Yards in fourth to the Twins at the Hubert H. Humphrey Metrodome in eleventh. The difference between the top and bottom teams' average home attendances was approximately 27 million, much less than in 1991 and 1996. Based on this variable, more equality existed across the league than in the early-to-mid 1990s.

The Mariners—who won their division by fourteen games—lost to the Yankees in the ALCS. Besides ranking second in revenue and sixth in payroll that season, Seattle's MLB team was led by all-star Ichiro Suzuki in batting average, hits, and stolen bases, pitchers Jamie Moyer and Freddy Garcia, and Bret Boone, Edgar Martinez, and Mike Cameron each with more than one hundred runs batted in (RBIs). Suzuki won Rookie of the Year and Most Valuable Player awards and Lou Piniella was named Manager of the Year. This was an outstanding, popular, and talented group of players which, led by Piniella, propelled the club to its victories in the regular season.

In 2006, the AL's attendance was 30,300 per game or 4 percent more spectators than before. The White Sox, Tigers, and Angels improved the most in attendance at home but others did not such as the Athletics at twelfth, Royals at thirteenth, and Rays at fourteenth.

The Orioles, Indians, Athletics, and Mariners also declined in rank, while the Yankees were first in the league with more than 52,000 spectators at its games in Yankee Stadium. Moreover, it became apparent to baseball fans and officials that the small-market Rays and Royals consistently experienced low attendances at Tropicana Field in Tampa Bay and Kauffman Stadium in Kansas City.

As of 2006, the Yankees were first in the league not only in attendance but also in revenue and payroll. During that season, they won the most games in the AL yet lost to the Tigers in the ALDS. Furthermore, the Rays and Royals each lost at least one hundred games and finished more than thirty-three games behind their division's leader. Based on these outcomes, the league's competitive balance continued to deteriorate despite revenue sharing plus a luxury tax on big market clubs.

In comparing MLB's 2006 and 2011 seasons, the AL's average attendance declined from 30,300 to 28,700, or by 6 percent. Once again, the Yankees ranked first followed by the Twins and Angels. Some clubs, however, had much smaller crowds at their home games including the Orioles, White Sox, Athletics, and Mariners but not the Red Sox, Royals, Rays, and Rangers. In other words, this group of small, midsized, and large market teams had different results in attracting fans to games at their ballparks in 2011.

In addition to their home attendance that season, the Twins also improved from a financial perspective. Their revenues ranked seventh and their payroll fifth among fourteen clubs. Nonetheless, they placed last in their division, thirty-two games behind the Tigers, and had the worst winning percentage in the league. Simply put, Minnesota's MLB team shifted from existing as another club in a small market to being midsized and therefore superior especially compared to the Rays, Royals, and Athletics.

As they did in 1991, the Blue Jays had the highest attendance among all clubs in the AL in 2016. While the league's average was 28,800, the Yankees ranked second and Angels third in attendance at their ballparks and then from thirteenth to fifteenth, respectively, the Indians at Progressive Field, Athletics at Oakland Stadium, and Rays at Tropicana Field.

Relative to 2011, home attendances significantly decreased for the White Sox, Indians, and Twins but increased for the Royals and Blue Jays in 2016. Regarding their performances in the season, the Indians defeated the Blue Jays in the ALCS while the White Sox and Twins finished with losing records and the Royals finished at .500. Despite a payroll ranked fourteenth, attendance thirteenth, and revenue ninth in the league, the Indians came within one game of winning the World Series.

From most to least, teams' attendances tend to range from the Yankees, Angels and Red Sox to the Indians, Royals, Athletics, and Rays. This, in turn, negatively affects the second group in payroll, revenue, and other ways both financially and competitively throughout seasons. Meanwhile the Astros, who play their home games in a relatively midsized-to-large market, were successful on the field in 2015–2017 yet ranked below average in payroll but not attendance.[10]

National League

Organized twenty-five years before the AL, the NL consisted of eight teams in 1876. Because of business problems and poor attendance, however, each of them struggled, including the Hartford Dark Blues and Louisville Grays. In 1901, these two professional baseball leagues joined to form a group and established MLB.

As the sport became increasingly popular in metropolitan areas across America during the twentieth century, MLB continued to expand by adding more clubs. In fact, each league had teams with sites in small, midsized, and large markets. This, in turn, caused differences between them especially from a financial perspective. As a result, some had more success than others in regular seasons and postseasons. This section of the chapter focuses on important topics of the NL and parity of its members during various seasons.

---

10 *With respect to the AL's 2017 season, home attendances averaged 28 million and varied or deviated by 7 million. While the Blue Jays ranked first, Yankees second and Angels third, the smallest number of spectators attended home games of the Indians, Athletics, and Rays. For various reasons, teams' average attendances trended downward from 2016 to 2017and then to 26 million in 2018. Such clubs as the Orioles, Tigers, Royals, Rangers, and Blue Jays had much smaller crowds at their home games in 2018 but not, for example, did the Indians, Astros, and Yankees. With respect to teams attendances, see such scholarly articles as Young Hoon Lee and Rodney Fort, "Attendance and the Uncertainty-of-Outcome Hypothesis in Baseball," Review of Industrial Organization (December 2008): 281–295; Brian Soebbing, "Competitive Balance and Attendance in Major League Baseball: An Empirical Test of the Uncertainty of Outcome Hypothesis," International Journal of Sport Finance (May 2008): 119–126; Allen Barra, "By the Numbers: Imbalanced Logic," Wall Street Journal (30 August 2002): W.5.; Maury Brown, "Rainouts Impacting MLB Attendance Early in Season," www.forbes.com cited 7 September 2017; Ben Langhorst, "What Do Your Fans Want? Attendance Correlations With Performance, Ticket Prices, and Payrolls," www.sabr.org cited 8 September 2017.*

Table 5.4 contains the gross revenues of teams in the NL during six specific years. Besides listing values in millions, it reveals how each of them ranked among the group each year and to what extent, if any, that influenced their performances in games of regular seasons and postseasons.

In 1991 (before revenue sharing), the average amount of the twelve NL teams was $54 million with a deviation of $15 million. While the large market New York Mets ranked first followed by the Los Angeles Dodgers and Chicago Cubs, the midsized-to-small-market Pirates, Braves, and Expos each had revenues below $46 million. Thus, those of seven teams or 58 percent of the group were ranked below the league average.

Despite their relatively low revenues from operations, the Pirates won the ED and Braves WD while the Dodgers finished second, Cubs fourth, Mets fifth, and Expos sixth in their respective division. After the Braves defeated the Pirates in the NL Championship Series (NLCS), they lost to the AL's Minnesota Twins in the World Series, who had ranked twelfth in revenue. Based on these results, NL teams with the most revenue did not compete for titles because they lacked talented players or managers and therefore lost too many games of the 1991 season.

When MLB introduced revenue sharing in 1996 and after realigning into three divisions two years earlier, the Rockies, Dodgers, and Braves ranked first to third in revenues with the Reds, Expos, and Pirates twelfth to fourteenth. Since 1991, however, while the Mets fell from first to sixth, Giants from fifth to tenth and Phillies from seventh to eleventh, the Braves and Astros improved their rank among the group. Also, the league's average revenue increased by $8 million or 14 percent per team and the deviation in revenue slightly changed from $15 million to $17 million. This meant that the redistribution of amounts within the group was about the same when comparing 1991 to 1996.

Based, in part, on their financial ability to build or rebuild their rosters, the NL's Braves, Cardinals, and Padres won their respective divisions in 1996. Thus, the high-revenue Rockies and Cubs and low-revenue Reds, Expos, and Pirates failed to qualify for the playoffs although later the Dodgers lost to the Braves and Padres to the Cardinals in the NLCS. Soon thereafter, the Braves won the NL pennant but were then defeated by the Yankees in the World Series. As reflected in table 5.4, the Padres were the only midsized-to-small-market club in the league's postseason.

Table 5.4 Gross Revenues, National League by Team, Selected Years

Team	Year (Revenue Rank)					
	1991	1996	2001	2006	2011	2016
Arizona Diamondbacks	NA	NA	127 (7)	154 (10)	186 (12)	253(11)
Atlanta Braves	40 (11)	79 (3)	160 (2)	182 (8)	203 (7)	275(8)
Chicago Cubs	64 (3)	76 (4)	130 (5)	197 (3)	266 (1)	434(2)
Cincinnati Reds	49 (6)	45 (12)	87 (14)	146 (12)	185 (13)	229(14)
Colorado Rockies	NA	95 (1)	129 (6)	151 (11)	193 (11)	248(12)
Houston Astros	46 (9)	62 (7)	125 (8)	184 (6)	196 (9)	NA
Los Angeles Dodgers	79 (2)	88 (2)	143 (3)	211 (2)	230 (5)	462(1)
Montreal Expos	39 (12)	41 (13)	63 (16)	NA	NA	NA
Miami Marlins	NA	56 (8)	81 (15)	122 (16)	148 (16)	206(15)
Milwaukee Brewers	NA	NA	108 (10)	144 (14)	195 (10)	239(13)
New York Mets	91 (1)	68 (6)	169 (1)	217 (1)	225 (6)	332(4)
Philadelphia Phillies	48 (7)	50 (11)	94 (12)	183 (7)	249 (2)	325(5)
Pittsburgh Pirates	45 (10)	40 (14)	107 (11)	137 (15)	163 (14)	265(9)
San Diego Padres	47 (8)	53 (9)	93 (13)	160 (9)	162 (15)	259(10)
San Francisco Giants	50 (5)	52 (10)	142 (4)	185 (5)	231 (4)	428(3)
St. Louis Cardinals	59 (4)	70 (5)	123 (9)	186 (4)	233 (3)	310(6)
Washington Nationals	NA	NA	NA	145 (13)	200 (8)	304(7)

Note: Abbreviated is not applicable (NA). Arizona Diamondbacks entered the NL in 1998 and Colorado Rockies in 1993. Expos moved from Montreal to Washington, D.C. in 2005 and nick-named the Nationals. Florida Marlins joined the NL in 1993 and became the Miami Marlins in 2012. Brewers shifted from the AL Central to NL Central in 1998. Houston Astros shifted from the NL West to AL West in 2013.

Source: "MLB Franchises Revenues and Expenses," www.baseballchronology.com cited 23 August 2017 and "The Business of Baseball," www.forbes.com cited 24 August 2017.

With respect to the distribution of revenues in 2001, the Mets ranked first, Braves second, and Dodgers third but in twelfth to fourteenth place were, respectively, the Phillies, Padres, and Reds. Because of expansion teams in Phoenix and Miami and new ballparks in Atlanta, Houston, Milwaukee, Pittsburgh, and San Francisco between 1996 to 2001, the league's average revenue increased by $55 million or 88 percent and its deviation by $12 million or 70 percent. Consequently, there were above-average changes in cash flows and earnings for such wealthy clubs as the Mets and Giants but also for the small-market Pirates.

In the NL's 2001 season, the Braves, Astros, and Diamondbacks each won their divisions and in the league's division series, the Diamondbacks defeated the wild card Cardinals and then later the Yankees in the World Series. Although only seventh in revenue with the Astros eighth and Cardinals ninth, the Diamondbacks likely had benefitted from being a new and relatively popular team and the recipient of revenues from the Mets and perhaps Braves and Dodgers.

While such teams as the Braves, Rockies, and Brewers substantially declined in rank from 2001 to 2006, the Phillies, Padres, and Cardinals increased because of their additional revenues from operations at home games. Somewhat similar to previous years, the large market Mets, Dodgers, and Cubs continued to have the highest amounts but lowest included the Brewers, Pirates, and Marlins. Again, the league's average revenue rose by more than $50 million or 44 percent but alternatively the deviation or variability in amounts among the sixteen teams decreased by $2 million or 7 percent.

During NL's 2006 postseason, the Cardinals defeated the mediocre Padres and the Mets beat the wealthy Dodgers. After the Cardinals won the NLCS, they beat the powerful Detroit Tigers in five games in the World Series. Given these results, revenue sharing had little to no impact on which clubs qualified for the playoffs since the low-revenue Brewers, Diamondbacks, Marlins, Nationals, Pirates, and Rockies experienced problems and each lost the majority of their games in the regular season.

From 2006 to 2011, the league's average revenue increased from $169 million to $204 million or more than 20 percent. The Cubs, Phillies, and Cardinals ranked first to third but then the small-market Pirates, Padres, and Marlins from fourteenth to sixteenth. While such clubs as the Brewers and Nationals improved in rank, others like the Astros fell from sixth to ninth, Dodgers from second to fifth, and Mets from first to sixth. Along with average revenue during the period, the deviation or variation in amounts increased by $5 million or approximately 18 percent.

Regarding MLB's 2011 season, the small-market Brewers defeated the Diamondbacks but then lost to the Cardinals in the NLCS. Other mediocre clubs–with below-average revenues–such as the Rockies, Reds, Pirates, and Padres each had more losses than wins in their division and so did the Cubs and Mets who ranked in the top six. Apparently, revenue sharing benefitted the Brewers and Diamondbacks but not all small-market teams.

In 2016, the league's average revenue increased to $304 million or by 49 percent. Because of a new lucrative television contract, higher tickets sales, and additional sponsorships, advertising fees, and memorabilia sales, NL clubs earned significantly more revenue. Following the large market Dodgers with most revenue were the Cubs and Giants while the Brewers, Reds, and Marlins had the lowest amounts. Also, the small-market Pirates and Padres each received about $100 million more than in 2011. Across the league in 2016, the deviation in revenue was $79 million compared to $32 million five years earlier and only $15 million in 1991.

Other than the Nationals, there were no small or midsized market teams in the wild card game and NLCS. Simply put, millions in revenue sharing did not improve these clubs enough to be competitive and as a result, six of them finished the regular season in their division below .500. Because of less parity in the league as of 2016, fans of such teams as the Marlins, Pirates, and Padres may attend fewer games in the future because of poor performances by their hometown baseball club. Moreover, it will be a challenge for these teams to resign their star players and successfully bid for free agents.[11]

---

11 *From 2016 to 2017, NL teams' average gross revenues increased by $17 million or 5 percent. For the league's 2017 season, the Dodgers ranked first followed by the Cubs and Giants. The Brewers, Reds, and Marlins had the smallest revenues. Also, the average variation in revenue amounts increased by $9 million or 11 percent. From a financial perspective, this gap indicates less parity among teams in the league.*

TEAM PAYROLLS

At the beginning of each MLB season, several publications report the payrolls of AL and NL teams based on their rosters as of opening day. Originally obtained and compiled by baseball's commissioner's office, these amounts typically include such things as players' termination pay, prorated shares of signing bonuses and earned incentive payments, and buyouts of options and cash transactions.

This data is important for fans because it reflects the commitment and ability of teams to invest in various players, impacts each club's performances in regular and postseason games, and affects the competitive balance of a league during a season. Usually, prosperous and wealthy teams that exist in large metropolitan areas such as Chicago, Los Angeles, and New York tend to have higher payrolls than those located in midsized and small markets.

In this section, table 5.5 contains the payrolls of NL clubs on opening day as of six equally spaced MLB seasons. To compare and analyze them, these amounts are ranked from highest to lowest each year depending on the number of teams within the league. Although payrolls were rounded into millions of dollars and appear in the table, there are no ties in rank among teams given the original amounts.

Based on data for MLB's 1991 season, the league's average payroll was approximately $24 million with the Dodgers and then Mets and Giants having the highest amounts while the Braves ranked tenth, Phillies eleventh, and Astros twelfth. Other clubs with above-average payrolls were the Cubs and Reds but not the Expos, Pirates, Padres, and Cardinals. Nevertheless, the Braves and Pirates won their division while the Dodgers finished second, Mets fifth, and Giants fourth. Thus, players on the former two teams were really underpaid relative to others in their division.

From 1991 to 1996, the NL's average payroll increased from $24 million to $31 million or about 29 percent. Because of success in previous seasons, the Braves ranked first in amount spent on players followed by the Reds and Cardinals but alternatively, those of the Expos, Mets, and Pirates actually declined compared to 1991. Besides the Braves, the Astros and Cardinals also had significantly higher amounts paid to players on their roster on opening day of the season.

Table 5.5 Payrolls, National League by Team, Selected Years

Team	*Year (Payroll Rank)*					
	1991	1996	2001	2006	2011	2016
Arizona Diamondbacks	NA	NA	85 (4)	59 (12)	53 (14)	87 (10)
Atlanta Braves	20 (10)	48 (1)	91 (3)	90 (5)	87 (8)	60 (14)
Chicago Cubs	26 (4)	30 (7)	64 (7)	94 (3)	125 (2)	174 (2)
Cincinnati Reds	25 (3)	40 (2)	48 (11)	60 (11)	75 (10)	89 (9)
Colorado Rockies	NA	34 (4)	71 (6)	41 (15)	88 (7)	85 (11)
Houston Astros	11 (12)	26 (11)	60 (9)	92 (4)	70 (11)	NA
Los Angeles Dodgers	33 (1)	34 (5)	109 (1)	98 (2)	104 (6)	192 (1)
Montreal Expos	20 (9)	15 (14)	34 (16)	NA	NA	NA
Miami Marlins	NA	30 (8)	35 (15)	14 (16)	56 (13)	69 (12)
Milwaukee Brewers	NA	NA	45 (12)	57 (13)	85 (9)	69 (13)
New York Mets	32 (2)	23 (12)	93 (2)	101 (1)	118 (3)	133 (6)
Philadelphia Phillies	20 (11)	28 (9)	41 (13)	88 (8)	172 (1)	45 (15)
Pittsburgh Pirates	23 (6)	21 (13)	57 (10)	46 (14)	45 (16)	100 (7)
San Diego Padres	22 (7)	27 (10)	38 (14)	69 (9)	45 (15)	100 (8)
San Francisco Giants	30 (3)	34 (6)	63 (8)	90 (6)	118 (4)	171 (3)
St. Louis Cardinals	21 (8)	38 (3)	78 (5)	88 (7)	105 (5)	139 (5)
Washington Nationals	NA	NA	NA	63 (10)	63 (12)	140 (4)

Note: Payrolls are in millions. Based on actual amounts each year, there were no ties in rank among teams' payrolls. Abbreviated is not applicable (NA). Arizona Diamondbacks entered the NL in 1998 and Colorado Rockies in 1993. Expos moved from Montreal to Washington, D.C. in 2005 and nicknamed the Nationals. Florida Marlins joined the NL in 1993 and became the Miami Marlins in 2012. Brewers shifted from the AL Central to NL Central in 1998. Houston Astros shifted from the NL West to AL West in 2013.

Source: "MLB Payrolls," www.umich.app.box.com cited 31 August 2017; "The Business of Baseball," www.forbes.com cited 24 August 2017; "2016 Total Payroll," www.usatoday.com cited 31 August 2017.

Although the Padres won the league's WD but then were defeated in the NLDS, other low-payroll teams had losing records including the Marlins, Pirates, and Mets, but not the Astros or Expos. In contrast, the high-payroll Braves, Cardinals, and Dodgers were successful, in part because their players had financial incentives to pitch effectively, produce runs, and win games in the regular season. The Rockies, meanwhile, finished above .500 and outperformed the Giants in the WD. Thus, the competitive balance within the NL continued to be influenced mostly by large rather than midsized or small-market clubs.

Between 1996 and 2001, the league's average payroll increased by $32 million or 103 percent. The Dodgers had the largest payroll at $109 million and the Marlins' $35 million ranked fifteenth. Because of the sport's popularity and substantially more television revenue, the majority of clubs paid their players significant amounts compared to 1996. The smallest changes, however, occurred for the Reds, Expos, Marlins, and Padres as opposed to the Braves, Dodgers, Cardinals, and Mets. In other words, much greater variation in payrolls divided the small from the large market teams.

There were no NL teams with payrolls less than $60 million in MLB's 2001 postseason. The four-year-old Diamondbacks ranked fourth in payroll in the league and won their NLDS game and the NLCS, and then the World Series by defeating the AL Yankees. This data suggests that midsized-to-large market clubs, with above-average payments to their players, had dominated the league's regular season since the Marlins, Expos, Reds, Pirates, Padres, and Rockies each finished below .500. Thus, competitive parity worsened in 2001 relative to 1996 and 1991.

From 2001 to 2006, the NL's average payroll increased from $63 million to $72 million or 14 percent. The Mets at $101 million and the Dodgers and Cubs had the three highest amounts while the Pirates, Rockies, and Marlins ranked lowest in the league after significantly reducing their expenses. In comparison, such small- to midsized market teams as the Reds, Astros, Brewers, Phillies, and Padres each expanded their budgets and paid players more income from operations. Finally, after moving from Montreal to Washington and being renamed the Nationals, the club's payroll almost doubled, putting them into tenth place.

During MLB's 2006 postseason, the Padres were the only NL team with a payroll less than $70 million. In fact, most clubs ranked tenth to sixteenth in the league had losing records and finished third or worse in their division. The Cubs, however, had the worst record despite a relatively high payroll of $94 million. Because some players failed as batters, pitchers, or fielders due to coaching and management problems and perhaps injuries, such teams as the Cubs simply underperformed in games rather than producing enough runs to win them.

In 2011, the Phillies ranked first of sixteen clubs by having the highest payroll in the NL at approximately $172 million. While the Cubs and Mets were next in amounts paid to their players, four other teams each had payrolls below $57 million including the small-market Diamondbacks, Pirates, and Padres. Overall, the league's average amount was $88 million or 22 percent more than in 2006. Only those of the Diamondbacks, Braves, Astros, Pirates, and Padres declined from five years earlier.

Besides the Diamondbacks, the NL's Brewers, Cardinals, and Phillies also competed in the NLDS and after defeating the Brewers in the NLCS, the Cardinals won the World Series. Thus, two clubs each had above-average and below-average payrolls in the league's postseason. To some extent, this indicated more parity competitively than in 1991, 1996, 2001, and 2006. Remarkably, after winning the most games in the regular season (102) and having a roster of several excellent players, the Phillies were unable to continue their success and lost in the NLDS. In addition, the high-payroll Cubs and Mets each had more losses than wins in the regular season while the Giants and Dodgers placed second and third, respectively, in the WD.

From 2011 to 2016, the NL's average payroll increased from $88 million to $110 million or by 25 percent. While the Dodgers, Cubs, and Giants had the three highest amounts, the bottom payrolls included the Phillies at $45 million, Braves at $60 million, and Brewers and Marlins each at less than $70 million. Except for the Marlins, these included significant cuts for the other three teams while payrolls of the Nationals, Padres, and Pirates each expanded by approximately 122 percent. Because of a television deal and higher revenues from operations, most NL teams became more prosperous since 2011.

In the league's 2016 postseason, the payrolls of the five NL clubs were first (Dodgers), second (Cubs), third (Giants), fourth (Nationals), and sixth (Mets). The Cardinals, who ranked fifth, finished second in the Central Division and only one game behind the two wild cards, the Giants and Mets. Alternatively, the other nine clubs had losing records and finished between fifteen and thirty-six games behind the division winners. According to these results, midsized and small-market clubs with average to below-average payrolls failed to compete effectively enough to qualify for the playoffs. Comparatively, there was substantial deviation across the NL with respect to these teams' payroll amounts and their performances.[12]

HOME ATTENDANCES

Each MLB season, several factors determine in different ways the actual attendances of teams at their home games. These include such things as the growth, population, and per capita or disposable income of households in the local market, team's competitiveness and win-loss record among others in its and other divisions during the regular season, age and location of the ballpark and its amenities, number and popularity of star players who play on a team, range of ticket prices for seats at home games, and whether other professional clubs exist within or near the metropolitan area.

With respect to this topic, table 5.6 contains the distribution of home attendances of NL clubs and how they compared to each other in six specific seasons. This and such data in other tables of the chapter as their revenues and payrolls, as well as their performances as reported in Table A5.2 of the appendix, denotes the extent of parity or competitive balance among them while located at home sites during a period of years.[13]

12 *In MLB's 2017 season, NL teams' payrolls averaged $129 million. This was $19 million or approximately a 17 percent increase from 2016. It's almost certain, however, that players' payrolls will not expand as much in future years. In fact, the average fell by $1 million in 2018 except for such clubs as the Diamondbacks, Cubs, and Brewers. Topics regarding MLB team salaries and payroll include Dennis Lin, "New International Cap Could Benefit Teams like Padres," TCA Regional News (4 December 2016): 1; Daniel Glazer, "Ballpark Figures," Wall Street Journal (29 August 2002): A.12; "MLB Salaries Top $3 Million," Pittsburgh Post-Gazette (14 December 2010): D.6; David Biderman, "The Count: Designated Hitters = Baseball's Most Overpaid?" Wall Street Journal (7 December 2009): B.8; "Baseball Salary Comparison by Club," New York Daily News (2 December 2009): 71.*

13 *Table A5.2 reveals how much NL teams succeeded in various five-year periods. According to the data, the most prominent of them in consecutive periods were the Braves twice, Cardinals, Phillies, and Giants. Other clubs who ranked next highest in performances included the Dodgers and Diamondbacks. Alternatively, the worst at winning championships were the Rockies, Brewers, and Pirates.*

Table 5.6 Average Home Attendances, National League by Team, Selected Years

Team	*Year (Attendance Rank)*					
	1991	1996	2001	2006	2011	2016
Arizona Diamondbacks	NA	NA	33.8 (9)	25.8 (14)	25.9 (12)	25.2 (11)
Atlanta Braves	26.4 (6)	35.8 (3)	34.8 (7)	31.8 (9)	30.0 (9)	25.1 (12)
Chicago Cubs	27.9 (4)	27.3 (5)	35.1 (6)	39.0 (4)	37.2 (5)	39.9 (4)
Cincinnati Reds	29.2 (2)	22.9 (8)	23.7 (13)	26.3 (12)	27.3 (10)	23.3 (14)
Colorado Rockies	NA	48.0 (1)	39.0 (2)	25.9 (13)	35.9 (7)	32.1 (6)
Houston Astros	14.7 (11)	24.3 (7)	35.8 (5)	37.3 (6)	25.5 (13)	NA
Los Angeles Dodgers	41.3 (1)	39.3 (2)	37.2 (4)	46.4 (1)	36.2 (6)	45.7 (1)
Montreal Expos	13.7 (12)	19.9 (11)	7.6 (16)	NA	NA	NA
Miami Marlins	NA	21.5 (10)	15.7 (15)	14.3 (16)	19.0 (16)	21.4 (15)
Milwaukee Brewers	NA	NA	34.7 (8)	28.8 (10)	37.9 (4)	28.5 (9)
New York Mets	27.8 (5)	19.6 (12)	32.8 (10)	43.3 (2)	30.1 (8)	34.8 (5)
Philadelphia Phillies	24.6 (7)	22.2 (9)	22.8 (14)	34.2 (7)	45.4 (1)	23.6 (13)
Pittsburgh Pirates	24.5 (8)	16.6 (14)	30.8 (11)	23.2 (15)	24.2 (15)	28.1 (10)
San Diego Padres	22.2 (9)	27.0 (6)	29.7 (12)	32.8 (8)	26.4 (11)	29.0 (8)
San Francisco Giants	21.4 (10)	17.2 (13)	40.8 (1)	38.6 (5)	41.8 (2)	41.5 (3)
St. Louis Cardinals	29.1 (3)	32.7 (4)	38.4 (3)	42.5 (3)	38.1 (3)	42.5 (2)
Washington Nationals	NA	NA	NA	26.5 (11)	24.8 (14)	30.6 (7)

Note: Average home attendances are in thousands. Abbreviated is not applicable (NA). The Colorado Rockies were an expansion team in 1993 and Arizona Diamondbacks in 1998. Prior team names include Florida Marlins to Miami Marlins in 2012. Houston Astros shifted from the NL to AL West in 2013, Milwaukee Brewers from the AL to NL Central in 1998, and Expos from Montreal to Washington, D. C. in 2005 and nicknamed the Nationals.

Source: "MLB Team Attendances," www.baseballpilgramages.com cited 28 August 2017.

In MLB's 1991 season, the NL's average attendance was 25,200. Among the 12-team group, the top three clubs in attendance were the Dodgers, Reds, and Cardinals with the Giants, Padres, and Astros at the bottom of the distribution. Besides enthusiastic and big crowds at their home games, the Dodgers also ranked first in payroll and second in revenue. However, despite mediocre attendances, the Braves and Pirates had the most successful season in the league and not the Dodgers or Cardinals who finished second in their division and Reds fifth in the WD.

Comparing 1991 to 1996, the league's average attendance had increased by 1,500 per game or approximately 6 percent. Being a relatively new franchise and popular in the Denver metropolitan area, the four-year-old Rockies had the highest attendances followed by the Dodgers and Braves. Alternatively, the Mets, Giants, and Pirates ranked twelfth, thirteenth, and fourteenth. In 1996, fewer spectators attended home games of such teams as the Cubs, Reds, and Dodgers than in 1991 but not those of the Astros, Expos, and Padres.

Despite differences in attendances at their ballparks, the Braves, Cardinals, and Padres each won their division. After defeating the Cardinals in the NL Championship Series (NLCS), the Braves lost to the Yankees in the World Series. In the early-to-mid 1990s, Atlanta's MLB team dominated the NL in victories and titles and also ranked high in payroll and revenue. Simply put, there was significant inequality in competitiveness and results between a few successful franchises and others in the league.

In 2001, the NL's average attendance of 30,800 had increased by 4,100 per game or 15 percent compared to 1996. While the Giants improved from thirteenth to first and Cardinals fourth to third, the Rockies fell in rank from first to second. Despite the league's higher average attendance than five years earlier, some clubs actually experienced smaller audiences at their ballparks such as the Braves, Rockies, Dodgers, and Marlins. In fact, the Expos' attendance numbers fell by more than 50 percent.

Partly because they ranked fourth in payroll, seventh in revenue and ninth in home attendance, and frequently depended on outstanding pitchers' Curt Shilling and Randy Johnson, the Diamondbacks defeated the Cardinals in the NLCS and then won the World Series in 2001. As a result, competitive balance temporarily shifted to midsized clubs and away from such large market teams as the Cubs, Dodgers, Mets, and Giants.

The league's average attendance had increased by only 1,500 people or almost five percent in 2006 relative to 2001. During the most recent of these years, the Dodgers, Mets, and Cardinals ranked highest with more than 42,000 in attendance each game, and with least number of spectators were the Marlins, Pirates, and Nationals. Interestingly, the Giants fell from first to fifth and Rockies second to thirteenth in 2006 as the Expos transferred to Washington in the NL after its 2005 season. According to table 5.6, the Cubs' and Cardinals' home attendances have been most consistent and least variable in rank among all NL teams.

Despite being mediocre in attendance, payroll, and revenue in 2006, the Padres played but lost to the Cardinals in the National League Division Series (NLDS). Otherwise, several of the small-to-midsized market clubs finished with losing records when compared to the Mets, Cardinals, and Dodgers. Because the former group had disappointing seasons, their attendances and financial results were below average compared to their competitors.

For the first time in decades, the NL's average attendance declined by 700 per game in 2011 compared to five years earlier. Although the Phillies were first, Giants second, and Cardinals third that season, other clubs significantly fell in rank including the Astros, Dodgers, Mets, Padres, and Nationals. Despite differences in payroll and revenues among the sixteen teams, some maintained their rankings in attendances such as the Braves, Marlins, and Pirates.

The small-market Brewers—fourth in home-game attendance, ninth in payroll, and tenth in revenue—won their division but were later defeated by the Cardinals in the NLCS. As in previous years, usually three or more midsized-to-large-market clubs qualified for the postseason and only one from the bottom one-fourth of the league. For the most part, this inequality exists because of such things as differences in markets' population and per capita income, teams' home attendances, revenues and payrolls, and other demographic and economic variables at sites in each league.

While the league's average attendance remained at about 31,400 per game in 2016, the Dodgers, Cardinals, and Giants each drew more than 41,000 people to home games in their ballparks. Among those in the NL, the least popular teams in fan support included the Phillies, Reds, and Marlins. In addition, very small changes in ranking attendances occurred for the Diamondbacks, Cubs and Rockies, but not the Brewers, Mets, and Nationals.

In MLB's 2016 postseason, there were no small-market, low-attendance teams from the NL. In fact, nine teams or 60 percent of the league's total had more losses than wins. The Reds and Padres were the worst in performances and their attendances ranked fourteenth and eighth, respectively, while their payrolls and revenues finished in the lower part of the league. For several years, including those in table 5.6, this has been the trend in these variables for one or more clubs in the NL and, as shown in table 5.3, for some others in the AL.[14]

Major League Baseball

To compare MLB's leagues and the extent of competitive balance between them during six distinct seasons, table 5.7 shows the amounts and distribution of three variables that represent their teams in some way. Next is a brief analysis of each variable including reasons for how much and why they differ during these periods of the sport.

First, except for 2016, average revenues were higher in the AL than the NL in five seasons. They ranged from $3 million in 2006 to $16 million in 2011. The two largest differences in average revenue changes between the leagues, however, occurred from 2006 to 2011 ($13 million) and then 2011 to 2016 ($9 million).

14 *On average, NL teams' home attendances remained approximately the same from MLB's 2016 to 2017 season. Similarly, so did the variation in attendances among the league's fifteen teams. In 2017, home games of the Dodgers, Cardinals, and Giants were most popular among fans to attend but not those, for example, of the small-market Marlins, Reds, and Pirates. From their 2017 to 2018 season, however, NL teams' average attendance fell by 1,000. The Reds, Marlins, Mets, Pirates, and Giants each declined by 2,000 per game at home while such clubs as the Brewers and Phillies played before larger crowds in 2018 than 2017. Topics regarding MLB team attendances include: Peter Grant, "Braves' Stadium is a Winner, Owner Says," Wall Street Journal (10 October 2018): B6; Tyler Kepner, "Strikeouts Turn Into Baseball's Latest Crisis," Wall Street Journal (19 August 2018): 4B; Michael Parsons, "Opening Day Far Too Global for True Fans," Florida Today (12 February 2014): 2; Bill Shaikin, "MLB Boss: Expansion Could be on the Table," The Patriot (16 July 2015): S.6; Brian Soebbing, "Competitive Balance and Attendance in Major League Baseball: An Empirical Test of the Uncertainty of Outcome Hypothesis," International Journal of Sport Finance (May 2008): 119–126; Scott Tainsky and Jason Winfree, "Discrimination and Demand: The Effect of International Players on Attendance in Major League Baseball," Social Science Quarterly (March 2010): 117; Hoon Lee Young and Rodney Fort, "Attendance and the Uncertainty-of-Outcome Hypothesis in Baseball," Review of Industrial Organization (December 2008): 281–295.*

During the first five-year period, for example, AL teams' revenues increased from $172 million to $220 million while the NL's only increased from $169 million to $204 million. This happened, in part, because home games of such teams as the Yankees, Red Sox, Twins, and Rangers were extremely popular among fans in the local market and therefore generated significant amounts of operating income from concession, ticket, and merchandise sales. In the second five-year period, NL teams as a group were more successful in producing revenue from their games, especially those of the large-market Cubs, Dodgers, and Giants. Also, after the 2015 season, the mediocre Astros transferred from the NL to AL.[15]

Table 5.7 Competitive Balance, AL and NL Teams Average Data, Six Years

	American League			National League		
Year	**Revenues**	**Payrolls**	**Attendances**	**Revenues**	**Payrolls**	**Attendances**
1991	60	24.3	28.3	54	24.0	25.2
1996	69	32.8	26.1	62	31.1	26.7
2001	127	67.2	29.1	117	63.7	30.8
2006	172	83.4	30.3	169	72.3	32.3
2011	220	97.7	28.7	204	88.5	31.6
2016	297	125.1	28.8	304	110.7	31.4

Note: Abbreviated are American League (AL) and National League (NL). Revenues and payrolls are average amounts in millions of dollars during six equally-spaced MLB seasons. Attendances are averages per team in thousands.

Source: "MLB Franchises Revenues and Expenses," www.baseballchronology.com cited 23 August 2017; "The Business of Baseball," www.forbes.com cited 24 August 2017; "MLB Payrolls," www.umich.app.box.com cited 31 August 2017; "2016 Total Payroll," www.usatoday.com cited 31 August 2017; "MLB Team Attendances," www.baseballpilgramages.com cited 28 August 2017.

15 *For articles about MLB teams' revenues, see Dennis Punzel, "Selig Relishes Game's Parity," Wisconsin State Journal (20 April 2016): C.1.; Michael Wenz, "A Proposal for Incentive-Compatible Revenue Sharing in Major League Baseball," Journal of Sport Management (November 2012): 479; Elizabeth Gustafson and Lawrence Hadley, "Revenue, Population, and Competitive Balance in Major League Baseball," Contemporary Economic Policy (April 2007): 250–261; Maury Brown, "MLB Sees Record Revenues Approaching $10 Billion for 2016," www.forbes.com cited 7 September 2017; Billy Witz, "Winning Yankees Aren't Faring Nearly as Well at the Box Office," www.nytimes.com cited 8 September 2017.*

Second, throughout the years in column one of table 5.7, the average payrolls of AL teams were greater than those in the NL. The smallest and largest differences in payrolls between the leagues happened, respectively, in 1991 and 2016. While almost identical in 1991 at approximately $24 million, the gap increased in 2016 when AL teams like the Orioles, Tigers, Royals, Mariners, and Blue Jays signed free agents to lucrative deals and also re-signed veteran players to increasingly larger contracts. But in the NL, payrolls actually declined for several teams including the Phillies from $172 million in 2011 to $45 million in 2016.

Third, except in 1991, NL teams' average attendances exceeded those in the AL. Regarding specific numbers and years, the differences ranged from 600,000 in 1996 to 2.9 million in 2011. During the mid-1990s, home games of the Orioles, Indians, Mariners, and Rangers ranked high in attendances in the AL as did those of the NL's Braves, Cubs, Rockies, and Cardinals. Then from 2006 to 2011, home games of such NL clubs as the Dodgers, Giants, and Cardinals attracted relatively more fans on average than those of the AL's Yankees, Angels, and Rangers despite the relatively small crowds who watched the Diamondbacks, Reds, and Marlins play in the NL and Athletics and Rays in the AL.

To conclude, the revenues, payrolls, and attendances in the AL and NL were each factors in measuring the competitive balance between these leagues and clubs within them. As mentioned before, other ways to evaluate parity in MLB are a combination of the actual standard deviation, actual and idealized standard deviations, Gini coefficient, Herfindahl–Hirschman Index, Lorenz curves, analysis of variance statistics, concentration ratios, and relative entropy.[16]

16 *Besides definitions of measurements in Note 2, the "idealized" standard deviation (ISD) is the quotient of the actual standard deviation of results in a season divided by 0.5/ÖN, where N is equal to the number of games in a season. This works well for baseball and other sports that compare results on a one-zero basis but not those that award points for ties. See, for example, David Haddock and Louis Cain, "Measuring Parity: Tying Into the Idealized Standard Deviation," www.researchgate.net cited 29 October 2018; "How to Calculate the Noll-Scully Competitive Balance Measure," www.transportationanalysis.blogspot.com; Bart van der Voort, "Measuring Balance of American Leagues," www.competitive-balance.blogspot.com.*

CHAPTER 6

Team Relocations

After experiencing internal corruption and leadership problems, the Western League (WL) folded, but then sportswriter Ban Johnson revived it during the early 1890s. Renamed the American Baseball League in 1899, it had teams in eight cities: Buffalo, Chicago, Cleveland, Detroit, Indianapolis, Kansas City, Milwaukee, and Minneapolis. During 1900, the clubs based in Buffalo, Indianapolis, Kansas City, and Minneapolis withdrew from the league because of financial problems or other reasons. To replace them, Johnson allowed franchises in Baltimore, Boston, Philadelphia, and Washington to join his organization as new members. In the following sections of the chapter, team relocations of the league occurred between 1901 and 2016.[1]

AMERICAN LEAGUE

Milwaukee Brewers I → St. Louis Browns → Baltimore Orioles II

As franchises in the American League (AL) in 1901, the eight teams played their games at home within urban places whose populations ranged from second (Chicago) to fifteenth (Washington). Finishing in eighth place and thirty-five games

1 *See W.C. Madden and Patrick J. Stewart, The Western League: A Baseball History, 1885 Through 1899 (Jefferson, NC: McFarland, 2002) and Warren N. Wilbert, The Arrival of the American League: Ban Johnson and the 1901 Challenge to National League Monopoly (Jefferson, NC: McFarland, 2007).*

behind the Chicago White Sox, the Milwaukee Brewers drew only 139,000 people to their home games at 10,000-seat Lloyd Street Grounds in Milwaukee. Because of the club's dismal performance and poor attendance, Brewers' owners Henry and Matthew Killilea decided to sell their franchise after the season for $50,000 to a syndicate of investors.[2]

Unable to attract and excite baseball fans in the Milwaukee area, the group moved its franchise to St. Louis—ranked fourth in population—which, besides Chicago, was the largest city that allowed ballgames to be played on Sundays. After being nicknamed the same as a National League (NL) club that existed in St. Louis during the early-to-mid-1890s, the Browns played their home games at 30,500-seat Sportsman's Park and while there, challenged the NL's St. Louis Cardinals for the support of baseball fans in eastern Missouri.[3]

The Browns' home attendance in the 1902 season was approximately 272,300—which ranked fifth among the eight clubs in the AL and was 20 percent greater than the 226,400 fans that had attended Cardinals games in 14,500-seat Robison Field. The Browns almost won a pennant in 1902 by finishing second in the league while the Cardinals ended in sixth and more than forty-four games behind the Pittsburgh Pirates. For several years after 1902, the Browns had few winning seasons. Nevertheless, the club frequently outdrew the Cardinals at home games and also attracted more fans than such AL teams as the Cleveland Indians, Detroit Tigers, and Washington Senators.

Based on history, it was a smart business decision for the syndicate to move its franchise from Milwaukee to the St. Louis area in 1902. The Brewers struggled to win their games while playing in the minor WL during the mid-to-late-1890s and 1900; failed to establish a large fan base as part of the AL in 1901; and were not a profitable baseball enterprise in southeastern Wisconsin. In contrast, the St. Louis

---

2 *Three references are Frank P. Jozsa Jr., Major League Baseball Expansions and Team Relocations: A History, 1876–2008 (Jefferson, NC: McFarland, 2010) and American League Franchises: Team Performances and Business Success (New York, NY: Springer, 2015), and Frank P. Jozsa Jr. and John J. Guthrie Jr., Relocating Teams and Expanding Leagues in Professional Sports: How the Major Leagues Respond to Market Conditions (Westport, CT: Quorum Books, 1999).*

3 *The movement of the Brewers from Milwaukee to St. Louis after the 1901 MLB season is discussed in "Milwaukee Brewers," www.mlb.com cited 1 September 2017 and "St. Louis Browns," www.baseball-library.com cited 1 September 2017.*

metropolitan area contained thousands of people who loved baseball more than they did any other professional or amateur sport. While the AL was transformed from a minor to major league, this relocation of an AL franchise from a city in the Midwest to eastern Missouri resulted in benefits for the league and also for other AL clubs with respect to their home attendances, gate receipts, and popularity.

During its fifty-two years entertaining fans at home in St. Louis, the Browns were a very marginal and largely unsuccessful team. After being sold and then resold between the mid-1910s and late 1940s, a syndicate headed by entrepreneur Bill Veeck purchased more than 55 percent of the franchise and the club's stadium in 1951 from the DeWitt brothers for $1.4 million and later acquired an additional 21 percent for $350,000.

Veeck's strategy was to force the Cardinals to leave eastern Missouri, which seemed possible since their owner Fred Saigh had legal problems with the government about his income taxes. However, that failed when beer mogul August Busch and his subsidiary purchased the Cardinals franchise and replaced Saigh.

Veeck—who was a very popular man in the sport during the mid-to-late 1940s where his promotions in Cleveland attracted a record number of baseball fans—tried some unique stunts in St. Louis. He hired a little person named Eddie Gaedel to be a hitter in a Browns game against the Tigers, and he occasionally allowed fans in the grandstands to co-manage his team by holding up cards that signaled to Browns' players to bunt, hit, steal a base, and do other things. These tactics, however, angered MLB's commissioner and other AL team owners, and failed to attract many spectators to the club's home games in Sportsman's Park.

In 1953, Veeck was reportedly broke while the Browns finished eighth and more than forty-six games behind the New York Yankees. When the league twice denied Veeck's bid to relocate his franchise to Baltimore, he sold a majority of it that year to a syndicate who represented an area of Maryland for $2.5 million and also transferred Sportsman's Park to multimillionaire Busch for $850,000. After the Cardinals pledged about $300,000 for the Browns' movement to a city near the east coast, a syndicate of new owners from Baltimore, including brewer Jerry Hoffberger, attorney Clarence Miles, and Mayor Tommy D'Alesandro, moved the team from St. Louis into a recently-renovated 53,750-seat ballpark named Memorial Stadium and changed its name to the Baltimore Orioles.

During the 1950s, the population of the Baltimore area increased from 1.4 to 1.8 million while St. Louis' expanded from 1.7 to approximately 2 million. It seemed, therefore, that St. Louis could successfully host only one MLB club during those and future years whereas the AL Senators in Washington failed to attract fans from southern neighborhoods in Baltimore.

As a result, baseball's Orioles had a potentially larger market to exploit during the mid-to-late 1950s than did the Browns in St. Louis from the late 1940s to early 1950s. Moreover, other areas in the United States with a population of one million or more such as Atlanta, Denver, Houston, Miami, San Diego, and Seattle were not developed enough as baseball towns in those years. Consequently, the league's approval to permit relocation of an existing team out of St. Louis into Baltimore in 1953 was a good decision. In the long run, it resulted in relatively more attendances at AL teams' home and away games, and also brought additional cash flows, revenues, and profits for them in years since the late 1950s.

Baltimore Orioles I → New York Highlanders/Yankees

After completing its season in 1899, the NL reduced its size from twelve to eight teams. One of the clubs eliminated by the league was the Baltimore Orioles. When Ban Johnson reorganized the AL in late 1900 and early 1901, he admitted the Baltimore Orioles which was managed by John McGraw but owned—for the most part—by Harry Goldstein, S. Mahon, and Sidney Frank.

During the league's 1901 and 1902 seasons, respectively, the club finished fifth and eighth in the league, and its attendances at Oriole Ballpark in Baltimore averaged 157,500 per season—the lowest in the league. Furthermore, Johnson got mad when McGraw secretly transferred from managing the Orioles to managing the NL New York Giants and then raided the Orioles roster to acquire its best players for his Giants team. This caused the AL to intervene and assume partial control of the Orioles' franchise.

When the 1902 AL season concluded, Goldstein and his group of investors offered their club for sale. Within a short time, a syndicate headed by ex-saloonkeeper Frank Farrell and New York gambler Bill Devery purchased the Orioles for $18,000 from Goldstein and then appointed coal dealer Joseph Gordon to be a front man. Later, the syndicate installed him as the franchise's first president.

In early 1903, AL and NL officials met to settle their disputes and coexist in the sport. One outcome of that conference was that the NL agreed to allow an AL team to locate and play their home games somewhere in the New York metropolitan area. In response to that deal, Farrell moved the Orioles from Baltimore to Manhattan and renamed them the New York Highlanders.[4]

In June 1903, a rickety and wooden 15,000-seat stadium nicknamed Hilltop Park–formally known as American League Park–was constructed for $75,000 between 165th and 168th Streets in northern Manhattan, only a few blocks away from the NL Giants' Polo Grounds. The Highlanders received their nickname because of Hilltop Park's location on one of the island's highest points and also a British military unit–The Gordon Highlanders–which referred to team president Joseph Gordon. For several years, however, the Highlanders were sometimes called the New York Americans. In 1913, the team's name changed to the New York Yankees, who for the next ten years played their home games in the 38,000-seat Polo Grounds as tenants of the NL Giants.

The Highlanders soon became a popular and successful sports team in New York. For example, the club finished second in the AL seasons of 1904, 1906, and 1910. Also, after attracting only 211,000 to its home games in 1903, the club's attendance at Hilltop Park increased to more than 434,000 per season during 1904, 1906, and 1909, and continued to average between 242,000 and 620,000 each year after 1912 while playing at New York's Polo Grounds.

In retrospect, the movement of this franchise from Baltimore to New York was a smart decision by its owners especially after the Orioles finished the 1902 season in eighth place. In fact, the club could not survive for more than a few years in Baltimore because of its inferior performances within the league and some financial problems, and also due to the small number of passionate baseball fans who lived in that area. Even though the AL and several of its teams struggled to become prominent baseball organizations during the early 1900s, the New York area was populated enough to support another MLB club besides the NL Giants.

---

4 *For this important relocation, see Marty Appel, "New York Yankees: Pride, Tradition, and a Bit of Controversy," in Peter C. Bjarkman, ed., Encyclopedia of Major League Baseball: American League Team Histories (New York, NY: Carroll & Graf Publishers, 1993).*

In short, the relocation of a team from Baltimore to New York in 1903 contributed to the AL becoming a major organization in the sport. If that move, alternatively, had been approved to a smaller and lower-income area such as Buffalo, New Orleans or Newark, it would have been decades before the league would be as or more popular and prestigious than its counterpart, the NL.

Philadelphia Athletics → Kansas City Athletics → Oakland Athletics

Between 1901 and the early 1950s, Connie Mack served in several different positions within the Philadelphia Athletics organization besides being the franchise's majority owner. At one time or another, he held such titles as field manager, general manager, and president. In other words, Mack kept the club operating—but not necessarily profitable—for more than fifty years.

After World War II ended, Mack donated 30 percent of the team to his sons Connie Jr., Earle, and Roy. When Connie became too old to devote more time to the franchise and could no longer perform his duties, the club became somewhat leaderless as the family argued about who should be the organization's coaches, executives, and players. This was apparent, for example, in 1950 when Earle and Roy Mack mortgaged the team's 33,600-seat ballpark named Shibe Park and borrowed enough money to buy out the minority interests of their mother, Connie Jr., the heirs of original owner Ben Shibe, and the McFarland family. Unfortunately, the franchise's concession operator, Sportservice, had to provide funds to the Mack brothers to pay the team's operating expenses and some bank debts.

Throughout the spring and summer of 1954, a few wealthy investors from Dallas, Los Angeles, and Philadelphia expressed a willingness to purchase the Athletics and perhaps its stadium. Another bidder was a vending machine executive from Chicago named Arnold Johnson whose real estate holdings included Yankee Stadium. In fact, Johnson agreed to be a front man for a syndicate from Kansas City to purchase the team from Mack's family and move it to that metropolitan area in the Midwest. When the AL turned down an offer for the Athletics from eight Philadelphia businessmen in late 1953, Johnson and his group became even more enthused and optimistic about owning the franchise and then relocating it to a site in Kansas City.[5]

In November 1954, Johnson presented his bid to the league's team owners at a meeting in New York. As testimony, he cited the success of the NL Braves' transfer from Boston to Milwaukee and the movement of the former Browns from St. Louis to Baltimore. Moreover, in his remarks, Johnson emphasized his dedication to the Kansas City area and also his commitment to sell his investment in Yankee Stadium.

That compromise convinced Detroit Tigers owner Spike Briggs to approve Johnson's bid, which was then passed in a six-to-two vote by the league. A few days later, 91-year-old Connie Mack signed his name on the back of a stock certificate representing 302 shares that, in turn, transferred ownership of the team to Johnson and his syndicate. Within a few months, Mack's former club moved to the Kansas City area and became known as the Kansas City Athletics.

In the end it was disunity, infighting, and mistrust among family members, along with Connie Mack's inability to operate the team's business after his health had declined that most likely caused the Athletics to gradually fail as a team in Philadelphia. Moreover, the ambition, determination, and persistence of Johnson and his group from Kansas City, and the Athletics' pathetic performances and poor attendances at home games played in Shibe Park persuaded the AL to approve the relocation of this franchise into a small-to-midsized area in northwest Missouri. Since other regions in America such as Atlanta, Denver, and Houston were not yet fully developed or experienced enough as sports markets to host one or more MLB franchises, Kansas City was an appropriate and sensible site for the Athletics in 1954.

Additionally, the Philadelphia area's sports fans enthusiastically cheered for, supported, and respected performances of the popular NL Phillies and National Football League (NFL) Eagles rather than the AL Athletics. Although Philadelphia had been an above-average sports market since the 1920s–1930s, the Athletics could not overcome their increasingly poor image and inferior reputation in that market as a subpar MLB team. Nevertheless, fans remember Connie Mack as a legend in the

---

5 *See, for example, "Philadelphia Athletics-Kansas City Athletics-Oakland A's: Three Families and Three Baseball Epochs" in Encyclopedia of Major League Baseball: American League Team Histories (1993): 293–357.*

sport for his great leadership and historical contributions to the game during years when baseball dominated as a professional sport in the United States.

From 1955 to 1967, the Athletics finished no higher than fifth in the AL. Furthermore, the club failed to develop a productive farm system and periodically traded several of its talented players to the Yankees and other teams. It was in 1960, however, that owner Arnold Johnson died and his heirs sold more than 50 percent of their interest in the franchise to insurance executive Charlie Finley for $1.9 million. Within a few months of that year, Finley acquired the remaining share of the club from Roy Mack's widow for $1.8 million.

During the next seven years in Kansas City, Finley tried a number of unusual but ridiculous promotions to entice more local baseball fans to attend the Athletics' home games. Although he took credit for them, many of these stunts had been implemented before by Bill Veeck while he owned the Indians in Cleveland and Browns in St. Louis. In addition, Finley sold his best ballplayers after each season—primarily to the Yankee—while his teams struggled to win games in the league. According to local baseball fans and reporters in the media, the Athletics owner had deliberately fielded bad teams in order to justify moving his franchise from Kansas City to another area. Meanwhile, the annual attendance at the Athletics home games declined from 1.4 million in 1955 to 963,000 in 1959 and then fell to 726,000 in 1967.

There were other problems associated with Finley's activities, decisions, and intentions. For example, he frequently criticized his managers in postgame interviews and publicly denounced players at clubhouse meetings. In turn, they usually ignored or simply rejected these insults from him. Also, it became apparent to some people that Finley intended to move the Athletics because the franchise had reportedly not made a profit from the late 1950s to early 1960s. As a result, season tickets sales to homes games gradually declined while local baseball fans participated in other events during summer months. To some extent, visiting teams also realized that Finley's teams were demoralized and not competitive, and thus, they consistently defeated the Athletics in single games and weekend series.

After his club finished tenth and twenty-nine games behind the Red Sox in 1967, Finley requested and received permission from the AL to move his franchise from

Kansas City to Oakland, California. Even though voters in Missouri's Jackson County approved a multimillion-dollar bond issue to construct a new baseball stadium there, Finley had already spoken to city officials in several cities including Dallas and Louisville to determine if any of them were interested in hosting his team.

Since the city of Oakland had successfully supported a professional baseball team in the Pacific Coast League before the Giants moved from New York to San Francisco in 1958, Finley believed that another MLB could exist within the Bay Area. He met with the community's decision-makers and agreed to lease Oakland Coliseum from them for the 1968 MLB season. To ensure their support, Finley also told these officials he would establish his residence in Oakland and predicted the Athletics (nicknamed the A's) would attract more than one million each season to the club's home games and soon win an AL pennant.

Because of a five-year, $5 million radio and television contract in Oakland rather than the $56,000 earned from a media contract in Kansas City, a low-rent lease of the city's Coliseum—which they shared with the NFL Raiders—and a large sports market within the Bay Area that included the NL San Francisco Giants, Finley made an excessive amount of money for several years from investing in the Athletics. In fact, this occurred while the team's home attendances at games increased to more than 800,000 in 1968; 900,000 in 1971; and then to one million in 1973. Moreover, the club performed much better in Oakland than it had in Kansas City, finishing second in the league's West Division in 1969 and 1970 and first in 1971–1975, and also winning three each AL pennants and World Series in 1972–1974. After refusing two offers in 1977 to sell the A's for, respectively, $10 million and $12 million, Finley sold the franchise in 1980 for $12.7 million to Walter Haas, Jr., his son Wally, and his son-in-law Roy Eisenhardt.

The potential financial rewards and business opportunities from relocating his franchise from Kansas City to Oakland after the 1967 MLB season suggests, in part, that Finley was unable to negotiate a more attractive deal with city officials from Dallas and Louisville, and also from such places as Denver, Milwaukee, New Orleans, San Diego and Seattle. For sure, these were also above average to superior markets for the Athletics to perform, but Finley decided that an area in northern California was where his club would be most profitable and likewise successfully compete as a franchise in the AL. When a representative from the Yankees switched his vote from no to yes on the second ballot during a league meeting in October 1967, the Athletics' move to the west coast made Finley a wealthier man.

According to various readings in the literature, Finley—like Veeck and other owners of MLB franchises—was a shrewd character and a ruthless businessman who knew and cared more about the commercial aspects of professional baseball than the emotions, feelings, and opinions of his managers, players, and fans, and also sports writers and economists. Although this style of management did not succeed for Finley in Kansas City, as a strategy it improved his club's performances, prosperity, and value in Oakland.

Washington Senators I → Minnesota Twins

For most MLB seasons that the original Senators' teams played while based in the nation's capital, Clark Griffith and his family controlled the franchise. From the time Griffith became its manager in 1912 and acquired a 50 percent share of it seven years later to the mid-to-late 1950s, the ball club was operated primarily as a closed family business. During its 60-year history in Washington, the Senators won three AL pennants and, in 1924, a World Series after defeating the NL New York Giants in seven games. Most other seasons, however, the team did not perform well with its attendances at home games lingering at or near the bottom of the league.

After Griffith died in 1955, his nephew Calvin inherited 50 percent of the franchise. Calvin was a visionary businessman, who, for financial reasons, appeared intent on moving his team to an area in the upper Midwest. In part, his strategy was inspired by the Dodgers' and Giants' relocations from New York to the west coast in 1958 and by plans for future AL and NL expansions into a number of sports markets. In fact, Calvin spoke to insiders about the potential of big league baseball existing somewhere in Minnesota. He knew, for sure, that the sport was popular there since Ted Williams had played with the Minneapolis Millers, as did such Hall-of-Famers as Carl Yastrzemski, Duke Snider, and Willie Mays.

A decision permitting the Senators to leave Washington for Minneapolis occurred in late 1960 at a meeting of the league held in New York's Savoy-Hilton Hotel. At that conference, AL franchise owners expressed a strong interest in competing against the NL for markets within the Midwest to offset the senior league's expansions into southern and northern California during the late 1950s.

In closed-door sessions, Griffith argued before the group that his team could not survive much longer in Washington. Consequently, he requested permission to transfer his franchise to Minneapolis. Although many owners feared an outrage from local politicians and baseball fans in the District of Columbia, the AL approved the Senators' movement to another area in early 1961. To minimize criticism from the media for their decision, the owners confirmed that a new franchise would replace the former Senators for the 1961 MLB season. After relocating to the Minneapolis area, the Senators team was renamed Minnesota Twins.[6]

Despite movement of the National Basketball Association (NBA) Lakers from the Twin Cities to Los Angeles in 1960, Minneapolis became an increasingly popular sports town and metropolis for other professional sports teams. The NFL Vikings, for example, started playing there in 1960 and a few years later, so did the American Basketball Association (ABA) Minnesota Pipers and National Hockey League (NHL) North Stars.

In 1961, the Twins began to play their home games at 45,900-seat Metropolitan Stadium, which was located in the city of Bloomington, Minnesota. For that MLB season, the club won only seventy games and finished seventh in the league but also featured a combination of veterans and a number of competitive and talented young ballplayers who eventually became stars for the team in future years.

Being the league's fifth relocation since 1901, this transfer of a sixty-year-old franchise from one area to another in the early 1960s had occurred for several reasons. First, Clark Griffith's death in 1955 provided an opportunity for his nephew Calvin to abandon Washington and increase the team's profits elsewhere, or alternatively, to reduce its losses in a smaller sports market. Second, the retirement of such great Senators' players as pitcher Walter Johnson and fielders Goose Goslin, Joe Cronin, and Mickey Vernon resulted in fewer victories and smaller attendances for the club at home games during the 1950s. Third, AL franchise owners needed to reinvigorate their organizations and radically restructure them after movements of the NL Braves, Dodgers, and Giants during the 1950s and to prepare for expansions planned in the early 1960s.

6 *This relocation is thoroughly covered in Frank P. Jozsa Jr.'s Major League Baseball Expansions and Team Relocations: A History, 1876–2008 and also his American League Franchises: Team Performances and Business Success.*

Fourth, after the departure of the Senators to Minneapolis in 1961, a new expansion team that played in Washington excited baseball fans in the area and created some additional revenues for the nine existing teams in the league. Fifth, Minneapolis expected to be an above-average and popular market for professional teams throughout the 1960s even though the NBA Lakers had left in 1960. In short, for nearly six decades the Twins have been moderately competitive, especially at home in Minneapolis and therefore, the franchise succeeded to continue as a business despite poor performances of its predecessor as an enterprise in most MLB seasons between 1901 and 1960.

Los Angeles Angels → California/Anaheim Angels/ Los Angeles Angels of Anaheim

As a four-year-old expansion franchise in Los Angeles, the Angels struggled in games against its opponents in the AL and attendances at its home ballpark exceeded a million in only one of the seasons. Former singing cowboy, movie star, and multimillionaire Gene Autry—who then owned the club—realized during 1963–1965 that his franchise could not reach its highest potential in value as long as the Angels continued to rent and play their home games in Walter O'Malley's Dodger Stadium in Los Angeles.

While leasing and competing in that facility, Autry's Angels had several problems. The Angels were seen as an inferior option for the area's baseball fans, who preferred to root for the popular and successful Dodgers. According to Autry, this meant less exposure, gate receipts, and revenues for his team and the other AL clubs that played the Angels in regular-season games at Dodger Stadium.

Two other issues had adversely affected the cash flows and profits of the Angels while being tenants in Dodger Stadium during the 1961-1965 MLB seasons. First, O'Malley charged the Angels for expenditures of any type even though there were no tangible benefits or rewards associated with these charges. For example, the Angels paid 50 percent for all supplies and other items used at the ballpark even though the club's attendances each season equaled about one-half to two-thirds of the Dodger's. Second, any parking lot repairs for labor and material expenses at the stadium were charged to the Angels. These costs were later rescinded by O'Malley after being told that Autry's team did not receive any share of the ballpark's parking revenues. Thus, these and other infractions and mistakes caused the Angels owner to not renew his lease of the stadium with the Dodgers when it expired in 1965.

Autry's first choice was to immediately move his team to Long Beach where the city would build the club a new stadium. That deal failed, however, because government officials there insisted on renaming the team the Long Beach Angels. Then, the nearby city of Anaheim created a plan for a modern facility that would open before the start of the 1966 MLB season. Although Anaheim was located within Orange County—which was approximately thirty miles from downtown Los Angeles and contained 150,000 people—municipal officials there offered to construct a new 45,000-seat stadium for the Angels.

After Autry accepted the deal, the Angels signed a thirty-year lease for the building followed by three ten-year options of it. When the new ballpark opened in April 1966, more than 31,000 fans bought tickets to attend the team's first home game in Anaheim. That crowd was larger than any of the club's games played in 1965 at Chavez Ravine—which was property occupied by Dodger Stadium in the Los Angeles area.[7]

Anaheim Stadium provided some short-run benefits for the newly named California Angels. Between 1966 and 1970, for example, the club's average attendance at home games increased to more than one million and in 1967, the team finished fifth in the AL and then third in its division in 1969 and 1970. Given the franchise's problems while playing games in Dodger Stadium during the early 1960s, Autry made a strategic decision to not renew his lease of that facility and then moved the Angels from its original site in Los Angeles into a modern ballpark located thirty miles south in Anaheim.

Although the Angels played their home games within a relatively small city, there were approximately six to seven million people that lived within twenty-five to thirty-five miles of Anaheim Stadium. Besides the population of the area, moving his club such a short distance from Los Angeles in early 1966 required much less of a hassle and cost for Autry than if relocating it somewhere else in the west, or to an area within the Midwest or on the east coast.

---

7 *The history of the Angels franchise and their home sites is in Mark Stewart, The Los Angeles Angels of Anaheim (Chicago, IL: Norwood House Paper Editions, 2008) and "Los Angeles Angels of Anaheim," www.wikipedia.com cited 5 September 2017.*

Seattle Pilots → Milwaukee Brewers II

As an AL expansion team in the Seattle area, the Pilots failed miserably after playing one season. Besides finishing sixth in the West Division in 1969, the club's attendance at its home games in 25,420-seat Sick's Stadium ranked last in the league at less than 678,000. During regular season games, the Pilots' ballplayers–who were primarily retreads and castoffs from other clubs–wore bizarre caps and uniforms on the field while their opponents scored more than 700 runs to their team's 639. As a result, the franchise suffered a huge operating loss.[8]

During late 1969, majority stockholder and President William Daley offered to sell the Pilots to the highest bidder. Soon thereafter a private corporation composed of several Milwaukee businessmen and thirty-five-year-old car dealer Bud Selig offered $10.8 million for the Pilots, which was approximately $5 million more than the original price of the franchise. But then a syndicate led by James Douglas and Westins Hotel owner Eddie Carlson bid $11.5 million for the club. However, the latter offer was rejected by the AL because of the group's outstanding financial problems.

In early 1970, the Pilots borrowed more than $600,000 from the AL to pay their debts. Even so, the franchise declared bankruptcy while in spring training and only one week before the scheduled start of MLB's 1970 season. Eager to sell his team in a hurry and without any delays, Daley sold it for $10.8 million to Selig's group who–within a few weeks–moved their franchise to Milwaukee and renamed it the Milwaukee Brewers. Interestingly, this was only the second time since 1901 that any city in the U.S had lost a professional team after performing only one season in the big leagues.

Although the NL Braves left Milwaukee for Atlanta, Georgia in early 1966, it was apparent to some in the sport that this city in southeast Wisconsin had more than enough fans to support a professional baseball team at least for several MLB seasons and perhaps decades. First, the Braves' annual attendance at County Stadium exceeded one million for five years and two million for another four of them. After some of the club's most productive ballplayers retired or were traded to another team

---

8 *Sources in the literature include Kenneth Hogan, The 1969 Seattle Pilots: Major League Baseball's One-Year Team (Jefferson, NC: McFarland, 2006) and James Quirk and Rodney D. Fort, Pay Dirt: The Business of Professional Team Sports (Princeton, NJ: Princeton University Press, 1992).*

in the league during the early 1960s, attendance at its home games in Milwaukee still topped 750,000 each in 1962 and 1963, and 900,000 in 1964.

Second, Selig and his group made a competitive, impressive, and well-financed proposal to the AL for the Pilots. In turn, the league needed to make an immediate decision to approve a sale of the franchise and also the movement of it from Seattle to Milwaukee. Besides, a bid from another syndicate for the Pilots did not meet the league's requirements regarding the condition of its balance sheet and other financial statements. Third, natural intra-league rivalries between the Brewers and such competitors as the Twins and White Sox could quickly develop and thereby excite baseball fans in each of the three markets, and thus, increase their attendances and gate receipts when playing each other.

The relocation of this AL franchise from Seattle to a small-to-midsized city in the upper Midwest proved to be an instant success. Within the first three weeks of April 1970, more than 4,000 season tickets were sold to fans in the Milwaukee area along with another 2,000 ticket plans each priced at $150–$375. When the Brewers returned from their first road trip, in excess of 8,000 people greeted them at the airport while 37,000 attended the club's opening game at home against the Anaheim Angels. Despite being a very mediocre club until the late 1970s–after which it won more games and finished higher in the league's East Division–the Brewers drew more than 900,000 to County Stadium in 1970, and also at least one million in 1973 and again in 1975–1980 and after 1982. Therefore, the relocation from Seattle to Milwaukee in 1970 improved the operation of the AL from a business viewpoint and also its financial potential.

Washington Senators II → Texas Rangers

As an expansion franchise in the AL, the Senators struggled to win its regular season games and never placed higher than fourth in the league's East Division. The team's annual attendances at 27,400-seat Griffith Stadium and 45,000-seat RFK Stadium in Washington varied between 535,000 and 918,000 during each of eleven seasons while being sold and resold to different groups of investors.[9]

9 *James R. Hartley, Washington's Expansion Senators (1961–1971) (Germantown, MD: Corduroy Press, 1998) and Encyclopedia of Major League Baseball: American League Team Histories.*

In 1969, Democratic National Committee Treasurer Robert Short purchased 90 percent of the Senators for approximately $9 million from a syndicate that owned it. As a sports entrepreneur and capitalist, he had acquired the NBA Minneapolis Lakers during the late 1950s and then moved the team to Los Angeles in 1960. Five years later, Short sold the basketball club for $5 million to Jack Kent Cooke.

As another asset in Short's portfolio, the Senators served primarily as a corporate tax shelter that could be depreciated at its full value over five years. Therefore, after the club's terrible performances since being an expansion team in 1961 and Short's well-publicized statements of moving it soon to another metropolitan area, baseball fans in Washington became angry, bitter, and disillusioned about the future of their hometown franchise. In fact, during one game, a few fans ran onto the field at RFK Stadium and for doing that the umpire forfeited it to the visiting Yankees. Also, some spectators held up obscene banners before, during, and after home games, and others made derogatory gestures to the Senators' coaches and ballplayers. Thus to keep the franchise in operation, Short had decided to move it out of the Washington area.

When the 1970 MLB season concluded, Short tried to sell the Senators for $12 million to a syndicate and also threatened to not renew his lease of the ballpark from the city. The former effort failed, however, because no investors would agree to Short's asking price. After a series of secret discussions with Arlington, Texas Mayor Tom Vandergriff, Short announced he would move his franchise there when other AL team owners agreed to the club's relocation by a vote of 10–2. As a condition to relocate within the Dallas-Fort Worth area, Short consented to pay six Texas League franchises $40,000 apiece for invading their territory, and he also agreed to host an annual exhibition game against an all-star team from that minor baseball league.

To pay off the majority of his debts in Washington while establishing a market after moving to Arlington, Short received more than $7 million in cash from an arrangement with Vandergriff in exchange for ten years of broadcast rights within the area. That transaction plus Arlington's 10,000-seat Turnpike Stadium were additional reasons for Short's team to exist in the Dallas-Fort Worth sports market. Built in 1965 as a home site of the AA Spurs in the Texas League, the ballpark had been constructed according to MLB specifications, located within a natural bowl, and needed only minor renovations to expand its capacity by thousands of seats.

Between October 1971 and April 1972, the ballpark was renamed Arlington Stadium and its capacity expanded to 43,500 seats to accommodate MLB's Texas Rangers. As these changes occurred, however, Short sold 90 percent of his interest in the franchise for $10 million to a group of investors headed by businessman Brad Corbett. Although the Rangers finished sixth in the AL West Division in 1972 and 1973, one year later attendance at Arlington Stadium increased to 1.1 million and remained above one million until 1981, and then stabilized between one and two million in 1982 and again in many years thereafter.

Table 6.1 contains the MLB seasons and performances of AL teams before and after they moved from their original homes. In average winning percentage (win%) at their post-move sites, each of them improved except for the Kansas City Athletics. Regarding specific performance data, the New York Highlanders/Yankees ranked first among the group in numbers of playoffs, pennants, and World Series. Alternatively, Kansas City's Athletics won zero championships in thirteen seasons, St. Louis Browns one in fifty-two, and Milwaukee Brewers II one in twenty-eight.

Table 6.1 Team Performances, American League Relocations, Selected Data

Teams	Seasons	Win%	Playoffs	Pennants	World Series
Milwaukee Brewers I	1901–1901	.350	0	0	0
→ St. Louis Browns	1902–1953	.433	1	1	0
→ Baltimore Orioles II	1954–2018	.513	13	6	3
Baltimore Orioles I	1901–1902	.436	0	0	0
→ New York Highlanders/Yankees	1903–2018	.568	54	40	27
Philadelphia Athletics	1901–1954	.478	8	9	5
→ Kansas City Athletics	1955–1967	.404	0	0	0
→ Oakland Athletics	1968–2018	.516	19	6	4
Washington Senators I	1901–1960	.465	3	3	1

(continued)

Table 6.1 continued

Teams	Seasons	Win%	Playoffs	Pennants	World Series
→ Minnesota Twins	1961–2018	.495	12	3	2
Los Angeles Angels	1961–1965	.476	0	0	0
→ Calif./Anaheim Angels/LAAA	1966–2018	.502	10	1	1
Seattle Pilots	1969–1969	.395	0	0	0
→ Milwaukee Brewers II	1970–1997	.479	2	1	0
Washington Senators II	1961–1971	.418	0	0	0
→ Texas Rangers	1972–2018	.495	8	2	0

Note: Abbreviated is California (Calif.) and the Los Angeles Angels of Anaheim (LAAA) and average winning percentage (win%). Playoffs, pennants, and World Series are self-explanatory. Although in the regional Los Angeles metropolitan area, Anaheim is in Orange County. The Angels moved from Dodger Stadium in Los Angeles into Anaheim Stadium in 1966. The Milwaukee Brewers II switched from the American League Central Division to the National League Central Division as of 1998.

Source: "Franchise History," www.baseball-reference.com cited 8 September 2017 and "Teams," www.mlb.com cited 8 September 2017.

Besides the Highlanders/Yankees, other successful clubs that had moved, for example, were the Oakland Athletics and Baltimore Orioles II in win% and also playoffs, pennants, and World Series. While the Minnesota Twins and California/Anaheim Angels/Los Angeles Angels of Anaheim (LAAA) ranked fourth and fifth, respectively, in number of playoffs, they were less competitive in winning pennants and World Series.

Other than Kansas City Athletics and St. Louis Browns teams, the Milwaukee Brewers II won one championship in the postseason and California/Anaheim Angels/LAAA and Texas Rangers each two. Based on results in the table, New York Highlanders/Yankees and then the Oakland Athletics and Baltimore Orioles II have been the three most successful relocations while the most disappointing in the group includes the Kansas City Athletics followed by the St. Louis Browns and Milwaukee Brewers II.

NATIONAL LEAGUE

To end the rowdiness, alcohol abuse, and gambling that troubled professional baseball before the mid-1870s, businessman William Ambrose Hulbert founded the National League of Professional Baseball Clubs (NL) at a meeting in New York City's Grand Central Hotel during February 1876. It consisted of franchises in Boston, Chicago, Cincinnati, Louisville, Hartford, New York, Philadelphia, and St. Louis. Thus, team relocations occurred within the league between 1876 and 2018.[10]

Cleveland Blues → St. Louis Maroons → Indianapolis Hoosiers

The NL consisted of six franchises in 1878. One year later, three new teams joined the league including the Cleveland Blues. Meanwhile, franchises based in Indianapolis and Milwaukee dropped out because they each finished at least seventeen games behind the Boston Red Stockings (later renamed Braves). These changes not only increased the number of clubs from six to eight but also committed them to play complete regular season schedules and control their debts and other liabilities.[11]

As an expansion team, the Blues finished no higher than third place during its six seasons in the NL and that result, in turn, caused attendance and financial problems for franchise owner C.H. Bulkley. After the Blues finished seventh and forty-nine games behind the Providence Grays in 1884, Bulkley sold his club for $2,500 to Henry Lucas in early 1985. However, when Lucas purchased the Blues, former owner Bulkley had apparently sold the club's ballplayers to the American Association's (AA) Brooklyn Bridegrooms. Despite a series of court cases against Bulkley's action, Lucas moved his team from Cleveland to a midsized sports market in East St. Louis and nicknamed it the St. Louis Maroons.

The Browns, a popular team in the AA, had played at a site in St. Louis since 1882 and successfully drew a relatively large number of fans each season to its home

10 *See the Official Major League Baseball Fact Book 2005 Edition (St. Louis, MO: Sporting News, 2005).*

11 *For this and other team relocations, read Charles C. Euchner, Playing the Field: Why Sports Teams and Cities Fight to Keep Them (Baltimore, MD: John Hopkins Press, 1993) and Kenneth L. Shropshire, The Sports Franchise Game: Cities in Pursuit of Sports Franchises, Events, Stadiums, and Arenas (Philadelphia, PA: University of Pennsylvania Press, 1995).*

games. Because other NL and AA teams existed in very large cities like New York and Philadelphia and other AA clubs played at home in midsized Baltimore, Cincinnati, and Pittsburgh, Lucas determined that St. Louis was a big enough city to host another big-league club besides the Browns.

But in the NL's 1885–1886 seasons, respectively, the Maroons finished eighth and then sixth while the Browns easily won AA pennants. In a series of games between the AA and NL champions, the Browns defeated the Chicago White Stockings twice and declared their ball club should be recognized as the best in professional baseball. Consequently, because of the Browns' great success and the Maroons' weak performances each season, Lucas sold his franchise in early 1887 to an investor from Indianapolis, Indiana who then moved the team there and renamed it Indianapolis Hoosiers.

Owned by John Brush, the Hoosiers played the 1887–1889 seasons in the NL and finished eighth and then seventh twice. Although they competed in weekday home games at Indianapolis's Athletic Park, the Hoosiers staged Sunday games outside the city limits at Bruce Grounds because of blue laws. Due to an inferior win-loss record, poor attendance, and financial problems, the club folded after its 1989 season and Brush became part-owner of the NL Giants franchise.

Brooklyn Dodgers → Los Angeles Dodgers

When real estate executive and practicing attorney Charles H. Bryne entered a baseball team he owned from Brooklyn into the short-lived Interstate League, it won a pennant in 1883. One year later, Bryne transferred his club to the AA where it played with such nicknames as the Brooklyns, Brooklyners, Brooks, and, for the media and majority of sports fans, as the Bridegrooms.

After a few seasons in the AA, the team defeated the St. Louis Browns for the league's championship. Then in a nine-game series, the Bridegrooms lost 6–3 to the New York Giants which had won the NL pennant in 1889. When another baseball team from Brooklyn joined the newly organized Players League in 1890, the Bridegrooms shifted from the AA into the NL.

During the mid-to-late 1890s and very early 1900s, the team's nickname gradually changed from Bridegrooms to Superbras to Robins and finally to Dodgers. These different changes in names resulted from baseball games being played at Eastern Park where several trolley lines had converged in Brooklyn. Thus, the team's name, Trolley Dodgers, evolved into merely Dodgers.

Between 1900 and the early 1940s, this franchise was sold and resold, and also incurred huge debts and nearly bankrupted in 1938. Even so, it started to generate profits when Larry McPhail took over as the club's president. In 1942, Branch Rickey replaced McPhail while Walter O'Malley became the club's lawyer and later a minor owner of it. Before 1950, O'Malley gained control of the franchise from Rickey, in part, by purchasing the stock of other owners.

Since the early 1910s, the club's home-game attendances at 31,500-seat Ebbets Field in Brooklyn frequently ranked between first and third in the league. Then in 1954–1957, the Milwaukee Braves drew more two million fans each season to its home games at County Stadium. The incredible support for the Braves within a small baseball market impressed Dodgers owner O'Malley and motivated him to complain about the condition of his ballpark in the media and also to such officials as the Commissioner of Parks in Brooklyn. In O'Malley's view, the Commissioner did not respect him for demanding public land for free to construct a new facility for his team. Thus, the surge in attendance in Milwaukee indicated to O'Malley that the Braves would have enough fans, resources, and money to challenge and possibly outperform the Dodgers each season in the NL.

Besides improvement of the Braves' environment, the Dodgers, Giants, and Yankees each played their home games within the New York metropolitan area. During 1953–1957, the average winning percentages and home attendances of these three teams were, respectively, .613 and 1.1 million, .497 and 814,000, and .642 and 1.5 million. On average, Dodgers teams outplayed those of the Giants in these five seasons. Nevertheless, the Brooklyn club had to share America's most lucrative commercial market with its rival in the NL and also with the Yankees and local teams in other professional sports.

In MLB's 1956 and 1957 seasons, the Dodgers scheduled and played several home-away-from-home games in Jersey City's 24,000-seat Roosevelt Stadium. These events reflected the ongoing dispute and bitter feud between O'Malley and a number of politicians within the local community about the proposal to allocate public land and replace Ebbets Field with a new, modern ballpark.

When his discussions with the city became hopeless, O'Malley negotiated so hard with officials from another large metropolitan area such that he was given the title to some prime real estate near downtown Los Angeles in sunny southern California. After being awarded this valuable property, O'Malley's team in Brooklyn moved to the west coast and became the Los Angeles Dodgers in early 1958. As a result, Ebbets Field was then sold by the city to businessman Marvin Kratter for $3 million.[12]

Relocating from Brooklyn to Los Angeles provided an immediate financial bonus and was an excellent long-run investment for the Dodgers franchise and its various groups of owners, coaches, managers and ballplayers. While the team played four years in the city's 93,600-seat Memorial Coliseum, its attendances there increased to almost two million per season. Then in 1962, 56,000-seat Dodger Stadium opened and the club's attendances at home games zoomed to 2.2–2.7 million each year until 1967. To some sports economists, the move of the Braves to Milwaukee was an example of a lagging market in Boston while the Dodgers' exit from Brooklyn occurred because of an opportunity for the team to play in greener pastures within a fast-developing and prosperous area near the US west coast.

New York Giants → San Francisco Giants

The New York Gothams joined the NL as an expansion franchise in 1883. Two years later, the club was renamed Giants and then in 1890–1891, it had financial troubles and merged with another team from New York that also competed in the Players League. Between the late 1890s and mid-1950s, the Giants franchise became owned and then resold by such well-known baseball entrepreneurs as John Brush, Charles Stoneham and his son Horace, and John McGraw.[13]

Before the late 1950s, the club had won seventeen NL pennants and five World Series while, in part, playing its home games in various ballparks including different versions of the Polo Grounds. Thus, the franchise thrived financially while located in New York and also played competitively in regular season games as a rival of the crosstown Brooklyn

---

12 *For more information about this movement, see Neil J. Sullivan, The Dodgers Move West: The Transfer of the Brooklyn Baseball Franchise to Los Angeles (New York, NY: Oxford University Press, 1987).*

13 *See, for example, "San Francisco Giants," www.mlb.com cited 6 September 2017 and Andrew Goldblatt, The Giants and the Dodgers: Four Cities, Two Teams, One Rivalry (Jefferson, NC: McFarland, 2003).*

Dodgers. In fact, the Giants became a popular and successful team in the early 1950s because of the performances of such great hitters as Willie Mays, Alvin Dark, and Bobby Thompson, and pitchers Sal Maglie, Johnny Antonelli, and Larry Jansen.

During the late 1940s to 1951, the Giants attendances at its home games in the 56,000-seat Polo Grounds exceeded one million per season. Then, between 1952 and 1957, the club attracted less than 900,000 to its ballpark each year except in 1954 when it won a NL pennant and then a World Series after defeating the AL Cleveland Indians in four consecutive games. Meanwhile, Dodgers owner O'Malley expressed a strong interest in moving his club out of Brooklyn after clashing with government officials there about having to play some games in tiny, outmoded Ebbets Field. Similarly, Giants owner Horace Stoneham began to look for another home for his team since the Polo Grounds were scheduled to be demolished and then replaced by a housing project. An interesting but unfulfilled strategy, Stoneham considered renting Yankee Stadium for one or more years because the Yankees had played their home games in the Polo Grounds for ten years (1913–1922).

When O'Malley decided to move the Dodgers to Los Angeles, Stoneham announced that he received an attractive offer to transfer the Giants from New York to somewhere within the Bay Area of northern California. Because his team's attendances at the Polo Grounds fell from 1.2 million in 1954 to less than 630,000 in 1957, and due to the impending departure of the Dodgers from Brooklyn to southern California, Stoneham received approval from the league to move his club into the Bay Area before opening day of the 1958 MLB season.

After that relocation occurred, the Giants teams played home games for two years in San Francisco's 22,900-seat Seals Stadium. Because of the anticipation, enthusiasm, and excitement of baseball fans in that sports market, the Giants attendances at Seals Stadium increased to more than 1.2 million people in 1958 and also in 1959. Then in 1960, a new 63,000-seat ballpark named Candlestick Park opened in San Francisco and the Giants' attendance increased to 1.7 million and remained greater than 1.5 million during most MLB seasons of the mid-1960s. Besides playing at home before large crowds, the team also won the NL pennant in 1962 after beating the Dodgers in the league's playoffs. Then in a close multigame series with the Yankees, the Giants lost 1–0 in game seven despite the powerful hitting of superstars like Willie Mays, Orlando Cepeda, and Willie McCovey.

Besides these two teams' home attendances and ballparks and also their revenues, other factors contributed to the movement of the Dodgers and Giants into California sports markets in the late 1950s. First, some members of the US Congress questioned why MLB had not added new clubs and expanded into existing or other domestic baseball territories. With at least two big-league clubs playing at home in California in 1958 and more thereafter, organized baseball had, in part, responded to Congress' concerns about unoccupied sports markets within two relatively large areas on the west coast.

Second, the longstanding Pacific Coast League (PCL) and start-up Continental League (CL) were each determined to form a third major league in professional baseball. With relocation of NL clubs from the New York area to Los Angeles and San Francisco in 1958, these movements ruined the PCL's plan whereas expansion by the AL and NL during the early 1960s eliminated the hopes of CL officials to organize and field new teams in a major league. In fact, the CL folded in 1960–1961 while being organized by attorney William Shea and future New York Mets owner Joan Payson.

Boston Braves → Milwaukee Braves → Atlanta Braves

From 1876 to 1952, the Boston Red Stockings/Beaneaters/Doves/Pilgrims/Braves franchise existed in the NL. During these seventy-seven seasons of competition, these teams as a group won ten NL pennants. Then in 1914, the Braves played well enough to defeat the AL Philadelphia Athletics in four games and win its first and only World Series.[14]

Despite these victories and also being runner-up to the AL Cleveland Indians in the 1948 World Series, the Braves tended to finish below third in the league during a majority of its MLB seasons. Consequently, these dismal performances and a series of financial difficulties caused a high turnover of sports entrepreneurs and various groups to temporarily own the franchise while in Boston.

14 *This topic is discussed in "Milwaukee Braves," www.sportencyclopedia.com cited 6 September 2017; Evan Weiner, "Lou Perini Should be in Baseball's Hall of Fame With Walter O'Malley," www.mcnsports.com cited 7 September 2017; "Atlanta Braves," www.mlb.com cited 8 September 2017; Glen Gendzel, "Competitive Boosterism: How Milwaukee Lost the Braves," Business Review, Vol. 69, No. 4 (Winter 1995): 530–566.*

After a series of sales and repurchases, a syndicate headed by Lou Perini—that included his brothers and a few other investors—bid and acquired almost 100 percent of the team in 1944. Eight years later, the Perinis bought out the franchise's co-owners and assumed total control of the Braves enterprise.

During the late 1940s and early 1950s, some circumstances and events occurred that provided a great incentive and wonderful opportunity for the Perini's to shift the NL Braves from Boston to Milwaukee following the 1952 MLB season. First, the club ranked no higher than fourth each season from 1949 to 1952 while the AL Boston Red Sox placed second, third twice, and sixth in the AL. Second, during these four seasons, the Braves' and Red Sox's average attendances at their home games were, respectively, 698,000 at Braves Field and 1.3 million at Fenway Park. Third, each teams' average pre-tax profits for three years—1948–1949 and 1952 (profits were unavailable in 1951)—were estimated at $−308,000 for the Braves and $−140,000 for the Red Sox. In comparison, the Braves' performed much worse and also were less popular and incurred larger operating losses than the Red Sox.

Besides significant differences between these two Boston-based professional baseball franchises, MLB changed its rules in 1952. These changes meant that team movements (and expansions) became a concern for only the league involved and not the other—except for invasion of another team's territory—and that the relocation of clubs required merely a three-fourths favorable vote and not the unanimous consent of the league's members. In other words, the approval for any NL and AL franchises to move from one area to another, and for either league to expand, became simpler and much easier to obtain from decision-makers within organized baseball.

A new 28,000 permanent seat—36,000 capacity— but publicly funded baseball facility named Milwaukee County Stadium was completed during the early 1950s for the Milwaukee Brewers, which was the NL Braves' AAA minor-league club located in southeast Wisconsin. Also, sometime before or after the Perini brothers received approval from MLB to relocate their franchise from Boston to Milwaukee, they successfully negotiated a sweetheart lease with government officials in Milwaukee. As a result, the Perini's received permission to rent County Stadium from the city for $1,000 per year. The team, however, agreed to amend its contract with the city and thereby accepted an increase in rent for the ballpark from $1,000 to $25,000 in 1953 and again in 1954.

In retrospect, the movement of the Braves to Milwaukee in early 1953 generated significantly more fans, revenues, and profits for the Perinis' franchise. Furthermore, it compelled the brothers to spend additional amounts of money to increase the payrolls of the team's coaches and ballplayers, and for more investment in the club's minor-league system and development programs. Invariably these expenditures resulted in a World Series championship for the Braves in 1957 and another NL pennant in 1958.

Undoubtedly the relocation also provided an opening and pathway for other baseball clubs to change their home sites—especially away from metropolitan areas in the east toward some sports markets in the Midwest and west—and for the expansion of teams in both leagues of MLB. In the long run, the Braves' move also provided an opportunity for various municipalities in the US to invest public money in order to finance the construction of modern ballparks for a majority of big-league clubs, especially during the mid-to-late 1900s and early 2000s.

After a steady decline in attendances at County Stadium and mediocre-to-below-average performances of their team after its championship seasons in Milwaukee, the Perinis sold a majority of the franchise's stock for $6.2 million in 1962 to a group of investors that consisted of the Braves president and general manager John McHale, and also of six former minority owners of the Chicago White Sox including William Bartholomay and Thomas Reynolds, Jr. Four years later, these owners jointly decided to vacate the Milwaukee area—where the local and regional broadcast market was tiny—and move the Braves to Georgia and then rename them the Atlanta Braves.

For several years after moving from Boston to Milwaukee during the early 1950s, the Braves became one of the most competitive, successful, and prosperous teams in the NL. Between 1953 and 1960, for example, the club's annual attendances at County Stadium exceeded two million during four of these years and at least 1.4 million in another four of them. Besides winning consecutive NL pennants, the Braves also defeated the Yankees 4–3 to win a World Series title in 1957. While it existed for thirteen years in the Milwaukee area, the franchise became the only team in MLB history to play more than one season and never finish with a winning percentage less than .500.

There are other important facts to remember about the Braves' commercial success while operating in southeast Wisconsin. First, the club was profitable for several years because of the total revenues it collected from paid admissions, concession receipts, and parking fees at the ballpark, and also from advertising, sponsorships, and local and regional television and radio contracts. Second, some sports historians estimate that the team's arrival in 1953 generated millions of dollars in new business for local companies and that this relocation caused numerous investments within Milwaukee's infrastructure that improved the city's roads, schools, water systems, and real estate values. Third, the Braves franchise established excellent communications and good relations within the community by contributing money and their ballplayers' leisure time to local charities, social campaigns, and many of the city's youth organizations. Indeed, these were intangible benefits, rewards, and also goodwill from the Braves that likely affected people including ethnic groups in the area.

After the team's huge success in the mid-to-late 1950s, the Braves organization experienced different baseball, business, and internal problems that gradually led to its final season as a MLB franchise within a midsized sports market of southeast Wisconsin. A few of these issues originated during the very early years of the 1960s. For example, after accumulating approximately $8 million in profits since 1953, the club had a financial loss in 1962 due, in part, to a 30 percent decline in attendances at its home games in County Stadium. As a result, the Perinis sold 90 percent of their franchise's stock for $6.2 million to a Chicago-based group of investors led by Bill Bartholomay. This was the highest price ever paid for a MLB team that did not own its home-site ballpark.

Another issue for the Braves was the Dodgers and Giants business. These were profitable and very successful franchises because their revenues and economic values greatly appreciated since relocating to big markets in California during early 1958. Also, some of the Braves' most talented ballplayers had aged, been traded, or retired from the game after the late 1950s. This, in turn, caused many diehard baseball fans in Milwaukee to become less enthusiastic and not attend or to simply ignore the team's home games after 1961.

About one or two years after the club was sold in 1962, the Braves' new ownership group decided that leaving Milwaukee for another city in America was the practical and most profitable option to pursue for their franchise. They realized the geographic limitations and boundaries of Milwaukee's advertising market of 2.5 million households given the location of Chicago to the south, Minneapolis to the west, and Lake Michigan to the east. Furthermore the group was not optimistic about reviving the Braves fan base in Milwaukee, or interested in investing millions of additional dollars to sign expensive free agents from other teams and improve the competitiveness of the club, or to increase the salaries of managers and players who performed on their minor-league teams. Consequently, Braves' owners contacted government officials and business leaders in several cities of the US to determine whether they would or could host their floundering Milwaukee baseball franchise.

In 1964–1965, there were a total of twenty MLB teams located in seventeen different metropolitan areas of the US. As such, the largest sports markets in the nation without baseball clubs—and their rank in population during these years—were Nassau-Suffolk (9), Dallas-Fort Worth (12), and Newark (15), and then Atlanta (18), Seattle (19), and San Diego (23). After negotiating with representatives from these and other places, Bill Bartholomay's investment group selected Atlanta to be the next home of the Braves. The decision involved demographic, economic, and sport-specific issues.

One, during spring 1964, Atlanta started constructing an $18 million, 52,000-seat ballpark to be finished and opened in early 1965. When the AL Kansas City Athletics decided to relocate to Oakland, California rather than to central Georgia, the Braves became a potential tenant of the city's new ballpark—Atlanta Stadium. Even so, a year remained on the club's lease at County Stadium in Milwaukee which became an obstacle in the Braves' plans to exit the city.

Two, some important financial factors influencing the Braves' move from Milwaukee into the Atlanta area included an immediate increase in television revenues of $1 million per year, more advertising income from such large corporate sponsors as Coca-Cola and local banks, and an expanded media network that extended hundreds of miles to the east and southeast coast and also to communities in the south and southwest within Florida and other southern states.

Three, Milwaukee was a city with blue-collar job losses from being located within the Rust Belt whereas Atlanta was experiencing economic development, employment growth, and an expanding population as workers in manufacturing and households vacated declining areas in the nation's Midwest and northeast to live in the southeast. Four, throughout the 1960s, some of Atlanta's prominent civic, corporate, and government leaders established a policy many business people referred to as competitive boosterism. In other words, these officials combined their knowledge, talents, and resources to actively participate in luring industries and investment projects from other cities for the purpose of economic development.

Besides the construction of Atlanta Stadium and new roads, freeways, and skyscrapers and other complexes and facilities within the metropolitan area, activities included (a) the involvement and support of Atlanta Mayor Ivan Allen, Jr. and local businessmen, (b) investments in programs within schools of higher education such as Atlanta University, Georgia State University and Georgia Institute of Technology, and (c) development of a countywide mass transit system. For the most part, these improvements in infrastructure were financed primarily with local and state taxpayer money and with donations, gifts, and grants from various corporations in the region.

Within a few months after the NL initially approved Milwaukee's MLB team to relocate to Atlanta, 29-year-old Bud Selig—the son of Wisconsin's biggest Ford dealer—filed an injunction in a state court to force the Braves to play home games in Milwaukee for the 1965 MLB season. Because of various efforts from those who agreed and did not agree with the franchise's potential move, the club's current lease of County Stadium, and criticism from sports reporters in local, regional, and national media, the NL reversed its decision and denied the Braves' request to relocate from Milwaukee in early 1965. Consequently, the Braves played their final season in Milwaukee and finished fifth in the league and eleven games behind the Los Angeles Dodgers. When the season concluded, Bartholomay moved his baseball team to the largest city in Georgia and renamed it the Atlanta Braves.

The final legal battle to prevent the Braves' movement to Atlanta ended in December 1966 when the US Supreme Court voted 4–3 against hearing this case. Thus, the judges let stand the decision of the Wisconsin Supreme Court to allow the club's exit from Milwaukee. In the end, MLB and its member franchises were more prominent, prosperous, and successful during the 1970s and years thereafter because of the Braves move in 1966 from small-to-midsized-market Milwaukee to a fast-developing and expanding sports market based in Atlanta.

Montreal Expos → Washington Nationals

Since the club's first MLB season in the NL, the Montreal Expos struggled throughout their 36-year history to win enough games to qualify for the league's playoffs. Although Expos teams won two East Division titles, they normally finished with more losses than the Cardinals, Mets, Phillies, and others. According to sports historians, the Expos' decline began four years after a syndicate headed by John McHale and Charles Bronfman sold the franchise for $86 million to another group that included such diversified investors as a food chain and credit union, city of Montreal, and province of Quebec.

To revisit part of its history, in early August of 1994, the Expos had MLB's best winning percentage at .649 putting them six games ahead of the Atlanta Braves in the NL East Division. However. on August 12th, a general strike by ballplayers occurred causing teams' owners to initiate a lockout thus cancelling MLB's regular season and postseason. As a result, baseball's reputation was damaged among fans along with the Expos' efforts to construct a new ballpark in Montreal.

For personal reasons, some local owners of the franchise decided not to invest more of their money or resources to increase the team's payroll or retain its most productive players. Later, owner Claude Brochu said the Expos had an excellent team that would have won a NL pennant in 1994 and then appear in MLB's World Series. Undoubtedly, Brochu's prediction was based, in part, on the performances of such Expos as Manager of the Year Felipe Alou and talented players as Ken Hill, Moises Alou, and Marquis Grissom.

After the strike ended in early 1995, Expos' general manager Kevin Malone spent the next two years releasing many of the team's best fielders, hitters, and pitchers. Besides Hill, Alou, and Grissom, the other men that left the Expos in 1995–1996 included Larry Walker, John Wetteland, Mel Rojas, and Pedro Martinez.

A few years later, American art dealer Jeffrey Loria purchased the franchise from Brochu and named his stepson David Samson its executive vice president. Then, Loria spent more than $10 million to acquire just three ballplayers. That sum, in turn, amounted to 50 percent of the club's total payroll in 1999. For that season and the next one, the Expos played well enough to finish fourth in the

East Division. In short, the strike in 1994 led to the team's ownership problems and deterioration of its fan base, and also to problems in selling television broadcast rights to local, regional, and national networks, and to cable and satellite companies.

During early 2002, MLB became majority owner of the Expos and operated the franchise while it finished second but nineteen games behind the Atlanta Braves in the East Division. To expand the game internationally, MLB assigned the Expos to play some of its home games in 2003 and 2004 at a small but popular ballpark in Puerto Rico.

As these baseball seasons opened and closed, the league made various contacts and negotiated with them to assist moving the Expos out of Montreal into a sports market within the US or elsewhere. Indeed, MLB officials considered such domestic areas for the franchise as Charlotte in North Carolina, Norfolk in Virginia, and Portland in Oregon. Furthermore, three non-US cities that MLB likely evaluated as potential sites for the ball club were San Juan in Puerto Rico and both Mexico City and Monterrey in Mexico. Consequently in late 2004, MLB chose Washington, DC as the new home of the Expos because of the area's previous experience with professional baseball teams and also the commitment of politicians there to build the team a modern ballpark at a convenient place for sports fans to attend its home games.

During December 2004, the Expos' relocation from Montreal to Washington, DC was approved in a 28–1 vote by other owners of MLB franchises. Baltimore Orioles owner Peter Angelos voted against the move since his team performed at home within the area, which in his view existed as a single baseball market although there were obvious differences in cultures, populations, household incomes, and commercial activities between the two cities.[15]

Angelos, however, feared that his investment in the Orioles would dramatically decline if a competitor was permitted to enter his team's area. In contrast, several

15 *For this relocation, read "Montreal Expos," www.mlb.com cited 10 September 2017; "Washington Nationals," www.wikipedia.com cited 10 September 2017; Frank P. Jozsa Jr., Baseball, Inc.: The National Pastime As Big Business (Jefferson, NC: McFarland, 2006) and also National League Franchises: Team Performances and Business Success (New York, NY: Springer, 2015); "Teams," www.mlb.com cited 8 September 2017.*

critics, including some owners, disagreed with Angelos since the Orioles had shared its market with the former Washington Senators for eighteen years. This dispute, in turn, also disturbed baseball fans in Washington who remembered that the Griffith family, as longtime owners of the Senators, allowed the AL St. Louis Browns to move from Missouri to eastern Maryland in early 1954.

After threatening to file lawsuits against MLB and also making public announcements about protecting his franchise's territorial rights by preventing an invasion into the DC area by another team, Angelos and league officials successfully negotiated their dispute. Thus, the parties made a deal that ensured no financial harm would come to the Orioles from the entry of an existing baseball team from Montreal recently renamed the Washington Nationals.

According to a crucial aspect of this unique settlement, the Orioles agreed to form a new sports network that produced and distributed games for each of these two franchises on local affiliates and cable and satellite systems. In other words, Angelos and his new network legally controlled the television and radio rights for broadcasting both Orioles and Nationals regular season games. The network, however, was not available for all cable providers meaning that Nationals' fans who lived in the DC area could not watch the majority of the team's games on television in the 2005 and 2006 MLB seasons.

Another short-term but controversial problem regarding the team's relocation from Montreal was Washington Mayor Anthony Williams' financial plan for a new ballpark. Initially, he committed the city to pay a portion of the estimated $600 million or more of the cost for the facility without any subsidies from municipal or regional governments in Maryland and Virginia.

After a series of proposals to amend the plan in late 2004 and throughout 2005, MLB finally signed a lease with the nation's capital city in March of 2006 for a new ballpark.

With respect to the lease, the league accepted a cap of $611 million to be spent for the ballpark that DC's council had decided to impose, agreed to contribute $20 million to offset the stadium's construction costs, and stipulated that any excess tax revenues from the ballpark would be allocated for debt service of bonds and also for the payment of any cost overruns. Given these three specific conditions, a contract was approved by the council to build a state-of-the-art, 41,000-seat ballpark for the team to open for the 2007 MLB season.

A final issue concerned the sale of the Expos franchise by MLB and then choosing a new group of investors to own and operate it. Because of delays as a result of negotiating with DC officials and signing a lease for the new ballpark, MLB had little time to evaluate the proposals submitted by several syndicates. But in the summer of 2006, the league sold the team for approximately $450 million to the Lerner Enterprise Group which was headed by wealthy real estate developer Theodore N. Lerner.

During the fall of 2006, Comcast Corporation committed to broadcast the Nationals' games on its cable network. For certain, the relocation from Montreal to Washington was a complicated deal that involved such elements as determining the current boundaries of markets and values of professional baseball teams, deciding how to equitably finance and share construction costs and any overruns of a new stadium, efficiently but fairly allocating broadcast rights of two major sports club, and concluding the sale and purchase of an existing MLB franchise in Montreal.

Table 6.2 consists of five original NL teams and their seasons and performances before and after moving to different sites. Of the group, the Milwaukee Braves had the highest win%, followed by the Los Angeles Dodgers and San Francisco Giants. The Dodgers also ranked first in numbers of playoffs, pennants, and World Series. In contrast to them, the St. Louis Maroons had the lowest win% and zero playoffs and championships while the Indianapolis Hoosiers and Washington Nationals also failed to win any titles through MLB's 2018 season.

Another club with some success has been the Atlanta Braves. They ranked second in playoffs, third in pennants, and tied for third with the Milwaukee Braves in World Series. Besides Maroons and Hoosiers teams, the Nationals have below-average results but as of 2018 won their division title and expect to eventually advance in the postseason.

Table 6.2 Team Performances, National League Relocations, Selected Data

Teams	Seasons	Win%	Playoffs	Pennants	World Series
Cleveland Blues	1879–1884	.440	0	0	0
→ St. Louis Maroons	1885–1886	.342	0	0	0
→ Indianapolis Hoosiers	1887–1889	.368	0	0	0
Brooklyn Dodgers	1890–1957	.516	9	13	1
→ Los Angeles Dodgers	1958–2018	.539	23	11	5
New York Giants	1883–1957	.553	14	17	5
→ San Francisco Giants	1958–2018	.518	12	6	3
Boston Braves	1876–1952	.478	2	10	1
→ Milwaukee Braves	1953–1965	.563	2	2	1
→ Atlanta Braves	1966–2018	.513	20	5	1
Montreal Expos	1969–2004	.484	1	0	0
→ Washington Nationals	2005–2018	.498	5	0	0

Note: Abbreviated is average winning percentage (win%). Playoffs, pennants, and World Series are self-explanatory. Brooklyn's team was nicknamed Dodgers in 1913 and 1932–1957, but also Bridegrooms (1890–1898), Superbas (1899–1913), and Robins (1914–1931). New York's NL team was nicknamed Gothams (1883–1885) and Giants (1886–1957). Besides nicknamed Braves in 1912–1935 and 1941–1952, Boston's NL team was also nicknamed Red Stockings (1876–1882), Beaneaters (1883–1906), Doves (1907–1910), Rustlers (1911–1911), and Bees (1936–1940).

Source: "Franchise History," www.baseball-reference.com cited 8 September 2017 and "Teams," www.mlb.com cited 8 September 2017.

To conclude this chapter, the movement of MLB teams from one site to another transformed the sport mostly in good ways. Based on information in the tables, most clubs were more competitive following their relocation and also improved financially, in part, because of larger attendances at home games. They earned enough revenue to compensate and reward players on their roster and perhaps invested in a new ballpark or renovated the current facility. This, in turn, expanded their fan base, popularity, and monetary value as business enterprises both in the short and long term.

CHAPTER 7

League Expansions

Besides a metropolitan area's location, population, and its growth rate, other factors that affect the longevity of new teams in Major League Baseball (MLB) are whether they earned enough revenue to generate profit, their win-loss record and any championships they won, number of fans and size of their market, attendances at home games in regular seasons, politics, and support from businesses and other organizations in the community. Based on information in the literature including articles, books, studies, reports, and websites, this chapter discusses the founding of each expansion franchise as a member of either the American League or National League of MLB and also their historical performance and success.[1]

AMERICAN LEAGUE

Los Angeles (1961)

Since 1940, there had been conversations, rumors, and expectations among baseball executives regarding the eventual placement of an American League (AL) team

1 *For more details about expansion teams in MLB, see Frank P. Jozsa Jr., Major League Baseball Expansions and Team Relocations: A History, 1876–2008 (Jefferson, NC: McFarland, 2010); Frank P. Jozsa Jr. and John J. Guthrie Jr., Relocating Teams and Expanding Leagues in Professional Sports: How the Major Leagues Respond to Market Conditions (Westport, CT: Quorum Books, 1999); James Quirk and Rodney D. Fort, Pay Dirt: The Business of Professional Team Sports (Princeton, NJ: Princeton University Press, 1992).*

within or very near the Los Angeles metropolitan area (LA). The league, for example, denied a request by the owner of the Browns to move his team from St. Louis to LA in 1940. One year later, however, MLB approved the club's relocation, but the bombing of Pearl Harbor in Hawaii by Japan prevented that move. During the 1950s, AL officials again considered a transfer of the Browns to LA before permitting them to relocate and play at home in the Baltimore area.

Others in MLB had discussed temporarily moving the AL Athletics from Philadelphia to Kansas City and then a few years later permanently to LA, but when the National League (NL) Dodgers and Giants left the New York area for Los Angeles and San Francisco in 1958, and the Continental League (CL) announced plans to organize and place some teams on the west coast of the United States (US), MLB decided to put a new AL team in LA and another in the nation's capital city.

As denoted in tables A7.1 and A7.2 of the appendix, LA ranked second in population among US metropolitan areas during the early 1960s and also experienced above-average population growth. Furthermore, the area had hosted four other professional sports teams including the National Football League (NFL) Rams and National Basketball Association (NBA) Lakers. Nevertheless, it was potential competition from clubs in the CL and a decision by the NL to locate new teams in Houston and New York City in 1962 that were important factors for the AL to approve expansion into LA and compete for baseball fans there against the successful and popular NL Dodgers.

A syndicate headed by former celebrity, cowboy actor, and movie star Gene Autry purchased the rights for an expansion franchise from the AL in 1960–1961 for a fee of $2.1 million. Besides that group, MLB Hall of Famer Hank Greenberg and his partner Bill Veeck–who was a maverick, promoter, and a former owner of the AL St. Louis Browns–and also Chicago insurance executive and owner of the AL Oakland Athletics Charlie Finley had bid for a franchise. For various reasons, they each failed, in part, because Greenberg and Veeck's offer was opposed by Dodgers owner Walter O'Malley, who did not want to compete with Veeck for sports fans in LA, while a conflict of interest occurred since Finley had previously acquired majority control of the Athletics.[2]

---

2 *An interesting source to read is Richard E. Beverage, "Los Angeles Angels–California Angels: A Cowboy's Search for Another Champion," in Peter C. Bjarkman, ed., Encyclopedia of Major League Baseball: American League Team Histories (New York, NY: Carroll & Graf Publishers, 1993).*

As a rich, well-known actor and entrepreneur in the entertainment and media business, Autry owned and controlled Golden West Broadcasters which included radio and television enterprises based in LA. Furthermore, he was a stockholder in a Pacific Coast League (PCL) baseball team named the Hollywood Stars, and his wealth exceeded an estimated $300 million. In short, Autry and his group possessed the ambition, money, and power to successfully outbid other groups and become the initial owner of the AL's expansion team in LA.

One of the first tasks for Autry's syndicate was to name their new team. Since the Spanish words *Los Angeles* translate into English as *the Angels*, Autry paid O'Malley approximately $300,000 for the right to use Angels as a nickname for his team because the Dodgers' owner had controlled a former PCL team in the city with the same name. When this transaction was completed, the Los Angeles Angels were identified and officially established as an expansion team in the AL.

To open its first season, the club played home games in 1961 at Wrigley Field in South Los Angeles, which was also the local ballpark of the PCL's Angels. One year later, the AL's Angels were allowed to play their home games in Dodger Stadium, a baseball facility referred to as Chavez Ravine. At that ballpark, however, they were a tenant of the Dodgers and thus, the Angels could not generate a distinct, large, and independent fan base. Moreover, O'Malley imposed severe lease conditions on them while playing their home games in Dodger Stadium. As a result, during the mid-1960s, Autry attempted to negotiate with city officials in Long Beach for the construction of a new, taxpayer-funded baseball stadium. When these talks failed, Autry successfully negotiated an agreement for a new stadium to be built in Anaheim, a suburban city of LA but within Orange County.

In 1966, Autry's syndicate transferred its club—then named California Angels—to Anaheim and remained the franchise's owner for thirty-one consecutive seasons. When the Disney Corporation bought the team from Autry and his associates in early 1997, its name was changed to Anaheim Angels. That name reflected, in part, the location of Disney's headquarters and the company's popular theme park in California's Orange County.

During the early 2000s, Disney had other important commercial interests to manage and operate. Thus, the company sold its MLB franchise to Mexican billionaire Arte

Moreno. In turn, he planned to publicize and exploit the state's largest media market by renaming his team from Anaheim Angels to the Los Angeles Angels of Anaheim (LAAA). Despite protests from local baseball fans and a lengthy lawsuit filed by the city of Anaheim, the name of Moreno's team has remained the same since 2005.

Washington, DC (1961)

Between 1901 and 1960, the Washington Senators won three AL pennants and, in 1924, a World Series. Nevertheless, the Senators' dismal performances and low attendances at their dilapidated ballpark in DC convinced owner Clark Griffith to vacate the nation's capital after MLB's 1960 season and move his team to the Minneapolis area in Minnesota.[3]

Previously, Congress had held open hearings and threatened to lift MLB's antitrust exemption if the baseball organization did not amend its policy and increase the number of franchises to more than sixteen. Consequently, after several meetings during the late 1950s to early 1960s, the league conceded to political pressure to avoid public relations problems and therefore approved the entry of new AL clubs within the LA and Washington, DC metropolitan areas.

Because it ranked seventh in population and experienced a very high growth rate during the 1950s, the DC area was an appealing site for the AL to place a new team. Certainly, MLB foresaw the Senators being an intra-league rival for the nearby Baltimore Orioles and successfully competing for local sports fans with the NFL Redskins but with no local NBA or National Hockey League (NHL) clubs. Furthermore, other than the cities of Newark, Houston, and Buffalo, there was at least one AL or NL club located within the largest and midsized populated areas of the US. Even though the Senators would likely perform poorly in its league and struggle financially for a few years, potential profits from expansion and the political pressure from Congress after the relocation of the former Senators team to Minneapolis in 1960 compelled MLB to choose Washington as a prime location for an AL expansion team.

---

3 *See "Washington Senators–Minnesota Twins: Expansion Era Baseball Comes to the American League," in Peter C. Bjarkman, ed., Encyclopedia of Major League Baseball: American League Team Histories, 487–535 and "Washington Senators," www.baseball-reference.com cited 19 September 2017.*

A powerful and savvy group led by Richard Quesada—an administrator in the Federal Aviation Administration—purchased the rights to this franchise from MLB for $2.1 million. Although Quesada knew very little about operating a professional sports team, he had political connections in the DC area and raised enough financial capital to bid for and acquire a new AL expansion franchise. Later, however, he played only a minor role in the organization as an owner; in fact, Quesada sold his interest in the team to another investor during the early 1960s. The Senators played one season in Griffith Stadium and then, in the mid-to-late 1960s, performed at home in a $20 million DC stadium which was renamed Robert F. Kennedy Memorial Stadium.

In retrospect, Washington was not an optimal area to host the Senators ball club during the 1960s. The original Senators teams floundered there because they finished at or near the bottom in most AL seasons, drew more than a million people in attendance to their home games in only one year (1946), remained a distant second in popularity to the NFL Redskins, and otherwise earned a reputation for a famous saying: "Washington—first in war, first in peace, and last in the American League." Long-time owner Clark Griffith—who had failed to invest enough resources into the team—caused the Washington Senators to lose the majority of their games, except when the club won AL pennants in 1924–1925 and 1933, and a World Series in 1924.

It was a bit optimistic for MLB to expect a new team and its organization to be successful in the short run after its predecessor had a history of poor performances, below-average home attendances, and debilitating financial problems. For eleven seasons, the expansion Senators franchise failed to realize the business, demographic, economic, and social advantages of being located in the nation's capital.

Kansas City (1969)

After his team finished no higher than sixth place in thirteen AL seasons while playing at home within the Kansas City area, owner Charlie Finley moved the Athletics to Oakland, California following the 1967 MLB season. Finley's decision was severely criticized by Missouri Senator Stuart Symington and publicized in the media from late 1967 through 1968. In fact, Symington demanded that MLB authorize and put a team in his state to replace the former Athletics.

As denoted in tables A7.1 and A7.2 of the appendix, the Kansas City area ranked twenty-fifth in population during the late 1960s, had experienced mediocre economic and population growth, and hosted a popular American Football League team nicknamed the Chiefs. In contrast to the superior attributes of the LA area and population growth of Washington as a city as of 1961, Kansas City appeared to be less than an optimal place for a MLB club from business, economic, and demographic perspectives.

In the end, Symington's influence, power, and prestige as a US Senator intimidated MLB and its officials. In 1969, he persuaded the league to locate one of its two AL expansion teams in Kansas City rather than within a larger metropolitan area such as Phoenix in Arizona, Tampa-St. Petersburg in Florida, or Denver in Colorado. MLB's decision was made, in part, because wealthy businessman Ewing Kaufman was a resident of Kansas City and, as such, he had the wherewithal and enough financial capital to pay MLB a fee of $5.5 million for the right to own an expansion franchise. Besides the involvement of Symington and contribution of Kaufman, the Athletics' former ballpark—named Municipal Stadium—was available in Kansas City to host the new team's eighty-one home games in each regular season.[4]

Given the city's ownership of a 46-year-old, 35,500-seat stadium that met MLB ballpark requirements, one of Kaufman's first decisions was to nickname his team in order to generate enthusiasm and excite baseball fans in the area. Since the popular American Royal Livestock Show had performed in Kansas City for approximately seventy years, Kaufman decided to name his club the Kansas City Royals. As of their 2018 season, the Royals have won seven West Division titles, four AL pennants, and in both 1985 and 2015, a World Series.

Why did MLB select the Kansas City area to be a site for an AL expansion team in 1969? Factors include the area being home to a former AL team for thirteen years; US Senator Symington's implicit threat to challenge baseball's antitrust exemption in the federal courts; the availability of an old but well-known big-league stadium in the city; baseball's confidence, respect, and trust in Ewing Kaufman as a franchise

---

4 *Readings include "Kansas City Royals," www.mlb.com cited 19 September 2017 and Frank P. Jozsa Jr., American League Franchises: Team Performances and Business Success (New York, NY: Springer, 2015).*

owner; and a way for MLB to complete its organizational plans of expanding the AL and NL by two teams each in 1969.

Seattle (1969)

For several years, the Seattle area in Washington State had been involved in some way with professional team sports. It was home, for example, to a minor league baseball team named the Seattle Rainiers of the PCL. Furthermore, the area contained an NBA expansion club named Seattle SuperSonics and also was previously considered as a potential relocation site for the AL Cleveland Indians. Finally, during the late 1960s, Seattle was the third most populated area on the west coast after Los Angeles and San Francisco.

In addition, an impressive ownership group had formed in Seattle to campaign for and promote professional baseball, raise millions in financial capital, and seriously bid for an existing or expansion AL team. The group's leaders were Dewey Soriano, a former president of the PCL, and William Daley, who had owned the Cleveland Indians from 1956 to 1966. In 1968, King County voters approved the issuance of a municipal bond to fund the construction of a new baseball stadium in the area which would become the home ballpark of the expansion Seattle Mariners. Based on these and other factors, MLB chose Seattle as one of two cities to host an AL expansion team that adopted Pilots as its nickname in 1969.[5]

As noted in tables A7.1 and A7.2, during the late 1960s, the Seattle area ranked nineteenth in population, experienced above-average economic growth, and contained a population nearly equal to Minneapolis, which was home of the AL Minnesota Twins. Unfortunately, however, the Pilots began their inaugural season in 1969 by playing games at home in 31-year-old, 18,000-seat Sick's Stadium.

There were several huge and unique problems associated with this facility. As a ballpark of the minor league Rainiers, it was too small in capacity and had become obsolete by the mid-to-late 1960s. For example, there were several delays in increasing Sick's Stadium's capacity by 30,000 seats before the 1969 MLB season

5 *Paul D. Adomites, "Seattle Pilots–Milwaukee Brewers: The Bombers, the Bangers, and the Burners," in Peter C. Bjarkman, ed., Encyclopedia of Major League Baseball: American League Team Histories (New York, NY: Carroll & Graf Publishers, 1993): 422–444.*

had started, and although many of its seats had been installed by June of that year, most of them obstructed views for spectators. In addition, the ballpark's scoreboard did not operate on opening day and the water pressure fell in the building's toilets and faucets after the first few innings of the Pilots' home games. Because of these issues and an extremely inferior team, the Pilots' attendances at home in the 1969 season frustrated MLB officials and did not meet the expectations of its owners. This, in turn, caused the club to struggle financially and it did not perform competitively against its AL rivals.

Despite the area's rank and above-average growth in population, it was a colossal mistake for MLB to approve an AL expansion team to play in Seattle during the late 1960s. Sick's Stadium needed major renovations that opponents of the project and thousands of local taxpayers would not support. Furthermore, the team experienced immediate financial problems because for three years it forewent its share of revenues from baseball's national television contract, and the team agreed to provide other AL owners at least two percent of its gate receipts collected from home games. After a payment of $5.3 million to MLB for its expansion fee, poor attendance, and accumulating losses during the 1969 season, the Pilots gradually depleted their cash account and dollars of reserves from a bank loan. As a result, the value of the franchise plummeted to less than $15 million before 1970.

In hindsight and given the failure of the Pilots in Seattle's sports market, baseball officials should have initially selected the Milwaukee area as an expansion site for an AL team to perform in 1969. Besides hosting the NL Braves for thirteen seasons, that city was represented by an enthusiastic, knowledgeable, and wealthy business group headed by automobile dealer Alan 'Bud' Selig.

Based on the popularity of fifteen-year-old County Stadium, a local baseball fan base that consisted of tens of thousands, and the contributions of profitable corporate sponsors such as those in the beer industry, the Milwaukee area had the demographics, economic power, and infrastructure to successfully host a new AL franchise in organized baseball. For reasons stated before, MLB selected the Seattle area for an expansion team rather than Milwaukee. That, in turn, was an extremely bad managerial decision.

Seattle (1977)

With the Pilots bankrupted after their 1969 MLB season, a syndicate controlled by thirty-five-year-old Bud Selig purchased the team from MLB in 1970 for about $11 million and moved the franchise to Milwaukee where it performed as the Milwaukee Brewers in the AL's West Division. As a result of that relocation, the city of Seattle, King County, and Washington State sued baseball's AL for a breach of contract. At the trial, league officials agreed to place an expansion team in Seattle if the prosecution dropped its lawsuit. After about a year of intense negotiations, the AL authorized the placement of a new club at a site in the Seattle area, which voided the lawsuit.[6]

As denoted in table A7.2 of the appendix, between 1969 and 1977, the Seattle area's population had decreased in rank from nineteenth to twenty-third as did the rankings of AL clubs in Baltimore, Boston, Cleveland, Kansas City, and Minneapolis. Even so, in 1974, the NFL Seahawks had joined the NBA SuperSonics as another professional sports team based in Seattle of King County. Consequently, the decisions made by the owners of these teams suggest this area in the northwest section of Washington State had appealed to professional sports leagues as a prime site for at least one of their franchises.

As a result, Hollywood actor Danny Kaye—as spokesperson and principal member of a syndicate—paid a fee of $6.2 million to MLB in 1976 for the right to own and operate an AL expansion team and locate it in the Seattle area. Thus, Kaye and his colleagues nicknamed their new club Mariners to start the 1977 MLB season and have it compete against other teams in the AL's West Division.

There are two interesting features of Kaye's expansion team. First, the Mariners were chosen as a nickname to reflect the prominence of marine culture in the Seattle area. Second, from 1977 to 1998, the club played its home games in a multipurpose $67 million, 59,500-seat stadium named the Kingdome. This facility was baseball's largest ballpark until it was replaced in July 1999 by Safeco Field, a $517 million, 46,600-seat ballpark with a retractable roof.

---

6 *"Seattle Mariners," www.baseball-reference.com cited 19 September 2017.*

As mentioned earlier for the expansion Seattle Pilots, construction of the Kingdome experienced delays during the late 1960s and early 1970s, in part, because of lawsuits filed by groups who opposed the use of taxpayer money to finance it. Although these legal disputes continued in the courts, the Mariners played their home games—and so did the NFL Seahawks—in the Kingdome.

In short, Seattle was a reasonably attractive and viable place to host a baseball expansion team as of the mid-to-late 1970s. Indeed, it was the city's new ballpark and productive economy, and the area's above-average population growth and strong job market that convinced the AL to choose a group that represented Seattle and not areas in Denver, Phoenix, or Tampa Bay-St. Petersburg to host the AL's thirteenth team.

Toronto (1977)

Prior to the late 1970s, a few owners of baseball clubs considered the Greater Toronto Area (GTA) to be a prime site for their MLB team. In fact, the NL San Francisco Giants were interested in relocating there until businessman Bob Lurie purchased the franchise in 1976 and then committed to maintain its location at a site in that west coast city. Nonetheless, the Giants' intentions became news in the media and created such excitement that the city of Toronto decided to renovate Exhibition Stadium—the home of the Canadian Football League (CFL) Argonauts—in order to accommodate games played by teams in professional baseball.

To add a seventh team to the AL's East Division and thus align it with the league's West Division during the mid-1970s, baseball officials evaluated the GTA and other areas as potential sites. Subsequently, for a fee of $7 million in the mid-to-late 1970s, the AL awarded an expansion franchise to a group of sports investors that consisted of Canada's Labatt's Breweries, businessman Howard Webster, and the Canadian Imperial Bank of Commerce. Later, a name-the-team contest was held in Toronto and Labatt's Blue became one choice selected by the area's sports fans. Ironically, Labatt's Blue was also the name of a top beer brand of Labatt's Breweries who, in part, hoped the team's name would be shortened to Blues and accordingly, provide free advertising for a popular product of the company. Within a few years, however, a majority of Toronto's baseball fans identified the expansion team as the Jays. As a result, the club's official and public nickname evolved into the Blue Jays.[7]

During the mid-to-late 1970s, the GTA had a large and expanding population and an economy that experienced job growth within Canada, consisted of many households with relatively high incomes and wealth, and contained local industries whose prosperity had significantly increased historically. Since the Montreal Expos had become moderately popular for about eight years as an expansion team in the NL East Division, MLB decided to expand and approve a new team within the GTA rather than in a metropolitan area of the US.

Some other options in the US for a new MLB team during the late 1970s likely included Denver in Colorado, Miami in Florida, and Washington in the District of Columbia. Although each of these areas had midsized or midsized-to-large populations, they also contained popular professional sports teams such as the NFL Broncos and NBA Nuggets in Denver, NFL Dolphins in Miami, and NFL Redskins and NBA Bullets in Washington. Apparently, and perhaps realistically, MLB thought that the presence of the NHL Maple Leafs and CFL Argonauts in Toronto would not significantly threaten business opportunities and potential success of a new baseball club in that area.

Tampa Bay (1998)

Since the 1980s, several civic and business leaders and some prominent newspaper journalists and reporters in Tampa Bay had attempted to lure MLB to their area because the city is located on the mid-coast of Florida. This area is a destination for tourists and also a home site of the NFL Buccaneers and NHL Lightning; contains a large number of retirees and thousands of senior citizens; and hosts various entertainment activities and events each month of a year. Furthermore, for decades, some MLB clubs have spent their preseason in the area by operating spring training camps and playing exhibition baseball games within or near Tampa Bay and St. Petersburg.[8]

---

7 *See, for example, "Toronto Blue Jays," www.baseball-reference.com cited 19 September 2017 and "Teams," www.mlb.com cited 8 September 2017.*

8 *Some interesting facts about decisions and consequences of AL expansion in 1998 are in Albert Theodore Powers, The Business of Baseball (Jefferson, NC: McFarland, 2003) and "Tampa Bay Rays," www.mlb.com cited 20 September 2017.*

During 1990, the Florida Suncoast Dome—now named Tropicana Field—was built for baseball games in St. Petersburg, a city located only a few miles south of Tampa Bay. In 1992, there was speculation that San Francisco Giants owner Bob Lurie had attempted to sell his NL club to investors in Tampa Bay, who would then move their team from San Francisco to play its home games at the Suncoast Dome in St. Petersburg. Three years after that deal failed, MLB decided to expand again into a metropolitan area of Florida, subsequent to the expansion of the Marlins into Miami in 1993. Thus in 1995, the league awarded an AL expansion franchise to a group of investors from Tampa Bay that was headed by businessman Vincent J. Naimoli.

Soon after MLB's announcement of expansion was publicized to—and welcomed by—sports fans across Florida and the southeast, owner Naimoli and his organization nicknamed their team the Tampa Bay Devil Rays and then sold the naming rights to their stadium in St. Petersburg to an orange juice and soft drink company in the private sector named Tropicana Products. To prepare the ballpark for opening day of the 1998 MLB season, $70 million in taxpayer money was used to renovate the building and increase its seat capacity to approximately 45,000.

Based on such factors as population growth, steady increases in per capita and household income, and ideal weather conditions, MLB made the prudent business decision in 1995 to permit a new AL team to locate in the Tampa Bay-St. Petersburg area. During that year, Phoenix in Arizona was also granted an expansion team by MLB.

As these expansions occurred, the data revealed that in the mid-1990s Washington in D.C., Riverside in California, and Portland in Oregon were the only US metropolitan areas ranked among the top twenty-five in population without an MLB club. In short, this suggested that the AL (and NL) might decide to consider expansion sites in less populated areas of the US where minor league baseball was popular such as Indianapolis in central Indiana, San Antonio in southeast Texas, Nashville in northwest Tennessee, and Columbus in central Ohio.

Table 7.1 contains the performances of AL expansion teams from their first season in the league through 2018. In winning percentage, they ranged from 50 percent for the Los Angeles/Anaheim Angels to 39 percent for the Seattle Pilots. The Blue Jays and Royals also won more than 48 percent of their regular-season games but not the Senators, Mariners, or Devil Rays/Rays.

Table 7.1 American League Expansion Teams, Seasons, and Performances, Selected Years

			Performances			
Team	Year	Seasons	Playoffs	Divisions	Pennants	World Series
Los Angeles/Anaheim Angels	1961	58	10	9	1	1
Washington Senators	1961	11	0	0	0	0
Kansas City Royals	1969	50	9	7	4	2
Seattle Pilots	1969	1	0	0	0	0
Seattle Mariners	1977	42	4	3	0	0
Toronto Blue Jays	1977	42	7	6	2	2
Tampa Bay Devil Rays/Rays	1998	21	4	2	1	0

Note: Team is self-explanatory. Year is each team's first season in the American League. The Angels' fifty-eight seasons include their performances while located in Los Angeles and Anaheim. The Pilots played one season in Seattle and then moved to Milwaukee in 1970. Performances include these teams' number of playoffs, division titles, pennants, and World Series since their expansion year through MLB's 2018 season.

Source: The World Almanac and Book of Facts (New York, NY: World Almanac Books, 1930–2016); "World Series History," www.baseball-almanac.com cited 18 September 2017; "Teams," www.baseball-reference.com cited 8 September 2017.

Based on their other performances as reported in the table, the Angels were first in number of playoffs and division titles, Royals in pennants, and Royals and Blue Jays in a tie with two World Series championships each. In comparison, the Pilots and Senators performed worst because of inferior players on their rosters, a lack of experienced, smart, and talented managers, and poor team chemistry. According to these results, the Angels, Royals, and Blue Jays significantly outplayed the four other AL expansion clubs and were competitive during many of their seasons in the league.

NATIONAL LEAGUE

Between 1876 and 1900, there were fifteen NL expansion teams located in thirteen different urban areas with two each in Cleveland and Indianapolis. Seven, or 47 percent, of them occurred in the 1870s while eight, or 53 percent, happened in the 1980s. Based on table A7.3 in the appendix, the population of these teams' areas ranged in rank from first (New York) to thirty-second (Syracuse) and their average annual growth rate varied between a low of 1.8 percent in Syracuse to a high of 14 percent in Kansas City. Except for franchises with sites in Indianapolis, Kansas City, Milwaukee, and Syracuse, the other eleven competed for more than one season in the league. Next are NL expansion teams after 1900 followed by their performances.

Houston (1962)

From when the Texas League formed in 1888 until a minor league team nicknamed the Houston Buffaloes (or Buffs) moved to the American Association in 1959, that area in Texas had been involved in some way with organized baseball. For example, the city's Buffalo Stadium—when built in 1928—was considered by many experts in the sport to be the finest stadium in the US minor leagues. Nevertheless, during the mid-to-late 1950s, a few of Houston's most prominent business leaders, investors, and politicians joined forces and made a concerted effort to lure a big-league team into the area even though MLB officials showed little interest.[9]

To accomplish their goal of locating a franchise in the metropolitan area, a few prominent people organized and jointly led a regional campaign to promote expansion within southeast Texas. That effort resulted in the formation of the Houston Sports Association (HSA) in 1957. Initially, the three individuals most responsible for this organization included public relations expert George Kirksey—who in 1952 had tried to convince St. Louis Cardinals owner Fred Saigh into selling his franchise to a Houston-based group—and also banker William A. Kirkland and Craig Cullinan, the son of a wealthy oil baron.

9 *"Franchise History: Major League Baseball Comes to Houston," www.wikipedia.org cited 20 September 2017 and Frank P. Jozsa, Jr. and John J. Guthrie Jr., Relocating Teams and Expanding Leagues in Professional Sports: How the Major Leagues Respond to Market Conditions.*

After several exploratory meetings with major league franchise owners, these promoters from Houston were told to secure the necessary funds to build a new baseball stadium in the area. To achieve that objective financially, Harris County voters approved a $20 million bond issue in 1958 for the construction of a new ballpark.

Because of meetings with current franchise owners and a decision to provide financing, it appeared to the HSA that the city would be awarded a new MLB team by current baseball owners or the transfer of an existing one within one to three years. After the entry of an MLB team did not occur in 1959–1960, entrepreneurs in the HSA became frustrated. As a result, they joined with promoters in other non-MLB cities to organize another major baseball organization and name it the Continental League (CL).

During early 1960, oil and real estate multimillionaire R.E. "Bob" Smith and former Houston mayor and Harris County judge Roy Hofheinz began to play an increasingly important role in the operations of the HSA and ultimately, these men won control of it. Close-knit business partners who trusted each other, Smith owned a large number of financial resources while Hofheinz knew a great deal about public land use and the construction and maintenance of municipal facilities. Meanwhile, in mid-to-late 1960, Congress discussed baseball's exemption from the US antitrust laws but then failed by four votes to pass the Kefauver bill, which stipulated that MLB be included in this legislation.

Alarmed by competition from other ball clubs in a proposed CL and also because of the narrow defeat of Senate Bill 3483 in Congress, an expansion committee within MLB met and agreed to admit two new clubs each into the NL and AL no later than 1961–1962. Thus, any metropolitan areas targeted by the CL as potential markets would be preferred locations for expansion teams in MLB.

One of these places was Houston while others included the Los Angeles, New York, and Washington DC areas. Consequently, during the 1960 World Series played between the NL Pittsburgh Pirates and AL New York Yankees, and after existing team owners had evaluated all bids submitted by individuals and syndicates, the NL awarded expansion franchises to ownership groups from Houston and New York City. As a result of MLB's decision to expand in size during 1961–1962, the CL eventually dissolved.

In early 1961, the HSA purchased the minor-league Buffs franchise and soon thereafter, this group gained control of Houston's expansion team that initially was nicknamed Colt .45s and eventually became the Astros. Among the leaders of the Colt .45s were general manager and veteran baseball executive Gabe Paul and field manager Harry Craft, who had coached the Buffs during its final season in the Texas League. As such, Houston's expansion team was assigned to compete against its rivals in the NL until 1969, when it became a member of the league's West Division.

After playing three NL seasons in hastily constructed, 32,600-seat Colt Stadium and then being renamed the Houston Astros in 1964, the club moved one year later to the 54,300-seat Astrodome, a spectacular air-conditioned, domed stadium built in Houston. Financed with taxpayer money, this ballpark was completed largely because Judge Hofheinz successfully sold a concept of it to the local community and also bragged about the grandeur, image, and prestige of the facility to owners of other NL franchises. Despite numerous promotions and costly marketing efforts, within ten years the Astros' debts exceeded $30 million and for financial reasons, Hofheinz declared bankruptcy. As a result, such creditors as Ford Motor Credit Corporation and General Electric seized control of Hofheinz's assets, which included the Astros franchise. In 1979, a syndicate headed by John McMullen purchased Houston's MLB team and the Astrodome's lease from creditors for $19 million.

From a demographic and financial perspective, the NL's decision to expand into the Houston area in 1962 appeared then to be a forward-looking, smart, and timely strategy. The area's population of 1.4 million ranked seventeenth in the US, and the city's economy had experienced above-average economic growth. Nevertheless, these reasons for expansion into Houston and elsewhere during the early 1960s appeared to be secondary since the threat of a rival baseball league, and Congressional hearings on the sport's antitrust exemption, had been the primary factors that influenced MLB's decision.

New York (1962)

Before the departure during late 1957/early 1958 of the Dodgers to Los Angeles and Giants to San Francisco, 1882 was the last year a NL team had not been based in the New York area. This, in part, caused the city's mayor, Robert Wagner, to appoint a small committee of prominent people to investigate the possibility of persuading an existing NL team to relocate into the area. Indeed, this group tried but failed in its attempts to attract the league's Philadelphia Phillies, Pittsburgh Pirates, and Cincinnati Reds.

In 1959, committee member and attorney William Shea and baseball veteran Branch Rickey organized an eight-team Continental League that included at least one franchise placed in New York. In large part, formation of this new league and the US government's scrutiny of baseball's exemption from the country's antitrust laws compelled NL officials to unanimously pass a resolution and thus award an expansion team to a syndicate which would locate it somewhere within an area that included New York City.[10]

To bid for and ensure the entry and location of a NL expansion team into the city, the New York Metropolitan Baseball Club, Inc. was created sometime in late 1959 to early 1960. This syndicate, which consisted of principal owner Joan Whitney Payson, former New York Giants director and Wall Street broker M. Donald Grant, and a few other wealthy investors, developed plans and consolidated its resources to successfully purchase a new franchise from MLB in 1960 for $1.8 million. To manage the business operations of the new club, Grant hired former New York Yankees general manager George Weiss to be its first president.

For many decades, the New York Standard Metropolitan Statistical Area (SMSA) ranked first in population and its economy included the nation's largest financial companies and several international, commercial, and investment banks. Therefore, the area's baseball fans and its businesses and politicians had the financial capital and resources to enthusiastically support another MLB franchise besides the AL's powerful and highly valued Yankees. Soon after Payson and her group became owners of their new NL franchise, they nicknamed it the Mets.

Even though the New York State Assembly had voted in early 1961 for a bond to fund a new ballpark in Flushing Meadows for the Mets, the decision was too late. Thus, the club had to play its home games in its first two regular seasons after expansion before a total of 1.9 million spectators in the 55,000-seat Polo Grounds.

10 *"Pete Cava, "New York Mets From Throneberry to Strawberry: Baseball's Most Successful Expansion Franchise," in Peter C. Bjarkman, ed., Encyclopedia of Major League Baseball: National League (New York, NY: Carroll & Graf Publishers, 1993), 342–393.*

Then in 1964, the Mets moved their local games to 56,700-seat Shea Stadium and the team's attendance immediately increased to an average of 1.8 million per year. During its early years in the league, the Mets were managed by a gnarled, bow-legged legend with a great personality named Casey Stengel. In addition to his fifty years of experience in the game, Stengel had coached the New York Yankees to seven World Series championships between 1949 and 1960.

In the end, it was challenges from teams in a newly established Continental League and threats from Congress to eliminate organized baseball's exemption from the antitrust laws that primarily affected MLB's decision to expand into the New York area during the early 1960s. However, another crucial factor in placing an expansion team in New York–and then effectively getting it organized and prepared for the 1962 MLB season–was the political leadership of Mayor Robert Wagner, the power and wealth of Joan Payson and Donald Grant, and the baseball experience of president George Weiss and later, the team's manager, Casey Stengel. Without their interest in and dedication to the city as a sports metropolis, New York may not have received a NL team for years after 1962.

Montreal (1969)

Throughout the 1940s and 1950s, a popular Brooklyn Dodgers minor-league Canadian-based baseball team named the Montreal Royals existed as a member of the International League. Such great Hall of Fame ballplayers and former Dodgers as infielder Jackie Robinson, outfielder Duke Snider, and catcher Roy Campanella each played for the Royals, which, at least during one season, had attracted more than 600,000 to its home games and earned a profit that exceeded $300,000. After the Dodgers moved from Brooklyn to Los Angeles in late 1957/early 1958, the Montreal Royals terminated their affiliation with the Dodgers.

An attempt to bring a MLB club to Montreal began in the early-to-mid-1960s. That effort was led, in part, by Canadian Gerry Snyder, who served as a member of Montreal's City Council from the district of Snowdon. During his twenty-six-year tenure in government, Snyder chaired the city's executive committee, became the mayor's liaison to people in the community who spoke English, and contributed numerous hours to bring the 1976 Summer Olympic Games and Formula One Grand Prix of Canada to sites in Montreal.

In late 1967, Snyder presented a bid to an expansion committee of MLB for a new team to be placed in Canada's second most populated metropolitan area. In complete support of Snyder's bid from the NL was Los Angeles Dodgers' owner Walter O'Malley. That year, he was the chairman of baseball's expansion committee and for nearly two decades, his team had an affiliation with the minor-league Montreal Royals. Consequently, five months after Synder's bid, NL president Warren Giles announced that Montreal was awarded a franchise to play in the league's East Division as of the 1969 MLB season.[11]

Following Giles' announcement, the NL demanded a payment of $1.1 million—or about 10 percent of its franchise initiation fee—from the new team's group of investors. Furthermore, the league required that the expansion franchise's ownership be organized and financially secure, and also for it to play its home games within an adequate ballpark in the Montreal area for the club's regular season in 1969 and possibly thereafter.

Within weeks, the league's requirements became a significant issue when Montreal multimillionaire Jean Luis Levesque withdrew his support of, and participation in, this baseball project. To replace Levesque, Gerry Snyder then convinced Seagram Ltd.'s stockholder and wealthy businessman Charles Bronfman to guarantee and provide enough Canadian and US dollars to purchase the expansion franchise from the NL. As a result of Synder's efforts, Bronfman bought a majority interest in the club, and later became the group's chairman of the board of directors.

The next task for the ownership group was choosing an appropriate, clever, and marketable nickname for their new expansion team in Montreal. Since a club in Kansas City nicknamed the Royals already existed in the AL's West Division, the new owners held a name-the-team contest to attract input of baseball fans in Montreal. After considering such nicknames as the Nationals and Voyageurs, the owners decided to select Expos because it was pronounced the same whether in French or

11 *"Montreal Expos," www.baseballalmanac.com cited 21 September 2017 and Frank P. Jozsa Jr., National League Franchises: Team Performances and Business Success (New York, NY: Springer, 2015). For more news about anticipation of expansion into the city, see Pat Hickey, "Blue Jays Back in Montreal Amid High Hopes for New Team," Montreal Gazette (1 April 2017): E.1; Kevin Mio, "Montreal a 'Frontrunner' for Expansion, MLB's Manfred Says," Montreal Gazette (7 May 2016): D.3; "Montreal Mayor Coderre Delighted That Baseball Commissioner Supports Expansion," The Canadian Press (25 September 2015): 1.*

English. Moreover, the 1967 World's Fair, or Expo 67, was a huge success when it occurred in the Montreal area.

Another crucial obstacle to overcome was the construction of a large and suitable ballpark that met MLB's standards regarding its architecture, capacity, location, safety, and other features. Being the former home of the Montreal Royals, Delorimier Downs was rejected for being too small even for temporary use while a local facility named the Autostade required more than 10,000 seats, a dome, and other expensive renovations that discouraged city officials from using it as a home ballpark for the Expos.

During mid-summer of 1968, NL president Giles and MLB Commissioner Bowie Kuhn travelled to northwest Montreal to attend a local amateur baseball game played at 2,000-seat Jarry Park. After he was recognized and enthusiastically cheered by fans while at the game, Giles approved Jarry Park as a temporary site for home games of the Expos. However, the city had less than one year to adequately renovate it and significantly increase the number of seats.

For approximately $4 million (Canadian) and within four months, Jarry Park's capacity was expanded by adding 26,000 makeshift seats and 5,000 parking spaces. The Expos hired veteran baseball executive John McHale to operate the franchise and he recruited former Philadelphia Phillies coach Gene Mauch as the club's first field manager.

After baseball's fall expansion draft in 1968 to acquire players and before completing renovation of Jarry Park, the Expos played their first game in New York's Shea Stadium on the opening day of the 1969 MLB season against the Mets and won it 11–10. Then on April 14, 1969, the Expos defeated the St. Louis Cardinals 8–7 before 29,180 spectators at Jarry Park and millions of Canadians who watched it on television or listened on the radio. The Expos continued to play their home games in refurbished Jarry Park until 1977, when 46,000-seat Olympic Stadium opened for the team in Montreal.

Based on these facts and other information discussed thus far in this section, it was certainly a huge risk for the NL to approve the Montreal area as a site for an expansion franchise during the late 1960s. Indeed, ice hockey had always been

Canada's national pastime while American baseball ranked as an inferior team sport among that nation's athletes, communities, and fans. Before 1969, the minor-league Montreal Royals terminated their affiliation with the Los Angeles Dodgers; at least one major Canadian investor withdrew his support of the new expansion franchise as a baseball project; three ballparks within Montreal did not meet MLB's requirements; and many sports events in Canada were broadcast on television and the radio in French and not English.

Despite these and other obstacles, the Expos played their home games in Montreal for thirty-six big-league years but failed to win a NL pennant or compete in a World Series. After MLB's 2004 season, the club was sold to a new group of investors and then moved to Washington, DC by its existing owners.

San Diego (1969)

Since the mid-to-late 1930s, a minor-league baseball team named the San Diego Padres had performed in the Pacific Coast League (PCL) in sunny California where the club was successful and won several PCL championships. Then in the mid-1950s, prominent and well-known businessman C. Arnholdt Smith—whose commercial investments included banking, tuna fishing, real estate, and an airline—purchased the Padres and moved his club from Lane Field in San Diego to the city's beautiful Westgate Park. Meanwhile, a majority of voters in the area approved a multimillion-dollar bond issue to build 50,000-seat San Diego Stadium in which the PCL Padres and NFL Chargers would play their home games.[12]

When MLB initially announced that the NL would increase by two new teams in 1969, Smith organized a syndicate to bid for the rights to own one of the league's expansion franchises. Besides Smith, a former Brooklyn and Los Angeles Dodgers executive named Emil J. "Buzzie" Bavasi also led a campaign to bring MLB to San Diego. Bavasi convinced baseball club owners that the metropolitan area's population of approximately1.4 million residents would support a MLB team. Furthermore, he pointed out that the city's location on the west coast had ideal weather conditions and a wonderful climate, San Diego had been a great sports city and baseball site

12 *David L. Porter, "San Diego Padres: The Saga of Big Mac and Trader Jack," in Encyclopedia of Major League Baseball: National League, 465–512, and "San Diego Padres," www.mlb.com cited 22 September 2017.*

for decades, and the local ballpark contained enough capacity to host big-league games.

As a further incentive to obtain a franchise from the NL and have it succeed, Smith agreed to borrow enough money to pay a fee of $12.5 million to the league. Moreover, he persuaded the city of San Diego to establish an association that would advertise, market, and otherwise promote the team within the metropolitan area. Thus, it was Smith who provided financial support and convinced city officials interested in the project to host a new MLB team, while Bavasi contributed his experience, knowledge, and talent from being involved in professional baseball operations for more than twenty-five years. During May 1968, a NL expansion franchise was unanimously awarded to Smith and his syndicate.

For a few years, the Padres struggled financially and competitively against the Los Angeles Dodgers for support from southern California's baseball fans, and to earn an identity and recognition among MLB franchise owners of being a viable major league enterprise. Furthermore, the Padres did not receive a share of the league's television revenues until 1972 while it tried to lure San Diegans from their other outdoor sports activities like fishing, golf, and tennis.

Besides the team's cash flow, marketing, operational, and attendance problems at home games in San Diego Stadium, Smith was indicted for tax evasion in 1973. As a result, a group of investors offered to purchase the Padres franchise and move it to Washington, DC for the 1974 MLB season. However, Smith refused to deal with them and instead sold his team for $12 million to McDonald's co-founder Ray Kroc who was committed to keeping the team in the San Diego area.

As denoted in tables A7.3 and A7.4 in the appendix, San Diego ranked twenty-third in population among all US metropolitan areas during the late 1960s. Moreover, it was a prime market both commercially and demographically because of sustainable economic growth and commercial development. In addition, thousands of people in the area participated in recreational activities and likewise attended outdoor sports events. Although businesses in the community did not originally support a big league franchise, eventually many of their employees and customers decided to attend home games in MLB's regular seasons, become loyal baseball fans, and financially contribute in different ways to Padres' teams each year.

In the end, it was visionaries such as Arnholdt Smith and Buzzie Bavasi who combined their experience, financial capital, prestige, and power to bring an expansion team into the San Diego area. Although the club has been sold and resold since former owner Ray Kroc's death in 1984, the Padres have won five West Division titles and two NL pennants but zero World Series during its 50-year history.

Denver (1993)

Between 1990 and 1992, the population in Denver and their per capita income increased, respectively, by approximately six and nine percent, while in 1990, the area ranked twenty-fourth in total population. In professional sports, the former Super Bowl champions NFL Broncos had played their home games in the city since 1970 and as of 1976, so did the competitive NBA Nuggets and NHL Rockies. Likewise, each of them had been popular and well-respected professional teams that performed each season in games at their respective stadiums before relatively midsized-to-large groups of fans. Thus, through the early 1990s, the Denver metropolitan area had experienced a multiyear history of hosting elite sports franchises.

During the early to mid-1980s, a number of talented NL Pittsburgh Pirates ballplayers used illegal drugs including steroids and were given a one-year suspension from the game by MLB Commissioner Peter Ueberroth. Soon after those suspensions but before a public-private syndicate had purchased Pittsburgh's club for $22 million from owner John Galbreath and Warner Communications in 1985, rumors circulated within baseball's community that the Pirates might move their operations from Pittsburgh to Denver. Although that relocation did not occur, a Colorado Baseball Commission based in Denver succeeded in getting the city's voters to approve a 0.1 percent sales tax in order to finance a new baseball stadium that would qualify as a big-league ballpark and in turn, attract a MLB team to the metropolitan area.

Sometime in 1990, Colorado Governor Roy Romer organized an advisory committee to recruit an ownership group who would efficiently prepare a realistic bid and then submit it to MLB for an expansion franchise. The group selected by the committee was composed of various Denver executives from such local and regional businesses as the Phar-Mor drugstore chain, Hensel Phelps Construction, and the Rocky Mountain News.

After presenting their bid to existing owners of NL teams at a meeting during the summer of 1991, Denver was approved as a site for a new professional team to play beginning in the 1993 MLB season. For an expansion fee of $95 million, the Colorado Rockies signed a lease to perform their home games at the NFL Broncos' Mile High Stadium as planned in 1993–1994, or until the construction of the club's new ballpark, Coors Field, was completed in the Denver area.[13]

Before the Rockies played their first MLB game, an accounting and embezzlement scandal occurred at Phar-Mor. As a result, Ohio beverage distributor John Antonucci and Phar-Mor's chief executive officer Michael I. Monus resigned from the team's organization and then sold their shares of the franchise to other investors. Trucking company executive Jerry McMorris replaced them, becoming head of the new franchise's ownership group and spokesperson of the team's management. Unfortunately, McMorris' trucking business failed in 1999 and furthermore, he had disagreements and serious disputes with other members of the franchise's syndicate. Consequently, McMorris' share of the club was purchased by others in the group in 2005. Three years later, businessmen Charlie and Dick Monfort gained control of the Rockies.

Despite a number of ownership problems since 1993, baseball's Rockies have been as popular in Denver as the NFL Broncos, NBA Nuggets, and NHL Rockies. In fact, the MLB club set attendance records at home games in 1993 and again in 1995–1998, as it gradually established a large fan base in the area.

In retrospect, MLB made a prudent and wise decision in approving an expansion team for the Denver area in 1991. Although the baseball franchise has experienced some troubles because of problems among its previous owners, the executive management and various leaders of the team's operations have seemingly stabilized the Rockies and improved their opportunities to be a profitable business enterprise and successful entertainment company.

The major challenge each season, of course, is for the NL Rockies to compete in the playoffs, win their first division title, another league pennant, and then a World

---

13 *See "Colorado Rockies," www.mlb.com cited 23 September 2017 and also the team's history in baseball-reference.com and sportsencyclopedia.com.*

Series. To accomplish its goals in the sport, the club needs to defeat the Los Angeles Dodgers, San Diego Padres, and San Francisco Giants in enough games at their ballparks and win the majority of games played at Coors Field.

Miami (1993)

During early 1990, Blockbuster Entertainment Corporation's chief executive officer H. Wayne Huizenga spent an estimated $30 million when he purchased 15 percent of the NFL Dolphins and 50 percent of this professional football team's home facility—75,000-seat Joe Robbie Stadium. Besides those assets, Huizenga also announced to the media that he wanted to acquire, invest in, and own a MLB franchise and then locate it at a site in the Miami area. Meanwhile, MLB had stated its goal of increasing the NL from twelve to fourteen clubs for the 1993 season. A major concern of Huizenga's, however, was to convince the league that his experience, expertise, and vision as a businessman reinforced his idea that the best place to locate a new baseball team was in Miami rather than in the Jacksonville, Orlando, or Tampa Bay area.

After successfully presenting a bid to a committee of MLB team owners, the NL awarded Huizenga an expansion franchise that would be based in Miami for a fee of $95 million. That decision meant that $100 million Joe Robbie Stadium—later renamed Pro Player Park, Pro Player Stadium, and then Dolphin Stadium—had to be converted to a multipurpose facility.[14]

Since NFL Dolphins founder Joe Robbie had anticipated that a professional baseball team would eventually find a home based in Miami, he assured baseball officials that his stadium had an extremely wide field to accommodate future MLB games. As a result, some seats in Joe Robbie Stadium were placed more than 800 feet from home plate while seats in the upper deck were far away from the ballfield. Consequently, Huizenga renovated Robbie Stadium by reducing its capacity for baseball games from 67,000 to approximately 44,000 and then later to approximately 36,000. Within three years of naming his baseball team the Florida Marlins, Huizenga purchased

---

14 *For more information about the Florida/Miami Marlins, read Frank P. Jozsa Jr. and John J. Guthrie Jr., Relocating Teams and Expanding Leagues in Professional Sports: How the Major Leagues Respond to Market Conditions and Frank P. Jozsa Jr., Major League Baseball Expansions and Team Relocations: A History, 1876–2008.*

the remaining 85 percent of the Dolphins franchise and 50 percent of Joe Robbie Stadium.

Another issue that affected Huizenga's new team was excessively hot and humid summers in south Florida. Indeed, these conditions made it very uncomfortable or even unbearable for most spectators, and particularly senior citizens, who attended many Marlins games during afternoons and weekends. To solve this ongoing problem, Huizenga received a waiver from MLB and the Entertainment Sports Programming Network (ESPN) that allowed his team to play some of its home games during Sunday evenings. Years before the Marlins requested and received their waiver, the AL's Texas Rangers had obtained a similar agreement from big-league baseball regarding a portion of its weekend games at Ameriquest Field in Arlington.

To conclude this section of the chapter, the seventh and final NL expansion franchise—and a discussion of its local and regional markets for professional baseball—is presented next. Then, it is followed by reviewing the performances of this team, the Marlins, and the other five NL clubs existing at sites before them.

Phoenix (1998)

Since the 1940s, the Phoenix area has increased tremendously in population and has also served as a spring training site for various MLB teams. Because of these advantages, an attempt to host a big-league club in the area occurred during the late 1980s when the owners of an AAA minor-league team and an affiliate of the San Francisco Giants named the Phoenix Firebirds, asked the NFL Cardinals' owner Bill Bidwill to share a proposed 70,000-seat domed stadium in the city. That request failed after Bidwill signed a lease with Arizona State University to use Sun Devil Stadium as a home football field when his Cardinals moved from St. Louis to Phoenix in 1988.

During 1993, the majority owner of the NBA Suns, Jerry Colangelo, announced to the media that he had assembled a business group named Arizona Baseball, Inc. that would apply for a MLB expansion franchise. After two years of work on a comprehensive and detailed proposal, the group submitted its bid to the league in early 1995. Subsequently, the bid received enthusiastic support from Chicago White Sox and Chicago Bulls owner Jerry Reinsdorf and from the acting baseball commissioner, Bud Selig. In part, the bid impressed them because Colangelo and Reinsdorf were good friends but also because it included plans for the construction of a retractable roof stadium to be named Bank One Ballpark.

After MLB evaluated this and other offers from investors and syndicates, Colangelo's Arizona Baseball, Inc. was awarded a new MLB franchise for the 1998 season. As a result, this decision required that the ownership group must pay an entry fee of $130 million to MLB. Initially, the expansion team was assigned to the AL's West Division. However, for business, demographic, and sport-specific reasons, Colangelo insisted his team play in the NL West Division.[15]

First, Phoenix was located near San Diego and close enough to Denver and Los Angeles to establish rivalries; second, similar demographic characteristics existed between the fast-growing economies and populations of Denver and Phoenix; third, tourists from San Diego had visited areas within southwest Arizona for decades; fourth, a history of relationships had developed between the Firebirds in Phoenix and NL Giants in San Francisco; and fifth, hundreds of baseball games of the Dodgers, Giants, and Padres had been broadcast for years into the markets of Phoenix and Tucson. In short, these factors convinced MLB officials to put Colangelo's franchise in the NL's West Division.

To identify their new team, Colangelo's ownership group held a name-the-team contest that appeared in early 1995 on a full-page of the *Arizona Republic*. For a

---

15 *"Teams," www.mlb.com cited 8 September 2017 and the Official Major League Baseball Fact Book 2005 Edition (St. Louis, MO: Sporting News, 2005).*
Some interesting but also relevant topics in articles about expansion in MLB are as follows: Bob McManaman, "Manfred Talks DH, Expansion and Trump," Arizona Republic (23 February 2016): C.3; Tyler Kepner, "Commissioner, Pointing to Growth, Says He is Open to First Expansion Since 1998," New York Times (15 July 2015): B9; Bill Shaikin, "MLB Boss: Expansion Could be on the Table," The Patriot (16 July 2015): S.6; Mike Dodd, "MLB's Growth Spurt Began 50 Years Ago," USA Today (8 April 2011): C.1; Carlos Frias, "Power Surge: Expansion Jolts Number of Home Runs," The Atlanta Journal (25 April 2002): F.1; Joseph Duarte, "Neverland: Attempts to Bring Baseball to Disney's World Appear Over," Houston Chronicle (3 March 2002): G.2; Tracy Ringolsby, "Expansion Backfired on Baseball," Cincinnati Post (9 November 2001): 1C; Glenn Dickey, "Baseball is Doing Its Homework on Expansion," San Francisco Chronicle (30 August 2000): E.6; John Delcos, "Baseball Needs Fewer Teams, Not More Divisions," The Journal News (14 May 2000): C.3. More recent articles about expansion in baseball include: Evan Weiner, "MLB Expansion is on the Table," www.thesportdigest.com cited 1 November 2018; Chris Mitchell, "MLB Needs to Expand; Here's Where," www.fangraphs.com cited 1 November 2018; Jay Jaffe, "If MLB Considers Expansion, What Would a 32-Team Look Like," www.si.com cited 1 November 2018; Dakota Randall, "MILB President Thinks MLB 'Will Happen' But 'Not Imminent'," www.nesn.com cited 1 November 2018.

prize of two lifetime season tickets to the team's home games, the winning entry was the Diamondbacks, a species of snake that injects large amounts of venom into its victims.

Based on that nickname, Colangelo wanted to market and promote his expansion club to a statewide fan base and not limit its appeal to one city or area. Thus, he decided to call the team Arizona Diamondbacks and not Phoenix Diamondbacks. In the end, this was a clever strategy since fans in other areas of the state embraced the word *Arizona* in the team's title rather than the state's largest city and capital, Phoenix.

Some other plans of the expansion franchise involved the city of Tucson, Arizona. Being a ninety-minute drive from Phoenix, Tucson became home of the Diamondbacks' spring training camp and the Tucson Sidewinders, which was the Diamondbacks' top minor-league affiliate. To generate interest in the franchise from baseball fans in other areas of the southwest besides Phoenix and Tucson, the Diamondbacks signed broadcast deals with radio stations and television networks based in several cities such as Flagstaff and Prescott in Arizona, and Las Vegas in Nevada.

Other innovations of the new team implemented during the mid-1990s and early 2000s included motor coach trips for fans from Tucson to Bank One Ballpark to attend the Diamondbacks' home games, and public appearances by various sports broadcasters, management representatives, and a number of players before midsized and small groups in communities within Arizona. In short, Colangelo's vision was to expand the team's market far beyond the Phoenix area, and according to some officials in baseball, he succeeded in that effort.

During the early-to-mid-1960s to late 1990s, the seven NL expansion franchises highlighted in this section were more popular and prosperous than were their seven counterparts in the AL. Indeed, the AL Senators relocated to Minneapolis after existing for eleven years in Washington, DC while the Pilots folded in Seattle after one season, and in 1970, the club filed for bankruptcy and then moved their operations to Milwaukee.

Although the Angels relocated from Los Angeles to Anaheim in 1965, the other four AL clubs have each remained at their original sites. In contrast to expansion franchises in the AL, the seven new clubs in the NL each struggled in various years since expansion, but for one reason or another, they recovered and each of them has continued to perform at home games before millions of baseball fans from within their metropolitan areas and surrounding markets. This includes the Houston Astros, who switched from the competitive NL Central to AL West after their 2012 season.

Table 7.2 includes the performances of expansion teams from their first season in the league to 2018. Prior to 1901, the most successful teams were the New York Gothams/Giants, Providence Grays, and Detroit Wolverines, while those with winning percentages less than 35 percent were the Milwaukee Grays, Syracuse Stars, Kansas City Cowboys, and Washington Nationals. In 1888 and 1889, the Giants won NL pennants and defeated teams from the American Association in postseason playoffs. However, the Philadelphia Quakers/Phillies and eleven other NL clubs failed to win a title between 1876 and 1900.

Table 7.2 National League Expansion Teams, Seasons, and Performances, Selected Years

			Performances			
Team	**Year**	**Seasons**	**Playoffs**	**Divisions**	**Pennants**	**World Series**
Pre-1901 Expansions						
Indianapolis Blues	1878	1	0	NA	0	NA
Milwaukee Grays	1878	1	0	NA	0	NA
Providence Grays	1878	8	2	NA	2	NA
Buffalo Bisons	1879	7	0	NA	0	NA
Cleveland Blues	1879	6	0	NA	0	NA
Syracuse Stars	1879	1	0	NA	0	NA
Troy Trojans	1879	4	0	NA	0	NA
Worcester Ruby Legs	1880	3	0	NA	0	NA
Detroit Wolverines	1881	8	1	NA	1	NA
New York Gothams/ Giants	1883	75	4	NA	17	5

Team	Year	Seasons	Performances Playoffs	Divisions	Pennants	World Series
Philadelphia Quakers/ Phillies	1883	136	14	12	7	2
Kansas City Cowboys	1886	1	0	NA	0	NA
Washington Nationals	1886	4	0	NA	0	NA
Indianapolis Hoosiers	1887	3	0	NA	0	NA
Cleveland Spiders	1889	11	0	NA	0	NA
Post-1900 Expansions						
Houston Colt .45s/ Astros	1962	51	11	6	1	0
New York Mets	1962	57	9	6	5	2
Montreal Expos	1969	36	1	1	0	0
San Diego Padres	1969	50	5	5	2	0
Colorado Rockies	1993	26	5	0	1	0
Florida/Miami Marlins	1993	26	2	0	2	2
Arizona Diamondbacks	1998	24	6	5	1	1

Note: Team is self-explanatory. Year is each team's first season in the National League or its expansion year. The column Seasons is the total number of baseball seasons of each expansion team in the National League. NA is not applicable. The initial World Series between winners of the American League and National League was played in 1903. Major League Baseball teams did not play in divisions until 1969. Divisions, pennants, and World Series are number of titles won by these teams since their expansion year. The New York Gothams were nicknamed Giants in 1885; Philadelphia Quakers the Phillies in 1890; Houston Colt .45s the Astros in 1964. Florida Marlins became Miami Marlins in 2012. Data does not include Astros' performances in the American League from MLB's 2013 to 2018 season.

Source: The World Almanac and Book of Facts, 1930–2016; "World Series History," www.baseball-reference.com cited 18 September 2017; "Teams," www.mlb.com cited 8 September 2017.

Regarding post-1900 expansion franchises in the NL, the Houston .45s/Astros and Arizona Diamondbacks each had the highest winning percentage at approximately 49 percent while the lowest at 46 percent included the San Diego Padres, Colorado Rockies, and Florida/Miami Marlins. In the table, the distribution also denotes NL teams' number of seasons and which in the group qualified for the most and least playoffs and winning or not winning division titles, pennants, and World Series. After MLB's 2018 season, such clubs as the Padres and Rockies may eventually improve enough to challenge the Dodgers, Giants, and Diamondbacks in the league's West Division and finally become a champion for the first time.

Since the Expos moved from Montreal to Washington DC in 2005, there has been a movement in the Canadian city to attract a MLB franchise and local support for building a ballpark downtown. Furthermore, during September 2017, MLB Commissioner Rob Manfred mentioned Portland, Oregon as a potential site for a new franchise. In fact, there was an ownership group in Portland that had financing along with support for a ballpark, partially funded by a $150 million grant. Approved by the state of Oregon to help finance a ballpark, the grant may still be available. As such, there is a growing consensus that baseball will expand into thirty-two teams, which in turn, may or may not lead to realignment and adjustment in the grant may still be available. As such, there is a growing consensus that baseball will expand into thirty-two teams, which in turn, may or may not lead to realignment and adjustment in schedule.

CHAPTER 8

Franchise Business

Besides being competitive and performing in regular-season and perhaps one or more postseason games within the American League or National League, a Major League Baseball (MLB) team is also a franchise or business organization. From this perspective, its economic goal is to maximize profit from operations based on the difference between total revenues and total costs.

There are several internal and external variables or factors that may or may not influence the operations of a baseball franchise—such as the Atlanta Braves and Boston Red Sox—in both the short and long run. In the book *Business Inc.*, the author identifies and then discusses different tasks that MLB organizations are involved in and must responsibly complete including those in such office departments as accounting, finance, human resources, international relations, legal, management, and marketing.[1]

As members of a group of clubs or league in the professional sports industry, each MLB enterprise is controlled by an owner or ownership syndicate and consists of executives, at least one general manager, and many other personnel and staff.

1 *See Frank P. Jozsa Jr., Baseball, Inc.: The National Pastime As Big Business (Jefferson, NC: McFarland, 2006). Three other prominent books about the topic include James Quirk and Rodney D. Fort, Pay Dirt: The Business of Professional Team Sports (Princeton, NJ: Princeton University Press, 1992); Kenneth L. Shropshire, The Sports Franchise Game: Cities in Pursuit of Sports Franchises, Events, Stadiums, and Arenas (Philadelphia, PA: University of Pennsylvania Press, 1995); Michael Lewis, Moneyball: The Art of Winning an Unfair Game (New York, NY: W.W. Norton & Company, 2004).*

Besides solving problems and making optimum decisions, these individuals are also responsible for any duties, requirements, and tasks that directly or indirectly affect their team as an organization within a community.

In order for readers of *The Making of Modern Baseball* to learn about the activities, operations, and accomplishments of MLB franchises and also important performances as commercial, for-profit businesses, this chapter discusses their results in various seasons. Besides cultural, demographic, and sport-specific data from the literature, there are descriptive, practical, and actual statistics, along with other types of quantitative information in tables within the chapter and appendix. This includes economic, financial, and other relevant topics and relationships concerning these different professional baseball organizations and recent facts about their location, history, and success while based in a small, midsized, or large market.

AMERICAN LEAGUE

Team Attendances

In the American League (AL) during regular seasons, teams play home games in their ballparks to entertain people who purchase tickets at various prices for seats and organizations that lease luxury suites. This generates gate receipts and operating income which, in turn, contributes to total revenue.[2]

To measure and determine to what extent different teams in the league attracted fans to their games and to compare them to each other, table 8.1 reveals the average home attendances of sixteen AL clubs as of ten seasons in five-year increments. What does the data denote about one or more of them?

---

2 *Besides the supplement in Pay Dirt, historical home attendances of MLB teams are available in "Rodney Fort's Sports Business Data," www.umich.app.box.com cited 6 October 2017; "MLB Attendance Reports," www.espn.com cited 6 October 2017; "MLB Attendance & Team Age," www.baseball-reference.com cited 6 October 2017.*

As reported in table 8.1, average attendance increased per team from approximately 13,000 in 1971 to 28,000 in 2016, or by 115 percent. Based on data for ten seasons of the period, the average declined in 1996, 2011, and 2016 relative to the previous five years. Thus, the overall trend of the group was positive because the sport expanded and more fans attended games of teams even though some had losing records within their division.[3]

Despite higher ticket prices, the Yankees ranked first in attendance four times while such clubs as the Orioles, Red Sox, Angels, Mariners, and Blue Jays had the most at least once. Alternatively, the lowest averages tended to occur in seasons for the Indians, Royals, Athletics, and Rays. Between these two groups were such clubs as the White Sox, Tigers, and Rangers.

For various reasons, some teams had unusually large and small changes in attendances within consecutive seasons of the table. For example, the Athletics increased in rank from eleventh in 1976 to fourth in 1981; White Sox from tenth in 1986 to second in 1991; Angels from eighth in 2001 to second in 2006; and Blue Jays from tenth in 2011 to first in 2016. Such things as performing in new or renovated ballparks at home, winning a majority of games within their division, competing for a league title, pennant, or World Series, or simply playing with better ballplayers on the roster caused them to attract larger crowds to games at their ballparks.

In contrast, the average attendances of a few teams declined and they drastically fell in rank. This was apparent for the Orioles from 2001 to 2006; Yankees from 1986 to 1991; Mariners from 2001 to 2006; and Twins from 1971 to 1976 and again from 2011 to 2016. These clubs went from being successful and productive to having worse seasons and smaller attendances due to changes in coaches, injuries to key players, more competition within their division, failing to entertain fans in games, and higher ticket prices.

---

3 *From the 2016 to 2017 MLB season, the AL teams' home attendances remained relatively constant at 28,000 per game. Similarly, so did the deviation in attendances among the group. Because of poor performances, higher ticket prices, and other reasons, ten clubs in the league failed to attract more fans to their home games in 2017 compared to 2016. See Table 5.3 for how teams ranked in attendances in six of their seasons.*

Table 8.1 Average Home Attendance, American League Teams, Selected MLB Seasons

	Seasons									
Team	**1971**	**1976**	**1981**	**1986**	**1991**	**1996**	**2001**	**2006**	**2011**	**2016**
Baltimore Orioles	13.2	13.0	18.6	24.9	31.5	44.4	38.6	26.5	21.6	26.8
Boston Red Sox	20.9	23.4	20.0	26.5	31.6	28.5	32.4	36.1	37.7	36.4
Chicago White Sox	20.4	11.4	19.3	17.5	36.2	20.5	22.0	36.5	24.7	21.9
Cleveland Indians	7.3	12.0	12.2	18.1	12.8	41.2	39.6	24.6	22.7	19.6
Detroit Tigers	19.6	18.3	20.8	23.4	20.2	14.4	24.0	32.0	32.6	31.1
Houston Astros	NA	NA	NA	NA	NA	NA	NA	NA	NA	28.4
Kansas City Royals	11.2	20.7	27.2	28.6	26.6	17.8	18.9	17.1	21.2	31.5
LA Angels of Anaheim	11.4	12.5	26.6	32.3	29.8	22.6	24.7	42.1	39.0	37.2
Milwaukee Brewers	8.9	12.4	17.8	15.9	18.4	16.3	NA	NA	NA	NA
Minnesota Twins	11.9	8.8	7.6	15.4	28.3	17.7	22.2	28.2	39.1	27.0
New York Yankees	13.2	25.1	31.6	28.3	23.0	27.7	40.8	51.8	45.1	29.9
Oakland Athletics	11.2	9.6	23.2	15.8	33.5	14.1	26.3	24.4	18.2	18.7
Seattle Mariners	NA	NA	11.1	12.5	26.5	33.8	43.3	30.6	23.4	27.9
Tampa Bay Rays	NA	NA	NA	NA	NA	NA	16.0	16.9	18.8	15.8
Texas Rangers	NA	14.3	15.1	20.8	28.3	35.4	34.9	29.4	36.3	33.4
Toronto Blue Jays	NA	NA	14.2	30.3	49.4	31.8	23.6	28.4	22.4	41.8
Washington Senators	8.0	NA	NA	NA	NA	NA	NA	NA	NA	NA

Note: Average attendance is in thousands. This season is not applicable (NA) for the team. Abbreviated is Major League Baseball (MLB) and Los Angeles (LA).

Source: "MLB Attendances," www.baseball-reference.com cited 22 September 2017 and Chapter 2 in Frank P. Jozsa Jr., Baseball in Crisis: Spiraling Costs, Bad Behavior, Uncertain Future (Jefferson, NC: McFarland, 2008).

Three years after shifting from the National League Central Division (CD) to the AL West Division (WD), the Astros ranked eighth in attendance in 2016, sixth in 2017, and third in 2018. After finishing in fifth and then fourth place of its division, the team was second in 2015 and third in 2016. One year later, Houston won the WD with the best record in the league and its first World Series. Led by manager A.J.

Hinch and such sluggers as Jose Altuve, Carlos Correa, and George Springer, along with pitchers Dallas Keuchel, Charlie Morton, and Brad Peacock, the team became popular and fun to watch in games at home in its midsized-to-large market.

In MLB's 1971 season, the Washington Senators finished thirty-eight games behind the Orioles in the East Division (ED) and eleventh in attendance among twelve teams in the league. After forfeiting their final game to the Yankees in the ninth inning, fans swarmed out of their seats in the stands and began tearing up RFK Stadium. A few months later, the franchise moved to the city of Arlington and became the Texas Rangers.[4]

There are other interesting and important results to highlight regarding the numbers in table 8.1. The Rays' average attendances, for example, have varied in rank from thirteenth in 2011 to fifteenth in 2016. Since 1998, this small-market club has won only two division titles and one league championship. Besides problems with its inferior ballpark and performances against rivals in the AL's ED, the franchise struggled to attract fans to most home games at Tropicana Field. This trend will likely continue unless the team's owner invests more resources in the organization to recruit and hire talented, but expensive, free agents.

Based on its six seasons in the table, the Brewers' attendances at County Stadium ranked from eighth in 1976 to thirteenth in 1991. Other than winning consecutive division titles in 1981–1982, the club usually finished between third and seventh in its division. After such great players as Paul Molitor and Robin Yount retired, the franchise could not revive or stimulate its fan base. As a result, the team moved from the AL's Central Division (CD) to the NL's in 1998. Since then, the club's average attendances have increased to more than 30,000 per game, with the team finishing second to fourth in the CD despite competition from the Cardinals and Cubs.

The Blue Jays' average attendances have really changed based on its eight seasons in the table. They ranked first or second in 1986, 1991, and 2016, fifth in 1996, eighth in 2006, and tenth or worse in the other three years. The club's fan base mostly attended Toronto's games during the late 1980s and early 1990s when it

4 *References are James R. Hartley, Washington's Expansion Senators (1961–1971) (Germantown, MD: Corduroy Press, 1998) and "Washington Senators," www.baseball-reference.com cited 19 September 2017.*

won four division titles and consecutive World Series in 1991–1992. When the Blue Jays finished second to the Red Sox in 2016 despite losing to the Indians in the AL Championship Series (ALCS), their attendance exceeded 41,000 per game. Besides being successful in games, the team was very popular among fans during these seasons.[5]

From the 2016 to 2017 MLB season, the average attendances of AL teams increased from 28,400 to 28,500 per game, or by less than one percent. While the Yankees ranked first, Blue Jays second, and Angels third, the White Sox were thirteenth, Athletics fourteenth, and Rays fifteenth. Such clubs as the Yankees, Indians, and Astros improved in rank but, for example, the Orioles, Royals, and Tigers did not. Among AL postseason teams in 2017, their home attendances increased except for the Red Sox and Twins (wild card). Besides that data, the average variation or spread in attendance of the fifteen teams was constant from year to year at 7,200. In other words, results were very similar in 2016 and 2017 with respect to this baseball variable.[6]

In comparison to MLB's 2017 season, however, average attendance in 2018 decreased by approximately 7 percent, or from 28,500 to 26,600. Although the Yankees and Astros had more fans at their home games on average in 2018, the other thirteen clubs failed to attract more people to games in their ballparks. This included such division winners as the Red Sox and Indians and the wild card Athletics. Unfortunately, the league's average in 2018 was the lowest since 1996 despite growth in the US and Canadian economies and higher disposable and household income in these countries. Regarding their average deviation in home attendances, AL teams increased by 1,000 per game from 2017 to 2018 because of significant changes in performances by some of them like the Orioles, Astros, Royals, and Blue Jays.

---

5 *"Toronto Blue Jays," www.mlb.com cited 6 October 2017, "Toronto Blue Jays Team History and Encyclopedia," www.baseball-reference.com cited 6 October 2017, and "Blue Jays Timeline," www.toronto.bluejays.mlb.com cited 6 October 2017.*

6 *See AL teams' attendance data for MLB's 2017 season at "The Business of Baseball," www.forbes.com cited 5 November 2018.*

Financial Data

Similar to enterprises and other organization in various sectors of the US economy, MLB franchises generate financial information annually from operations to determine their current status and progress as businesses in the professional sports industry. For tax and other reasons, this data is contained in documents such as balance sheets, cash flow accounts, and earnings statements. Prepared and maintained by staff accountants, these records are audited periodically and submitted to various government agencies to verify their accuracy, authenticity, and legality.

While the actual financial results for big-league baseball teams appear publicly in journals, magazines, and newspapers, they are incomplete, are usually outdated, and do not reveal enough information to thoroughly analyze these organizations from business and economic perspectives.

Rather than collect them from different sources in the literature, this and another section of the chapter used financial results and estimates published in *Forbes*. This is convenient and practical, and also an appropriate and realistic way to learn more about, compare, and rank MLB franchises financially, within the AL in table 8.2 and later in table 8.5 for those in the NL.[7]

As reflected in column two of table 8.2 for MLB's 2017 season, the revenue of AL franchises averaged approximately $309 million and the amounts varied or deviated from each other by $103 million. While the Yankees ranked first followed by the Red Sox and Astros, the Royals, Athletics, and Rays had the lowest revenue. According to data in the column, 10, or approximately 66 percent of the group, each earned amounts below the average. Thus, the four big-market teams in areas of New York, Boston, Houston, and Los Angeles received a total of $1.753 billion or 36 percent of all revenue, in the league during 2017. These clubs, in turn, attracted large numbers of fans to home games at their ballparks and charged them relatively high ticket prices.

---

7 *For other financial results of AL franchises, see chapters in books by Frank P. Jozsa Jr. including Baseball, Inc.: The National Pastime As Big Business; American League Franchises: Team Performances and Business Success (New York, NY: Springer, 2015); and Major League Baseball Organizations: Team Performances and Financial Consequences (Lanham, MD: Lexington Books, 2016).*

Table 8.2 Financial Data, American League Franchises, 2017 MLB Season

			Financial Data		
Franchise	**Revenue**	**Operating Income**	**Gate Receipts**	**Player Expenses**	**Valuations**
Baltimore Orioles	252	−26	54	183	1,200
Boston Red Sox	453	86	192	209	2,800
Chicago White Sox	266	30	48	119	1,500
Cleveland Indians	284	31	76	144	1,045
Detroit Tigers	277	−46	70	216	1,225
Houston Astros	347	77	137	141	1,650
Kansas City Royals	245	−17	64	168	1,015
LA Angels of Anaheim	334	25	95	188	1,800
Minnesota Twins	261	23	70	133	1,150
New York Yankees	619	14	278	220	4,000
Oakland Athletics	210	15	33	99	1,020
Seattle Mariners	288	−2.4	63	174	1,450
Tampa Bay Rays	219	23	28	98	900
Texas Rangers	311	30	77	171	1,600
Toronto Blue Jays	274	−1.3	83	180	1,350

Note: Financial data is in millions of dollars. Except for valuations, the amounts are for franchises' 2017 season. Revenue is net of stadium revenues used for debt payments. Operating income equals earnings before interest, taxes, depreciation, and amortization. Gate receipts include club seats. Player expenses include benefits and bonuses. Valuations are based on the current stadium deal without deductions for debt.

Source: "The Business of Baseball," www.forbes.com cited 22 September 2018.

In addition to the Royals, Rays, and Athletics, the AL's White Sox, Orioles, and Twins also had dismal results. Although the Twins were a wild card in the postseason, they and the Rangers, Tigers, and Mariners ranked among the worst in attendances at games at their ballparks. In addition, these franchises failed to generate substantial revenue in other ways such as from concessions, apparel and merchandise sales, parking fees, and broadcasting rights to their games on local and regional television networks.

Each franchise's operating income—earnings before interest, taxes, depreciation, and amortization—is displayed in column three of the table. The average and deviation of the group's data was $16 million and $36 million based on the distribution of amounts of the fifteen teams in the table. While the Red Sox, Astros, and Indians ranked first to third, the Royals, Orioles, and Tigers had the worst results with negative operating incomes.

The amounts of ten, or approximately 66 percent, of the teams were positive or above zero dollars in operating income based primarily on their gross income and relatively low operating expenses. But the high-revenue Yankees ranked only tenth and Mariners twelfth, in part, because of their generous players' salaries and other franchise expenses. This suggests that the league's clubs in Boston, Houston, and Cleveland operated more efficiently than those in other markets.

Except for the Royals (thirteenth), the other clubs' revenue and operating income were ranked differently. Also, the small-market Athletics, Twins, and Rays were in the top ten in operating income but not in revenue. Despite generating relatively low cash flows from operations, they committed to budgeting constraints and thereby avoided overspending and unnecessary expenses, allowing them to be more efficient than some other teams.

Because two AL franchises each had operating incomes that exceeded $76 million and the other thirteen no more than $31 million per team, there was a $36 million variation among them regarding this financial statistic. In part, the negative amounts of the Orioles, Tigers, Royals, Mariners, and Blue Jays caused this deviation to occur besides the financially inefficient Yankees.

In column four of table 8.2, the league's average gate receipts were approximately $91 million and deviated by $66 million among the group. Based mostly on their market size, attendances, average ticket prices, and performances in games during the 2016 MLB season, the Yankees finished first, Red Sox second, and Astros third in gate receipts. For the lowest amounts, the teams were the Rays, Athletics, and White Sox. Respectively, these three teams ranked fifteenth, fourteenth, and thirteenth in receipts.

Other aspects of this financial variable are: First, only four AL franchises in the group had more than $94 million in gate receipts, while eleven of them received less than the average amount. Second, the Yankees and Red Sox combined collected $470 million at the gate, or approximately 34 percent of the league's total. Third, although the Tigers and Twins tied for eighth in gate receipts, their revenues and operating incomes were each different in columns two and three. Fourth, besides the Red Sox's and Yankees' more than 40 percent in gate receipts to revenue, the other teams each had smaller proportions. Thus, the majority of teams in the league greatly depended on multiple sources for their revenue rather than simply tickets sales.

In column five of the table, the average player expenses of these fifteen teams was approximately $169 million and had a standard deviation, or variation, of $35 million for the 2017 MLB season. Although expected, the Yankees placed at the top with the Red Sox close at third. However, the Tigers ranked second because of huge multi-year contracts with such players as Miguel Cabrera, Ian Kinsler, Victor Martinez, and Omar Infante. Alternatively, the Indians, Athletics, and Rays had the least amounts of these expenses.

While the Athletics and Rays failed to qualify for the playoffs in MLB's 2017 season, the Astros won the AL championship and their first World Series. One year later, Cleveland easily won the CD, but the Tigers, Mariners, and Rays each finished in the middle of their division. The Yankees ended second to the Red Sox in the ED and qualified for the playoffs as a wild card.

Although ranked below average, at twelfth in player expenses, the Astros had a winning record in 2016 and one year later, won their first World Series, in part, because the club's most talented players remained healthy and productive at their on-the-field positions in regular season games and postseason series. This, in turn, likely resulted in higher player's expenses, especially for such players as Jose Altuve, Carlos Correa, and George Springer. Otherwise, they might become free agents or too expensive in salaries and therefore be traded to another team.

Besides the Tigers, players on rosters of the Orioles, Angels, and Blue Jays were each overpaid as groups, but not those on the Astros, Indians, and Twins. This observation is based on their performances in recent seasons and also in comparison to amounts paid in salaries to players on rival teams. Across the league in 2017, the ratio of player expenses to revenue was 54 percent, with the former three clubs above and the latter below that average percent.

In table 8.2, the most important financial statistic is each franchise's valuation in column six. These amounts—which averaged $1.58 billion—represent each team's estimated net worth as an enterprise based on several factors including its location, historical performances, attendances and gate receipts at home games, ballpark and its amenities, years in the league, revenue, and operating income.

As of 2017, the most valuable AL franchise was the Yankees followed by the Red Sox and Angels. Except for their operating income, the Yankees ranked first financially while the second- place Red Sox were first in operating income, second in gate receipts and revenue, and third in player expenses, and the third-place Angels were fourth in revenue, gate receipts, and player expenses, and sixth in operating income. Thus, these teams' rank in valuation closely reflected their status with respect to other financial data in the table.

The least valuable AL franchises in 2017 were the Athletics at thirteenth, Royals fourteenth, and Rays fifteenth. Individually, the Athletics had ranked highest (ninth) in operating income and lowest (fifteenth) in revenue; Royals highest (eighth) in player expenses and lowest (thirteenth) in revenue and operating income; and Rays highest (tied for seventh) in operating income and lowest (fifteenth) in gate receipts. In short, the data was consistent in measuring and determining the value of these teams.

If other factors are included in the analysis, such as the location and quality of teams' ballparks and their home attendances and performances, the valuations in table 8.2 accurately denote the worth of the fifteen AL franchises in 2017 from a business perspective. Whether these teams would actually sell in the market above or below their valuation depends on intangible benefits such as goodwill and competition between potential buyers.

Franchise Valuations

To continue highlighting and analyzing financial data, four elements comprise the specific value or worth of a MLB franchise. These are the sport and its market, stadium, and brand. *Forbes* magazine publishes this data annually based on information from various sources including the teams. In this section, table 8.3 contains a breakdown of valuations for AL clubs as of 2017.

On average, the sport (column two) of professional baseball contributed approximately $459 million, or 29 percent of these teams' valuations, in 2017. Of the group, the Yankees had the highest amount, followed by the Athletics and White Sox. Although Tampa Bay ranked fifteenth, or last, in valuation, approximately 60 percent of the club's value came from simply being a franchise in the sport and thus benefiting from revenue-sharing more than the club's market, stadium, or brand. Regarding other proportions, for example, the sport was much less than 40 percent each of New York, Boston, and Los Angeles's valuations.

Based on other comparisons of the data in column two of the table, the Mariners, Astros, and Indians had the smallest amounts and ranked, respectively, thirteenth to fifteenth in the group. Simply put, the sport did not provide much in total dollars to the value of AL franchises in Seattle, Houston, and Cleveland as of 2017. However, it was the most important element for the Royals and Rays, but not the Tigers relative to their market, stadium, and brand.

For all franchises in table 8.3, the average amount of the sport variable was $459 million in the AL. While six, or 40 percent of the teams, were above average in dollars, the other nine, or 60 percent, had amounts below the average. Besides the variable for the Yankees, Athletics, and White Sox, the Red Sox, Rays, and Orioles were also allocated higher amounts than other franchises and the proportions of their valuations ranged from 14 percent for New York to 55 percent for Tampa Bay. Interestingly, the large-market Angels ranked ninth and midsized-to-small market Twins eighth regarding the distribution of amounts in column two.

The table's column three contains a distribution of the Market variable and its contribution to each team's value in the league as of 2017. Averaging $631 million or 37 percent more than the Sport in column two, the Yankees, Red Sox, and Angels ranked first to third, respectively, in amounts followed by the Astros, Rangers, and Mariners. The market–which includes such things as these franchises' location, metropolitan area's population and growth in population, and households' per capita income and wealth–was especially important to the valuation of AL clubs in New York, Boston, Los Angeles, Houston, and Seattle.

Table 8.3 Distribution of Valuation Variables, American League Franchises, 2017 MLB Season

Franchise	Sport	Market	Stadium	Brand	Total
Baltimore Orioles	474	444	162	124	1,200
Boston Red Sox	512	1,261	565	462	2,800
Chicago White Sox	524	593	215	168	1,500
Cleveland Indians	379	373	177	117	1,045
Detroit Tigers	419	445	122	139	1,225
Houston Astros	394	700	338	218	1,650
Kansas City Royals	438	292	199	86	1,015
LA Angels of Anaheim	446	826	307	221	1,800
Minnesota Twins	454	375	212	110	1,150
New York Yankees	535	1,923	838	704	4,000
Oakland Athletics	528	285	128	79	1,020
Seattle Mariners	417	623	244	166	1,450
Tampa Bay Rays	496	225	116	63	900
Texas Rangers	425	637	339	198	1,600
Toronto Blue Jays	458	467	281	144	1,350

Note: Abbreviated is Los Angeles (LA). Valuations variables are in millions. Sport is the portion of franchise's value attributable to revenue shared among all teams. Market is the portion of franchise's value attributable to its city and market size. Stadium is the portion of franchise's value attributable to its stadium. Brand is the portion of franchise's value attributable to its brand.

Source: "The Business of Baseball," www.forbes.com cited 22 September 2018.

In metropolitan areas like Kansas City, Oakland, and Tampa Bay, this variable was much less important in dollars than the sport in column two. For example, the Royals, Athletics, and Rays had far less worth financially from being in their respective market (column three) than participating as a franchise in MLB (column two). While the large-market Yankees and Red Sox each derived about 46 percent of their total value from the market variable, the Royals received approximately 29 percent, Athletics 28 percent, and Rays 25 percent. Based on the distribution of amounts in column three, some teams were more fortunate than others simply because of their location being within a large or midsized area rather than a small one.

In column four of table 8.3, the third element that affects AL teams' total value as a franchise is their stadium. In dollars for specific clubs, ranked first is Yankee Stadium for the Yankees in New York; second, Fenway Park for the Red Sox in Boston; and third, Globe Life Park for the Rangers in Arlington, Texas. These stadiums have plenty of amenities for fans at games, and they generate millions in revenue for the home club from advertising, sponsorships, and concessions, including food, memorabilia, and merchandise.

The MLB teams with the smallest amounts in value from their ballparks include the Tigers at Comerica Park in Detroit, Rays at Tropicana Field in Tampa Bay, and Athletics at Oakland Coliseum in Oakland, California. These stadiums have problems with such things as their age, location, size, and overall quality relative to others in the league. Simply put, they contribute only a minor amount to the worth of their tenants.

In the AL, as of 2017, the stadium variable contributed approximately $282 million, or 17 percent, on average to the value of the league's fifteen franchises. In contrast, it averaged $343 million, or 20 percent, for fifteen clubs in the NL. Across both leagues, some venues had similar valuations, such as the AL Orioles' Camden Yards and NL Diamondbacks' Chase Field, AL Mariners' Safeco Field and NL Braves' SunTrust Park, and AL Red Sox's Fenway Park and NL Dodgers' Dodger Stadium. Because the Athletics, Rays, and Marlins have the least valuable ballparks in MLB, they need to be replaced or renovated to attract more fans to their teams' home games.[8]

---

8 *Other readings about AL franchises operating as business enterprises include Robert Trigaux, "5 Numbers Show Tampa Bay Rays' Business as Competitive Off Baseball Field as on," Tampa Bay Times (17 April 2017): 1; Marc Topkin, "Per Forbes Estimates, Rays Franchise Value up to $825-million, Still Last," Tampa Bay Times (11 April 2017): 1; Morgan Campbell, "Blue Jays' Star Power Bolsters Rogers," Toronto Star (30 March 2013): S.11; Christian Red and Nathaniel Vinton, "Look Who's #1 Yanks on the Money: $2.3B," New York Daily News (28 March 2013): 65; Thomas Korosec, "Rangers Owners Hit Jackpot With Run to the World Series; Value of Team Could go up US$50-100M," National Post (30 October 2010): S.4; Angela Brown, "Sale of Rangers Provides Wake-Up Call for Leagues," Telegraph Herald (20 August 2010): B.3; Matthew Craft, "Moreno's Math," Forbes (11 May 2009): 1.*

On average, the brand variable was $200 million, or 13 percent, of the typical AL team's total value. The three highest and lowest contributions of brand occurred, respectively, for the Yankees, Red Sox and Angels, but the least for the Royals, Athletics, and Rays. The variation or deviation among clubs averaged $168 million and eleven, or 73 percent, of the clubs' brands were worth less than average. Consequently, there is a large difference between the upper and lower distribution of this variable within the AL because of various reasons including teams' fan base, history, and popularity in the sport.

Based on amounts of sport, market, stadium and brand variables, the Yankees had the highest total valuation of these elements followed by the Red Sox and Angels. At the bottom of the distribution were the Athletics at thirteenth, Royals at fourteenth, and Rays at fifteenth. While the Yankees ranked first for each variable, the Red Sox placed second except for sport and the Angels third in market and brand, fifth in stadium, and ninth in sport.

NATIONAL LEAGUE

Team Attendances

In the National League (NL), during regular seasons, teams play home games in their ballparks for those who purchase tickets at various prices for seats or organizations that lease luxury suites. This generates gate receipts and operating income for them as franchises which, in turn, contributes to their total revenue and estimated market value.[9]

To measure and determine to what extent different teams in the league attracted fans to their games and compare them to each other, table 8.4 reveals the average home attendances of seventeen NL clubs as of ten seasons in five-year increments. What does the data denote about them?[10]

---

9 *Idem, and see the supplement in Pay Dirt and information in "Rodney Fort's Sports Business Data," and also "MLB Attendance & Team Age."*

10 *See Table 5.6 for the distribution of NL teams and how they ranked among each other in home attendances for six specific MLB seasons.*

According to data in the table, the average attendances of teams in the league increased from approximately 17,700 in 1971 to 31,300 in 2016, or by 77 percent. Compared to each other in five-year increments, they declined in 1976, 2011, and 2016, but increased in other seasons with their averages higher because of growth in population and the sport, popularity of various teams within their markets, rivalries, new ballparks, and expansion of the league.

Table 8.4 Average Home Attendances, National League Teams, Selected MLB Seasons

	Seasons									
Team	**1971**	**1976**	**1981**	**1986**	**1991**	**1996**	**2001**	**2006**	**2011**	**2016**
Arizona Diamondbacks	NA	NA	NA	NA	NA	NA	33.7	25.8	25.9	25.1
Atlanta Braves	12.2	10.1	10.7	17.1	26.4	35.8	34.8	31.8	29.2	24.9
Chicago Cubs	20.4	12.6	9.7	23.2	27.8	27.2	35.1	39.0	37.2	39.9
Cincinnati Reds	18.5	32.4	20.2	20.8	29.2	22.9	23.7	26.3	27.3	23.3
Colorado Rockies	NA	NA	NA	NA	NA	47.7	39.0	25.9	35.9	32.1
Florida/Miami Marlins	NA	NA	NA	NA	NA	21.5	15.7	14.3	18.7	21.4
Houston Astros	15.5	10.8	25.9	21.4	14.7	24.3	35.8	37.3	25.5	NA
Los Angeles Dodgers	25.4	32.4	42.5	37.3	41.3	39.3	37.2	46.4	36.2	45.7
Milwaukee Brewers	NA	NA	NA	NA	NA	NA	34.7	28.8	37.9	28.5
Montreal Expos	16.1	8.0	27.4	14.1	13.7	19.9	11.9	NA	NA	NA
New York Mets	27.9	17.9	13.5	34.1	27.8	19.6	32.8	43.3	29.0	34.4
Philadelphia Phillies	18.6	30.6	29.7	24.1	24.6	22.2	22.8	34.2	45.4	23.6
Pittsburgh Pirates	18.7	12.6	10.6	12.3	24.5	16.4	30.8	23.2	23.9	27.7
San Diego Padres	6.8	18.2	9.4	22.2	22.2	27.0	29.7	32.8	26.4	29.0
San Francisco Giants	13.6	7.7	11.9	18.8	21.4	17.4	40.8	38.6	41.8	41.5
St. Louis Cardinals	19.5	14.9	19.0	30.5	29.1	32.7	38.3	42.5	38.1	42.5
Washington Nationals	NA	NA	NA	NA	NA	NA	NA	26.5	24.2	30.6

Note: Average attendances are in thousands. This season is not applicable (NA) for the team. Abbreviated is Major League Baseball (MLB).

Source: "MLB Attendances," www.baseball-reference.com cited 22 September 2017 and Chapter 2 in Frank P. Jozsa Jr., Baseball in Crisis (Jefferson, NC: McFarland, 2008).

While the Dodgers ranked first in attendances among the group in 60 percent of the ten seasons, so did the Mets in 1971, Rockies in 1996, Giants in 2001, and Phillies in 2011. In general, fans flocked to these teams' home games and enjoyed them each April to September based on such things as their successful performances in regular seasons and postseasons, because of the Rockies' twenty-four years in the league since 1993, actual or recent opening of a new ballpark with amenities, and other economic, demographic, and sport-specific factors.

Alternatively, those clubs with the smallest average attendances tended to be the Diamondbacks, Padres, Pirates, and Marlins, and also the Expos, until they moved from Montreal to Washington DC in 2004. In fact, they ranked in the bottom third of all teams during most seasons, and consistently ahead of them throughout various years of the forty-six-year period—besides the Dodgers, Mets, Rockies, and Giants—were the Cubs and Cardinals but not always the Braves, Reds, Astros, and Nationals.

For teams that joined the league after 1971, their average attendances ranged in rank from ninth to fourteenth (Diamondbacks), first to thirteenth (Rockies), tenth to sixteenth (Marlins), fourth to tenth (Brewers), and seventh to fourteenth (Nationals). Since they usually failed to win titles and championships, each of these clubs had a large variation in numbers of fans attending their home games during years in the NL.

Based on data in table 8.4, the Expos had ranked third in attendance in 1981 but from eighth to sixteenth in other seasons. After winning a second-half division title and in second place behind the Cardinals in MLB's 1981 season, Montreal lost to the Dodgers in a five-game playoff.

Despite a fifty-day strike in MLB about free-agent compensation, the Expos were competitive in the early 1980s as a result of sluggers Andre Dawson and Gary Carter, batters Warren Cromartie and Tim Raines, and pitchers Steve Rogers and Scott Sanderson. However, when the team's attendances at home games remained low during the late 1980s to early 2000s, the franchise was in trouble financially and potentially bankrupt. This situation forced its relocation from Montreal to Washington DC after MLB's 2004 season.[11]

---

11 *More facts about this relocation are in "Montreal Expos," www.mlb.com cited 10 September 2017; Brian Borawski, "National Attention: The Expos' 35-Year Journey to Washington D.C.," www.fangraphs.com cited 6 October 2017; "Montreal Expos: Team History," www.baseball-reference.com cited 6 October 2017.*

Other interesting but insightful results are evident with respect to data in the table. Across all seasons, teams' average attendances had the most deviation in 1981 and the least in 1971. During 1981, for example, the gap between the Dodgers and Padres was 33,100 fans per game but only 21,000 for the Mets and Padres in 1971. In comparison, a difference of 24,300 existed between the Dodgers and Marlins in 2016. Thus, home attendances of the highest-ranked team were about double the lowest during the period.

From the 2005 to 2011 season, the Nationals struggled to attract fans to their games. But since 2012, the club has won four division titles (including 2017) and finished second twice. Led by veteran managers Davey Johnson, Matt Williams, and Dusty Baker, average attendances increased in rank from fourteenth in 2011 to seventh in 2016. From a business perspective, the franchise also improved financially with a higher payroll for players on its roster.

Among attendances of all teams in the league in table 8.4's ten seasons, the Dodgers and Cardinals each ranked no worse than sixth while other midsized-to-large-market clubs had different results. The Cubs, for example, were eleventh in 1981, Phillies fourteenth in 2001, and Mets twelfth and Giants thirteenth each in 1996. For the highest-attended seasons of four small-market clubs, the Pirates' average attendance ranked fifth in 1971, Reds second and Padres fourth in 1976, and Marlins tenth in 1996. In short, these results denote differences in popularity between them when playing in their home markets and also how devoted local fans have been to attend games in various seasons.

In comparing the two leagues across same seasons in tables 8.1 and 8.4, NL teams had larger audiences in their ballparks except in 1991 when AL clubs averaged 28,200 per game, or 3,000 more than those in the NL. While the Expos and Astros each attracted less than 15,000 to their home games that season, the AL's Indians and Brewers combined attendances exceeded 30,000 per game. In addition, the Blue Jays had the highest average attendance in MLB with 8,100 more per game than the NL's Dodgers.

Although the Yankees, Red Sox, and Angels dominate the AL as a group in attendances, the Dodgers, Giants, and Cardinals combined have more spectators at their home games. Simply put, the former three clubs are marginally less popular at home ballparks in New York, Boston, and Anaheim than the latter in Los Angeles,

San Francisco, and St. Louis. In part, that is because of differences and similarities between them competitively, demographically, and financially.

With respect to the ten seasons in tables 8.1 and 8.4, the two leagues together had the highest attendances in 2006 at approximately 62,500 per game with the Yankees averaging 51,800 followed by the Angels, Dodgers, Mets, and Cardinals each with more than 42,000. That season, the Yankees won their ninth consecutive division title but lost to the Tigers in the AL Division Series (ALDS). Such popular New York players as Robinson Cano, Derek Jeter, Alex Rodriguez, and Johnny Damon were outstanding along with pitchers Chien-Ming Wang, Randy Johnson, Mike Mussina, and Mariano Rivera. Meanwhile, the four other clubs had winning records and attracted plenty of fans to their home games.[12]

For growth in 2006 compared to 2011 and then 2011 to 2016, MLB teams' average attendances dropped in the AL from 30,300 to 28,700 and then to 28,400, and in the NL from 32,200 to 31,400 and then to 31,300. Whether this downward trend will continue depends on the extent of parity or equality between small-, midsized-, and large-market clubs, population and per capita income of sports fans within these baseball markets, changes in ticket prices at ballparks, and competition among teams in each division of the leagues.

From the 2016 to 2017 MLB season, the average attendance of NL teams increased from 31,300 to 31,500 per game, or by less than one percent. Ranked first both years were the Dodgers, then Cardinals second, and Giants third. Teams with the least attendances at games in their home ballpark included the Marlins at fifteenth, Reds at fourteenth, and in 2017 the Pirates at thirteenth. Although they won their divisions, the Cubs were fourth and Nationals seventh in attendances at Wrigley Field in Chicago and Nationals Park in Washington, DC. Besides this group of clubs in the NL, the Diamondbacks, Braves, Rockies, Brewers, and Phillies played before larger crowds in games at their ballparks but not the Mets and Padres.

For various demographic, economic, and sport-specific reasons, the average attendance of NL teams declined to 30,500 per game from 2017 to 2018. Although

12 *See "New York Yankees," www.baseball-reference.com cited 6 October 2017 and "New York Yankees," www.mlb.com cited 6 October 2017.*

their rankings did not change much as a group from year to year, the Dodgers, then Cardinals, and Giants had the highest averages in 2018 while the lowest again were those of the Marlins, Reds, and Pirates. Since Brewers' games in Milwaukee became more popular after the club won its division but were defeated by the Dodgers in the NLCS, the Braves, Cubs, Dodgers, and Rockies also competed in the league's postseason. Similar to the AL, the NL's average attendance is at its lowest since 1996. Thus, MLB needs to be more entertaining as a sport for its fans and also find ways to improve competition in games between teams and not price tickets above their economic value. Otherwise, attendance will continue to fall in big-league ballparks of baseball markets.

Financial Data

Similar to enterprises and other organizations in various industries of the US economy, MLB franchises generate financial information annually from their operations to determine their current status and progress as businesses in the professional sports industry. This data is organized in documents such as balance sheets, cash flow accounts, and earnings statements. Prepared and maintained by staff accountants, these records are audited periodically and submitted to various government agencies to verify their accuracy, authenticity, and legality.

While the actual financial results for big-league baseball teams appear publicly in journals, magazines, newspapers, reports, and studies, they are incomplete, usually outdated, and do not reveal enough information to thoroughly analyze these organizations from business and economic perspectives. Rather than collect them from different sources in the literature, this chapter refers to financial results and estimates published in *Forbes*. This was a practical, appropriate, and realistic way to learn more about, and also compare and rank, MLB franchises financially within the NL.

In table 8.5 are five different but important financial variables or elements for fifteen NL franchises based on MLB's 2017 season. For the specific teams listed alphabetically in column one, their gross revenue appears in column two. Averaging $321 million per team in the league, the Dodgers had the most revenue with the Cubs second and Giants third. Each of them were competitive although the Giants were not in the playoffs. As a result, they earned more than $1.4 billion in revenue, or approximately 29 percent of the group's total that season.

The Marlins, Reds, and Brewers had the three smallest amounts of revenue. Despite relatively low ticket prices, these teams' attendances at home games were below the league average, in part, because of losing records in the regular season and also failing to attract spectators and entertain them at their ballparks. In addition, other midsized-to-small-market clubs, such as the Diamondbacks, Pirates, Rockies, and Padres, had ranked low in revenue from tickets and other sources such as advertising, parking fees, concessions, and apparel and merchandise sales.

Besides the Dodgers, Cubs, and Giants, five other NL teams earned between $300 million and $350 million in revenue. Indeed the Cardinals and Nationals—but not Phillies, Mets, and Braves—each had winning records and fans flocked to ballparks to attend home games in St. Louis and Washington, DC and spend their money. Ranked seventh in the league with $319 million in revenue, the Cardinals were effective and also popular and savvy enough to generate millions in cash in different ways despite finishing its season third in the CD but with a winning record.

Listed in column three of table 8.5 is NL teams' operating income or earnings before interest, taxes, depreciation, and amortization (EBITDA) received from MLB's 2017 season. The group's average was $38 million or approximately $23 million more than those in the AL. Despite less revenue than the Dodgers, the Cubs had the highest EBITDA by far at $102 million followed by the Phillies and Giants.

The Padres and Marlins had the worst results in operating income. The costs to operate these franchises greatly exceeded the income in their 2017 season because of such things as high salaries—compared to productivity—paid to those who played for San Diego and due to relatively small attendances at home games in Miami. Although other teams had fewer liabilities and personnel problems, the Padres and Marlins were very inefficient and undisciplined from a financial perspective for these and other reasons.

Such franchises as the Diamondbacks, Brewers, and Pirates ranked much higher in operating income than revenue while the reverse occurred for the Braves, Mets, and Nationals. Because of commitments to responsibly budget their operations and discipline in controlling spending internally, the former group had relatively better results in EBITDA than NL clubs in Atlanta, New York, and Washington, DC, especially with respect to this financial variable.

Table 8.5 Financial Data, National League Franchises, 2017 MLB Season

Franchise	*Financial Data*				
	Revenue	Operating Income	Gate Receipts	Player Expenses	Valuations
Arizona Diamondbacks	258	34	49	118	1,210
Atlanta Braves	336	46	79	141	1,625
Chicago Cubs	457	102	214	186	2,900
Cincinnati Reds	243	14	46	118	1,010
Colorado Rockies	266	15	73	148	1,100
Los Angeles Dodgers	522	68	188	261	3,000
Miami Marlins	219	−53	27	143	1,000
Milwaukee Brewers	255	67	66	85	1,030
New York Mets	336	17	104	171	2,100
Philadelphia Phillies	329	91	84	119	1,700
Pittsburgh Pirates	258	35	60	118	1,260
San Diego Padres	266	2	55	102	1,270
San Francisco Giants	445	84	180	198	2,850
St. Louis Cardinals	319	40	129	165	1,900
Washington Nationals	311	11	101	186	1,675

Note: MLB is Major League Baseball. Financial data is in millions of dollars. Except for valuations, other amounts are for franchises' 2017 season. Revenue is net of stadium revenues used for debt payments. Operating income equals earnings before interest, taxes, depreciation, and amortization. Gate receipts include club seats. Player expenses include benefits and bonuses. Valuations are based on the current stadium deal without deductions for debt.

Source: "The Business of Baseball," www.forbes.com cited 22 September 2018.

Unlike the other thirteen NL franchises but similar to the AL's Royals, the Marlins, Cardinals, and Giants each ranked the same individually in both revenue and operating income at respectively fifteenth, seventh, and third. Being organized fiscally, their general managers were able to establish and maintain standards regarding the allocation of funds for operations rather than spend unnecessarily. While the league's ratio of operating income to revenue averaged approximately 12 percent, Chicago's and Milwaukee's, for example, were superior at more than 22 percent.

The third financial variable to highlight in the table is gate receipts of NL teams from their home games in MLB's 2017 season. While the average was $97 million, six clubs exceeded that amount including the Cubs, Nationals, and Dodgers. In fact, each of them had winning records and played before large crowds at home in Wrigley Field, Nationals Park, and Dodger Stadium. Although their ticket prices were relatively high, these clubs were popular and fans loved and supported them throughout the season.

In contrast to those franchises, the Marlins and then Reds and Diamondbacks had the smallest gate receipts in the league. Simply put, the Marlins and Reds—but not the Diamondbacks— were neither good teams for fans or exciting to watch at home games in their ballparks. Other problems such as overpriced tickets and lack of talented players also contributed to their relatively low attendances and gate receipts. Interestingly, the Diamondbacks improved enough to be a wild-card team in 2017 while the Marlins and Reds each finished more than nineteen games behind their division leaders in the NL's regular season.

The league's ratio of average gate receipts to revenue was approximately 30 percent. It was relatively high for such clubs as the Cubs, Mets, and Cardinals, but not for the Reds, Rockies, and Padres. Among teams, the variation in attendances and their ticket prices were reasons for differences in the ratio besides performances between rivals in their and other divisions.

The deviation or spread in gate receipts of NL franchises exceeded $56 million in MLB's 2017 season. In the AL, it was $65 million because of large differences in gate receipts between the Yankees and Rays and the Athletics and White Sox, for example, compared to less between the Cubs and Marlins, Diamondbacks, and Reds. This inequality indicates why large-market teams in the sport have a financial advantage which, in part, affects their ability to increase payroll by signing free agents and qualifying for postseasons.

Column five of table 8.5 lists the player expenses of NL clubs with respect to their 2017 season. The amounts averaged $150 million and they deviated by $45 million among the fifteen teams. Ranked first in the group were the Dodgers and then Giants with a tie for third between the Cubs and Nationals. Of all MLB teams, Dodgers had the highest payroll at approximately $261 million, the Giants were fourth at $198 million and Cubs and National were each sixth at $186 million. Some interesting facts about the distribution in the NL: Los Angeles paid $14 million less than in 2016; San Francisco spent more than $94 million on pitchers; and Miami took a big leap forward from one year earlier with a payroll of $143 million and from fourteenth to eighth place.

In contrast, the Diamondbacks, Reds, Pirates, and Brewers ranked twelfth to fifteenth in payroll expenses. Among clubs in both leagues, they were tied for twenty-sixth, and then thirtieth in payroll. Interestingly, the Brewers' amount declined from $98 million, or twentieth place, in 2015 while the Marlins' increased from thirtieth, or $60 million, and Diamondbacks from twenty-fifth, or $83 million. Despite these changes, the Marlins and Brewers failed to make the playoffs during the two seasons.

The biggest gap in payroll expenses among NL clubs in 2017 was between the Dodgers and Brewers at $176 million whereas in the AL, the Yankees and Rays' amounts differed by $122 million. If these gaps continue to increase between large- and small-market teams in each league after 2017, there will be less parity and likely more inequality among teams in each league economically and perhaps competitively in future MLB seasons.

Although average payroll expenses were less by $19 million in the AL than NL in MLB's 2017 season, the latter league had a larger deviation between them by $10 million. To illustrate, the Mets at $171 million and Angels at $188 million each ranked fifth in their respective league while the Phillies at $119 million and Royals at $168 million were each tenth. As a result, for those ranked the same, NL teams tended to have smaller amounts but more deviation from their league's average and also less parity with respect to payroll expenses.

The valuations of NL franchises appear in column six of table 8.5. Their average was approximately $1.7 billion and deviated by $709 million. Based on other financial data and their location and recent history of performances, the Dodgers, Cubs, and Giants ranked first to third, and the Brewers, Reds, and Marlins from thirteenth to fifteenth.

Besides valuations, the Dodgers also ranked first in revenue and player expenses, Cubs first in operating income and gate receipts, and Giants second in players expenses and third in revenue, operating income, and gate receipts. Although ranked at or close to the bottom among NL clubs, the other financial data had the Marlins at eighth to fourteenth, Brewers fifth to fifteenth, and Reds twelfth to fourteenth. As a result, this distribution denotes the highest and lowest valued teams in the league as of 2017.

In comparison to the average of fifteen franchises in the AL, the NL's were $120 million greater in valuation. Ranked fifth, for example, the Cardinals at $1.9 billion exceeded the Rangers by 23 percent, while ranked first, the Dodgers had $1 billion less in value than the Yankees.

Despite the Yankees at $4 billion and Red Sox at $2.8 billion, the typical NL club had more revenue, operating income, and gate receipts but smaller player expenses than its counterpart. In addition, the AL's Indians, Royals, Athletics, and Rays each had valuations below $1.1 billion with the Brewers, Marlins, and Reds being the only NL teams below that amount. Simply put, these were reasons for differences in financial data between and among the leagues and their franchises in MLB.

The average deviation in valuations among AL teams was larger than those in the NL by $106 million, or 15 percent. This occurred, for the most part, because amounts varied more between large-, midsized-, and small-market clubs in the AL than in the NL. In other words, the Yankees and Red Sox dominated and had relatively impressive results financially among their group of clubs, and also to a greater extent than did the Dodgers and Cubs. This explains the concept of franchise valuations and why and how much they differed across MLB in a recent period.

Franchise Valuations

To continue with reporting and analyzing financial data, four elements comprise the value or specific worth of a MLB franchise. These are the sport and its market, stadium, and brand. *Forbes* publishes this type of data annually based on information from various sources including the teams. In this section, table 8.6 contains a breakdown of valuations for each NL club as of 2017.

Table 8.6 Distribution of Valuation Variables, National League Franchises, 2017 MLB Season

Franchise	Sport	Market	Stadium	Brand	Total
Arizona Diamondbacks	496	433	166	115	1,210
Atlanta Braves	400	667	340	218	1,625
Chicago Cubs	525	1,255	635	486	2,900
Cincinnati Reds	444	305	195	86	1,010
Colorado Rockies	433	351	212	100	1,100
Los Angeles Dodgers	476	1,481	541	503	3,000
Miami Marlins	653	195	97	55	1,000
Milwaukee Brewers	423	313	204	90	1,030
New York Mets	517	829	474	279	2,100
Philadelphia Phillies	428	754	292	226	1,700
Pittsburgh Pirates	477	450	200	133	1,260
San Diego Padres	496	411	248	115	1,270
San Francisco Giants	531	1,207	728	385	2,850
St. Louis Cardinals	493	715	447	245	1,900
Washington Nationals	446	674	372	183	1,675

Note: Valuation variables are in millions. Sport is the portion of franchise's value attributable to revenue shared among all teams. Market is the portion of franchise's value attributable to its city and market size. Stadium is the portion of franchise's value attributable to its stadium. Brand is the portion of franchise's value attributable to its brand.

Source: "The Business of Baseball," www.forbes.com cited 22 September 2018.

In column two of the table is the amount that the sport, as an element, contributed to the valuations of these franchises (column six) as of 2017. While the average was $482 million, or 28 percent per team, the most in dollars were for the Marlins, Giants, and Cubs. Relative to their total values, the sport was 65 percent of Miami's team and approximately 18 percent each of the worth of the Giants and Cubs. Thus, professional baseball as a competitive team sport in southeast Florida is very important proportionately to the Marlins revenue and financial results in MLB.

The sport, alternatively, contributed the least in dollars to the valuations of the Phillies, Brewers, and Braves. Revenue sharing among all teams is simply not very important to these clubs from a financial perspective. Besides them, other clubs whose amounts were relatively small include the Reds, Nationals, and Rockies. Although the percent of sport to valuation for each of these teams varies greatly among some of them, their worth as business enterprises also depended on other factors.

While the variable in column one—sport—was approximately 28–29 percent on average of franchise valuations in both leagues, the NL's exceeded the AL's by $23 million. Furthermore, these leagues' deviations in amounts were, respectively, $61 million and $49 million. In other words, more variation in dollars caused by the sport occurred among teams in the NL than AL. The gap in amounts, for example, between the Yankees ($535 million) and Indians ($367 million) was much smaller than that of the Marlins and Brewers ($253 million). These amounts, in turn, represent the sport's influence on the financial worth of each franchise.

Another variable in the table is market (column three) and its impact on NL teams' valuations (column six). As expected, its amounts were largest for clubs in big cities including the Dodgers in Los Angeles, Cubs in Chicago, and Giants in San Francisco. Each of these franchises' allocation of the variable was more than $1.1 billion and at least 42 percent of their total valuation. Others in the league whose values were significantly impacted by their city and market size or market were the Mets, Phillies, and Cardinals.

As of 2017, the Brewers, Reds, and Marlins benefitted least and ranked at the bottom of the distribution with respect to the market variable. More important to them than city and market size, the sport and revenue sharing within the league contributed the greatest amounts to these three franchises valuations but not their stadium or brand. The Diamondbacks, Padres, and Rockies also gained relatively little from the market at their home sites in Phoenix, San Diego, and Denver.

While the NL's market variable averaged $669 million and AL's $631 million, it had a smaller difference in deviation between the two leagues than $57 million. To clarify, variation in the distribution of market amounts due to city and market size— among, for example, the first, fifth, tenth, and fifteenth ranked clubs in each group of teams— varied more in the AL than NL.

The amounts of the stadium variable of each NL franchise are in column four of table 8.6. Across all of them, they averaged $343 million, or 20 percent of their valuation, compared to $482 million, or 28 percent, for the sport and $669 million, or 39 percent, for the market. While the Giants, Cubs, and Dodgers had the highest amounts of the group, the lowest dollars in valuations from their stadium included the Reds (thirteenth), Diamondbacks (fourteenth), and Marlins (fifteenth). As a result, games played in AT&T Ballpark, Wrigley Field, and Dodger Stadium contributed more value to their teams than those in the Great American Ballpark, Chase Field, and Marlins Park.

In comparing four variables within the table, stadium ranked highest for the Braves, Rockies, and four other clubs, lowest for the Diamondbacks and Pirates, and tied with three other variables in rank for the Marlins and one for the Cardinals. Regarding two other franchises, stadium is among the four variables tied for first for the Mets and also first for the Braves with their brand. This element of the total, in turn, denotes which NL clubs had most and least amounts based on such things as the location, size, and amenities of their home ballparks.

The deviation in amounts of the stadium variable equaled $185 million for NL teams and $192 million among those in the AL. Despite being applicable to the same professional sport, they differed by $7 million for several reasons including the age, capacity, and construction cost of these facilities and the market and performances of clubs that occupied them at their home site.

From a business perspective, the fourth variable—brand—is very important to the total financial worth of MLB franchises. For those in the NL, it averaged $200 million or 13 percent of their franchise's valuation. While the Cubs, Dodgers, and Giants had the most lucrative brands, the least lucrative amounts belonged to the Brewers, Reds, and Marlins. Besides their market, the distribution of brands also reflects these clubs' revenue, operating income, and gate receipts from home games in a season.

In comparison, the brand variable was $14 million more on average for NL franchises than those in the AL. Besides amounts of the Yankees and Red Sox and also $221 million for the Angels, the NL's four smallest amounts as a group exceeded combined brand values of the AL's Royals, Twins, Athletics, and Rays. Interestingly, the Diamondbacks and Indians had somewhat similar amounts and so did the Cubs,

Dodgers and Red Sox, and the Nationals and Rangers. This data, in part, denotes how fans view them within the sports business and their organization's brands from a marketing and public relations perspective.

The sum of each NL franchise's sport, market, stadium, and brand variables is their total valuation in column six of table 8.6. The league's average value was $1.70 billion per team compared to $1.58 billion in the AL. This is a relatively small difference proportionately and in amounts, which indicates the parity that exists in total valuations of fifteen clubs each within two groups of MLB.

Regarding primarily NL franchises and the distribution of their amounts, significant results were as follows: first, the Dodgers ranked as the most valuable team in 2017 followed by the Cubs and Giants; second, the least in value included the Marlins at fifteenth, Reds at fourteenth, and Brewers at thirteenth; third, six, or 40 percent of the NL clubs, were above the league average in value and the other nine below-average; fourth, the average deviation in valuations among the group equaled $709 million per team or $106 million less than those in the AL; fifth, the gap between the top-ranked Dodgers and bottom-ranked Marlins was $2 billion, but in the AL, $3.1 billion when comparing Yankees to the Rays.[13]

Tables A8.1 and A8.2 in the appendix contain financial data for twenty-eight MLB franchises as of their 1997 season. To reveal and compare average amounts of data for the AL and NL for that season, respectively, their average revenue was $83 million and $74 million; operating income $2.6 million and $2.4 million; payroll $42 million and $37 million; and value $202 million and $185 million. These results indicate that, as a group, AL teams on average were financially superior to those in the NL.[14]

13 *Other information and facts about NL franchises and their history as businesses is in Russ Wiles, "Cardinals Rank 42 in World Value List," Arizona Republic (14 July 2016): A.6; Travis Sawchik, "Report: Pirates' Estimated Value at $500 Million," Pittsburgh Tribune (24 October 2013): 1; "Long-Term Deal Hurting Marlins Contract With Fox Sports Florida Under Market Value While Other Teams Cash in," South Florida Sun (10 March 2013): C.1; Steven Marcus, "Mets' Value Could Rise After Dodgers' $2B Sale," Newsday (29 March 2012): A.63; Josh Kosman, "Mets Stakes Sold [Exclusive] Owners Raked in $240M, Paid Down Debt," New York Post (20 March 2012): 23; Tom Van Riper, "Return of the Rockies," Forbes (20 August 2011): 1; David Waldstein, "Mets' Value Declines, Forbes Says," New York Times (24 March 2011): B.3.*

14 *"MLB Data 1998 (1997 Season)," www.forbes.com cited 6 October 2017.*

In 1997, the AL's Yankees, Orioles and Indians, and also NL's Rockies, Braves, and Dodgers each ranked first to third in value within their group. In contrast, the lowest-ranked clubs included the Athletics, Royals, and Twins in the AL, and Pirates, Phillies, and Expos in the NL. While the Yankees had the most revenue and payroll and the highest value of all franchises, they ranked second to the Rockies in operating income.

Television Deals

Big-market teams in MLB have a financial advantage regarding revenues at the gate, but increasingly their advantage also comes from television revenue from local cable networks. They continue to sign billion-dollar deals that include an ownership stake, although determining how to divide that money among the group could be difficult for them.[15]

When hearing about differences in television deals, we often think of them in terms of the average annual value they equally provide to the owner or owners and indirectly to the players of MLB franchises. That is a familiar term in baseball since most player contracts are structured to be paid evenly over the course of the television contract. That practice is less common under other circumstances, however, with deals often paying a smaller sum at the beginning of a contract and increasing over time. In fact, television contracts are often structured this way.

Teams and networks make money from getting their broadcasts to appear within the standard cable lineup and charging a per-subscriber fee. The result is that more homes mean more money to give to teams. That is not only a big-market advantage. Teams also reap benefits from owning a stake in the network, assuming it's profitable. By and large, the bigger-market teams have been able to negotiate more favorable set-ups when it comes to ownership.

---

15 *See Craig Edwards, "Estimated TV for All 30 MLB Teams," www.fangraphs.com cited 6 October 2017. Readings about this topic are Maury Brown, "MLB Sets Record For Revenues In 2017, Increasing More Than $500 Million Since 2015," www.forbes.com cited 3 November 2018; "MLB TV Revenue–Santa Claus Keeps Coming to Town," www.foxsports.com cited 3 November 2018; "MLB's Most Valuable Television Deals," www.forbes.com cited 3 November 2018; Dan Perry, "MLB Seems to Think Its Broadcast Audience is More Important Than Fans at the Ballpark," www.cbssports.com cited 3 November 2018; Wayne Friedman, "2018 MLB's TV National Ad Revenues Remain Stable," www.mediapost.com cited 3 November 2018.*

For the most part, MLB teams receiving an ownership share of a television network are in the big markets. Only the San Diego Padres, and maybe the St. Louis Cardinals, are each located in a small television baseball market. Although the Cardinals might be in a small market television-wise, they operate on a larger scale due to attendance. Their deal with an ownership stake did not begin until the 2018 MLB season.

The ownership shares are incredibly important when it comes to revenue-sharing in the AL and NL because any money gained as an owner of a network is shielded from revenue-sharing, as are figures that MLB provides when calculating players' share of revenue. In the appendix, table A8.3 for the AL and table A8.4 for the NL show 2016 estimated revenue, start and end years of each television deal, amount of the deal if known, and ownership stake. Here is an overview of information contained in the tables.

Regarding 2016 estimated revenues of the AL and then NL deals, they averaged $57 million and $50 million and also deviated among teams by $27 million and $44 million. The top three franchises in amounts were the AL's Angels, Yankees, and Red Sox, and NL's Dodgers, Cubs, and Phillies. Teams with the least revenue included the Rays, Royals, and Twins, and in the NL, the Marlins, Rockies, and Brewers. Thus, the television revenues of clubs in the biggest markets exceeded those in midsized and small markets.

Based on start to end dates as of 2016, the television deals averaged seventeen years in the AL and eighteen in the NL and each deviated among teams by six years. The Yankees and then Orioles, and also the Dodgers, Mets, Phillies, and Giants had the longest contracts in their respective league while teams with the least number of years included the Indians, Tigers, and Rays each at ten years, and similarly the Reds and Rockies. These contracts were negotiated and influenced the financial rewards and risks of both teams and networks.

In amounts per team (column five in the tables), the AL's Yankees ranked first, Angels second, and Mariners third and in the NL, they were the Dodgers, Phillies, and Giants. Furthermore, seventeen, or 56 percent of the MLB franchises, had an ownership stake in the television network. This included, for example, the AL's Red Sox in NESN and Mariners in Root Sports Northwest and the NL's Mets in Sports Net NY and Padres in Fox Sport San Diego. Alternatively, thirteen other MLB clubs were not owners in regional sports networks.

To conclude this chapter, there have been tremendous changes in the financial status and wealth of big-league franchises especially since the mid-to-late 1990s. Because of new and improved collective bargaining agreements between the players' union and leagues, contracts with players and their teams, more expensive and modern ballparks with additional amenities, MLB and teams' renewal of contracts with local, regional and national television networks, international exposure of the game, and the relocation and expansion of teams, these things transformed the sport in different but also important, unique, and profitable ways from an economic perspective. Although various major and minor risks, rewards, and problems exist in the operation of MLB and their franchises, the leagues will prosper in the future across American sports markets and within at least one province in Canada.

CHAPTER 9

League Ballparks

One very important way that Major League Baseball (MLB) franchises generate revenue for the organization during the regular season is getting people to purchase tickets for seats at home games played in their ballparks. In order to compete for and win division and league titles and one or more World Series, team officials invest the cash flows from ticket sales and other sources to recruit better players and resign those whose contracts have expired by negotiating and paying them affordable but, if required, above-average salaries. Thus, each American League (AL) and National League (NL) club attempts to be successful financially, in part, by attracting audiences from its market and entertaining them at games given the amenities, location, size, and other characteristics of their ballpark.[1]

For several reasons, there have been conflicts between MLB teams, politicians, and communities regarding the renovation or replacement of a local but current ballpark. Besides the decision to renovate or replace them, other problems are, for example, who will finance the project, what amount of dollars are needed to complete it, and how and when to budget and schedule tasks regarding construction of a new—or renovation of an existing—facility. Each of these decisions is complex, controversial,

1 *For more information about this topic, see Frank P. Jozsa Jr., Major League Baseball Organizations: Team Performances and Financial Consequences (Lanham, MD: Lexington Books, 2016); James Quirk and Rodney D. Fort, Pay Dirt: The Business of Professional Team Sports (Princeton, NJ: Princeton University Press, 1992); Kenneth L. Shropshire, The Sports Franchise Game: Cities in Pursuit of Sports Franchises, Events, Stadiums, and Arenas (Philadelphia, PA: University of Pennsylvania Press, 1995).*

and usually involves both public officials and private organizations. Once the project starts, however, it is urgent to finish it as designed, funded, and planned.

Being something that has impacted the sport and truly transformed professional baseball, this chapter focuses on the ballparks of teams in each league as of MLB's 2018 season. The discussion not only includes general information about them as venues but also reveals how they rank based on different criteria. For other specific data, the attendances at and gate receipts from these teams' home games are reported in sections of previous chapters within *The Making of Modern Baseball*.[2]

AMERICAN LEAGUE

Angel Stadium

During their history of MLB seasons, the Angels played home games at Wrigley Field (1961), Dodger Stadium (1962–1965), and Anaheim Stadium (1966–1997)—renamed Edison International Field in 1998—and then six years later, Angel Stadium of Anaheim or simply Angel Stadium. Since it opened in 1966, the facility has hosted many events other than baseball including professional football games.

---

2 *The description of current and former big-league ballparks or stadiums are covered in such readings as "The Fields of Major League Baseball," www.ballparksofbaseball.com cited 13 October 2017, "The History of Major League Ballparks," www.cnn.com cited 13 October 2017, and "Ballparks, Baseball Stadiums & Field of Dreams," www.baseball-almanac.com cited 13 October 2017. The evaluation of specific American League and National League teams' ballparks are in the following articles: "Ranking All 30 MLB Ballparks," www.nbcsports.com cited 13 October 2017 for Angel Stadium, Minute Maid Park, Oakland Coliseum, Tropicana Field, Chase Field, Nationals Park, Petco Park, and PNC Park; Matt Meltzer, "All 30 Major League Baseball Stadiums, Ranked," www.thrillist.com cited 13 October 2017 for Camden Yards, Rogers Centre, Citi Field, and SunTrust Park; "America's Best Baseball Stadiums," www.travelandleisure.com cited 13 October 2017 for Comerica Park, Kauffman Stadium, Safeco Field, Marlins Park, and Miller Park; Thomas Boswell, "How Thomas Boswell Ranked All 30 MLB Ballparks, and Grouped Them in Four Tiers," www.washingtonpost.com cited 13 October 2017 for Fenway Park, Globe Life Park, Yankee Stadium, Coors Field, and Great American Ballpark; Ted Berg, "All 30 MLB Stadiums, Ranked," www.usatoday.com cited 13 October 2017 for Progressive Field and Target Field; Jeff Goldberg, "MLB Ballparks, From Oldest to Newest," www.ballparkdigest.com cited 13 October 2017 for Guaranteed Rate Field, Citizens Bank Park, Dodger Stadium, and Wrigley Field; Andrew Joseph, "All 30 MLB Stadiums, Ranked," www.usatoday.com cited 13 October 2017 for AT&T Ballpark and Busch Stadium.*

In the 1970s, the National Football League (NFL) Rams moved from the Los Angeles Coliseum to Anaheim Stadium and by the 1980 sports season, the ballpark became a multipurpose facility and thus home to both the Angels and Rams. It was enclosed and expanded by 23,000 seats, increasing capacity to more than 65,000. Also, a new scoreboard was installed on the façade of the outfield roof when the Big A scoreboard moved to the parking lot. Additional upgrades included new executive and media boxes, and a sound system.

During January 1994, an earthquake damaged Anaheim Stadium when the Sony jumbotron fell from the roof in left field, crashed into the upper deck, and destroyed hundreds of seats. After their 1994 season, the Rams moved from Los Angeles to St. Louis, Missouri allowing the Angels to convert their facility back to one that exclusively hosted baseball games.

After renovations in the mid-1990s, the ballpark improved for fans. As of 2018, there were many amenities in it including the Pepsi Perfect Game Pavilion, dugout-level seating, and three club restaurants. These are the Knothole Club–a sports bar located on the club level down the right field line; Diamond Club–an upscale restaurant with outdoor seating; and the Homeplate Club–which overlooks the main entrance to the ballpark.

> *"Though the basic foundation of the stadium opened nearly 50 years ago, it was gutted and rebuilt in the '90s, so it doesn't feel at all like an old ballpark. This is just a pleasant place to watch a ballgame. The weather is usually fantastic. The home team is usually good. The stands are usually packed. And Disneyland is only five minutes away. What more do you need?"*[3]

---

3 *See Note 2 for remarks and specific views about American League ballparks including such sources as "Ranking All 30 MLB Ballparks;" "All 30 Major League Baseball Stadiums, Ranked;" and "How Thomas Boswell Ranked All 30 MLB Ballparks, and Grouped Them in Four Tiers."*

Camden Yards

Located in northeast Baltimore, Memorial Stadium was not a typical multipurpose baseball facility, with seats too distant from the field and structurally obsolete by the late 1980s. Therefore, MLB's Orioles and city officials developed a plan to build a new ballpark in downtown Baltimore on land that once occupied the saloon of Babe Ruth's father. They hired architect Joseph Spear of HOK Sport to design a new stadium similar to ballparks of the early 1900s with steel columns, beams, and trusses instead of concrete.

When it opened in April 1992 for the club's first home game that season, upper deck fans in Oriole Park at Camden Yards could see the city's skyline and eight-story high B&O Warehouse. The stadium's infrastructure consists of a three-tier grandstand that stretches from behind home plate, down the third base line to the left field pole and also down the first base line. The original 48,000 seats were replaced with larger green ones before the 2011 MLB season.

> *"Wanna feel old? The first retro ballpark that opened its doors in 1992 and changed the way ballparks were built is now the 10th oldest in the sport. It's only filling a little over half of capacity these days, but it's still got one of the best environments for taking in a game. Boog Powell's BBQ in right-center remains an absolute must-eat if you're there (in fact, Bleacher Report ranks Camden Yards No. 1 for food)."*

Comerica Park

Prior to MLB's 2000 season, the Tigers played their home games in two ballparks: Bennett Park (1901–1911) and then Navin Field (1912–1937)—renamed Briggs Stadium in 1938 and again twenty-three years later to Tiger Stadium. At each facility, the club's attendances per game ranged from a low of 2,200 to a high of 6,300 at Bennett Park; 203,000 to 1.1 million at Navin Field; 580,000 to 1.9 million at Briggs Stadium; and 816,000 to 2.7 million at Tiger Stadium.

In 1992, new owner Mike Illitch initiated many cosmetic improvements to the ballpark, primarily the Tiger Den and Tiger Plaza. While the former was an area in the lower deck between first and third base that had padded seats and waiters, Tiger Plaza was constructed in the old players' parking lot and consisted of several concessionaires and a gift shop.

After the 1994 MLB players' strike, plans were made by officials to construct a new ballpark in Detroit although many fans in the community preferred and campaigned to not abandon the old stadium. After a few years, ground was broken and construction began during mid-to-late 1997 to build a new ballpark and replace historic but outdated Tiger Stadium.

Completed for opening day in early April 2000, more than 40,000 fans attended the Tigers first game at Comerica Park. Consisting of three levels, almost every seat in the main grandstand has a view of downtown Detroit. Fans may walk along the main concourse without losing sight of the playing field. In center field, there are several fountains that produce liquid fireworks after a home run. Along the left center field wall are statues of such Hall of Fame players as Ty Cobb, Al Kaline, and Hank Greenberg. Besides a large high-density (HD) video scoreboard, the ballpark features a Ferris wheel and merry-go-round.

> *"Kids score big at Comerica Park thanks to its 50-foot Ferris wheel and the tiger-clad carousel at the base of the food court; come on Sunday, and kids 14 and younger ride for free. But grown-ups have a playground of their own at the 1940s-style Cigar Bar of the Tiger Club, stocked with 20 cigar varieties and a baby grand. Whether you've got club access or nosebleed seats, you'll appreciate the Bellagio-like liquid fireworks—a synchronized light and music fountain that shoots up 150 feet in the air through more than 900 nozzles to celebrate each home run."*

Fenway Park

After becoming a charter member of the AL in 1901, the Red Sox—known then as the Americans—built Huntington Avenue Grounds (HAG) on the site of a wasteland in Boston. A rickety wooden ballpark, HAG contained approximately 11,000 seats. While Americans and then Red Sox teams played there for a total of eleven MLB seasons, attendance averaged between a low of 4,100 per game in 1901 to a high of 8,900 in 1909.

Due to security problems including potential fires and injuries to spectators at HAG, Red Sox owner and real estate magnate John Taylor decided to build a new ballpark near downtown Boston. After he sold himself a parcel of land in the Fens as a site, the ballpark's construction began in September 1911 and ended before the team's 1912 season. Because of the new ballpark, the team's market value increased, causing Taylor to sell 50 percent of it in 1912 to Jim McAleer and Robert McRoy for $150,000.

Named for its location, Fenway Park had 27,000 seats with the main steel and concrete grandstand extending from behind home plate down the base lines and connecting with wooden bleachers in the outfield. A fire, unfortunately, occurred during May 1926 destroying the wooden bleachers along the left field foul line. Seven years later, Fenway Park was extensively renovated. After another fire in January 1934 destroyed most of the construction, the ballpark was rebuilt and then reopened for the MLB season.

Since 2003, there have been several major improvements and upgrades completed at the ballpark. These involved such things as the Green Monster wall and additional club seats, the State Street Pavilion, and a new video scoreboard. To accommodate fans, seating capacity increased to more than 37,000 for day and night games.

> *"Now that Fenway Park has been renovated, it's almost as good as its reputation. No matter how many times you go, it doesn't get old. Lot of great seats. But a lot of awful seats, too, in the right field bleachers and far down the right field line. The neighborhood is more BoSox Theme Park now than it used to be when it was gritty, authentic and the phrase Red Sox Nation hadn't been invented. But, if you're a baseball fan, or even if you're not, it is magical."*

Globe Life Park

From 1972 to 1993, the Rangers played their home games in Arlington Stadium. However, because of Texas's summer heat and humidity, the ballpark was the hottest one in MLB. Thus, almost all Rangers' home games, even those on Sundays, were played at night. As a result, the team began lobbying for a new stadium in the late 1980s and then during October 1990, the Rangers and city of Arlington agreed to build it.

After construction began in April 1992 and then ended twenty-three months later, The Ballpark in Arlington—renamed Ameriquest Field in 2005, Rangers Ballpark in Arlington in 2008, and finally Globe Life Park (GLP) in 2014—opened for the team's 1994 season. Designed with ideas from bygone stadiums, the 48,100-seat ballpark resembles Brooklyn's Ebbets Field with its red brick façade and arches. Besides a brick Wall of Fame containing information about every Rangers team, it is the only retro ballpark with enclosed seats and a four-story office complex surrounding the playing field.

More specifically, GLP's amenities include such things as luxury suites divided into tiers; a large video scoreboard located above the home run porch in right field; a Rangers Baseball Hall of Fame that contains team artifacts and captures the franchise's history; the Kid's Zone, which provides interactive games for kids and all-you-can-eat seats in the upper home run porch; an expanded home plate club; the Capital One club; and a new merchandise store.

> *"Despite being in the middle of nowhere, I enjoyed both World Series I covered there. The outfield grandstands have a good, traditional feel. Unfortunately, it is right next to the Jerry Jones Ego Museum, the most hideous wretched excess in sports. But it makes the Rangers' park look tasteful by comparison."*

Guaranteed Rate Field

From 1901 to 1909, the White Stockings/White Sox clubs played their home games in Chicago's 15,000-seat South Side Park. In 1910, the 28,000-seat White Sox Park—renamed Comiskey Park in 1913—opened and the team competed in games there until 1990. When that facility became outdated, a new, publicly financed, 44,300-seat ballpark was built for the White Sox across 35th Street and south of its predecessor. Opened in 1991, it was also called Comiskey Park but then renamed U.S. Cellular Field in 2003 and, thirteen years later, Guaranteed Rate Field.

Since the early 1990s, the team's ballpark has been renovated several times, including its seats, decks, concourses, and sight lines. Its amenities include a multilevel, interactive fundamentals skills deck in left field and a two-level fan deck in center field, which provides a panoramic view of the playing field. Good locations exist throughout the outfield concourse for fans to mingle or view statues of former great White Sox players such as Frank Thomas and Nellie Fox. During summers, a popular area for spectators is the Rain Room where a cool mist relieves the heat.

> *"The replacement for Comiskey Park on Chicago's south side and known for much of its history as U.S. Cellular Field, it had the misfortune of being designed by Populous the year before the firm broke through with the design of Baltimore's Camden Yards, which set the standard for ballpark design for the next 25 years. Guaranteed Rate Field's design lacked the charm of ballparks to follow and underwent a series of renovations in the 2000s to rectify issues that plagued the facility from its inception."*

Kauffman Stadium

Municipal Stadium was the home site of baseball's Kansas City Athletics (1955–1967) and the Royals (1969–1972), Negro League's Monarchs during 1923–1931 and 1937–1954, and the NFL Kansas City Chiefs from 1963 to 1971. While the gridiron at Municipal Stadium extended over the baseball diamond into right centerfield, portable bleachers were placed in left field. In 1976, the building was demolished and the area containing it redeveloped to become a single-family housing neighborhood.

Construction on the Truman Sports Complex, which included the Royals' ballpark and Chiefs' Arrowhead Stadium, began during mid-July 1968. Originally known as Royals Stadium—then Kauffman Stadium since 1993—the team played its first game there in April 1973. The ballpark is very colorful, with approximately 40,700 seats, all facing second base and arranged in three tiers in maroon, gold, and orange. This was the AL's first ballpark with Astroturf as its playing surface. The most unique feature of the stadium is the water fountains beyond the outfield fence since people know Kansas City as the City of Fountains. The fountains stretch more than 300-hundred feet horizontally and have a 10-foot-high waterfall that descends from an upper cascade pool that serves as a background for two water pools. A twelve-story scoreboard, in the shape of the Royals' crest, is located beyond the center field fence.

From 2007 to 2009, the Royals sponsored a two-year, $256 million renovation of Kauffman Stadium. Phase I included new bullpens, expansion of seats in the Crown Club and Dugout Suites, and an LED auxiliary scoreboard in the left field wall. The crown scoreboard in centerfield was replaced by a new high-definition video scoreboard. Renovations continued on to the dugout level concourse and exterior to widen concourses at all levels and also on the outfield plaza to connect the entire ballpark. Other attractions for fans at Kauffman Stadium include a kids' area known as the Little K, a right-field sports-bar themed restaurant named Taste of KC, and the Royals' Hall of Fame in left field.

> *"The Kansas City Royals' Kauffman Stadium is not new, but it's experienced a recent surge in fan appreciation. Thanks in part to a $250 million renovation finished in 2009, the sixth-oldest stadium in the majors (it opened in 1973) now offers one of the sport's best game-day experiences."*

Minute Maid Park

Following MLB's Houston Colt .45s' seasons at Colt Stadium (1962–1964), the NL Astros played their home games at the Astrodome (1965–1999). By the early-to-mid-1990s, however, the stadium lacked the amenities of new retro ballparks and had an Astroturf field with numerous seats distant from the field.

When franchise owner Drayton McLane threatened to move his club elsewhere, voters approved a referendum in late 1996 to fund the construction of a new ballpark on a 25-acre site in downtown Houston. Built with steel and concrete in addition to a brick and limestone exterior, the 40,900-seat ballpark features a retractable roof plus a 50,000-square-foot sliding glass door that provides a view of the city's skyline with or without an open roof.

Originally known as Enron Field before the Enron Corporation went bankrupt during 2000–2001, the facility received its current name, Minute Maid Park, in 2002. Besides a huge HD video scoreboard, a wild-west steam locomotive, and 20-degree-angled Tal's Hill, the ballpark includes such attractions as Phillips 66 Homerun Alley, the team's store named The Shed, and a FiveSeven Grille in honor of former players Jeff Bagwell and Craig Biggio.

> *"OK, it's quirky. Really quirky. Maybe too much so. There's Tal's Hill in center field, which is an accident waiting to happen. There's a way-too-short wall in left field, plus an odd angle back to the bullpens in deep left-center. There's a locomotive filled with fake giant oranges above the wall. But in spite of all that, it really is a nice park, especially when the roof is open."*

Oakland Coliseum

From 1968 to 1997, the MLB Athletics (A's) played their home games at the Oakland Coliseum (OC)—renamed Network Associates Coliseum during 1998–2004, McAfee Coliseum in 2005–2008, Oakland Coliseum in 2009–2011, O.co Coliseum in 2012–2015, and OC again in 2016–2017. During these MLB seasons, the club's annual attendance exceeded two million only eleven times.

A three-tiered stadium, the OC was built in a circular shape with many seats stretching from the foul poles and bleachers beyond the outfield fence. Two Diamond Vision video scoreboards exist above both the left and right field bleachers. Few renovations occurred until the NFL Raiders returned from Los Angeles to Oakland in 1995. The stadium was expanded with outfield bleachers replaced by a four-tier section of 22,000 seats and video boards installed above the stadium rim down the left and right field base lines.

After renaming its ballpark four times, the team closed the third deck of O.co Coliseum beginning in 2006. This decision moved fans closer to the field and made games more intimate. Although it has 60,000 seats, the stadium's capacity is actually about 41,100. Some fans arrive for games on the Bart Metro transportation system to tailgate, discuss baseball strategy, and mingle with each other.[4]

> *"The shame is that this once was a nice stadium. Back before Al Davis built the monstrosity that has overtaken the center-field bleachers as an upper deck for his Raiders, the Coliseum offered up gorgeous views of the mountains in the distance. These days, there are no mountains to be seen, only a decrepit stadium that feels even older than it is. Have we mentioned the recurring raw sewage problem? The A's and their fans deserve so much better than this, but they remain stuck in limbo while MLB tries to find a way to let them relocate to San Jose, encroaching on territory the Giants claim is solely theirs."*

Progressive Field

Historically, the Indians played their home games at League Park (1901–1915), Dunn Field (1916–1927), League Park/Cleveland Stadium (1928–1946), and then Cleveland Stadium (1947–1993). In 1985, David and Richard Jacobs purchased the Indians and hoped to build a new ballpark and improve the team's value.

A few years after voters approved a bond issue in 1990, a 43,000-seat ballpark was built as part of an urban renewal project along with the Quickens Loan Arena for the National Basketball Association (NBA) Cleveland Cavaliers. Named Jacobs Park

---

4 *In March 2017, the NFL Raiders announced plans to relocate to Las Vegas, Nevada. As a result, a new sports stadium will be built in Oakland and open in 2020. Since the Raiders would likely play two or three more seasons at the Coliseum, this makes it the last multipurpose stadium. Based on the Raiders' plans to move, the A's want a new ballpark. The team expected to announce plans for their preferred site in Oakland by the end of 2017 or in 2018. For plans regarding a new ballpark, see Andy Dolich, "Where Consultant Says A's Will Build Their Ballpark," East Bay Times (7 September 2018): A.8; Christopher O'Donnell, "Much Riding on Ybor City Ballpark Design," Tampa Bay Times (10 July 2018): 1; David DeBolt, "Oakland and A's Begin Talks of New Ballpark," East Bay Times (17 May 2018): B.1; Gary Peterson, "A's Have Unique Idea to Get Fans to New Ballpark," East Bay Times (13 April 2018): B.3.*

from 1994 to 2007, Progressive Insurance purchased naming rights in 2008 for $3.6 million per year for sixteen years and then renamed the Indians' ballpark, Progressive Field.

Although fans may enter Progressive Field from several gates, many come through Gate C in center field. Revamped following the club's 2014 season, Gate C connects the ballpark to downtown Cleveland and contains Heritage Park, which is the Indians' Hall of Fame that features statues of such former great players as Bob Feller and Jim Thome.

After MLB's 2015 season, the Indians began phase two of their renovations to Progressive Field, completing them in the spring of 2016. These included building a new enclosed club behind home plate on the main level of the ballpark that features a glass front for viewing games. Another amenity, the main concourse, was opened from home plate to left field so fans never lose sight of the game. Additionally, the existing videoboard was replaced with a new, large HD video scoreboard.

> *"It's funny: So many of today's ballparks were borne of backlash to the cookie-cutter municipal parks of the 1950s and 60s, then wound up feeling somewhat humdrum when roughly half the league opened new baseball-only stadiums. Progressive Field–still "The Jake" to many–is a cozy park in a downtown location with few particulars that stand out. It's fine."*

Rogers Centre

After playing their home games in Toronto's 30,900-seat Exhibition Stadium for twelve years, the Blue Jays moved into the new retractable-roof SkyDome in 1989. Sixteen years later, Rogers Communication purchased the ballpark for $25 million and renamed it Rogers Centre. Located in downtown Toronto next to the CN Tower, it has five levels of seats that extend from right centerfield to home plate and then to left center field. All lower-level seats are movable and can form a football gridiron to host games of the Canadian Football League (CFL) Toronto Argonauts. Interestingly, the pitcher's mound rises and lowers hydraulically when not needed for baseball.

During late 2015, the team announced the installation of a dirt infield at Rogers Centre. This eliminated the dirt cutouts around the bases. In addition, there is a possibility of installing a grass field at the ballpark in 2018 or sometime thereafter. That depends on several factors including the Argonauts moving to another site in Toronto. In addition to the ballpark's retractable-roof, field turf, and large video scoreboard, the area also includes Rogers Centre Renaissance Hotel with approximately seventy, or one-fifth, of its rooms overlooking the playing field.

> *"Back in the early 90s, when the concept of a retractable roof was almost as crazy as a phone you could carry in your pocket, this was the coolest stadium in baseball. Now, not so much. The Blue Jays just pulled themselves back to relevance in the last few years, but 2015's playoff run seems like a distant memory for Jays fans. A team with almost no playoff hopes is filling the dome at about a 55% clip, which is why Rogers Centre has slipped a spot this year to 29."*

Safeco Field

For more than two decades, sports fans watched MLB's Seattle Mariners play their home games at the concrete and sterile Kingdome. Although it was revolutionary when it opened in the late 1970s, by the early-to-mid-1990s a new wave of ballparks were being built, which made the Kingdome an outdated yet semi-popular facility.

The Mariners, therefore, wanted a new state-of-the-art ballpark for their fans, and the franchise needed it as a way to increase revenue because of financial losses in 1993 and 1994. Since a new ballpark was seen as a way to solidify the city's sense of community and lead to economic development, the team would not sign a long-term lease to remain in Seattle if ground was not broken for a modern stadium by 1996.

In 1994, the King County Stadium Alternatives Task Force was established after tiles from the Kingdome's roof crashed onto several seating areas forcing the team to play on the road for the rest of the season. Then in 1995, Washington state's governor, together with King County, developed the Public Facilities District to oversee site selection, design, construction, and management of a new ballpark. Although voters rejected a proposal to increase the sales tax in September 1995, one month later the state's legislature authorized funding for a stadium.

After choosing a site directly south of the Kingdome, the Mariners unveiled plans for their ballpark in early 1997. Besides following the same neo-traditional pattern as every new ballpark built in the 1990s, it featured a brick façade with natural grass and a retractable roof. The roof was necessary because of Seattle's rainy weather. As a result, 47,500-seat Safeco Field opened in mid-July 1999.

Safeco Field has several amenities and attractions including the Bullpen Market and such things as the Fan Walk's personalized bricks, local food vendors, an open-pit barbecue, and one of the best views of the game from behind the centerfield fence. Located at the end of the left field line on the upper deck, Lookout Landing provides incredible views of inside and outside the ballpark. In addition, there is an Outside Corner Picnic Patio, Children's Hospital Playfield, and supposedly the largest video board in baseball.

> *"Come early for happy hour at the newly opened 'Pen to get your fill of $5 beers and star-chef Ethan Stowell's oyster po'boys. Then settle into the stadium, which offers sunset views of the Puget Sound and Seattle skyline. It borders Pioneer Square, an area that includes artist studios, shops, and restaurants. Baseball-inspired works by Pacific Northwestern artists are on display, including a chandelier made from 1,000 resin baseball bats, located above the home-plate entry way. The 12-by-9-foot abstract bronze catcher's mitt is a popular photo-op as is the team mascot, the Mariner Moose, which can be found in the main concourse's Moose Den."*

Target Field

From 1961 to 1981, the Minnesota Twins played their home games at 48,000-seat Metropolitan Stadium and then another twenty-eight seasons at the 46,500-seat Hubert H. Humphrey Metrodome. After experiencing problems with the latter ballpark, including its deterioration and inability to generate enough revenue for the franchise, the state's legislature approved financing for the construction of a new ballpark in May 2006. According to the legislation, the county's share was about two-thirds of the cost while the Twins paid for the other portion of it. In September 2008, the Target Corporation acquired naming rights for twenty-five years at Target Field in downtown Minneapolis.

The 39,000-seat ballpark, which reflects Minnesota's urban sophistication and outdoor vitality, has a façade that consists of limestone while a canopy covers much of the upper deck seats. Most fans enter the building through Target Plaza—a park-like space located outside the right field entrance gate. This landscaped area features a 1,500-pound bronze glove, statues of famous Twins players, and a wall tribute to Minnesota ballparks and Metropolitan Stadium.

Besides heated concessions, restrooms, a restaurant and also lounge areas on each level of the ballpark, fans can gather for food and beverages inside the Legends Club Lounge, the Met Club, and the Town Ball Tavern which celebrates Minnesota's amateur baseball history. Themed concessions are also located throughout Target Field including Taste of Twins territory, Hennepin Grille, Senior Smokes, and Frankie V's Italian.

Before MLB's 2016 season, the Twins reconfigured the centerfield seating area into a multilevel fan space. Located directly below the Minnie and Paul figures in centerfield, the area features a Twins-themed pub with Minnesota-branded food options on the upper level. Named CATCH, the lower level area is premium space for season ticket members.

> *"But the Twins' home park, opened in 2010, has got all the staples of a great contemporary ballpark: skyline views, a relatively walkable (and bikeable) location, great (i.e., fried) local cuisine, and open concourses good for exploring and aimless wandering. Like most new parks, it has its quirky features, but none of them feel too forced."*

Tropicana Field

Finished in 1990, the publicly-financed Florida Suncoast Dome—renamed Thunderdome in 1992—was originally built for baseball although the team renovated the stadium to make it even more like a MLB ballpark. The $85 million renovation included, in part, wider concourses and installation of Astroturf, clubhouses, dugouts, additional luxury suites, restrooms, elevators, escalators, administrative offices, and a reduction in capacity from 48,000 to 45,000. After Tropicana Juice purchased naming rights, the stadium's name changed to Tropicana Field in 1996.

People enter the ballpark's main entrance through a giant rotunda reminiscent of Brooklyn's Ebbets Field. Inside, visitors are in the Centerfield Street area which includes a brew house, the team's store, the Capitan Morgan Deck, and Hitters Hall of Fame. Another feature at Tropicana Field is the 35-foot, 10,000 gallon Rays Touch Tank where spectators can touch an actual ray fish in water.[5]

> *"Built eight years before the region even had its own major-league team, the Trop has provided one of the worst environments in baseball history for 16 years now. It's the only permanent dome still being used in the majors. The lack of crowds leaves everything echoing throughout the park. And then there are the catwalks that hover over the field of play, with special ground rules written in case a batted ball strikes one of the four different rings. The Rays desperately want a new park, and they've been trying for years, but for now they remain stuck in this awful facility."*

Yankee Stadium

During mid-April 2009, the new 52,000-seat Yankee Stadium opened for the team's first home game of the MLB season. The ballpark has the appearance and tradition of the original stadium with a grandstand that consists of four levels. While the lower two levels include 30,000 seats, the third level contains more than fifty luxury suites and the fourth a split-level upper deck.

---

5 *For some relatively recent articles about the construction and financing of a new ballpark for the Rays, see Christopher O'Donnell and Meagan Betts, "Ballpark Lite: Spaced Great Less Filling," Tampa Bay Times (22 July 2018): 1; "Paying For Ballpark Will Take Teamwork," Tampa Bay Times (12 July 2018): 8; Christopher O'Donnell, "Rays Owner Boosts Hope," Tampa Bay Times (31 March 2108): 1; Shelly Sigo, "Bonds Likely to Fuel Cross-Bay Ballpark Move by Tampa Bay Rays," The Bond Buyer (22 February 2018): 1; "Rays Owner Wants New Ballpark," Charleston Gazette (10 February 2018): B.3.*

Among its features, historic Monument Park is located beyond the outfield fence in center field; a high-definition video scoreboard is in the outfield; hand-operated auxiliary scoreboards are part of the right-center and left-center fences; and other amenities include luxury, outdoor, and party suites, club seats, a martini bar and steakhouse, and picnic areas. In addition, a Yankees Museum displays memorabilia of their former great teams and players while a Hard Rock Café exists in the Grand Hall. Despite these things, the club's average attendances declined from the low 50,000s per game during the 2005–2008 MLB seasons to the low-to-mid 40,000s. Undoubtedly factors such as the team's performances and problems in the local economy influenced its home attendances.

> *"They almost ruined it with the 'new' Yankee Stadium. It will never be as good as the old place. In its worst elements, it's a crass cash factory for the rich. In its best elements, it still feels like it's Yankee Stadium, white façade and all. The park doesn't 'play' as well as it once did with far too many cheap home runs to right and right-center field."*

Table 9.1 contains some important and relevant characteristics of AL ballparks as of 2018. First, their average age was twenty-eight years with the three oldest being Fenway Park, Angel Stadium, and Oakland Coliseum while the most recent included Target Field, Yankee Stadium, Comerica Park, and Minute Maid Park.

Second, these ballparks' average capacity equaled 42,300 in 2018. From smallest to largest in number of seats was, respectively, the Rays' Tropicana Field and Blue Jays' Rogers Centre. Since being constructed, several of these facilities have been renovated and reduced in size to provide better and more convenient seats for fans to see games.

Third, the original but unadjusted cost to build these fifteen ballparks was $224 million as of 2018. They ranged in price from less than $1 million for Fenway Park in 1912 to $1.6 billion for Yankee Stadium in 2009. If any AL team or teams decide to construct a new ballpark and replace their current one, it will be very expensive and likely uneconomical for them to entirely finance the project. Thus, local and state government will likely pay all—or at least a large portion—of the new ballpark's construction cost.

Table 9.1 Teams Ballparks, American League, 2018 Major League Baseball Season

Ballpark (Team)	Year	Capacity	Cost	Pub%	Owner
Angel Stadium (Angels)	1966	45.4	24	100	City of Anaheim
Camden Yards (Orioles)	1992	45.9	110	96	MD Stadium Authority
Comerica Park (Tigers)	2000	41.5	300	63	County Stadium Authority
Fenway Park (Red Sox)	1912	37.6	<1	0	Boston Red Sox
Globe Life Park (Rangers)	1994	48.1	191	80	Sports Facility Authority
Guaranteed Rate Field (White Sox)	1991	40.6	137	100	Sports Facilities Authority
Kauffman Stadium (Royals)	1973	40.7	43	100	Jackson County
Minute Maid Park (Astros)	2000	40.9	248	68	County Sports Authority
Oakland Coliseum (Athletics)	1968	41.1	25	100	Alameda County
Progressive Field (Indians)	1994	35.2	169	88	Cuyahoga County
Rogers Centre (Blue Jays)	1989	50.5	500	63	Rogers Communications/BJ
Safeco Field (Mariners)	1999	47.5	517	72	County Stadium Authority
Target Field (Twins)	2010	39.0	545	64	Hennepin County
Tropicana Field (Rays)	1998	31.0	115	100	City of St. Petersburg
Yankee Stadium (Yankees)	2009	50.2	1,600	0	New York Yankees

Note: Year is when the ballpark opened for the teams' home games. Capacity is in thousands. Cost is the ballparks' original construction cost in millions of US dollars. Abbreviated is Blue Jays (BJ), Maryland (MD), public (Pub), and percent (%). Pub is the proportion of the ballpark paid for by the public sector. The symbol < means less than the amount.

Source: "American League Ballparks," www.ballparksofbaseball.com cited 24 September 2018.

Fourth, according to column five in table 9.1, the public's share of AL ballparks' original cost averaged 78 percent. While five, or 33 percent of the group, were entirely financed by taxpayers and only two, or 13 percent, of them without money from the public sector (cities, municipalities, and states), the other eight, or 53 percent, used both public and private funds.

Fifth, based on information in column six of the table, the Red Sox own Fenway Park and the Yankees own Yankee Stadium. Although the Blue Jays control a portion of the Rogers Centre in Toronto, owners of the other twelve ballparks include such things as cities, counties, and stadium and sports authorities. Because of significant and increasing labor costs in the future, this suggests that a combination of public entities and teams will jointly finance the construction of new MLB ballparks that are primarily owned by government but operated by the team or another organization in the private sector.

NATIONAL LEAGUE

AT&T Ballpark

After leaving New York for San Francisco in late 1957, the Giants played their home games at Seals Stadium (1958–1959) and then Candlestick Park (1960–1995)–renamed 3Com Park during 1996–1999. Within this 42-year period, their attendances ranged from a low of 6,400 per game in 1974 to a high of 32,100 in 1993. Notorious for its windy conditions and also home of the NFL 49ers, 3Com Park became an inferior stadium and not a profitable investment as an asset for its owner.

After residents in San Francisco and neighboring Santa Clara and San Jose rejected referendums for the construction of a new ballpark during the late 1980s, the Giants announced plans in 1995 to build a new stadium in downtown San Francisco within the China Basin district. Privately financed by the team, construction began in late 1997 and was completed in April 2000. Originally known as Pacific Bell Park, it was renamed SBC Park in 2004 and then, two years later, AT&T Ballpark.

As fans approach this 41,900-seat ballpark, they see a steel and brick structure that features two clock towers with pyramid-shaped roofs topped by flagpoles. Once inside the ticket gates, expansive concourses allow people to easily find their seats. The main three-tier grandstand consists of green seats that extend from behind home plate down to both foul poles. While bleachers are located behind the left field fence, a walkway is above the right field fence because of the China Basin, aka McCovey Cove. A sidewalk between the water and right field commemorates historical moments in Giants history. Those without tickets may see games through a screened section of the right field fence.

Besides a video scoreboard behind the right field fence, spectators have other entertainment options. For example, the Coca-Cola Fan Lot is an interactive play area for children and adults to enjoy a slide into home plate from one of the four slides inside the Coca-Cola contour bottle. After a Giants player hits a home run, strobe lights flash inside the bottle, bubbles appear to float from the bottle's mouth, and green and white lights flash up and down the neon tubes running along its ribs. In addition, fans can stroll up to the world's largest baseball glove or view the Bay Area from the outfield area.

> *"The Giants left Candlestick Park after the 1999 season and moved into an absolutely spectacular stadium in AT&T Park. It's another picturesque stadium with the view of the Bay and home runs flying into McCovey Cove. It always smells like garlic fries, has a giant baseball glove in the outfield concourse, and brings one of baseball's best atmospheres."*[6]

Busch Stadium

Before 2006, the NL's St. Louis Browns played their home games at Sportsman Park (1892), Robison Field (1893–1898), and the Perfectos at Robison Field (1899). Renamed Cardinals, they performed at Robison Field (1900–1919), Sportsman's Park (1920–1952), Busch Stadium I (1953–1965), and Busch Stadium II (1966–2005). During this period, the club's attendances ranged from a low of 2,200 per game in 1897 to a high of 43,600 in 2005.

In June 2001, the Cardinals and state of Missouri signed a contract to construct a new ballpark in downtown St. Louis and adjacent to Busch Stadium II. Owned entirely by the Cardinals, Busch Stadium III was privately financed using a combination of private bonds—obligating the team—bank loans, cash from the franchise's owners,

---

6 *Idem. The first three Notes in this chapter also contain the same readings for descriptions and rankings of National League ballparks.*

and a long-term loan from St. Louis County. During 2004, the team and Anheuser-Busch signed a 20-year naming rights deal to the ballpark.

As fans approach the 46,700-seat ballpark, they confront a façade consisting of brick and steel with arched openings at the main entrances. There are main, loge, and terrace concourses and bleachers in both left and right field providing spectators with a view of action on the field. Beyond the outfield is the skyline of downtown St. Louis in addition to the Gateway Arch.

Busch Stadium III has several amenities. For example, there is the US Cellular Family Pavilion where fans enjoy interactive games and activities; Coca-Cola Rooftop Deck and Backstop Bar; Ballpark Village, which includes a three-story building containing a Hall of Fame Museum and Cardinals Nation Restaurant & Bar; and Budweiser Brew House, which showcases Anheuser-Busch's connection to the franchise featuring a beer garden and an estimated 100 different beers.

> *"Busch Stadium is nice, but it's essentially a new and improved version of the old Busch Stadium. It doesn't stand out enough to make it into the top 10, but it does rank among the top half of the league. Cardinals' fans are passionate–in an elitist sort of way, but still–so the atmosphere is always excellent. I'd just expect better beer for a stadium named after a mega brewer. Oh wait, I guess I shouldn't."*

Chase Field

When MLB awarded an expansion franchise to Phoenix, Arizona, construction began on a stadium in November 1995. Shaped like a massive airport hangar and originally named Bank One Ballpark, it was the first stadium built with a retractable roof because of extreme summer temperatures and also with a natural grass field to allow outdoor games late in the baseball season. After Bank One and JP Morgan Chase merged their operations in 2005, the $354 million ballpark was renamed Chase Field.

The Diamondbacks made their debut before a packed house at Bank One Ballpark on March 31, 1998. More than 3.6 million fans filled the 48,600-seat facility to see the team during its first year in the league. Regarding the ballpark's structure, a four-tier grandstand extends from the left field foul pole to home plate and around to the right field foul pole. Thousands of bleacher seats are behind both the left and right field fences and a 25-foot center field wall serves as the hitters' backdrop with the main video scoreboard above it. The ballpark's most unusual feature is a swimming pool located behind part of the right field fence.

Other than the pool, Chase Field has several other amenities. Overlooking left field and third base is Friday's Front Row Sports Grill, which offers food and provides entertainment. Although one of the youngest franchises in MLB, some Diamondbacks teams have been successful, including victories in four of seven games at Bank One Ballpark in the 2001 World Series against the AL Yankees. The newest addition to the ballpark is the $12 million, 136-feet wide by 46-feet high HD video scoreboard, installed in 2008.

> *"Similar in look to Miller Park, Chase Field has a retractable roof that splits open in the middle, plus panels beyond the outfield wall. This stadium, though, is massive, and can be seen from miles away, resembling a huge airplane hangar more than a ballpark. There are plenty of distractions, from restaurants and bars to the famous swimming pool behind the right field fence. Like Coors Field, it was built too big, back when ticket demand was sky-high. Now, the Diamondbacks have trouble coming close to sellouts even for big games against prime opponents."*

Citi Field

After two seasons at the Polo Grounds, the Mets played their home games in Shea Stadium from 1964 to 2008. While at these ballparks, the team's attendances ranged from a low of 9,600 in 1979 to a high of 49,900 in 2008. Although Shea Stadium was a multipurpose stadium that fans both loved and hated, it lacked the modern amenities of new ballparks built since the mid-to-late 1990s.

In 2006, the club revealed plans for a new ballpark and received approval to issue bonds for its construction. After officially breaking ground, it was built in the parking lot beyond the outfield fence of Shea Stadium. Financial service company, Citigroup

Incorporated, purchased naming rights to the new ballpark for $20 million annually over twenty years.

Named Citi Field, the 42,000-seat ballpark has 42 percent of its seats in the lower deck. The main three-tier grandstand extends from the right field pole to home plate and down to the left field pole into left center field. The stadium has at least fifty luxury suites and in right field, the Pepsi Porch seats more than 1,000 fans. The seating area, modeled after Detroit's Tiger Stadium, overhangs the playing field and allows for easy home runs.

Citi Field has such amenities as an enhanced outfield picnic area known as Taste of the City; an interactive Mets museum with club memorabilia and Hall of Fame displays; two HD video scoreboards; the famous Big Apple located behind the center field fence that rises each time a Mets player hits a home run; and a skyline atop a restaurant in center field.

> *"Yes, it's an upgrade from Shea, but just replacing something that's worn out doesn't make it great on its own. This is definitely the case with Citi, where even a center field Shake Shack and an NL pennant haven't done much to help the Mets' attendance, which, after last year's post-World Series novelty, dipped back to 68% of capacity. This is deserving for a team with the third-worst home record this decade."*

Citizens Bank Park

Before MLB's 2004 season, various Philadelphia Quakers and then Phillies teams played their home games chronologically at Recreation Park (1883–1886), Philadelphia Baseball Grounds (1887–1894), Baker Bowl (1895–1937), Shibe Park (1938–1952), Connie Mack Stadium (1953–1970), and Veterans Stadium (1971–2003). During this period, the club's attendance ranged from a low of 1,600 per game in 1902 to a high of 38,700 in 1993.

Because of Veteran Stadium's bad turf and problems sharing the facility with the NFL Philadelphia Eagles, the Phillies needed and wanted a new ballpark by the late

1990s. After considering at least three different sites including Chinatown, Liberty Yards, and property adjacent to Veterans Stadium, a site in the Philadelphia Sports Complex was chosen as the location for the club's new ballpark and for a new football stadium for the Eagles. Philadelphia's city council approved the construction of these venues—financed in part by a 2 percent rental car tax and largely paid by visitors to the metropolitan area. According to that deal, the Phillies organization agreed to pay for any construction overruns along with maintenance of the ballpark. Similar to most other teams in MLB, the Phillies sold naming rights to their ballpark to Citizens Bank for $95 million over twenty-five years.

Opened during mid-April 2004, 43,600-seat Citizens Bank Park consists of a lower deck, suite level, and upper deck. The main grandstand extends from the left field foul pole to home plate down to the right field foul pole and then into right center field. There is a break in the upper deck along the first base side, allowing the seating area to be closer to the ballfield. Additional seating is available behind the left field fence.

Besides the seating bowl and main HD video scoreboard, the ballpark has several amenities. These include a gigantic Liberty Bell to celebrate home runs and a festive outdoor entertainment area named Ashburn Alley. It features a street-fair type atmosphere complete with picnic areas; family-fun activities; treasured Philadelphia moments in baseball; enhanced concessions with plenty of Philadelphia flavor; clear views to the playing field; and a special viewing area overlooking the pitchers' bullpens.

> *"The new ballpark for the Phillies was built as part of a larger sports complex that also features Lincoln Financial Field for the Eagles and Wells Fargo Arena for the 76ers and Flyers. Designed by Populous, perhaps the most distinctive feature of CBP, other than its propensity to allow home runs, is its massive HD Daktronics video boards, which were installed in 2004 and 2005. The screen in left field measures 76 by 97 feet, making it the largest videoboard in the National League. Perhaps most notably, Citizens Bank Park would be the last new ballpark designed by Populous."*

Coors Field

During the late 1980s, the state of Colorado formed the Denver Metropolitan MLB Stadium to plan and build a new ballpark for the NL Rockies. Before the city was awarded an expansion franchise in 1991, voters in a six-county area approved a 1 percent sales tax to fund the ballpark. After MLB's decision to expand in Denver, construction began on the stadium in October 1992. When the team's attendance exceeded three million at Mile High Stadium in 1993 and 1994, the new ballpark's capacity was increased from 43,000 to 50,300.

Named Coors Field, it has an old-fashioned brick façade and on 20th and Blake Street, a large clock exists for fans to meet at prior to a game. The three-tiered grandstand extends from the left field foul pole to home plate and then down to the right field pole and around to center field. While purple seats exist throughout the entire upper deck, a 2,300-seat bleacher section called the Rockpile is located behind the center field backdrop. The main HD video scoreboard is beyond the left field bleachers and another one makes up part of the right field wall.

Coors Field has several amenities. These include 4,400 club seats; the Roundeus at the Sandlot Brewery; a microbrewery located at the right field entrance; the Diamond Dry Good gift shop; a merchandise store; and the Mountain Ranch Club that features upscale dining on six tiers located down the right field line. Completed in 2014, an extensive renovation project removed the majority of upper-deck seats in right field and replaced them with a two-level rooftop deck. This area contains the 5280 Craft Bar, CHUBurger Restaurant, and the VIP Cabana Terrace.

> *"Coors Field is very pretty, in a wonderful part of Denver, and on a clear day from the upper deck you can see the Rocky Mountains. But only from the upper deck and only on a clear day. Unfortunately, playing baseball in mile-high altitude is an abomination against the game. It's not Denver's fault, but it's a major demerit. Distant fences, to compensate for altitude, plus a too-large capacity, give Colorado 15,000 very remote seats."*

Dodger Stadium

During their first four seasons on the West Coast, the Dodgers played their home games in the 93,600-seat Los Angeles Memorial Coliseum. Before moving there in 1958, however, the city agreed to exchange 352 acres of land at Chavez Ravine for the team to build a privately-funded, 56,000-seat ballpark. Three years after its construction started in 1959, the $23 million Dodger Stadium opened to host MLB games.

Located a few miles from downtown Los Angeles, Dodger Stadium was constructed on a hillside with parking areas surrounding the facility. The ballpark has five seating levels extending from the left field foul pole to home plate and then down to the right field foul pole, except for the top deck. Bleachers are in both left and right field and feature a wavy top roof, and behind them are two jumbo hexagonal HD video scoreboards.

After several renovations during the 2000s including an expanded dugout section, two new Baseline Box Clubs, a team store, and other improvements, Dodger Stadium became an attractive, clean, and well-landscaped facility. Consequently, Dodgers' teams play in a relatively old and inexpensively built but valuable ballpark within a large and prosperous sports market.

> *"One of three ballparks to remain from the Major League's West Coast expansion in the late 1950s and 1960s, Dodger Stadium remains among the jewels in baseball, recently hosting the finals of the World Baseball Classic. Designed by Col. Emil Prager, Dodger Stadium was built in Chavez Ravine, overlooking the city of Los Angeles. It is the only ballpark in the Major Leagues to have not increased its seating capacity over its lifetime, holding roughly 56,000."*

Great American Ball Park

Before 2003, the NL's Reds played their home games at League Park (1890–1901), Palace of the Fans (1902–1911), Redland Field (1912–1933), Crosley Field (1934–1969), and Riverfront Stadium (1970–1995)—renamed Cinergy Field (1996–2002).

During this 113-year period, the team's attendances at home ranged from 1,800 per game in 1890 to 31,600 in 1994.

After the Reds and NFL Cincinnati Bengals shared Riverfront Stadium for almost three decades, Hamilton County voters approved a bond in 1996 to increase the county sales tax and fund a facility for each pro team. Then two years later, voters agreed to build the ballpark along the city's riverfront. The new 42,200-seat ballpark was built and named Great American Ball Park after Great American Insurance, who bought naming rights to it for $75 million over thirty years.

Adjacent to the Reds' Hall of Fame Museum, team store, and a garden remembering Pete Rose, the ballpark consists of three levels with the lower grandstand extending from the left field foul pole to home plate and around to the right field foul pole. The second deck has club seats, luxury suites, and a press box while the upper deck includes two large seating sections for fans.

The ballpark has several amenities. For example, there is a brewpub with a bar that includes memorabilia from the Big Red Machine era; dining options at the Fox Sports Ohio Championship Club, Handlebar at Riverfront Club, and Diamond Club; a two-story Riverboat Deck to be used as a party area; an LED video board above the Sun and Moon Deck seats; and statues of former ballplayers throughout the landscape.

> *"People say it was built on the cheap. They say it looks like the circus came to town with pinwheels and riverboat restaurants above the outfield. They say the Ohio River beyond right field is brown. They say it's an uphill walk back to downtown. They say... oh, gimme a break. I like it. It's an enthusiastic homer-happy little park that feels* open*—to the sky, weather, and views of the (muddy) river."*

Marlins Park

From 1993 to 2011 the Marlins played their home games at a multipurpose facility in Miami Gardens, Florida. It was initially named Joe Robbie Stadium (1993–1996) and then renamed Pro Player Stadium (1997–2004), Dolphins Stadium (2005–2008),

Land Shark Stadium (2009), and then Sun Life Stadium (2010–2011). During this 19-year period of MLB seasons, the club's attendance ranged from a high of 37,800 per game in 1993 to a low of 10,100 in 2002. Because of heat, humidity, and rain, and playing their games in a stadium partially built for football, the Marlins needed a modern ballpark with amenities to attract fans and generate more revenue from gate receipts.

Three years after city and county commissioners approved funds for a new ballpark, construction began on it but was temporarily delayed in 2011 by a lawsuit challenging the use of public money for the project. Eventually built for $515 million, Miami-Dade County paid the majority of the costs while the city of Miami contributed $13 million and the Marlins $155 million. Located in Little Havana on the site of the former Orange Bowl, 37,400-seat Marlins Park was completed in early 2012. Thus, the team moved from baseball's largest ballpark to its smallest.

Besides a retractable roof and outside glass panels, Marlins Park has several unique features. These include, for example, a tall structure behind the outfield's left-center field fence that has moving waves along the bottom and spins marlins, seagulls, and flamingos anytime a Marlins player hits a home run; a pool and a private seating area providing classic Clevelander food and entertainment for fans; and behind home plate on both sides of the backstop, twin 450-gallon saltwater aquariums containing up to fifty fish protected by bulletproof glass.

> *"The Little Havana-based Marlins Park, which debuted for the 2012 season, is already making a big splash—literally, with two 450-gallon tanks featuring nearly 100 tropical fish. Try the aquatic life yourself with a dip in the Clevelander's pool, a South Beach party outpost complete with animal-print-body-painted dancers and celeb DJs spinning at each game. A kaleidoscopic mosaic walkway, mango slaw-topped SoBe dogs, and a 73-foot marlin (and flamingo) sculpture that rotates to celebrate home runs also reflect Miami's flamboyant influence."*

Miller Park

While a member of the NL's Central Division (CD) for three years, the Brewers played their home games at Milwaukee's County Stadium. During this period the club's home attendances declined from 22,300 per game in 1998 to 21,200 in 1999 and then one year later, to 19,400. Built for the Milwaukee Braves in 1953, the 28,100-seat ballpark—later expanded to 53,200 seats—was obsolete and needed replacement by the mid-to-late 1990s.

After the Brewers unveiled plans for a retractable roof ballpark in late 1995 and got financial approval for its construction, fans at their games could watch it being built beyond County Stadium's outfield bleachers. Despite a tragic crane accident killing three workers and destroying part of the ballpark's first base side, it was completed in 2001.

Named after the Miller Brewing Company—which has naming rights for $2.1 million per year through 2020—41,900-seat Miller Park is a structure with a façade that consists of red brick, arched windows, and a clock tower at the home plate entrance. Directly outside of it are statues of such Milwaukee icons as Hank Aaron and Robin Yount. The 12,000-ton, seven-panel retractable roof has a unique fan-shaped design and opens or closes in ten minutes. Fans can buy their favorite Brewers merchandise at the team's relatively new store, and there is upscale dinning for them at the Johnson Controls Stadium Club on the club level down the left field foul line.

Some of the ballpark's unique amenities are the Hall of Fame; children's area and brewpub; open air patios and walkways; a T.G.I Friday's Front Row Sports Grill located in the left field area known as the Front Row; and the Miller Park Kids Zone—an 8,000-square-foot interactive play area that includes a replica of Bernie the Brewer's slide.

> *"Tailgating parties here rival those prior to NFL games, so don't be alarmed by that smoky haze visible from I-94. It billows up from thousands of grills sprawled across the 12,500-car lot where fans have been cooking up pregame chow. Come early because the line to the lot starts hours before the game. By the time you're inside, you may be ready for round two: helpings of the stadium's bratwursts, Polish sausages, chorizos, and bacon-wrapped hot dogs. Rally for your favorite link in the Famous Racing*

Sausages sprinting extravaganza on the field. And don't let any foul weather deter you; Miller Field's retractable roof can open and close in about 10 minutes."

Nationals Park

From the 2005 to 2007 MLB seasons, the NL's Washington Nationals played their home games at multipurpose Robert F. Kennedy Stadium (RFK). While there, the team's attendances steadily declined from 33,700 per game in 2005 to 23,900 in 2007. Built in 1961, RFK lacked many amenities of newer ballparks.

Before the Montreal Expos had moved to DC following their 2004 season, Washington city agreed to build a new ballpark for the team. After disputes among members of the DC council on how to finance the facility, the council and MLB negotiated a deal in 2006 that authorized public financing to construct the stadium.

Without naming rights as of 2017, 43,300-seat Nationals Park opened for big-league games in 2008. The ballpark, unlike traditional stadiums, has a sleek but modern design that features mostly glass and a steel façade. Similar to the Braves' former Turner Field in Atlanta, many fans enter through outfield areas that lead from the Navy Yard Metro Station. Open concourses exist throughout the ballpark with escalators and ramps delivering fans to their seats.

Nationals Park has many amenities. These include 1,800 padded luxury seats; 2,500 club seats, more than 1,000 suite seats, and a 500-seat founder's club; a baseball-inspired restaurant named PNC Diamond Club; Homestead's Grey Bar, which honors the Negro Leagues; a kid's play area with various games; the Red Porch where fans watch games from a different perspective; and several Kwanzan Japanese cherry trees in the center field plaza and left field concourse. In 2018, the ballpark hosted MLB's all-star game.

"Nationals Park, to its credit, is a very fan-friendly ballpark, with wide concourses and good field views from just about any seat. But it simply has no defining characteristic, no distinct charm. Think about it this way:

What's the first thing you think of when you think of Nationals Park? It's tough to come up with something. The big video board? The Red Porch area? The cherry blossoms that bloom for only a week or so in early-April? The distant view of the Capitol dome from a handful of sections in the upper deck? I just wish there was something that stood out about this place."

Petco Park

Before 2004, the Padres played their home games at 67,500-seat, multipurpose San Diego Stadium from 1969 to 1980—renamed Jack Murphy Stadium in 1981—and then at Qualcomm Stadium from 1997 to 2003. During this 35-year period, their home attendances ranged from a low of 6,300 per game in 1969 to a high of 31,500 in 1998.

While playing in an aging Jack Murphy Stadium and sharing it with the NFL San Diego Chargers, the Padres announced plans in 1996 to replace it. After the club played in but lost the 1998 World Series, local voters approved the construction of a new ballpark in downtown San Diego. Originally scheduled to open in 2002, funds for its completion were not allocated for more than a year. In November 2001, the city approved a $166 million bond to resume construction of it. Two years later, Petco Animal Supplies Inc. purchased naming rights to the stadium for $60 million over twenty-two years. As a result, Petco Park opened in 2004 for the Padres.

With its white steel and sandstone façade and palm and jacaranda trees along the perimeter, Petco Park has a southern California appearance. At the entrance, fans pass by a palm court and waterfalls, and the ballpark's blue seats are close to the field and angled toward the pitcher's mound. The three-tiered grandstand extends from the right field foul pole to home plate and down to the left field foul pole where a San Diego landmark—the Western Metal Supply Building—is part of the left field wall. While the Supply Building contains the team's store on the first floor, party and luxury suites exist on the second and third floors, and there is a restaurant on the fourth.

Petco Park has several amenities. These include an elevated but manicured grass park outside the stadium with lawn seats each at less than $10; a Padres Hall of Fame,

250-seat auditorium, kids entertainment zone, and a theater; a relatively new HD video board; and two levels of social space for fans in right center field modeled after beach piers and featuring pilings and decking constructed from recycled composite wood.

> *"For starters, you're in San Diego, so it's hard to go wrong, no matter what the place looks like. But the Padres did a fantastic job designing and building Petco Park, which combines modern niceties with some old-fashioned flair. For example, the Western Metal Supply Co. building, one corner of which serves as the left-field foul pole. Genius! There's also the beach area behind the center-field fence. And the neighboring Gaslamp District has been completely revitalized, a bustling corner of downtown San Diego that offers no shortage of places to go before and after Padres games."*

PNC Park

Before 2001, the NL Pirates played their home games at Recreation Park (1887–1890), Exposition Park (1891–1908), Forbes Field (1909–1969), and then Three Rivers Stadium (1970–2000). During this period, the team's attendances at home ranged from a low of 1,800 per game in 1914 to 25,300 in 1990.

When investor Kevin McClatchy purchased the franchise in 1996, he and the city established plans for a new ballpark. After financing was approved, construction began on the facility in 1999. Completed and named PNC Park after PNC Financial Services purchased naming rights, the 38,300-seat venue opened in April 2001.

One of baseball's smallest venues, PNC Park features two main seating decks. These extend from the right field foul pole to home plate and down to the left field pole with club seats in the lower section of the upper deck and a press box at the top, and luxury suites between decks. Fans can walk around the main concourse without losing sight of the field and sit in the left or right field bleachers to catch a home run while overlooking the bullpens. A scoreboard is part of the right field fence and a video scoreboard exists behind bleachers in left field.

The ballpark's amenities include a restaurant above the left field bleachers; two elaborate food courts–a smorgasbord and Pop's Plaza, named after former player Willie Stargell; accessible shops along General Robinson Street; an outer promenade known as River Walk that gives fans views of the city, river, and field; and in the right field corner, the Budweiser Bowie Bar where fans mingle, eat at Manny's BBQ, and enjoy an adult beverage while watching a game. In short, PNC Park has a quaint setting and provides excellent views of the downtown Pittsburgh skyline.

> *"It has everything: An unmatched vista of downtown Pittsburgh beyond the Allegheny River, the Roberto Clemente Bridge ushering fans back and forth, an intimate seating bowl with only two decks (the first ballpark built with fewer than three decks since Milwaukee's County Stadium in the 1950s) and just enough quirks to make games there distinct without threatening the quality of play. And after two decades of awful baseball, it's been great to see Pirates games become a real event inside the best ballpark in America."*

SunTrust Park

For fifty-one years, the Braves played in downtown Atlanta at two different ballparks: Atlanta Fulton County Stadium (1966–1996) and Turner Field (1997–2016). In 2013, the franchise decided to construct a new ballpark due to the high infrastructure costs needed to upgrade and renovate Turner Field and the inability to develop a mixed-use development surrounding the ballpark.

During September 2014, the Braves announced their new ballpark would be named SunTrust Park after agreeing to a twenty-five-year deal with SunTrust Bank. It is the centerpiece of a mixed-use development that also includes apartments, offices, restaurants, and other buildings. When visiting the ballpark, most fans enter through the outfield entrances from the Battery. Upon coming inside, fans encounter a sea of green seats enclosing the playing field.

Opened in 2017, SunTrust Park features such amenities as the three-level Chop House in right field, an area that features a restaurant, two party decks, and one group area directly on the field behind the outfield fence. In left center field is the Home Depot Clubhouse, a premium suite that looks like a tree house. It has bleacher-style seating in the front with garage style doors in the back. Behind the grandstand in left field is Hope & Will's Sandlot. This is a large kid-friendly area that has a zip-line and numerous baseball-themed activities and games.

> *"Poor Turner Field didn't even last 20 years before the Braves sought greener pastures out in Cobb County, a pleasant 10-mile drive from Downtown on a construction-riddled 285. But hey, they've got a bourbon bar in the stands! It's the newest park on the list, and the food offerings make the games tastier, but the Braves' losing home record this year has made this place feel just as empty at Turner Field. Maybe when the team returns to regular-season glory the drive will seem a little more worth it."*

Wrigley Field

Before 1916, this team played its home games at various ballparks in Chicago including the 23rd Street Park (1876–1877), Lakefront Park (1878–1884), West Side Park (1885–1890), South Side Park (1891–1893), and West Side Grounds (1894–1915). During this forty-year period, attendances ranged from a low of 1,300 per game in 1890 to a high of 8,500 in 1908 even though the club had appeared in five World Series against AL clubs and won two of them.

When businessman Charles Weeghman bought the Federal League (FL) Chicago Whales, he built his team a new 14,000-seat ballpark in the largely undeveloped north side of Chicago. Initially known as North Side Park until Charles renamed it Weeghman Field, the $250,000 ballpark originally had only one deck of a V-shaped grandstand with wooden bleachers in the outfield. The Whales played there for two seasons, finishing second in 1914 and first in 1915.

After the FL went bankrupt following its 1915 season, a syndicate led by Weeghman and mogul William Wrigley acquired the Cubs franchise for $500,000 with the NL contributing $50,000 of the price. One year later, they moved their team from West

Side Grounds to Weeghman Field, which was renamed Cubs Park in 1920 and then, six years later, Wrigley Field.

During the 1920s, the ballpark was renovated including its grandstands and bleachers plus ivy being planted along the base of the outfield wall. Since the opening of new bleachers in 1937, the facility's next big transformation began with a $575 million project in 2014. It will overhaul the entire ballpark within five years. Besides demolishing some bleachers and adding a new video board, for example, the exterior wall will be pushed back in order to expand the bleachers, widen concourses, and add more concessions. The project's other components include upgrading the steel infrastructure, installing a new roof to replace the existing wooden one, and returning the façade to its original 1930s appearance.

> *"The oldest ballpark in the National League, Wrigley Field was originally named Weeghman Park and Cubs Park before gum manufacturer William Wrigley renamed it after his company in 1927. Originally designed by architect Zachary Taylor Davis, Wrigley Field underwent more than a name change in 1927, as the grandstand was moved west—on rollers, no less!—and the upper deck was added in a major renovation. Wrigley's most iconic feature, the ivy growing on the outfield walls, wasn't added until 1934."*

Table 9.2 contains a few interesting and important characteristics of fifteen NL ballparks as of 2018. First, their average age was twenty-three years. The oldest and newest were, respectively, the Cubs' Wrigley Field and Braves' SunTrust Park. Almost 75 percent of the group initially opened in the 2000s and therefore, on average, are younger by four years than those in the AL.

Second, the average capacity of NL ballparks equaled 43,000 in 2018 and these ranged from Marlins Park being the smallest to Dodger Stadium being the largest. Since AL ballparks had a capacity of 42,000, teams in the leagues played their games before crowds in ballparks of nearly equal capacities. Interestingly, the Marlins at 37,400 and Rays at 31,000 had the smallest venues in their respective league.

Table 9.2 Teams Ballparks, National League, 2018 Major League Baseball Season

Ballpark (Team)	Year	Capacity	Cost	Pub%	Owner
AT&T Ballpark (Giants)	2000	41.9	357	0	China Basin BB Corporation
Busch Stadium (Cardinals)	2006	46.7	411	12	St. Louis Cardinals
Chase Field (Diamondbacks)	1998	48.6	354	71	County Stadium District
Citi Field (Mets)	2009	42.0	632	28	New York Mets
Citizens Bank Park (Phillies)	2004	43.6	458	50	City of Philadelphia
Coors Field (Rockies)	1995	50.3	215	75	Metro BB Stadium District
Dodger Stadium (Dodgers)	1962	56.0	23	100	Los Angeles Dodgers
Great American Ball Park (Reds)	2003	42.2	320	82	Hamilton County
Marlins Park (Marlins)	2012	37.4	515	70	Miami Dade County
Miller Park (Brewers)	2001	41.9	382	66	SE Wisconsin BB District
Nationals Park (Nationals)	2008	43.3	611	100	DC Sports Commission
Petco Park (Padres)	2004	41.1	449	57	City of San Diego
PNC Park (Pirates)	2001	38.3	216	70	Sport & Exhibition Authority
SunTrust Park (Braves)	2017	41.5	672	63	Exhibition Hall Authority
Wrigley Field (Cubs)	1916	41.1	<1	100	Chicago Cubs

Note: Year is when the ballpark opened for the teams' home games. Capacity is in thousands. Cost is the original construction cost in millions of US dollars. Abbreviated is baseball (BB), public (Pub), percent (%), metropolitan (metro), and southeast (SE). Pub is the proportion of the ballpark paid by the public sector. The Cobb-Marietta Georgia Coliseum Exhibit Hall Authority actually owns SunTrust Park. The symbol < means less than the amount.

Source: "National League Ballparks," www.ballparksofbaseball.com cited 24 September 2018.

Third, the least and most expensive NL ballparks built were Wrigley Field at less than $1 million in 1914 and SunTrust Park at $672 million in 2017. The group of them averaged $374 million in cost compared to $224 million for those in the AL despite $1.6 billion to construct Yankee Stadium, which opened in 2009.

Fourth, except for AT&T Ballpark in San Francisco, the public–cities, municipalities, states–contributed funds to construct the fourteen NL stadiums. While Busch Stadium, Citi Field, Dodger Stadium, and Wrigley Field are each primarily owned and operated by a team, the Brewers claim a part of Miller Park along with the Southeast Wisconsin Professional Baseball District. Other owners of ballparks from the public sector include various cities, counties, districts, and a sports commission.

To conclude this chapter, tables A9.1 and A9.2 in the appendix denote the capacities and home attendances of former and replacement ballparks of a sample of teams in the AL and NL. Regarding pre-move and post-move data of ballparks in the AL, their average capacities decreased from 49,600 to 45,900 and six, or 40 percent, of the teams moved to larger ballparks and the other nine, or 60 percent, to smaller venues. At their previous facilities, the Indians, Mariners, and Yankees (pre-2009) played in the biggest ballparks but not the Red Sox, Royals, and Rays. After teams moved to replacements within their metropolitan areas, the three largest and smallest in capacities were, respectively, Yankee Stadium (1923), Metrodome, and SkyDome, and Fenway Park, Target Field, and Comerica Park.

At their home ballparks, attendances of AL teams averaged 1.87 million and then increased to 2.33 million, or by 25 percent, after moving to replacements. Furthermore, at their post-move ballparks, the attendances of twelve clubs were higher, led by the Blue Jays, Orioles, and Twins but not the Red Sox and Yankees (twice). Thus, teams primarily shifted to ballparks with less capacity and had higher attendances at games in the majority of them.

Table A9.2 lists the pre- and post-move capacities and home attendances at ballparks of various teams in the NL. At pre- and post-move (replacement) ballparks, their average capacities were, respectively, 51,800 and 45,800. Five, or 42 percent, of the teams played their home games in bigger venues after moving but not the Dodgers and six other clubs. The latter group downsized their facilities to give fans a better view of games and allow them to be closer to the ballfield.

With respect to average attendances of NL teams, they increased from 1.78 million to 2.29 million at the replacement ballparks. The Rockies, however, were the only team with less attendance at Coors Field than at their prior site in the Denver metropolitan area. Comparing pre-move to post-remove results, the rank in attendances among teams changed most for the Giants (from fifth to third) but remained the same for the Cubs (twelfth), Mets (tenth), Cardinals (ninth), Rockies (first), Braves (second), and Pirates (eighth).

Based on the data in tables A9.1 and A9.2 of the appendix, the majority of MLB teams moved into new ballparks with fewer seats. Moreover, these clubs' attendances tended to increase at their home games following a move because of such things as more amenities at the replacement venue despite higher ticket prices and other costs.

CHAPTER 10

Other Things

BASEBALL ON TELEVISION

Pre-1980s

After the World's Fair displayed the new technology called television in 1939, the first two Major League Baseball (MLB) games—a doubleheader between the Cincinnati Reds and Brooklyn Dodgers at Ebbets Field—were broadcast with one stationary camera located behind home plate to give an extensive view of the field and another above the dugout on the third base side to pick up throws to first base. It was difficult to capture fast-moving plays, swinging bats looked like paper fans, and the ball was all but invisible during pitches and hits. Realizing the medium's potential, however, many MLB games were broadcast on television by the mid-to-late 1940s.

In 1947, the World Series was broadcast for the first time and had 3.9 million viewers with most of them coming from public places where people gathered to watch games. Three years later, the first televised all-star game was played at Chicago's Comiskey Park. As a result, MLB commissioner Happy Chandler and a player representative agreed to split radio and television rights from the World Series. Thanks to the spread of games on television, MLB attendances reached a high of twenty-one million by the late 1940s.

During mid-August 1951, WCBS-TV in New York aired the first baseball game in color while the National Broadcasting Corporation (NBC) provided the first coast-to-coast broadcast of a baseball game on October 1, as the Dodgers defeated the New York Giants in a tiebreaker game in which Bobby Thompson hit his famous shot heard 'round the world. A few years after NBC offered a World Series broadcast entirely in color in 1955, KTTV in Los Angeles broadcast the first baseball game played on the west coast.[1]

The first baseball game televised via satellite was in July 1962, and in 1965, the American Broadcasting Corporation (ABC) made history when former Dodgers player Jackie Robinson called a game—the first time ever by an African American. The network also made history later that year when it started the tradition of Saturday afternoon national broadcasts, a format that eventually turned into *Game of the Week*.

The World Series made broadcast history in 1971 when MLB commissioner Bowie Kuhn scheduled the first of them at night. He felt the game would attract a larger audience in prime time. The idea worked and eventually became the standard.

Under the initial agreement (1976–1979) with ABC, NBC, and MLB, the two networks paid a combined $92.8 million. The ABC network paid $12.5 million per year to show sixteen Monday night games in 1976 and eighteen in the next three years, plus half the postseason with the League Championship Series (LCS) in even numbered years and World Series in odd numbered years. NBC paid $10.7 million per year to show twenty-five Saturday *Games of the Week* and the other half of the postseason with the LCS in odd numbered years and World Series in even numbered years. By 1980, income from television accounted for a record 30 percent of the game's $500 million in revenue.

---

1 *Readings about the history and success of baseball on television include Stevie Larsen, "The History of Early Broadcasting: Early Television," www.baseballessential.com cited 14 October 2017; "First Televised Major League Baseball Game," www.history.com cited 16 October 2017; Eldon Ham, Broadcasting Baseball: A History of the National Pastime on Radio and Television (Jefferson, NC: McFarland, 2011); Frank P. Jozsa Jr., Baseball, Inc.: The National Pastime As Big Business (Jefferson, NC: McFarland, 2006).*

1980s–2000s

In 1980, most MLB teams took part in a one-year cable deal with network UA-Columbia. It involved the airing of a Thursday night *Game of the Week* in markets at least fifty miles from a big-league ballpark. Although MLB earned less than $500,000, the deal led to a new two-year contract for forty to forty-five games per season.[2]

During April 1983, MLB, ABC, and NBC agreed to terms in a six-year television package worth $1.2 billion. In it, the networks continued to alternate coverage of the playoffs (ABC in even numbered years and NBC in odd numbered years), the World Series (ABC to televise the World Series in odd numbered years and NBC in even numbered years), and the All-Star Game (ABC would televise it in even numbered years and NBC in odd numbered years) through the 1989 season, with each of the twenty-six clubs receiving $7 million per year.

By 1986, ABC only televised thirteen *Monday Night Baseball* games. This was in contrast to eighteen games scheduled in 1978. *Sporting News* believed that ABC paid MLB to not make them televise the regular season while Turner Sports Network (TSN) added that the network only wanted the sport for October anyway.

In December 1988, the Columbia Broadcasting System (CBS)—under the guidance of MLB commissioner Peter Ueberroth—paid approximately $1.8 billion for exclusive television rights for four years (1990–1993). In one of the largest agreements between baseball and broadcasting, the network paid about $265 million each year for the World Series, LCS, All-Star Game, and Saturday *Game of the Week*. Then in January1989, MLB signed a $400 million deal with the Entertainment Sports Programming Network (ESPN), who would broadcast more than 175 games beginning in 1990.

For the next four years, ESPN televised six games a week including those on Sunday, *Wednesday Night Baseball*, and doubleheaders on Tuesdays, Fridays, and

---

2 *James Walker and Robert Bellemy, Center Field Shot: A History of Baseball on Television (Lincoln, NB: Bison Books, 2008) and "Major League Baseball on Television," www.wikipedia.com cited 16 October 2017.*

holidays. The deal with CBS paid each team approximately $10 million a year. A separate deal with cable television also paid each MLB team an additional $4 million.

In addition, teams could also sign deals with local television stations. For example, the New York Yankees signed with a cable and satellite network that paid the team $41 million annually for twelve years. Reportedly, after the huge television contracts with CBS and ESPN were signed, clubs spent their excess millions on free agents.

In the end, CBS wound up losing approximately half a billion dollars from their television contract with MLB; CBS repeatedly asked MLB for a rebate, but it would not do it. After the fallout from CBS' financial problems from its four-year television contract with MLB, baseball decided to produce the telecasts. After a four-year hiatus, ABC and NBC returned to MLB under the umbrella of a revenue sharing venture called The Baseball Network or TBN.

Under the venture's six-year plan, MLB intended to receive 85 percent of the first $140 million in advertising revenue, or 87.5 percent of advertising revenues and corporate sponsorships from games until sales topped a specified level, 50 percent of the next $30 million, and 80 percent of any additional money. Prior to the plan, MLB was projected to take a 55 percent cut in rights fees and receive a typical rights fee from the networks.

When compared to the previous television deal with CBS, TBN was supposed to bring in 50 percent less of the broadcasting revenue. Furthermore, advertisers were reportedly excited about the arrangement with TBN because the new package included several changes intended to boost ratings, especially among young viewers.

Arranging broadcasts through TBN seemed, at least on the surface, to benefit NBC and ABC since it gave them a monopoly on broadcasting MLB games. It would also benefit the networks because they reduced the risk associated with purchasing broadcast rights outright. Thus, NBC and ABC attempted to create a loss-free environment for each other.

After NBC's coverage of the 1994 All-Star Game ended, the network scheduled six regular season games on Fridays or Saturdays in prime time. It had exclusive rights for the twelve regular season dates such that no regional or national cable service or over-the-air broadcaster could telecast a MLB game on those dates.

Baseball Night in America usually aired up to fourteen games based on the viewer's region—affiliates chose games of local interest to carry—as opposed to a traditional coast-to-coast format. ABC picked up where NBC left off by televising six more regular season games. These fell under the *Baseball Night in America* umbrella which premiered during July 1994. In even numbered years, NBC had the rights to the All-Star Game and both LCS while ABC would broadcast World Series and newly-created Division Series. In odd numbered years, the postseason and All-Star Game television rights were supposed to alternate.

The long-term plans for TBN crumbled, however, when players went on strike during mid-August 1994, forcing cancellation of the World Series. Eleven month later, ABC and NBC shared televising the 1995 World Series as a way to recoup revenue—with ABC broadcasting Games 1, 4, and 5 and NBC broadcasting Games 2, 3, and 6—and announced they were opting out of their agreement with MLB.

Both networks believed that, as the delayed 1995 baseball season opened without a labor agreement, there was no guarantee against another strike. Meanwhile, others argued that a primary reason for failure was abandoning localized markets in favor of more lucrative and stable advertising contracts afforded by turning to a national model of broadcasting.

The networks publicly vowed to cut their business relationship with MLB for the remainder of the twentieth century. Also in 1994, ESPN renewed its baseball contract for six years, or through the 1999 season. The new deal was worth $42.5 million per year and $255 million overall. Nevertheless, it was ultimately voided after MLB's 1995 season and ESPN had to restructure its contract.

Soon after the *Baseball Network* fiasco, MLB made a deal with Fox and NBC in November 1995. Fox paid a fraction of the money that CBS had for MLB's television rights. Unlike the *Baseball Network*, Fox returned to the format of televising regular season games—approximately sixteen weekly telecasts that normally began on Memorial Day weekend—on Saturday afternoons.

Fox, however, continued a format that the *Baseball Network* started by offering games based purely on a viewer's region. The network's approach had usually been to offer four regionalized telecasts with exclusivity from 1–4 pm in each time zone. But when Fox first got into baseball, its motto was "Same game, new attitude."

Under a new five-year deal (1996–2000) worth approximately $400 million, NBC did not televise any regular season games. Instead, the network broadcast the All-Star Game and the American League Championship Series (ALCS) in even numbered years and the World Series and National League Championship Series (NLCS) in odd numbered years, in addition to three Division Series games in each of these five years.

In 1996, ESPN also began a five-year contract with MLB worth $440 million. The sports network paid for the rights to a Wednesday doubleheader, Sunday night *Game of the Week*, and all postseason games not aired on Fox or NBC. In fact, MLB staggered times of first-round games to provide a full-day feast for viewers: ESPN could air games at 1 pm, 4 pm, and 11 pm Eastern Daylight Time (EDT), with the broadcast networks telecasting the primetime game.

Beginning in 1997, Fox entered a four-year joint venture with Liberty Media Cable. This resulted in the placement of a Thursday night baseball game on Fox Sports Net alongside an FX Saturday night game. Later, the Fox family replaced Fox Sports Net. Worth $172 million, the deal called for two games a week that aired on its choice of two weeknights other than Wednesday with no exclusivity.

During September 2000, MLB signed a six-year, $2.5 billion contract with Fox to show Saturday baseball, All-Star Game, selected Division Series games, and exclusive coverage of both LCS and the World Series. Under the previous five-year deal with NBC (1996–2000), Fox paid $115 million while NBC only paid $80 million per year. In this contract, Fox paid about $575 million and NBC $400 million.

The difference between the Fox and the NBC contracts implicitly valued Fox's Saturday *Game of the Week* at less than $90 million for five years. Before NBC officially decided to part ways with MLB—for the second time in twelve years—in September 2000, Fox's payment would have been $345 million while NBC paid $240 million. Before 1990, NBC had carried MLB games since 1947.

After weeks of speculation and rumors, on July 11, 2006 at the All-Star Game, MLB and the Fox Broadcasting Company announced a renewal of their current contract through 2013. The contract continued to award Fox exclusive rights to televise the World Series and the All-Star Game for the duration of the contract. The World Series begins on the Wednesday after the LCS ends.

The Outdoor Life Network (now NBC Sports Network) briefly considered acquiring the rights to baseball's Sunday and Wednesday games, which expired after the 2005 season. During September 2005, however, rights holder ESPN signed an eight-year contract with MLB, which was highlighted by the continuation of ESPN's *Sunday Night Baseball* series with additional, exclusive team appearances. Fox received exclusive rights to televise the ALCS in odd years beginning in 2007 and also exclusive rights to televise the NLCS in even years beginning in 2008. Additionally, Fox had the right to broadcast its regional Saturday *Game of the Week* package for twenty-six weeks up from eighteen under the previous contract.

Beginning in the 2008 MLB season, Time Warner's TBS gained rights to Sunday afternoon *Game of the Week*. The network could choose the games to carry and also select a single team up to thirteen times. These games were normally shown outside the participating teams' markets, thus, TBS won the option of producing an alternate game in those markets. The network also gained exclusive broadcast rights to the ALDS and NLDS, as well as any tiebreaking games. In addition, TBS got the rights to the *All-Star Game Selection Show*, meaning that ESPN—which previously carried it—could only broadcast information after it aired on TBS.

In October 2006, TBS received exclusive rights to televise the NLCS in odd years beginning in 2007, and exclusive rights to televise the ALCS in even years beginning in 2008. This contract was in effect through 2013. As part of the contract, TBS relinquished its rights to air Atlanta Braves games nationally after the 2007 season, by separating WTBS (now WPCH) from the TBS network, rebranding it *Peachtree TV* during October 2007. The new station would still broadcast Atlanta Braves games. These were available to local cable and satellite operators in the Southeast for the 2008 season. In addition, some Braves games appeared on TBS as part of the new package.

During August 2012, ESPN and MLB agreed on a new eight-year deal that greatly increased the network's studio and game content across its platforms. Also, it increased ESPN's average yearly payment from approximately $360 million to about $700 million. ESPN also returned to broadcasting postseason baseball beginning in 2014 with one of two wild-card games each season. The network alternated airing the AL and NL wild-card games each year and had the rights to all potential regular-season tiebreaker games starting in 2014.

One month later, *Sports Business Daily* reported that MLB agreed to separate eight-year television deals with Fox Sports and Turner Sports through the 2021 season. Reportedly, Fox paid about $4 billion over eight years and Turner $2.8 billion over eight years. According to these deals, Fox and TBS's coverage was essentially the same as in the 2007–2013 contract with the exception of Fox and TBS splitting coverage of the Division Series, which TBS had broadcast exclusively dating back to 2007. More importantly, Fox broadcast some of the games—such as the Saturday afternoon *Game of the* Week—on its all-sports channel, Fox Sports 1. Later, Fox sold some Division Series games to the MLB Network.

Besides affecting teams' revenue from ticket sales, broadcasting MLB games on television raised the sport's profile by bringing the game to people without having them watch it at a ballpark. People liked it so much that now every major league team has a regional television deal and MLB some national contracts with multiple networks. In fact, the Yankees earn millions by owning the YES network.

Executives in the league office continue to improve the televised product, which possibly is baseball's biggest overarching initiative. When the popularity of the all-star game waned, MLB decreed that the winning league would get home-field advantage in the World Series. And when instant replay was initially considered, the front league office believed it could lengthen games and, subsequently, hurt viewership. The speed-of-play argument is a catalyst for more changes in the future.[3]

---

3 *For more recent information about baseball on television, see Mike Farrell, "OTT Players Could Change Television's Sports Game," Multichannel News (4 September 2017): 14, 16; Jon Lafayette, "Wild Earnings Season Sets TV Companies on New Course," Broadcasting & Cable (14–17 August 2017): 32; Daniel Frankel, "TWC Further Sweetens SportsNet LA Deal," FierceCable (30 March 2016): 1; Joe Flint, "Dodgers TV Fiasco, a Game Changer," Wall Street Journal (30 September 2014: B.1; Ira Boudway, "Major League Baseball Says It's Close to Ending Online Blackouts," Business Week (18–24 August 2014): 1; Richard Sandomir, "Fox Sports Nears Deal to Add More Games," New York Times (20 September 2012): B.14; Dick Friedman, "TV Stars? They Might be Giants," Sports Illustrated (20 July 2011): 1.*

About television's effect on the game as of 2013, one writer wrote:

> *"MLB is a league adrift in the television landscape. It floats around from network to network as it's needed, but no major channel (again, MLB Network is terrific, but still) seems all that interested in bringing us back to the 90s, when Baseball Tonight was must-watch television, MLB highlights dominated SportsCenter, and the sport was still getting people to tune in week to week. They've got eight years until the next television contract is up. If they don't find a network that's going to promote the hell out of it and treat it on the same level as football and hoops, we'll be having this same conversation in 2021, and that's a problem."*[4]

STEROIDS ERA

The steroids era refers to a period of time in MLB when a number of players were believed to have used performance-enhancing drugs, which resulted in increased offensive output throughout the game from the late 1980s through the early 2000s. Though steroids have been banned in MLB since 1991, the league did not implement league-wide performance-enhancing drug (PED) testing until 2003. This meant that players using PEDs would not get caught. After years of allegations, a federal investigation into the Bay Area Laboratory Co-Operative (BALCO) and Jose Canseco's autobiography *Juiced* revealed how widespread PED use had become in baseball.[5]

---

4 *Steve Lapore, "Major League Baseball is Adrift on Television, But Will Ending 'Game of the Week' Solve the Problem?" www.sbnation.com cited 18 October 2017.*

5 *Readings on banned drugs in baseball include Michael Weiner, "Baseball's Testing Already the Toughest," USA Today (6 August 2013): A.6; Jacob Hayutin, "Should MLB Adopt a Zero Tolerance Policy for Steroid Use?" US News & World Report (July 2013): 1; Jason Anderson, "Vigilance Keeping Drugs Off Diamond," McClatchy Tribune Business News (17 June 2012): 1; Ira Boudway, "Major League Baseball's Anthony Bosch Problems is Not Going Away," Business Week (13–19 January 2014: 1. Also, see Jose Canseco's Juiced (New York, NY: William Morrow, 2006).*

BALCO SCANDAL

In 2003, federal agents targeted BALCO, a nutritional supplement firm in Burlingame, California suspected of distributing undetectable steroids to athletes. The case was turned over to a grand jury, which subpoenaed baseball players Barry Bonds, Jason Giambi, Gary Sheffield, and dozens of other alleged BALCO customers. Bonds testified that he took substances described to him as linseed oil and rubbing balm by his personal trainer, Greg Anderson, who was among the individuals indicted in the case.[6]

In his grand jury testimony, Giambi admitted to using steroids and human growth hormone (HGH) provided by BALCO during the 2002 and 2003 seasons. But since neither Giambi nor Bonds had tested positive by the league and players' testimonies were not reported publicly until a year or more after their grand jury appearances, no punitive action was taken by MLB.

While none of the players were charged with using PEDs, the BALCO case was one factor in spurring baseball to toughen its stance and institute a drug-testing program. In 2007, Bonds was charged with perjury and obstruction of justice relating to his statements to the grand jury. He pled not guilty on five counts, and appeals related to the case delayed the start of the trial until 2011. During the course of the trial, one of the counts was dropped; however, four still went to jury deliberations. Although deadlocked on three of the counts, the jury found Bonds guilty of obstruction of justice. He was sentenced to thirty days of house arrest, two years of probation, and 250 hours of community service.

MITCHELL COMMISSION

In March 2006, MLB commissioner Bud Selig asked US Senator George Mitchell to head a panel to investigate steroids use by major league players. The league announcement indicated the investigation would focus on the period beginning with

---

6 *"BALCO Fast Facts," www.cnn.com cited 15 April 2018; Mike Fish, "Bonds' Positive Steroid Test Discovered Among BALCO Evidence," www.espn.com cited 8 November 2018; "Sports and Drugs," www.sfgate.com cited 8 November 2018.*

2002, but that Mitchell—who also served as a director of the Boston Red Sox—would be free to explore anything or any time that was relevant to understanding the problem of steroids in baseball.[7]

During the next twenty months, Mitchell's team interviewed hundreds of people, but only two active players freely cooperated with the Mitchell investigation. These were the Toronto Blue Jays' Frank Thomas and New York Yankees' Jason Giambi, who would face disciplinary action from MLB if he did not cooperate.

Mitchell warned team owners that a lack of cooperation with his investigation would increase the chances of government involvement in the matter. Donald Fehr, head of the MLB Players Association (MLBPA), believed the investigation raised issues of privacy rights for players. He left it up to individuals whether to talk with the investigators, and most refused to cooperate.

In December 2007, Mitchell released a lengthy report that linked eighty-nine players including Bonds and Giambi with using illegal PEDs. He said illegal substances posed a serious threat to the integrity of the game and made several recommendations to strengthen MLB's drug policy such as an independent overseer, greater education, and increased testing.

Though his report was inhibited by limited cooperation and absence of subpoena power, Mitchell claimed that there was a collective failure to recognize the problem early on and criticized both the commissioner's office and the players union for knowingly tolerating PEDs. The report's findings were based on testimony from former players, league and club representatives, and other informants, along with more than 100,000 pages of seized documents.

Mitchell recommended that rather than disciplining the players listed in the report, the league should set up a stronger testing program. Selig praised Mitchell's work, yet noted that he would review each player's case and could be inclined to discipline them. He intended to implement as many of Mitchell's recommendations as possible that did not need to be collectively bargained with the players union. Fehr

---

7 *"Recommendations From the Mitchell Commission Report," www.espn.com cited 9 November 2018; "Mitchell Report: Baseball is Called Out," www.washingtonpost.com cited 10 November 2018; "Mitchell Report," www.baseball-almanac.com cited 11 November 2018.*

maintained that the investigation was not a fair one, but he did report that the union would be willing to explore the possibility of adjusting testing procedures before the agreement expired in 2011.

2003 Survey Testing

While steroids had been part of baseball's banned substance list since 1991, testing for major-league players did not begin until 2003, when MLB conducted surveys to help gauge the extent of PED use in the game. The agreement with the MLBPA called for one random test per player per year, with no punishments that year. If more than five percent of players tested positive in 2003, tougher testing would be implemented with penalties ranging from counseling for a first offense to a maximum one-year suspension for a fifth violation. If less than 2.5 percent of players tested positive in two consecutive years, testing would be dropped.[8]

In November 2003, the league revealed that 5–7 percent of 1,438 tests returned positive results. The tests began during spring training and were conducted anonymously on members of each club's forty-man roster. In retrospect, 240 of the same players had been tested again without notice at some point during baseball's 2003 regular season.

With the results announced, MLB commissioner Bud Selig said he was pleased to learn that there was not widespread steroids use in baseball. He did add, however, that since the 5 percent threshold had been reached, mandatory testing for steroid use would begin in the spring of 2004.

2004 POLICY

All major league players were subject to two tests (without prior notice) during the 2004 season including an initial test and a follow-up one five to seven days later. The drug-testing program was administered by a health policy and advisory committee, which included representatives for both the players association and MLB. Under terms of the drug policy in the 2002 collective bargaining agreement, all anabolic steroids deemed illegal by the US Food and Drug Administration were subject to testing.

---

8 *"A Timeline of MLB's Drug-Testing Rules," www.usatoday.com cited 12 November 2018; "Event Timeline: Drug Testing Policy," www.mlb.com cited 13 November 2018; "Performance-Enhancing Drugs in Baseball: A Timeline," www.cleveland.com cited 15 November 2018.*

According to MLB's policy, any player testing positive would immediately enter a clinical track to be treated for steroids use. If a player under treatment then failed another test and was convicted or pled guilty to the sale or use of a prohibited substance, that player would immediately be moved to the administrative track and be subject to discipline. Depending upon the repeated use of the drug, any player failing to comply with the treatment program could then be suspended from an initial fifteen days with a $10,000 fine to one year with a $100,000 fine.[9]

2005 POLICY

After a US Senate committee in 2004 advised Selig that his policy on drugs and steroids was not strong enough, the league and its players union announced a new policy in January 2005.

The new drug-testing agreement called for year-round testing of banned substances and suspensions ranging from ten days for a first offense to the commissioner's discretion for a fifth offense.

According to the changes, a player who tested positive for the first time would be suspended for ten days and his name would be released to the public. A thirty-day suspension without pay would be handed out for a second positive test, with sixty days given for a third offense and a one-year suspension for the fourth. In all, twelve major leaguers were suspended in 2005 with each receiving ten-game suspensions. Early in the 2005 season, Selig proposed even stricter changes to the policy, and in November of that year MLB and the MLBPA agreed on a fifty-game ban for a first offense, 100 games for a second offense, and a lifetime ban for a player testing positive a third time.[10]

2008 POLICY REVISIONS

Following recommendations made by US Senator George Mitchell in his investigative report examining steroids use in MLB, the league and its players' union again fortified the testing policy in 2008. Modifications to the league's joint drug

---

9 *Idem.*

10 *Idem.*

agreement included disbanding the advisory committee—management and union representatives—who administered the program. It was replaced by an independent program administrator (IPA) responsible for publicly reporting key statistics related to the program and maintaining records for longer periods than defined for previous administrators.

The new policy, expected to be in place through 2011, expanded the list of banned substances, added 600 tests per year bringing the total number to 3,600, and increased the number of off-season tests that could be conducted per year up to 375. Testing was also expanded to include the top 200 prospects in the amateur draft. Any prospects that tested positive would remain draft eligible, but teams would be notified of those results.

In the new agreement, the league vowed to help educate youths and families about the dangers of performance-enhancing substances. The players' union agreed to join in that effort and contribute $200,000 to an antidrug charitable, educational, or research organization. In exchange for those provisions, the league agreed not to discipline players implicated by Mitchell's investigation. The MLB and MLBPA also agreed to keep players' names private until discipline could be imposed and agreed to apprise players of any allegations and evidence against them before any investigatory interview.

2008 Congressional Hearing

The Mitchell report included New York Yankees pitcher Roger Clemens on its list of major leaguers linked to the potential use of illegal, performance-enhancing drugs. Mitchell's investigation based some results on statements by Clemens' former trainer, Brian McNamee, who claimed that he had previously injected Clemens with steroids and HGH.[11]

Just days after the report was released in December 2007, multiple Cy Young Award winner Clemens issued a categorical denial of personal steroids use in a statement through his agent. The following month, he filed a defamation lawsuit against

---

11 *"Clemens Hit Hard in Mitchell Report," www.si.com cited 9 November 2018 and Matt Snyder, "Watch: Clemens Goes Hard After the Mitchell Report, Makes Strong Accusations," www.espn.com cited 10 November 2018.*

McNamee—which was later dismissed by a federal judge. Both Clemens and McNamee were invited to appear in February 2008 before a House oversight committee. The committee also invited or sought depositions from Clemens' teammates Andy Pettitte and Chuck Knoblauch, and former New York Mets clubhouse attendant Kirk Radomski, who made allegations also noted in the Mitchell report.

Early in the congressional hearing, lawmakers read Clemens a sworn statement by Pettitte that Clemens had told him in 1999 or 2000 that he used HGH. Responding that Pettitte must have misremembered the conversation that occurred years earlier, Clemens went on to testify under oath that he had not used steroids or PEDs during his career.

Throughout the hearing, Clemens and McNamee contradicted each other about whether the pitcher had used any PEDs. McNamee said he injected Clemens more than a dozen times with steroids and HGH between 1998 and 2001, while Clemens said the injections were painkillers.

Committee members questioned the truthfulness of both Clemens and McNamee during the hearing. In the following weeks, Congress requested that the Department of Justice investigate whether or not Clemens lied under oath when he denied using PEDs.

A grand jury convened the following year to hear witness testimony and review evidence on the matter. In August 2010, Clemens was indicted by the grand jury on six counts relating to his deposition to the House oversight committee and statements he made during the hearings in February 2008—one for obstruction of justice, three for making false statements, and two for perjury. Clemens pled not guilty to the charges, and his trial began in July 2011. However, a mistrial was declared just days into the trial after prosecutors showed video that was previously ruled to be inadmissible. Clemens was re-tried in 2012, and found not guilty on all six counts.

ALEX RODRIGUEZ

In February 2009, New York Yankees star Alex Rodriguez admitted using steroids from 2001 to 2003 while playing for the Texas Rangers. His disclosure came days after a *Sports Illustrated* article reported that he was on a list of 104 players who tested positive for banned substances in 2003, when players were not subject to suspension.[12]

Rodriguez cited an enormous amount of pressure to perform after signing a huge contract with Texas as a major reason to turn to PEDs. He said he was naive and stupid in making the decision during a time when baseball was a different culture. Rodriguez averaged fifty-two home runs and a .615 slugging percentage during the 2001 and 2003 seasons, numbers markedly higher than his average offensive output in his other seasons in the league. He was also named the AL's Most Valuable Player in 2003.

MANNY RAMIREZ

Through August 2010, twenty-seven major league players received suspensions for violating MLB's joint drug prevention and treatment program. Among the high-profile players disciplined was the Los Angeles Dodgers' Manny Ramirez, who was suspended for fifty games under the league's revised drug policy in May 2009. Ramirez's suspension was for using HCG after high levels of testosterone were detected during a spring-training drug test. HCG is a fertility drug but is also used by athletes between cycles of steroids and has been banned by MLB since 2008.[13]

In a statement released by the MLBPA following the announcement of the suspension, Ramirez said the substance was medication for a personal health issue. Ramirez's agent, Scott Boras, added that the player did not test positive for steroids, but for

12 *Steve Fishman, "Chasing A-Rod," New York Times (2 December 2013): 1; Michael Schmidt, "Reports of Failed Tests Cast Doubt on Rodriguez," New York Times (5 November 2013: B.14; Jacob Hayutin, "Was Major League Baseball Right to Suspend Alex Rodriguez?" US News & World Report (August 2013): 1.*

13 *"Report: Manny, Ortiz Tested Positive," www.espn.com cited 17 October 2017 and Michael Schmidt, "Ortiz and Ramirez Said to be on '03 Doping List," www.nytimes.com cited 17 October 2017.*

a drug that was prescribed by a doctor for a medical condition. In accordance with league policy, Ramirez received a fifty-game ban, costing the thirty-six-year-old $7.7 million of his $25 million salary that season. The power-hitting outfielder returned to the Dodgers' lineup in July 2009. That same month, the *New York Times* was among the first publications to report that Ramirez was among the major leaguers who tested positive during the league's 2003 survey testing period.

In 2011, MLB notified Ramirez of an issue under the drug program, and rather than face a 100-game suspension—which would have been the first of its kind in the majors—Ramirez chose to retire. He returned in 2012, signed with the Oakland Athletics, and served a reduced 50-game suspension, but was not called up from the minor leagues prior to his release.

As those who played during the steroids era retired and became eligible for the Hall of Fame, players linked to steroid use have often fallen short of election. Former St. Louis Cardinals slugger Mark McGwire, who admitted to performance-enhancing drug use, failed to earn even 25 percent of the vote during his first four years on the ballot, and his support fell below 20 percent in the 2011 voting, the first held after his admission. Rafael Palmeiro, who failed a drug test in 2005 after famously denying steroid use in front of Congress, received just over 11 percent of the vote in 2011.

Did steroids make a difference in players' performances? In a statistical analysis comparing each baseball parameter among different eras, the average total number of home runs (HRs) hit per season during the steroid era (1993-2002) was 4,782 +/- 767 while in the post-steroid era (2003-2012) was 4,549 +/- 296, pre-steroid era (1983-1992) 3,443 +/- 425, and in the early pre-steroid era (1973-1982) 2,896 +/- 582 . There were no significant differences between the number of HRs hit per year in the AL and NL. When comparing the total number of HRs hit in MLB, there was no statistically significant difference between the steroid era and the other ten-year time frames.[14]

The hitters' average isolated power (ISO) was not statistically significantly different for the steroid era compared to the early pre-steroid era of 1973-1982, the

14 *See Brandon Erickson, "The Effect of the Steroid Era on Major League Baseball Hitters: Did it Enhance Hitting?" www.omicsonline.org cited 17 October 2017.*

pre-steroid era of 1983-1992, or the post-steroid era of 2003-2012. Also, the mean batting average was not significantly different between the pre-steroid era, steroid era, and post-steroid era. The mean batting average for players hitting over forty home runs per season was not statistically significantly different between the various eras. Finally, during the steroid era, the overall batting average for MLB as a whole did not change significantly compared to before and after the steroid era, despite the number of players who were hitting greater than forty home runs, and there were no statistically significant differences in batting average between the players who hit greater than forty home runs and MLB overall.[15]

Of his concerns about the relationship between number of HRs and PEDs during MLB's 2017 season, *Sports Illustrated* sportswriter Tom Verducci wrote:

> *"Baseball has become a game of too many home runs (squeezing out the game rallies, balls in play, base running and strategy) and performance-enhancing drug use is continuing as the players association and owners allow every player two cracks at juicing before throwing them out. The two sides proved they still aren't serious enough about ridding the game of PEDs by negotiating a collective bargaining agreement last off-season that did not touch penalties for such use. The game suffers and the juicers, by way of changed body chemistry, benefit."*[16]

RULE CHANGES

Designated Hitter

The idea of adding a tenth man to the baseball lineup to bat for the pitcher had been suggested as early as 1906 by the revered player and manager Connie Mack. In 1928, NL president John Heydler revived the issue, but the rule was rejected by AL management. By the early 1970s, Charlie Finley, the colorful owner of the Oakland

---

15 *Idem.*

16 *Tom Verducci, "The Numbers—and the Truth—About Baseball's PED Problems and Why it May Never go Away," www.si.com cited 17 October 2017.*

A's, had become the designated hitter (DH) rule's most outspoken advocate, arguing that a pinch hitter to replace the pitcher–a player that usually batted poorly, exceptions like the legendary Babe Ruth notwithstanding–would add the extra offensive punch that baseball needed to draw more fans.[17]

At a joint meeting of the two major leagues in Chicago on January 11, 1973–presided over by baseball commissioner Bowie Kuhn–MLB's franchise owners voted to allow the AL (which lagged behind the NL in both scoring and attendance) to put the DH rule into practice. The rule allowing a DH has always been controversial since some want the rule eliminated, others want the rule adopted in both leagues, and some want the rule to remain in its current state. The NL teams use a DH in road games during interleague play while AL teams have the pitcher bat in road games in interleague match-ups.

While critics of the DH suggest it was designed to allow poor fielders to remain in the game despite their defensive flaws, it has not always been used that way. Many DHs have been players who were capable but injury-prone fielders kept from fielding to preserve their health. Former Minnesota Twin Paul Molitor–the first Hall of Famer to play more games as DH than any other position–fell into this category.

Some teams do not have a regular DH and instead use it to give their regular position players a break from fielding. While New York Yankee Ron Blomberg was the first player to bat as a DH, Kansas City Royal Hal McRae became the first player to spend most of his career in that spot of the batting order. Other all-time leaders at the position include Seattle Mariner Edgar Martinez, Chicago White Sox Harold Baines, and Boston Red Sox David Ortiz, who is the career leader for hits, home runs, and RBIs at the position.

There are a few peculiarities to DH Rule 6.10 in MLB. First, the DH is optional. A team may decide to bat its pitcher and not use a DH in a game where it would normally be used. A few instances were Texas Rangers pitcher Ferguson Jenkins in October 1974 against the Minnesota Twins, Oakland A's pitcher Ken Holtzman in September 1975 against the California Angels, and Chicago White Sox pitcher Ken Brett in

---

17 *John Cronin, "The Historical Evolution of the Designated Hitter Rule," www.sabr.org cited 18 October 2017 and "Designated Hitter Rule," www.mlb.com cited 18 October 2017.*

July 1976 against the Boston Red Sox and in September 1976 against the Twins. New York Yankees pitcher Rick Rhoden was a DH in June 1988 against the Baltimore Orioles in a game in which he was not pitching.[18]

Second, the DH can play in the field. However, once a manager decides to play him on defense, the pitcher immediately takes over the batting spot of the defensive player which the DH replaced unless there are multiple substitutions, in which case the manager can decide where the pitcher will bat. The team then forfeits the use of the DH for the rest of the game. This happens a few times every MLB season and sometimes results in a pitcher being forced to bat in an AL game.

Third, the DH spot is locked in the batting order. If the DH bats, for example, fifth in the order, no substitution can be made to move him to fourth or sixth, or anywhere else. Any substitute for the DH, including pinch hitters and pinch runners, is automatically considered to be the new DH, and the restrictions outlined above apply to them as well. These substitutes are listed in the box score as Smith ph-dh or Smith pr-dh. This is how a number of AL pitchers end up with games as DH in their statistics. These are almost always the result of being used as a pinch runner for the DH.

The DH listed in a team's starting lineup must bat at least once before being substituted unless there is an injury or the opposite team's starting pitcher has been changed. This rule was added after the 1980 season to close a loophole discovered by Baltimore Orioles manager Earl Weaver. He would list one of his inactive starting pitchers in the starting line-up as a phantom DH, and then, when his first time to bat came up, Weaver could decide which of a number of players to use as a pinch hitter for his DH, depending on the situation–for example if there were men on base, if he needed a baserunner, and so on. Pitchers Steve Stone and Dennis Martinez were used most often in this capacity. Box scores from that time listed the pitchers as having played a game at DH, but after the amendment to the rule was adopted, these appearances were erased from these pitchers' records.

Whether there is momentum to change DH Rule 6.10 as of 2017, MLB Commissioner Rob Manfred recently said:

---

18 "Designated Hitter," www.baseball-reference.com cited 18 October 2017.

"On the other side of the ledger, [former] commissioner [Bud] Selig did a lot of great things, including reforming the governance of baseball and eliminating the league structures, beginning the process of having one baseball. I think those are really important reforms, but one of the things those reforms do is you lose this league identity. And the biggest remnant of league identity is the difference between DH and no DH. I think that's a significant issue. We may get over that. I'm not saying it's not possible. But it is a significant issue on the other side of the scale."[19]

One thing Manfred is proudest of in his first two years on the job is how all thirty owners have been encouraged to offer their opinions and to participate in the process. On issues like this, those voices surely will be emphatic on both sides. Regardless of how it plays out, baseball will be better off for having had the discussion. For now, though, it appears to be a long way from having the DH in both leagues. Nevertheless, expect to hear much more discussion in the future and that's a good thing.

Other Rule Changes

Prior to formation of the NL in 1876, rules in playing and scoring baseball games evolved from the original Knickerbocker rules. Examples of these include: 1850s, the game was won when one side scored twenty-one aces in nine innings and the highest scoring team won it; 1860s, home base and pitcher's box must be marked, each base runner must touch each base in making the circuit, and batting averages are included; 1870s, ball size and weight are regulated and remain the same to this date.[20]

From 1876 to the late 1890s, major-league rules were implemented during many years for teams in the NL. By decade, some of the more interesting of them were:

---

19 *Richard Justice, "DH Debate Picking up Steam," www.mlb.com cited 9 November 2018 and Tyler Kepner, "New Commissioner With a Long-Term Mission," www.nytimes.com cited 9 November 2018.*

20 *Other Knickerbocker rules, for example, were: 1850s, called strikes introduced and the baserunner no longer required to touch each base in order; 1860s, pitcher's box now twelve feet by four feet, no base made on a foul ball, Henry Chadwick's scoring system introduced, and bat size regulated. For additional rules, see "Baseball Rule Changes Timeline," www.baseball-almanac.com cited 18 October 2017.*

1870s, hitter exempted from a time at bat if he walked and a pitcher had to face a batsman before pitching to him; 1880s, baserunner out if hit by a pitched ball, four balls became a base on balls, championships decided on a percentage basis, coaches recognized by the rules for the first time ever, batter awarded first base when hit by a pitch, a sacrifice bunt statistically recognized; 1890s, a pitcher was required to place his rear foot against the slab, infield-fly rule adopted, and a held foul tip classified as a strike.[21]

During the twentieth century, numerous other rules were adopted in MLB. Here, for example, are some of them: 1900s, foul strike rule adopted by the AL and pitchers prohibited from soiling a new ball; 1910s, earned-run statistics and definitions added to rules and the cork center added to the official baseball; 1920s, all freak deliveries, including the spitball, outlawed and number of runs batted in included in the official score; 1930s, sacrifice fly brought back and defensive interference changed from an offense by a catcher to one by a fielder as well; 1940s, no rules or changes to them listed in *Baseball Almanac*; 1950s, players must remove their gloves when batting and no equipment showing on the field at any time; 1960s, pitcher's mound dropped five inches and the save rule added to official rules; 1970s, all major league players ordered to wear protective helmets and the save rule rewritten and changed again; 1980s and 1990s: no rules or changes in them listed in *Baseball Almanac*.[22]

To improve competitiveness, pace, safety, and other things about the game of baseball for teams and their coaches and also to make it more attractive, entertaining, and standardized for spectators, the following is a sample of specific rule changes adopted during MLB's 2015, 2016, and 2017 seasons.

---

21 *Idem. Additional major league rules, for example, included: 1880s, player reserve clause for the first time put into a contract, a staff of umpires introduced, one portion of the bat could be flat (one side), chest protectors worn by catchers and umpires came into use; and in 1890s, substitutions permitted at any point in the game, foul bunts classified as strikes, pitching distance increased from fifty feet to sixty feet six inches.*

22 *Idem. Some other major league rules adopted in the twentieth century were as follows: 1900s, catchers compelled to remain continuously under the bat and height of the pitcher's mound limited to fifteen inches higher than the level of the baselines; 1910s, cork center added to the official baseball; 1920s, frivolous ninth-inning uncontested steals in a one-sided game discarded and pitcher allowed to use a resin bag; 1930s, no fielder could take a position in line with a batter's vision with deliberate intent to in any way distract the batter; 1950s, regulations set up for minimum boundaries for all new parks, 325–400–325 feet; 1960s, strike zone shrunken to the area from the armpits to the top of the batter's knees; and in the 1970s, rule on glove size and color minutely outlined for standardization and baseball permitted to be covered with rawhide because of the shortage of horses.*

2015

Adopted in 2015, first, the pace of game program enforces the batter's box rule, requiring that all batters must keep at least one foot in the batter's box unless one of a group of exceptions occurs. The new rule at the Major League level mirrors 6.02(d), which was in place in Minor League Baseball in 2014.[23]

Second, the addition of timers measures non-game action and break time between innings and pitching changes during each Major League game. One timer will be installed on or near the outfield scoreboard, and a smaller timer will be installed on the façade behind home plate near the press box. Immediately following the third out of each half-inning, the timer will count down from 2:25 for locally televised games and from 2:45 for nationally televised games.

Third, pitchers are permitted to throw as many warm-up pitches as they wish prior to the point when thirty seconds remain on the clock; however, pitchers will be deemed to have forfeited any of their traditional eight warm-up pitches that they are unable to complete prior to the thirty-second deadline. Exceptions to these rules will be made in a variety of circumstances, including if the pitcher or catcher ended the prior half-inning at bat or on base.

Fourth, batters are encouraged to get into the batter's box with twenty seconds remaining on the timer, when the broadcasters return from commercial. The pitcher is expected to begin his motion to deliver the pitch as soon as the batter gets into the batter's box and becomes alert to the pitcher. Batters who do not enter the box prior to five seconds remaining on the timer and pitchers who do not begin the motion to deliver the pitch prior to zero seconds remaining on the timer will be deemed to have violated the break timing rules.

According to a report in the Associated Press, the new pace of play measures shaved six minutes off the average time of game in 2015. The average game lasted two hours and fifty-six minutes in that season, though it was two hours and fifty-three

---

23 *"MLBPA, MLB Announce Pace-of-Game Initiatives, Replay Modifications," www.mlb.com cited 18 October 2017.*

minutes in the first half of the season and an even three hours in the second half. Extra pitching changes with September call-ups surely contributed to that result.

2016

Implemented in 2016, first, runners have wide latitude coming into second base as long as they are close enough to touch the bag. Under new Rule 6.01(j), a runner must make a bona fide slide, which is defined as making contact with the ground before reaching the base, being able to and attempting to reach the base with a hand or foot, being able to and attempting to remain on the base at the completion of the slide (except at home plate), and not changing his path for the purpose of initiating contact with a fielder.[24]

Second, visits to the mound by managers and coaches—that previously had no time limit—are limited to thirty seconds and between-inning break times will match the commercial time of two minutes and five seconds for local broadcasts and two minutes and twenty-five seconds for nationally televised games. The break times were twenty seconds longer in the 2015 MLB season, but the change is expected to allow the resumption of play to more closely match the end of the breaks. The timer for mound visits will be the same in-stadium clock that measures the between-inning breaks. The timer will be set at thirty seconds and will begin counting down when the manager or coach has exited the dugout and the timeout for a mound visit has been granted by the umpire. Unless the manager (or coach) signals for a pitching change, he must leave the mound when (or before) the timer reaches zero seconds.

2017

First, the most notable of the new rule changes is the addition of no-pitch intentional walks, which caused a bit of controversy when initially announced by MLB. The new rule allows opposing managers to signal that they would like to issue the intentional walk, bypassing the tradition of the catcher standing up and calling for four balls. The no-pitch walk removes some potential chaos from the game, eliminating the possibility of a wild pitch or the opportunity for a batter to swing on a pitch that

24 Paul Hagen, "Slip Slidin' Away: New Rules Music to All Ears?" www.mlb.com cited 18 October 2017.

strays too close to the plate, but Commissioner Rob Manfred and MLB felt that was a small price to pay for speeding up the game.[25]

Second, in a change to MLB's replay system, a manager has thirty seconds after the play to call for a replay from the dugout, forcing them to make quicker decisions on whether or not they believe the umpire made the correct call. The second change to the replay rule allows managers to make challenges up through the seventh inning, which is an inning longer than previously allowed. There will also be a two-minute guideline for making decisions on the replays, which means fewer 10-minute delays of games, although there might be an increase of incorrectly reviewed plays.[26]

Third, a new rule prohibits pitchers from shifting or lifting their pivot foot during a pitch. If a pitcher does so with a runner on base then the delivery will be charged as a balk. If the bases are empty, it will go down as an illegal pitch and be called a ball. Also, third-base coaches will be required to stay in the third-base coach's box before every pitch, refining a rule that was already on the books, but rarely enforced. Coaches will still be allowed to run down the line to scream at runners during the play, as long as they do not interfere with the on-field action.[27]

Fourth, MLB prohibits the use of any markers on the field that could create a tangible reference system for fielders. In a game against the New York Mets, the Los Angeles Dodgers wanted to mark positions on the field where their defenders should line up. After using the laser rangefinder, the club wanted to use markers on the playing surface to define the desired positions for their outfielders and informed the Mets' grounds crew of their plans. The Mets instructed their grounds crew to erase or obliterate anything they saw on the playing surface. MLB does allow teams to use electronics prior to games to show their players where to line up on defense, but the new rule specifically prohibits using any kind of marker on the dirt or grass as the game is progressing.[28]

---

25 *See Mansur Shaheen, "Major League Baseball Unveils Official Rule Changes for 2017 Season," www.sbnation.com cited 18 October 2017.*

26 *Idem.*

27 *Idem.*

28 *The source is Adam Wells, "Full List of MLB Rule Changes for 2017 Season," www.bleacherreport.com cited 18 October 2017.*

TOMMY JOHN SURGERY

> *"My first pitch to [Montreal Expos Hal] Breeden was . . . strange. As I came forward and released the ball, I felt a kind of nothingness, as if my arm wasn't there, then I heard a pop from inside my arm, and the ball just blooped up to the plate. I didn't feel soreness or pain at this point, but just the strange sensation that my arm wasn't there. It was the oddest thing I'd ever felt while pitching. I shook my arm, more baffled than concerned. My next pitch would be the last one I threw in a big league game for the next twenty-one months."*[29]

Known as *ulnar collateral ligament reconstruction* (or UCL), the Tommy John surgery is a surgical operation in which a ligament in the medial elbow is replaced with a tendon from elsewhere in the body such as the forearm, hamstring, or foot. The procedure was developed by Dr. Frank Jobe in 1974 to repair the left arm of Los Angeles Dodgers pitcher John.[30]

The injury results from repetitive use of the elbow during the violent motions involved with throwing a baseball. In the surgery, the new tendon is implanted and woven in a figure-eight pattern through holes drilled in the humerus and ulna. A torn elbow ligament was the most common cause of what was simply called dead arm injury during most of the twentieth century.

At the time of the first operation, Jobe put John's odds of returning to pitch at 1 in 100 or 1 percent. After his 1974 surgery, John spent eighteen months rehabilitating his arm and returned to the Dodgers for the 1976 season. He continued to pitch in the major leagues until 1989 at age forty-six and won twenty or more games each in 1977, 1979, and 1980.

The chances of a complete recovery after the surgery are estimated at 85 to 90 percent. Rehabilitation takes approximately twelve to fifteen months for pitchers

---

29 *These statements appear on page 143 of author Tommy John's book, T.J.: My 26 Years in Baseball (New York, NY: Bantam Books, 1991).*

30 *Ben Zellner, "A History and Overview of Tommy John Surgery," www.osmsgb.com cited 19 October 2017 and "Ulnar Collateral Ligament Reconstruction (Tommy John Surgery) in the Throwing Athlete," www.orlandoortho.com cited 19 November 2017.*

and about six months for position players. When Jobe died in the spring of 2014, it was reported that a one-third of major-league pitchers had completed the surgery. During the 2000s, an average of sixteen major-league pitchers underwent the procedure each year including a record thirty-six in 2012.[31]

It is not uncommon for pitchers to throw harder after the surgery than they did before being injured. This results not because of the surgery, but from the rigorous rehabilitation that ensues following it. Another common myth is that the injury happens suddenly, the result of overuse one day or of plain bad luck. In fact, tests performed on pitchers indicate that the ligament becomes frayed over years of abuse, starting in youth baseball, and eventually snaps.[32]

Former Atlanta Braves player John Smoltz became the first pitcher elected into the Baseball Hall of Fame after undergoing the surgical procedure, when he was a first-ballot inductee in the 2015 Hall of Fame Election. He underwent the procedure in 2000, missed that season altogether, then returned as a closer for a few years, compiling over 150 saves, before finishing his career as a starting pitcher once again.[33]

---

31 *The majority of studies indicate that greater than 80 percent of MLB pitchers return to the major leagues after Tommy John surgery. However, the issue of defining what constitutes positive and negative outcomes is tricky in medical studies. It gets even more complicated if you try to use certain statistics, such as a pitcher's total wins, to evaluate his effectiveness. Success on a baseball field is not just about one person's performance. The team's defense and hitters influence pitcher's statistics and so does random chance. Even if fastball velocity does decrease after the surgery, it is also pretty common for pitchers to lose fastball velocity as they age. As with many science topics, the issue is complicated, and easy to misinterpret. See "Do Pitchers Get Better After Tommy John Surgery?" www.sporttechie.com cited 19 October 2017.*

32 *As of 2018, 57 percent of all Tommy John surgeries were done on kids aged fifteen to nineteen years old. Furthermore, only one in seven of these kids will fully recover. For more about these results, see Tommy John, "Why We Need to Change my Legacy," AARP Bulletin (September 2018): 34.*

33 *Graham Womack, "Tommy John on Baseball Hall of Fame: "I'm Being Held Back,"" www.sportingnews.com cited 19 October 2017. Tommy John completed his Baseball Writers Association of Americian (BBWAA) eligibility in 2009, peaking at 31.7 percent of the vote and well short of the 75 percent needed for enshrinement. He appeared on the Expansion Era Committee's ballots for the 2011 and 2014 elections. John has a good shot at induction at some point because of his win total, longevity, and being the first pitcher to have ulnar collateral ligament reconstruction. Said John: "My whole thing is, if you'd looked at the pitchers of my era on the number of ground ball outs to total outs, I had the best ratio in the history of baseball. I was very, very good at what I did, and I wasn't a strikeout pitcher. I was when I was in high school and all that. But I wasn't when I became a pro. So I'm being held back because I didn't conform to some sportswriter's idea of what is good and what is not good." Recent readings on this topic are Mike Mazzeo, "Yank Pick Coming Off Elbow Surgery," New York Daily News (13 June 2017): 49; Jane McCauley, "With All the 100 MPH Pitchers, How Long Will the Arms Last?" Charleston Gazette (31 March 2017): B.3; Mike Vorkunov, "Spring Sees Tommy*

BASEBALL EVENTS

Besides those things discussed in this and previous chapters, some all-time important events transformed the game of baseball in some way. Chronologically, a few of these were the formation of the National Association of Professional Base Ball Players (1870), Negro Baseball Leagues (1885), deadball era (early 1900s), Black Sox scandal (1919), Carl Mays' pitch and banning spitballs (1920), first MLB all-star game (1933), President Franklin D. Roosevelt and the Green Light Letter that encouraged the scheduling of a baseball season during World War II (1942), Jackie Robinson breaking the color barrier (1946), and the MLB strike (1994).[34]

In another study of big-league baseball, other historical events greatly influenced the game and transformed it for teams and their players and also fans. Some of them were the sale of player Babe Ruth by the Boston Red Sox to New York Yankees for $125,000 in 1920; Atlanta Braves' Hank Aaron establishing a MLB record by hitting his 715th home run in 1974; known as the shot heard 'round the world, New York Giants' Bobby Thompson slugged a three-run homer in the bottom of the ninth inning to win the NL pennant in 1951 over the Brooklyn Dodgers; Pittsburgh Pirate Bill Mazeroski's walk-off home run in the ninth inning of game seven of the 1960 World Series against the New York Yankees; in his luckiest man speech during Lou Gehrig Appreciation Day on July 4, 1939, he became the first MLB player to have his number retired and two years later died of Lou Gehrig's disease or ALS; and New York Yankees Joe DiMaggio and his fifty-six-game hitting streak in 1941.[35]

John Spike," USA Today (14 February 2017): C.5; David Carson, "Surgery Maness Had Could Help Pitchers Return Earlier," St. Louis Post Dispatch (11 January 2017): B.1.

34 *"The Important Events That Changed Baseball," www.timetoast.com cited 19 October 2017.*

35 *In no specific order, other famous and memorable all-time events in the game were the New York Yankees' Roger Maris hitting his sixty-first home run in 1961 and surpassing Babe Ruth's record; Baltimore Orioles' Cal Ripken playing in 2,130 consecutive games in September 1995 and setting a new major league record of 2,632; Yankees' Don Larsen pitching a perfect game against the Brooklyn Dodgers in the 1956 World Series; Yankees' Reggie Jackson blasting three home run in a 1975 World Series game and earning the Most Valuable Player award for his accomplishments; and Cincinnati Reds' Pete Rose breaking Ty Cobb's record of 4,192 hits in 1985 and ending his career with 4,256 of them. For more details, see Rocco Constantino, "The Top 200 Moments That Shaped MLB's History," www.bleacherreport.com cited 19 October 2017.*

APPENDIX

Table A5.1 *Championship Performances, American League by Team, Selected Years*

Team	1992–1996			1997–2001			2002–2006			2007–2011			2012–2016		
	DT	P	WS	DT	P	WS	DT	P	WS	DT	P	WS	DT	P	WS
Baltimore Orioles	0	0	0	1	0	0	0	0	0	0	0	0	1	0	0
Boston Red Sox	1	0	0	0	0	0	0	1	1	1	1	1	2	1	1
Chicago White Sox	2	0	0	1	0	0	1	1	1	1	0	0	0	0	0
Cleveland Indians	2	1	0	4	1	0	0	0	0	1	0	0	1	1	0
Detroit Tigers	0	0	0	0	0	0	0	1	0	1	0	0	3	1	0
Houston Astros	NA			NA			NA			NA			0	0	0
Kansas City Royals	0	0	0	0	0	0	0	0	0	0	0	0	1	2	1
LA Angels of Anaheim	0	0	0	0	0	0	2	1	1	3	0	0	1	0	0
Milwaukee Brewers	0	0	0	0	0	0	NA			NA			NA		
Minnesota Twins	0	0	0	0	0	0	4	0	0	2	0	0	0	0	0
New York Yankees	2	1	1	4	4	3	5	1	0	2	1	1	1	0	0
Oakland Athletics	1	0	0	1	0	0	3	0	0	0	0	0	2	0	0
Seattle Mariners	1	0	0	2	0	0	0	0	0	0	0	0	0	0	0
Tampa Bay Rays	NA			0	0	0	0	0	0	2	1	0	0	0	0
Texas Rangers	2	0	0	2	0	0	0	0	0	2	2	0	2	0	0
Toronto Blue Jays	2	2	2	0	0	0	0	0	0	0	0	0	1	0	0

Note: Abbreviated are each team's number of Division Titles (DT), Pennants (P), and World Series (WS) and also Los Angeles (LA) and Not Applicable (NA). Prior team names include California Angels (1965–1996), Anaheim Angels (1997–2004), and Tampa Bay Devil Rays (1998–2007). The Houston Astros shifted from the NL West to AL West in 2013 and the Milwaukee Brewers from the AL Central to NL Central in 1998.

Source: "Franchise History," www.baseball-reference.com cited 8 September 2017.

Table A5.2 *Championship Performances, National League by Team, Selected Years*

Team	1992–1996			1997–2001			2002–2006			2007–2011			2012–2016		
	DT	P	WS	DT	P	WS	DT	P	WS	DT	P	WS	DT	P	WS
Arizona Diamondbacks	NA			2	1	1	0	0	0	2	0	0	0	0	0
Atlanta Braves	4	3	1	5	1	0	4	0	0	0	0	0	1	0	0
Chicago Cubs	0	0	0	0	0	0	1	0	0	2	0	0	1	1	1
Cincinnati Reds	2	0	0	0	0	0	0	0	0	1	0	0	1	0	0
Colorado Rockies	0	0	0	0	0	0	0	0	0	0	1	0	0	0	0
Houston Astros	0	0	0	4	0	0	0	1	0	0	0	0	0	0	0
Los Angeles Dodgers	2	0	0	0	0	0	1	0	0	2	0	0	4	0	0
Montreal Expos	1	0	0	0	0	0	0	0	0	NA			NA		
Miami Marlins	0	0	0	0	0	0	0	1	1	0	0	0	0	0	0
Milwaukee Brewers	NA			0	0	0	0	0	0	1	0	0	0	0	0
New York Mets	0	0	0	0	1	0	1	0	0	0	0	0	1	1	0
Philadelphia Phillies	1	1	0	0	0	0	0	0	0	5	2	1	0	0	0
Pittsburgh Pirates	1	0	0	0	0	0	0	0	0	0	0	0	0	0	0
San Diego Padres	1	0	0	1	1	0	2	0	0	0	0	0	0	0	0
San Francisco Giants	0	0	0	2	0	0	1	1	0	1	1	1	1	2	2
St. Louis Cardinals	1	0	0	1	0	0	4	2	1	1	1	1	3	1	1
Washington Nationals	NA			NA			0	0	0	0	0	0	3	0	0

Note: Abbreviated are each team's number of Division Titles (DT), Pennants (P), and World Series (WS), and also Not Applicable (NA). The Expos moved from Montreal, Canada to Washington, D.C. in 2005 and were nicknamed the Nationals. The Florida Marlins became the Miami Marlins in 2012. The Brewers shifted from the AL Central to NL Central in 1998.

Source: "Franchise History," www.baseball-reference.com cited 8 September 2017.

Table A6.1 *Site Relocations, American League Teams, Selected Years*

Team Years		Metropolitan Area		Area Population	
Before	**After**	**Before**	**After**	**Before**	**After**
1901–1901	1902–1953	Milwaukee	St. Louis	285	575
1901–1902	1903–2018	Baltimore	New York	508	3,437
1901–1954	1955–1967	Philadelphia	Kansas City	3,016	814
1901–1960	1961–2018	Washington	Minneapolis	2,076	1,482
1902–1953	1954–2018	St. Louis	Baltimore	1,618	1,337
1955–1967	1968–2018	Kansas City	Oakland	1,201	2,942
1961–1965	1966–2018	Los Angeles	Anaheim	6,755	1,161
1961–1971	1972–2018	Washington	Arlington	2,910	2,377
1969–1969	1970–1997	Seattle	Milwaukee	1,424	1,403

Note: Team years are American League seasons at the pre-move site (Before) and post-move site (After). Area population is in hundreds of thousands and based on the nearest census year.

Source: The information is in various editions of The World Almanac and Book of Facts (New York, NY: World Almanac Books, 1930–2016) and Official Major League Baseball Fact Book 2005 Edition (St. Louis, MO: Sporting News, 2005).

Table A6.2 *Site Relocations, National League Teams, Selected Years*

Team Years		Metropolitan Area		Area Population	
Before	**After**	**Before**	**After**	**Before**	**After**
1879–1884	1885–1886	Cleveland	St. Louis	160	350
1885–1886	1887–1889	St. Louis	Indianapolis	350	105
1901–1957	1958–2016	Brooklyn	Los Angeles	14,186	6,038
1901–1957	1958–2016	New York	San Francisco	14,186	2,135
1912–1952	1953–1965	Boston	Milwaukee	2,369	871
1953–1965	1966–2016	Milwaukee	Atlanta	1,331	1,258
1969–2004	2005–2016	Montreal	Washington	3,684	5,290

Note: Team years are National League seasons at the pre-move site (Before) and post-move site (After). Brooklyn's population is actually for the New York City metropolitan area. Area population is in hundreds of thousands and based on the nearest census year.

Source: The table's information is in various editions of The World Almanac and Book of Facts (New York, NY: World Almanac Books, 1930–2016) and Official Major League Baseball Fact Book 2005 Edition (St. Louis, MO: Sporting News, 2005).

Table A7.1 *AL Expansion Areas and Years, Seven Teams' Markets, Selected Years*

		Population		Teams	
Metropolitan Area	**Year**	**Rank**	**Growth**	**MLB**	**Other**
Los Angeles	1961	2	16	2	3
Washington, D.C.	1961	7	38	1	1
Kansas City	1969	25	14	1	1
Seattle	1969	19	28	1	1
Seattle	1977	23	12	1	2
Toronto	1977	1	14	1	2
Tampa Bay	1998	21	9	1	2

Note: Abbreviated is American League (AL). Metropolitan area is the standard metropolitan statistical area (SMSA) of teams in their expansion year. Each SMSA's rank in population is listed in column three, while their approximate population growth rate in column four is a percent. The Greater Toronto Area (or Toronto) ranked first in population among all areas in Canada in 1977. The column titled MLB is the total number of Major League Baseball clubs in an SMSA during the expansion year. The column labeled Other includes the number of professional basketball, football, ice hockey, and soccer teams located in a metropolitan area during the expansion year.

Source: See various editions of The World Almanac and Book of Facts, Statistical Abstract of the United States, Survey of Current Business and Census of the Population, and Frank P. Jozsa, Jr. and John J. Guthrie, Jr., Relocating Teams and Expanding Leagues in Professional Sports: How the Major Leagues Respond to Market Conditions (Westport, CT: Quorum Books, 1999).

Table A7.2 *AL Teams, Population Rank of Their Areas in Expansion Year, Selected Years*

Area	1961	1969	1977	1998
Anaheim	–	20	18	17
Baltimore	12	13	14	19
Boston	7	8	10	10
Chicago	3	3	3	3
Cleveland	11	14	19	23
Dallas-Fort Worth	–	–	8	5
Detroit	5	5	5	9
Kansas City	21	**25**	29	26
Los Angeles	2	–	–	–
Milwaukee	–	–	28	–
Minnesota	14	14	15	16
New York	1	1	1	1
Oakland	–	6	6	12
Seattle	–	**19**	**23**	15
Tampa Bay	–	–	–	**21**
Toronto	–	–	**1**	1
Washington	**7**	7	–	–

Note: Abbreviated is American League (AL). The numbers in bold are the population rankings of the areas of expansion teams. Since United States census of areas' populations are performed in ten-year intervals, the population ranks of teams' areas for 1961, 1969, 1977, and 1998 were reported from, respectively, the census conducted in 1960, 1970, 1980, and 2000. The 1998 rank (17) of Anaheim is based on the population of Orange County since Anaheim was not listed as a metropolitan area in the late 1990s. The population of the Greater Toronto Area (or Toronto) was ranked first in 1980 and 2000 among all areas in Canada. A dash (–) means that an AL team did not exist in that area during the expansion year.

Source: See various editions of The World Almanac and Book of Facts; Official Major League Baseball Fact Book 2005 Edition; "Historical Metropolitan Populations of the United States," www.peakbagger.com cited 13 September 2017.

Table A7.3 *National League Expansion Areas, Years, and Characteristics, Selected Years*

		Population		Teams	
Market Area	**Year**	**Rank**	**Growth**	**MLB**	**Other**
Pre-1901 Expansions					
Indianapolis	1878	24	5.6	1	0
Milwaukee	1878	19	6.2	1	0
Providence	1878	20	5.3	1	0
Buffalo	1879	13	3.2	1	0
Cleveland	1879	11	7.4	1	0
Syracuse	1879	32	1.8	1	0
Troy	1879	29	2.1	1	0
Worcester	1880	28	4.1	1	0
Detroit	1881	18	7.6	1	0
New York	1883	1	2.5	2	0
Philadelphia	1883	2	2.3	2	0
Kansas City	1886	24	14.0	1	0
Washington	1886	14	5.6	1	0
Indianapolis	1887	27	4.0	1	0
Cleveland	1889	10	6.3	1	0
Post-1900 Expansions					
Houston	1962	17	5.9	1	1
New York	1962	1	1.0	2	5
Montreal	1969	2	2	1	2
San Diego	1969	23	3.1	1	2
Denver	1993	24	3.0	1	2
Miami	1993	11	2.3	1	2
Phoenix	1998	14	4.5	1	3

Note: Market area is an urban place or, as renamed later, a standard metropolitan statistical area (SMSA) of the teams in their expansion year. Year is each team's expansion year. The 1880 and 1890 population ranks of urban places were used to estimate, respectively, the ranks for years 1878–1883 and 1886–1889. The 1960, 1970, 1990, and 2000 population ranks of metropolitan areas were used to estimate, respectively, the ranks for years 1962, 1969, 1993, and 1998. The annual growth rate in each area's population was determined during 1870–1880, 1880–1890, 1960–1970, and 1990–2000 for the nearest expansion years. MLB is the total number of Major League Baseball clubs (including AL teams or those from alternative professional baseball leagues) in a market area during the expansion year. Other includes the number of professional basketball, football, ice hockey, and soccer teams located in these market areas during the expansion year. In 1969, Montreal's population ranked second to Toronto's in Canada.

Source: Official Major League Baseball Fact Book 2005 Edition (St. Louis, MO: Sporting News, 2005); Frank P. Jozsa, Jr. and John J. Guthrie, Jr., Relocating Teams and Expanding Leagues in Professional Sports: How the Major Leagues Respond to Market Conditions (Westport, CT: Quorum, 1999); James Quirk and Rodney D. Fort, Pay Dirt (Princeton, NJ: Princeton University Press, 1992); The World Almanac and Book of Facts (New York, NY: World Almanac Books, 1930–2016).

Table A7.4 NL Teams, Population Rank of Teams Areas in Expansion Year, Selected Years

1878	1879	1880	1881	1883	1886	1887	1889	1962	1969	1993	1998
4	4	4	4	**1**	1	1	**1**	1	1	1	1
5	5	5	5	**2**	2	2	2	2	2	2	2
8	8	8	11	4	3	3	3	3	**2**	2	2
19	**11**	11	13	5	5	6	6	4	3	3	3
20	**13**	13	**18**	11	6	13	**10**	6	4	4	4
24	20	20	20	13	**14**	14	13	8	6	5	5
	29	**28**	28	18	15	15	14	9	9	10	10
	32	29	29	20	**24**	**27**	27	16	10	**11**	11
								17	13	12	12
								18	20	15	**14**
									21	17	17
									23	19	18
										23	20
										24	22
											24
											35

Note: Abbreviated is National League (NL). The bold numbers are population rankings of the areas of expansion teams relative to the closest census year. Indianapolis, for example, ranked twenty-fourth in population in 1878 according to the census in 1880. In 1969, Montreal was an expansion market and its area's population ranked second in Canada. The other area ranked second in population that year was Los Angeles. The ranks of these two areas are also listed in NL expansion years of 1993 and 1998.

Source: "Population of the 100 Largest Urban Areas: 1870–1900," www.census.gov cited 15 September 2017; "Historical Metropolitan Populations of the United States," www.peakbagger.com cited 13 September 2017; The World Almanac and Book of Facts, 1930–2016; Official Major League Baseball Fact Book 2005 Edition; Frank P. Jozsa, Jr. and John J. Guthrie, Jr., Relocating Teams and Expanding Leagues in Professional Sports, 1999.

Table A8.1 *Distribution of Financial Data, American League Franchises, 1997 MLB Season*

Franchise	Revenue	(Rank)	OI	(Rank)	Payroll	(Rank)	Value	(Rank)
Baltimore Orioles	135	(2nd)	18.7	(2nd)	64.6	(2nd)	323	(2nd)
Boston Red Sox	92	(5th)	7.7	(6th)	40.6	(9th)	230	(6th)
California Angels	63	(10th)	−9.6	(12th)	46.6	(5th)	157	(8th)
Chicago White Sox	82	(7th)	−4.2	(10th)	41.8	(8th)	214	(7th)
Cleveland Indians	134	(3rd)	15.4	(3rd)	58.8	(3rd)	322	(3rd)
Detroit Tigers	51	(12th)	−0.4	(9th)	20.9	(13th)	137	(10th)
Kansas City Royals	68	(8th)	2.3	(8th)	33.8	(10th)	108	(13th)
Milwaukee Brewers	47	(13th-t)	−4.8	(11th)	26.5	(12th)	127	(11th)
Minnesota Twins	47	(13th-t)	−16.5	(13th)	32.1	(11th)	94	(14th)
New York Yankees	145	(1st)	21.4	(1st)	73.3	(1st)	362	(1st)
Oakland Athletics	56	(11th)	7.5	(7th)	12.8	(14th)	118	(12th)
Seattle Mariners	90	(6th)	11.4	(4th)	46.2	(6th)	251	(5th)
Texas Rangers	98	(4th)	9.1	(5th)	44.5	(7th)	254	(4th)
Toronto Blue Jays	67	(9th)	−20.5	(14th)	48.9	(4th)	141	(9th)

Note: Financial data is in millions. Abbreviated are Major League Baseball (MLB), operating income (OI), and tie (t) in rank. Gate receipts were not available.

Source: "The Business of Baseball," www.forbes.com cited 22 September 2017.

Table A8.2 Distribution of Financial Data, National League Franchises, 1997 MLB Season

Franchise	Revenue (Rank)	OI (Rank)	Payroll (Rank)	Value (Rank)
Atlanta Braves	120 (1st)	18.2 (2nd)	53.1 (1st)	299 (2nd)
Chicago Cubs	82 (6th)	8.1 (3rd-t)	30.7 (12th)	204 (4th)
Cincinnati Reds	50 (12th)	−19.9 (14th)	38.2 (7th)	136 (11th)
Colorado Rockies	117 (2nd)	38.3 (1st)	46.0 (5th)	303 (1st)
Florida Marlins	94 (3rd)	0.9 (7th)	52.4 (2nd)	159 (10th)
Houston Astros	88 (4th)	−-5.5 (11th)	34.9 (8th-t)	190 (6th)
Los Angeles Dodgers	51 (11th)	−11.2 (13th)	48.4 (4th)	236 (3rd)
Montreal Expos	44 (14th)	−3.7 (10th)	18.0 (13th)	87 (14th)
New York Mets	81 (7th)	8.1 (3rd-t)	34.9 (8th-t)	193 (5th)
Philadelphia Phillies	57 (10th)	−2.5 (9th)	31.3 (11th)	131 (13th)
Pittsburgh Pirates	49 (13th)	7.5 (5th)	15.4 (14th)	133 (12th)
San Diego Padres	58 (9th)	−6.7 (12th)	32.7 (10th)	161 (9th)
San Francisco Giants	70 (8th)	0.2 (8th)	43.0 (6th)	188 (7th)
St. Louis Cardinals	83 (5th)	2.4 (6th)	50.2 (3rd)	174 (8th)

Note: Financial data is in millions. Abbreviated are Major League Baseball (MLB), operating income (OI), and tie (t) in rank. Gate receipts were not available.

Source: "The Business of Baseball," www.forbes.com cited 22 September 2017.

Table A8.3 *American League Teams, Estimated Television Contracts, Selected Years*

		Television Deal			
Team	**2016 Revenue**	**Start**	**End**	**Amount**	**Ownership**
Baltimore Orioles	46M	2006	2028	NA	82
Boston Red Sox	80M	2006	NA	NA	80
Chicago White Sox	51M	2004	2019	NA	20
Cleveland Indians	40M	2013	2022	400M	0
Detroit Tigers	55M	2009	2018	500M	0
Houston Astros	60M	2013	2032	1.6B	0
Kansas City Royals	22M	2008	2019	240M	0
LA Angels of Anaheim	118M	2012	2031	3.0B	25
Minnesota Twins	37M	2012	2023	480M	0
New York Yankees	98M	2013	2042	5.7B	20
Oakland Athletics	41M	2009	2029	1.0B	0
Seattle Mariners	76M	2014	2031	1.8B	71
Tampa Bay Rays	20M	2009	2018	NA	0
Texas Rangers	56M	2015	2034	1.6B	10
Toronto Blue Jays	NA	NA	NA	NA	100

Note: Abbreviated is Los Angeles (LA), billions of dollars (B), millions of dollars (M), and not available (NA). Ownership is each team's percentage share of the television contract.

Source: Craig Edwards, "Estimated TV for All 30 MLB Teams," www.fangraphs.com cited 6 October 2017.

Table A8.4 *National League Teams, Estimated Television Contracts, Selected Years*

		Television Deal			
Team	**2016 Revenue**	**Start**	**End**	**Amount**	**Ownership**
Arizona Diamondbacks	50M	2016	2035	1.5B	100
Atlanta Braves	35M	2008	2027	NA	0
Chicago Cubs	65M	2004	2019	NA	20
Cincinnati Reds	30M	2007	2016	NA	0
Colorado Rockies	20M	2011	2020	200M	0
Los Angeles Dodgers	204M	2014	2038	8.3B	100
Miami Marlins	20M	2006	2020	270M	0
Milwaukee Brewers	24M	2013	2019	NA	0
New York Mets	46M	2006	2030	1.3B	65
Philadelphia Phillies	60M	2016	2040	2.5B	25
Pittsburgh Pirates	25M	2010	2019	NA	0
San Diego Padres	39M	2012	2031	1.0B	20
San Francisco Giants	54M	2008	2032	1.7B	30
St. Louis Cardinals	33M	2018	2032	1.0B	30
Washington Nationals	46M	2006	2028	NA	18

Note: Abbreviated is billions of dollars (B), millions of dollars (M), and not available (NA). Ownership is each team's percentage share of the contract. The Cardinals ownership stake begins in 2018 and not in the 2008 season.

Source: Craig Edwards, "Estimated TV for All 30 MLB Teams," www.fangraphs.com cited 6 October 2017.

Table A9.1 Replacement Ballparks, American League by Year, 1901–2017

		Capacity		Attendance	
Ballpark	**Year**	**Former**	**Replacement**	**Former**	**Replacement**
Fenway Park (Red Sox)	1912	11.5	36.3	.60	.50
Yankee Stadium (Yankees)	1923	55.0	58.0	1.18	.92
Angel Stadium (Angels)	1966	56.0	45.0	.72	1.27
Royals Stadium (Royals)	1973	35.5	40.6	.77	1.22
Metrodome (Twins)	1982	45.9	55.8	.76	1.13
SkyDome (Blue Jays)	1989	43.7	50.5	2.60	3.75
New Comiskey Park (White Sox)	1991	52.0	46.0	1.39	2.73
Camden Yards (Orioles)	1992	53.3	48.3	2.53	3.24
Ballpark in Arlington (Rangers)	1994	43.5	49.2	2.24	2.45
Jacobs Field (Indians)	1994	74.5	43.3	1.48	2.71
Safeco Field (Mariners)	1999	66.0	46.6	2.85	3.18
Comerica Park (Tigers)	2000	52.4	40.0	1.58	1.98
Minute Maid Park (Rays)	2000	42.2	40.9	2.70	3.05
Yankee Stadium (Yankees)	2009	56.9	50.2	4.29	3.71
Target Field (Twins)	2010	56.1	39.0	2.41	3.22

Note: Year is the initial season of the home team in the replacement ballpark. Capacity and attendance are, respectively, the average three-year ballpark capacities, in thousands, and attendances, in millions, of the home teams in their former and replacement ballparks.

Source: See websites www.mlb.com, www.ballparks.com, www.baseball-almanac.com, and www.ballparkwatch.com.

Table A9.2 Replacement Ballparks, National League by Year, 1916–2001

		Capacity		Attendance	
Ballpark	**Year**	**Former**	**Replacement**	**Former**	**Replacement**
Weegham Field/Cubs Park (Cubs)	1916	16.0	38.9	.27	.37
Dodger Stadium (Dodgers)	1962	94.6	56.0	2.04	2.51
Shea Stadium (Mets)	1964	55.0	55.6	1.00	1.74
Busch Stadium (Cardinals)	1966	30.5	49.7	1.18	1.93
Olympic Stadium (Expos)	1977	28.5	43.7	.86	1.65
Coors Field (Rockies)	1995	76.1	50.4	3.88	3.64
Turner Field (Braves)	1997	52.0	49.8	2.66	3.37
Enron Field (Astros)	2000	59.8	41.0	2.39	2.82
Great American Ball Park (Reds)	2000	39.0	42.1	1.88	2.11
Pacific Bell Park (Giants)	2000	58.0	41.0	1.89	3.29
Miller Park (Brewers)	2001	53.1	43.0	1.69	2.16
PNC Park (Pirates)	2001	59.0	38.4	1.65	1.95

Note: Year is the initial season of the home team in the replacement ballpark. For example, Weegham Park was built in 1914 and the Cubs played there beginning in 1916. Then, Weegham Park was renamed Cubs Park in 1920 and then six years later renamed Wrigley Field. Capacity and attendance are, respectively, the average three-year ballpark capacities, in thousands, and attendances, in millions, of the home teams in their former and replacement ballparks. The table excludes ballparks of the Arizona Diamondbacks, Florida now Miami Marlins, Philadelphia Phillies, and San Diego Padres. The Diamondbacks and Marlins have each played their home games in one ballpark, while the Phillies opened the 2004 season in 43,000-seat Citizens Bank Park and the Padres in 46,000-seat Petco Park. The table also excludes ballparks of failed NL franchises.

Source: See websites www.mlb.com, www.ballparks.com, www.baseball-almanac.com, and www.ballparkwatch.com.

BIBLIOGRAPHY

ARTICLES

Abisaid, Joseph. "Traditional Baseball Statistics Still Dominate News Stories." *Newspaper Research Journal* (June 2017): 158–173.

Adomites, Paul D. "Seattle Pilots–Milwaukee Brewers: The Bombers, the Bangers, and the Burners," in Peter C. Bjarkman, ed., *Encyclopedia of Major League Baseball: American League Team Histories* (New York, NY: Carroll & Graf Publishers, 1993): 422–444.

Aisch, Gregor, Quealy, Kevin, and Rory Smith. "Where Are the Best Pro Athletes From? Increasingly, From Somewhere Else." *New York Times* (7 January 2018): 5–7.

Anderson, Jason. "Vigilance Keeping Drugs Off Diamond." *McClatchy Tribune Business News* (17 June 2012): 1.

Appel, Marty. "New York Yankees: Pride, Tradition, and a Bit of Controversy," in Peter C. Bjarkman, ed., *Encyclopedia of Major League Baseball: American League Team Histories* (New York, NY: Carroll & Graf Publishers, 1993).

Barra, Allen. "By the Numbers: Imbalanced Logic." *Wall Street Journal* (30 August 2002): W.5.

Barrett, Devlin. "FBI is Looking Into Foul Play." *Wall Street Journal* (17 June 2015): A3.

"Baseball: A History of America's Favorite Game." *Publishers Weekly* (12 June 2006): 46.

"Baseball Salary Comparison by Club." *New York Daily News* (2 December 2009): 71.

Beverage, Richard E. "Los Angeles Angels–California Angels: A Cowboy's Search for Another Champion," in Peter C. Bjarkman, ed., *Encyclopedia of Major League Baseball: American League Team Histories* (New York, NY: Carroll & Graf Publishers, 1993).

Biderman, David. "The Count: Designated Hitters = Baseball's Most Overpaid?" *Wall Street Journal* (7 December 2009): B.8.

Blum, Ronald. "Major League Baseball." *Charleston Gazette* (24 December 2016): B.3.

Blum, Ronald. "Ohtani, Acuna Named Rookies of the Year." *Charlotte Observer* (13 November 2018): 2B.

Boudway, Ira. "Major League Baseball's Anthony Bosch Problems is Not Going Away." *Business Week* (13–19 January 2014): 1.

Boudway, Ira. "Major League Baseball Might Miss a Closed-Off Cuba." *Business Week* (22 December 2014): 1.

Boudway, Ira. "Major League Baseball Says It's Close to Ending Online Blackouts." *Business Week* (18–24 August 2014): 1.

Brady, Thomas. "Do Sabermetrics Suggest a Baseball Hall of Fame Revision?" *IIE Annual Conference Proceedings* (2012): 1–4.

Brown, Angela. "Sale of Rangers Provides Wake-Up Call for Leagues." *Telegraph Herald* (20 August 2010): B.3.

Brown, Eliot. "When the New Ballpark is Already Too Old." *Wall Street Journal* (18–19 June 2016): A3.

Budig, Gene. "Baseball on the Up and Up." *Charleston Gazette* (19 March 2013): A4.

Bushika, Joe. "America's Game no Longer." *North Adams Transcript* (26 April 2007): 1.

Campbell, Morgan. "Blue Jays' Star Power Bolsters Rogers." *Toronto Star* (30 March 2013): S.11.

Carson, David. "Surgery Maness Had Could Help Pitchers Return Earlier." *St. Louis Post Dispatch* (11 January 2017): B.1.

Cava, Peter. "New York Mets From Throneberry to Strawberry: Baseball's Most Successful Expansion Franchise," in Peter C. Bjarkman, ed., *Encyclopedia of Major League Baseball: National League* (New York, NY: Carroll & Graf Publishers, 1993), 342–393.

Cheng, Jonathan. "In South Korea, Baseball Becomes Girls Night Out." *Wall Street Journal* (17 October 2015): D6.

Coker, Margaret. "Baseball Goes to Bat to Ease Rules on Foreign Players." *The Atlanta Journal* (3 May 2006): A.1.

Coleman, Ronny. "Stats Are More Than Inside Baseball." *Fire Chief* (October 2008): 30, 32–33.

Cook, Ron. "Cubs Make Right Call, by Rule, of Course." *Pittsburgh Post* (3 April 2015): E.1.

Costa, Brian. "The CEO Who Gets to Hand Out World Series Rings." *Wall Street Journal* (23 February 2015): R4.

Costa, Brian. "Why Children Are Abandoning Baseball." *Wall Street Journal* (21 May 2015): D6.

Costa, Brian, and Ezequiel Minaya. "Taking Their Ball and Going Home." *Wall Street Journal* (5 May 2015): D5.

Costa, Brian, and Jared Diamond. "Baseball Learns Data's Downside." *Wall Street Journal* (4 October 2017): A1, A10.

Craft, Matthew. "Moreno's Math." *Forbes* (11 May 2009): 1.

Dahlberg, Tim. "Some Changes That Can Help Make Baseball Great Again." *Charlotte Observer* (19 April 2018): 3B.

De Avila, Joseph. "Ballpark Adds to Hartford's Fiscal Strain." *Wall Street Journal* (12 July 2017): A3.

DeBolt, David. "Oakland and A's Begin Talks of New Ballpark." *East Bay Times* (17 May 2018): B.1.

Delcos, John. "Baseball Needs Fewer Teams, Not More Divisions." *The Journal News* (14 May 2000): C.3.

Diamond, Jared. "Baseball Remembers How to Score Runs." *Wall Street Journal* (12 July 2016): D6.

Diamond, Jared. "How Players Use New Data Analytics." *Wall Street Journal* (21 September 2017): A16.

Diamond, Jared. "The Elusive Riddle of Team Chemistry." *Wall Street Journal* (13 July 2017): A12.

Diamond, Jared, and Brian Costa. "The Rise of Baseball's Superteams." *Wall Street Journal* (24 October 2017): A14.

Dickey, Glenn. "Baseball is Doing Its Homework on Expansion." *San Francisco Chronicle* (30 August 2000): E.6.

Dodd, Mike. "MLB's Growth Spurt Began 50 Years Ago." *USA Today* (8 April 2011): C.1.

Dolich, Andy. "Where Consultant Says A's Will Build Their Ballpark." *East Bay Times* (7 September 2018): A.8.

Duarte, Joseph. "Neverland: Attempts to Bring Baseball to Disney's World Appear Over." *Houston Chronicle* (3 March 2002): G.2.

Farrell, Mike. "OTT Players Could Change Television's Sports Game." *Multichannel News* (4 September 2017): 14, 16.

Fieser, Ezra. "Red Sox-Yankees Series Highlights Globalization of Baseball." *Christian Science Monitor* (8 April 2011): 2.

Fitzpatrick, Frank. "As International Players Arrive, Big 4 Tapping Into Global Markets." *Knight Ridder Tribune News Service* (2 November 2005): 1.

Fleming, Carl. "Foreigners Breaking Down the Barriers." *Infomart* (5 April 2001): 48.

Fishman, Steve. "Chasing A-Rod." *New York Times* (2 December 2013): 1.

Flint, Joe. "Dodgers TV Fiasco, a Game Changer." *Wall Street Journal* (30 September 2014): B.1.

"Foreign Players on the Rise in MLB." *Niagara Falls Review* (3 April 2003): B4.

Frankel, Daniel. "TWC Further Sweetens SportsNet LA Deal." *FierceCable* (30 March 2016): 1.

Frias, Carlos. "Power Surge: Expansion Jolts Number of Home Runs." *The Atlanta Journal* (25 April 2002): F.1.

Friedman, Dick. "TV Stars? They Might be Giants." *Sports Illustrated* (20 July 2011): 1.

Gay, Jason. "What Baseball Can Really Teach Kids." *Wall Street Journal* (24 June 2016): D8.

Gendzel, Glen. "Competitive Boosterism: How Milwaukee Lost the Braves." *Business Review*, Vol. 69, No. 4 (Winter 1995): 530–566.

Germano, Sara. "Under Armour Sets MLB Deal." *Wall Street Journal* (6 December 2016): B3.

Glazer, Daniel. "Ballpark Figures." *Wall Street Journal* (29 August 2002): A.12.

Gordon, Ian. "In the Strike Zone." *Mother Jones* (July/August 2014): 10, 12.

Grant, Peter. "Braves' Stadium is a Winner, Owner Says." *Wall Street Journal* (10 October 2018): B6.

Gregorian, Van. "Cheer If You Must, But Cardinals Report Hurts Everyone." *Charlotte Observer* (18 June 2015): 4B.

Gross, Stephen. "With MacPhail, Phils Finally Go to Sabermetrics." *Morning Call* (1 July 2015): C.1.

Gustafason, Elizabeth, and Lawrence Hadley. "Revenue, Population, and Competitive Balance in Major League Baseball." *Contemporary Economic Policy* (April 2007): 250–261.

Hayutin, Jacob. "Should MLB Adopt a Zero Tolerance Policy for Steroid Use?" *US News & World Report* (July 2013): 1.

Hayutin, Jacob. "Was Major League Baseball Right to Suspend Alex Rodriguez?" *US News & World Report* (August 2013): 1.

Hickey, Pat. "Blue Jays Back in Montreal Amid High Hopes for New Team." *Montreal Gazette* (1 April 2017): E.1.

John, Tommy. "Why We Need to Change My Legacy." *AARP Bulletin* (September 2018): 34.

Jozsa, Frank P., Jr. "Ranking the Hot Spots for Baseball Expansion." *Athletic Business* (April 1989): 48–50.

Kendal, Brent. "Justices on Deck in MLB Case?" *Wall Street Journal* (16 January 2015): A5.

Kennedy, Brendan. "Newest Jay Ready to Go to WAR." *Toronto Star* (2 April 2015): M.4.

Kepner, Tyler. "Commissioner, Pointing to Growth, Says He is Open to First Expansion Since 1998." *New York Times* (15 July 2015): B9.

Kepner, Tyler. "Strikeouts Turn Into Baseball's Latest Crisis." *Wall Street Journal* (19 August 2018): 4B.

Korosec, Thomas. "Rangers Owners Hit Jackpot With Run to the World Series; Value of Team Could go up US$50-100M." *National Post* (30 October 2010): S.4.

Kosman, Josh. "Mets Stakes Sold [Exclusive] Owners Raked in $240M, Paid Down Debt." *New York Post* (20 March 2012): 23.

Lafayette, Jon. "Wild Earnings Season Sets TV Companies on New Course." *Broadcasting & Cable* (14–17 August 2017): 32.

Lacques, Gabe. "Parity Soars in MLB." *The Poughkeepsie Journal* (13 June 2014): 17.

Lin, Dennis. "New International Cap Could Benefit Teams Like Padres." *TCA Regional News* (4 December 2016): 1.

Linker, Andrew. "International Players Continue to Influence Game Greatly." *The Patriot* (16 July 2007): T16.

"Long-Term Deal Hurting Marlins Contract With Fox Sports Florida Under Market Value While Other Teams Cash in." *South Florida Sun* (10 March 2013): C.1.

"Major League Baseball: Around the Horn." *Deseret News* (2 May 2010): D.10.

Marcus, Steven. "Mets' Value Could Rise After Dodgers' $2B Sale." *Newsday* (29 March 2012): A.63.

Mazzeo, Mike. "Yank Pick Coming Off Elbow Surgery." *New York Daily News* (13 June 2017): 49.

McCauley, Jane. "With All the 100 MPH Pitchers, How Long Will the Arms Last?" *Charleston Gazette* (31 March 2017): B.3.

McManaman, Bob. "Manfred Talks DH, Expansion and Trump." *Arizona Republic* (23 February 2016): C.3.

Miles, Bruce. "In Sabermetrics Value, Cubs Annihilate Mets." *Daily Herald* (17 October 2015): 3.

Mio, Kevin. "Montreal a 'Frontrunner' for Expansion, MLB's Manfred Says." *Montreal Gazette* (7 May 2016): D.3.

"MLB Salaries Top $3 Million." *Pittsburgh Post-Gazette* (14 December 2010): D.6.

"MLBPA Chief Blasts Yanks' Levine for Betances Remarks." *Buffalo News* (23 February 2017): C.34.

"Montreal Mayor Coderre Delighted That Baseball Commissioner Supports Expansion." *The Canadian Press* (25 September 2015): 1.

Moores, Alan. "Recreation and Sports." *The Booklist* (August 2006): 26.

Morton, Jim. "Major Baseball Mission." *Herald Sun* (2 July 2009): 75.

Murphy, David. "MLB Players Union Boss 'Optimistic' About Deal." *Tribune Business News* (1 March 2011): 1.

Needleman, Sarah H. "MLB in League With Riot Games." *Wall Street Journal* (17–18 December 2016): B3.

O'Donnell, Christopher. "Much Riding on Ybor City Ballpark Design." *Tampa Bay Times* (10 July 2018): 1.

O'Donnell, Christopher. "Rays Owner Boosts Hope." *Tampa Bay Times* (31 March 2108): 1.

O'Donnell, Christopher, and Meagan Betts. "Ballpark Lite: Spaced Great Less Filling." *Tampa Bay Times* (22 July 2018): 1.

Olivarez-Giles, Nathan. "Baseball's New Player: iPad." *Wall Street Journal* (30 March 2016): B5.

O'Neill, Heather. "Do Major League Baseball Hitters Engage in Opportunistic Behavior?" *International Advances in Economic Research* (August 2013): 215–232.

"Our Insane Ideas to Save Baseball." *Wall Street Journal* (26 October 2018): A12.

Parsons, Michael. "Opening Day Far Too Global for True Fans." *Florida Today* (12 February 2014): 2.

Passan, Jeff. "Baseball is Hurting Our Kids." *New York Times* (9 April 2016): 5.

"Paying For Ballpark Will Take Teamwork." *Tampa Bay Times* (12 July 2018): 8.

Peterson, Gary. "A's Have Unique Idea to Get Fans to New Ballpark." *East Bay Times* (13 April 2018): B.3.

"Philadelphia Athletics-Kansas City Athletics-Oakland A's: Three Families and Three Baseball Epochs" in *Encyclopedia of Major League Baseball: American League Team Histories* (1993): 293–357.

Porter, David L. "San Diego Padres: The Saga of Big Mac and Trader Jack" in *Encyclopedia of Major League Baseball: National League* (1993), 465–512.

Punzel, Dennis. "Selig Relishes Games Parity." *Wisconsin State Journal* (20 April 2016): C.1.

"Rays Owner Wants New Ballpark." *Charleston Gazette* (10 February 2018): B.3.

Red, Christian, and Nathaniel Vinton. "Look Who's #1 Yanks on the Money: $2.3B." *New York Daily News* (28 March 2013): 65.

Ringolsby, Tracy. "Expansion Backfired on Baseball." *Cincinnati Post* (9 November 2001): 1C.

"Sabermetrics Are Revolutionizing Baseball." *University Wire* (14 May 2014): 1.

Sandomir, Richard. "Fox Sports Nears Deal to Add More Games." *New York Times* (20 September 2012): B.14.

Sawchik, Travis. "Report: Pirates' Estimated Value at $500 Million." *Pittsburgh Tribune* (24 October 2013): 1.

Schieber, Noam. "A Baseball Prodigy, the Players' Union and a Lesson for Labor." *International New York Times* (8 April 2015): 17.

Schmidt, Michael. "Reports of Failed Tests Cast Doubt on Rodriguez." *New York Times* (5 November 2013): B.14.

Shaikin, Bill. "MLB Boss: Expansion Could be on the Table." *The Patriot* (16 July 2015): S.6.

Sherman, Joel. "Balance of Power: Baseball Tackles Football in Competitive Parity." *New York Post* (31 October 2010): 90.

Sigo, Shelly. "Bonds Likely to Fuel Cross-Bay Ballpark Move by Tampa Bay Rays." *The Bond Buyer* (22 February 2018): 1.

Soebbing, Brian. "Competitive Balance and Attendance in Major League Baseball: An Empirical Test of the Uncertainty of Outcome Hypothesis." *International Journal of Sport Finance* (May 2008): 119–126.

Strauss, Ben. "Major League Baseball to Let Cuban Players Sign Directly With Teams." *New York Times* (2 March 2016): 1.

Tainsky, Scott, and Jason Winfree. "Discrimination and Demand: The Effect of International

Players on Attendance in Major League Baseball." *Social Science Quarterly* (March 2010): 117.

Topkin, Marc. "Per Forbes Estimates, Rays Franchise Value up to $825-million, Still Last." *Tampa Bay Times* (11 April 2017): 1.

Trigaux, Robert. "5 Numbers Show Tampa Bay Rays' Business as Competitive Off Baseball Field as on." *Tampa Bay Times* (17 April 2017): 1.

Van Riper, Tom. "Return of the Rockies." *Forbes* (20 August 2011): 1.

Van Scyoc, Lee, and Kevin McGee. "Testing for Competitive Balance." *Empirical Economics* (May 2016): 1029–1043.

Vass, George. "The Wide World of Baseball." *Baseball Digest* (February 2003): 11–16.

Verducci, Tom. "Welcome to the New Age of Information." *Sports Illustrated* (5 April 2004): 50–54.

Vorkunov, Mike. "Spring Sees Tommy John Spike." *USA Today* (14 February 2017): C.5.

Waldstein, David. "How an M.L.B. Tour of Cuba Went From a Dream to Reality." *New York Times* (15 December 2015): 1.

Waldstein, David. "Mets' Value Declines, Forbes Says." *New York Times* (24 March 2011): B.3.

Waldstein, David. "Where Analytics Don't Add Up." *New York Times* (11 January 2018): 1, 9.

"Washington Senators–Minnesota Twins: Expansion Era Baseball Comes to the American League," in Peter C. Bjarkman, ed., *Encyclopedia of Major League Baseball: American League Team Histories* (1993): 487–535.

Weiner, Michael. "Baseball's Testing Already the Toughest." *USA Today* (6 August 2013): A.6.

Wenz, Michael. "A Proposal for Incentive-Compatible Revenue Sharing in Major League Baseball." *Journal of Sport Management* (November 2012): 479.

Wharton, David. "Union Chief Sets Baseball Players Free." *Baltimore Sun* (28 November 2012): D.4.

Wiles, Russ. "Cardinals Rank 42 in World Value List." *Arizona Republic* (14 July 2016): A.6.

Young, Hoon Lee, and Rodney Fort. "Attendance and the Uncertainty-of-Outcome Hypothesis in Baseball." *Review of Industrial Organization* (December 2008): 281–295.

BOOKS

Bjarkman, Peter C., ed. *Encyclopedia of Major League Baseball: American League Team Histories* (New York, NY: Carroll & Graf Publishers, 1993).

Bjarkman, Peter C., ed. *Encyclopedia of Major League Baseball: National League* (New York, NY: Carroll & Graf Publishers, 1993).

Canseco, Jose. *Juiced* (New York, NY: William Morrow2006).

Compton, Eric, and Jeff Shermack. *Baseball Stats* (New York, NY: Scholastic Inc., 1985).

Cook, Earnshaw. *Percentage Baseball* (Boston, MA: MIT Press, 1964).

Deford, Frank. *The Entitled: A Tale of Modern Baseball* (Naperville, IL: Sourcebooks Landmark, 2008).

Euchner, Charles C. *Playing the Field: Why Sports Teams and Cities Fight to Keep Them* (Baltimore, MD: John Hopkins Press, 1993).

Goldblatt, Andrew. *The Giants and the Dodgers: Four Cities, Two Teams, One Rivalry* (Jefferson, NC: McFarland, 2003).

Gray, Scott. *The Mind of Bill James: How a Complete Outsider Changed Baseball* (New York, NY: Three Rivers Press, 2006).

Ham, Eldon. *Broadcasting Baseball: A History of the National Pastime on Radio and Television* (Jefferson, NC: McFarland, 2011).

Hartley, James R. *Washington's Expansion Senators (1961–1971)* (Germantown, MD: Corduroy Press, 1998).

Hogan, Kenneth. *The 1969 Seattle Pilots: Major League Baseball's One-Year Team* (Jefferson, NC: McFarland, 2006).

James, Bill. *The New Bill James Historical Baseball Abstract* (New York, NY: Free Press, 2003).

John, Tommy. *T.J.: My 26 Years in Baseball* (New York, NY: Bantam Books, 1991).

Jozsa, Frank P., Jr. *American League Franchises: Team Performances and Business Success* (New York, NY: Springer, 2015).

Jozsa, Frank P., Jr. *Baseball Beyond Borders: From Distant Lands to the Major Leagues* (Lanham, MD: Scarecrow Press, 2013).

Jozsa, Frank P., Jr. *Baseball in Crisis: Spiraling Costs, Bad Behavior, Uncertain Future* (Jefferson, NC: McFarland, 2008).

Jozsa, Frank P., Jr. *Baseball, Inc.: The National Pastime as Big Business* (Jefferson, NC: McFarland, 2006).

Jozsa, Frank P., Jr. *Major League Baseball Expansions and Team Relocations: A History, 1876–2008* (Jefferson, NC: McFarland, 2010).

Jozsa, Frank P., Jr. *Major League Baseball Organizations: Team Performances and Financial Consequences* (Lanham, MD: Lexington Books, 2016).

Jozsa, Frank P., Jr. *National League Franchises: Team Performances and Business Success* (New York, NY: Springer, 2015).

Jozsa, Frank P., Jr., and John J. Guthrie, Jr. *Relocating Teams and Expanding Leagues in Professional Sports: How the Major Leagues Respond to Market Conditions* (Westport, CT: Quorum Books, 1999).

Lewis, Michael. *Moneyball: The Art of Winning an Unfair Game* (New York, NY: W.W. Norton & Company, 2004).

Madden, W.C., and Patrick J. Stewart. *The Western League: A Baseball History, 1885 Through 1899* (Jefferson, NC: McFarland, 2002).

Neyer, Rob. *Power Ball: Anatomy of a Modern Baseball Game* (New York, NY: Harper, 2018).

Powers, Albert Theodore. *The Business of Baseball* (Jefferson, NC: McFarland, 2003).

Quirk, James, and Rodney D. Fort. *Pay Dirt: The Business of Professional Team Sports* (Princeton, NJ: Princeton University Press, 1992).

Shropshire, Kenneth L. *The Sports Franchise Game: Cities in Pursuit of Sports Franchises, Events, Stadiums, and Arenas* (Philadelphia, PA: University of Pennsylvania Press, 1995).

Stewart, Mark. *The Los Angeles Angels of Anaheim* (Chicago, IL: Norwood House Paper Editions, 2008).

Sullivan, Neil J. *The Dodgers Move West: The Transfer of the Brooklyn Baseball Franchise to Los Angeles* (New York, NY: Oxford University Press, 1987).

The World Almanac and Book of Facts (New York, NY: World Almanac Books, 1930–2016).

Thomas, G. Scott. *The Best (and Worst) of Baseball's Modern Era* (New York, NY: Niawanda Books, 2016).

Vecsey, George. *Baseball: A History of America's Favorite Game* (New York, NY: Modern Library, 2008).

Walker, James, and Robert Bellemy. *Center Field Shot: A History of Baseball on Television* (Lincoln, NB: Bison Books, 2008).

Wilbert, Warren N. *The Arrival of the American League: Ban Johnson and the 1901 Challenge to National League Monopoly* (Jefferson, NC: McFarland, 2007).

Wright, Carl R., and Tom House. *The Diamond Appraised* (New York, NY: Simon & Schuster, 1989).

Zimbalist, Andrew. *May the Best Team Win: Baseball Economics and Public Policy* (Washington D.C.: Brookings Institution Press, 2003).

INTERNET SOURCES

"2012 American League All-Star Roster." www.espn.go.com cited 11 August 2017.

"2012 Hall of Fame Voting." www.baseball-reference.com cited 19 December 2012.

"2012 National League All-Star Roster." www.espn.go.com cited 11 August 2017.

"2013 Official Hall of Fame Ballot." www.baseball-reference.com cited 19 December 2012.

"2015 Average Salaries in Major League Baseball." www.mlbplayers.com cited 22 August 2017

"2016 Total Payroll." www.usatoday.com cited 31 August 2017.

"2017 MLB Awards." www.espn.com cited 17 November 2017.

"A Celebration of Baseball Unionism." www.nyujlpp.org cited 21 August 2017.

"A Timeline of MLB's Drug-Testing Rules." www.usatoday.com cited 12 November 2018.

"All-Time Leaders." www.mlb.com cited 1 August 2018.

"America's Best Baseball Stadiums." www.travelandleisure.com cited 13 October 2017.

"American League Ballparks." www.ballparksofbaseball.com cited 24 September 2018.

"American League Gold Glove Award Winners." www.baseball-reference.com cited 17 December 2012.

Anderson, Stuart. "27 Percent of Major League Baseball Players Are Foreign-Born." www.forbes.com cited 21 November 2018.

Armour, Mark. "Collective Bargaining Agreement (1968)." www.pursuitofpennants.wordpress.com cited 21 August 2018.

Armour, Mark, and Dan Levitt. "A History of the MLBPA's Collective Bargaining Agreement: Part 1." www.fangraphs.com cited 21 August 2018.

"Atlanta Braves." www.mlb.com cited 8 September 2017.

"BALCO Fast Facts." www.cnn.com cited 15 April 2018.

"Ballparks, Baseball Stadiums & Field of Dreams." www.baseball-almanac.com cited 13 October 2017.

"Batting Average Year-by-Year Leaders." www.baseball-almanac.com cited 24 November 2012.

"Baseball Hall of Fame." www.baseballhall.org cited 3 December 2017.

"Baseball Rule Changes Timeline." www.baseball-almanac.com cited 18 October 2017.

"Baseball Statistics." www.baseball-reference.com cited 27 July 2017.

"Baseball Statistics." www.fangraphs.com cited 27 July 2017.

"Baseball Statistics and Analysis." www.fangraphs.com cited 4 August 2017.

"Batting Average Year-by-Year Leaders." www.baseball-almanac.com cited 11 August 2017.

Berg, Ted. "All 30 MLB Stadiums, Ranked." www.usatoday.com cited 13 October 2017.

"Biography by Baseball Almanac." www.baseball-almanac.com cited 30 November 2012.

"Blue Jays Timeline." www.toronto.bluejays.mlb.com cited 6 October 2017.

Borawski, Brian. "National Attention: The Expos' 35-Year Journey to Washington D.C." www.fangraphs.com cited 6 October 2017.

Boswell, Thomas. "How Thomas Boswell Ranked All 30 MLB Ballparks, and Grouped Them in Four Tiers." www.washingtonpost.com cited 13 October 2017.

"Brotherhood of Professional Baseball Players." www.baseball-reference.com cited 16 August 2017.

Brown, Maury. "MLB Sees Record Revenues Approaching $10 Billion for 2016." www.forbes.com cited 7 September 2017.

Brown, Maury. "MLB Sets Record For Revenues In 2017, Increasing More Than $500 Million Since 2015." www.forbes.com cited 3 November 2018.

Brown, Maury. "Rainouts Impacting MLB Attendance Early in Season." www.forbes.com cited 7 September 2017.

"The Business of Baseball." www.forbes.com cited 22 September 2017.

"The Business of Baseball." www.forbes.com cited 22 September 2018.

"Clemens Hit Hard in Mitchell Report." www.si.com cited 9 November 2018.

"Colorado Rockies." www.mlb.com cited 23 September 2017.

Constantino, Rocco. "The Top 200 Moments That Shaped MLB's History." www.bleacherreport.com cited 19 October 2017.

Cronin, John. "The Historical Evolution of the Designated Hitter Rule." www.sabr.org cited 18 October 2017.

"Curt Flood Case Decided." www.history.com cited 22 August 2018.

"Deep List of Candidates Rounds Out Hall's List." www.losangeles.dodgers.mlb.com cited 30 November 2012.

"Designated Hitter." www.baseball-reference.com cited 18 October 2017.

"Designated Hitter Rule." www.mlb.com cited 18 October 2017.

"Do Pitchers Get Better After Tommy John Surgery?" www.sporttechie.com cited 19 October 2017.

Dorhauer, Adam. "The Unionization of Baseball." www.hardballtimes.com cited 16 August 2017.

Dreier, Peter. "The Fascinating Story of Major League Baseball's Players Union Stimulated by the Death of Jim Bunning." www.salon.com cited 21 August 2017.

Drellich, Evan. "MLB Changes Market Rank Formula in Revenue Sharing." www.bostonherald.com cited 29 August 2017.

Edwards, Craig. "Estimated TV for All 30 MLB Teams." www.fangraphs.com cited 6 October 2017.

Erickson, Brandon. "The Effect of the Steroid Era on Major League Baseball Hitters: Did it Enhance Hitting?" www.omicsonline.org cited 17 October 2017.

"Event Timeline: Drug Testing Policy." www.mlb.com cited 13 November 2018.

"*Federal Baseball Club v. National League.*" www.baseball-reference.com cited 16 August 2017.

"The Fields of Major League Baseball." www.ballparksofbaseball.com cited 13 October 2017.

Fish, Mike. "Bonds' Positive Steroid Test Discovered Among BALCO Evidence." www.espn.com cited 8 November 2018.

"First Televised Major League Baseball Game." www.history.com cited 16 October 2017.

"Franchise History." www.baseball-reference.com cited 8 September 2017.

"Franchise History: Major League Baseball Comes to Houston." www.wikipedia.org cited 20 September 2017.

Friedman, Wayne. "2018 MLB's TV National Ad Revenues Remain Stable." www.mediapost.com cited 3 November 2018.

Goldberg, Jeff. "MLB Ballparks, From Oldest to Newest." www.ballparkdigest.com cited 13 October 2017.

Grow, Nathaniel. "The MLBPA Has a Problem." www.fangraphs.com cited 21 August 2017.

"Grunk Very Good: A History of Baseball Statistics." www.blessyouboys.com cited 4 August 2017.

Haddock, David, and Louis Cain. "Measuring Parity: Tying Into the Idealized Standard Deviation." www.researchgate.net cited 29 October 2018.

Hagen, Paul. "Slip Slidin' Away: New Rules Music to All Ears?" www.mlb.com cited 18 October 2017.

"Historical Metropolitan Populations of the United States." www.peakbagger.com cited 13 September 2017.

"The History of Major League Ballparks." www.cnn.com cited 13 October 2017.

"How to Calculate the Noll-Scully Competitive Balance Measure." www.transportationanalysis.blogspot.com.

"The Important Events That Changed Baseball." www.timetoast.com cited 19 October 2017.

Jaffe, Jay. "If MLB Considers Expansion, What Would a 32-Team Look Like." www.si.com cited 1 November 2018.

Joseph, Andrew. "All 30 MLB Stadiums, Ranked." www.usatoday.com cited 13 October 2017.

"June 19, 1972: Flood v. Kuhn is Decided." www.blackthen.com cited 22 August 2018.

Justice, Richard. "DH Debate Picking up Steam." www.mlb.com cited 9 November 2018.

"Kansas City Royals." www.mlb.com cited 19 September 2017.

Kepner, Tyler. "New Commissioner With a Long-Term Mission." www.nytimes.com cited 9 November 2018.

Langhorst, Ben. "What Do Your Fans Want? Attendance Correlations With Performance, Ticket Prices, and Payrolls." www.sabr.org cited 8 September 2017.

Lapore, Steve. "Major League Baseball is Adrift on Television, But Will Ending 'Game of the Week' Solve the Problem?" www.sbnation.com cited 18 October 2017.

Larsen, Stevie. "The History of Early Broadcasting: Early Television." www.baseballessential.com cited 14 October 2017.

Lazlo, Rob. "How to Understand Baseball Stats in a Game." www.guysgirls.com cited 27 July 2017.

"LI." www.fangraphs.com cited 7 August 2017.

"Los Angeles Angels of Anaheim." www.wikipedia.com cited 5 September 2017.

"Major League Baseball on Television." www.wikipedia.com cited 16 October 2017.

"Major League Baseball Players Association." www.mlbpa.org cited 21 August 2017.

"Major League Baseball Players Association: Our History." www.mlbplayers.com cited 21 August 2017.

"Major League Baseball Team Rosters." www.espn.com cited 8 August 2017.

"Mariano Rivera Award." www.baseball-reference.com cited 13 November 2018.

Meltzer, Matt. "All 30 Major League Baseball Stadiums, Ranked." www.thrillist.com cited 13 October 2017.

"Milwaukee Braves." www.sportencyclopedia.com cited 6 September 2017.

"Milwaukee Brewers." www.mlb.com cited 1 September 2017.

Mitchell, Chris. "MLB Needs to Expand; Here's Where." www.fangraphs.com cited 22 November 2018.

"Mitchell Report." www.baseball-almanac.com cited 11 November 2018.

"Mitchell Report: Baseball is Called Out." www.washingtonpost.com cited 10 November 2018.

Mitrosilis, Teddy. "Foreign-Born Players in Baseball's Hall of Fame." www.thepostgame.com cited 5 November 2012.

Mitrosilis, Teddy. "Silver Slugger Award Winners—American League." www.baseball-reference.com cited 17 December 2012.

"MLB Attendance." www.baseball-reference.com cited 22 September 2017.

"MLB Attendance Reports." www.espn.com cited 6 October 2017.

"MLB Attendance & Team Age." www.baseball-reference.com cited 6 October 2017.

"MLB Attendances." www.baseball-reference.com cited 22 September 2017.

"MLB Awards." www.mlb.com cited 17 November 2017.

"MLB Data 1998 (1997 Season)." www.forbes.com cited 6 October 2017.

"MLB Franchises Revenues and Expenses." www.baseballchronology.com cited 23 August 2017.

"MLB Most Valuable Player MVP Awards & Cy Young Awards Winners." www.baseball-reference.com cited 11 August 2017.

"MLB Payrolls." www.umich.app.box.com cited 31 August 2017.

"MLB Players Association Hires Sports Litigation Expert Meyer." www.foxsports.com cited 21 November 2018.

"MLB Rookie of the Year Awards." www.baseball-reference.com cited 11 August 2017.

"MLB Team Attendances." www.baseballpilgramages.com cited 28 August 2017.

"MLB TV Revenue–Santa Claus Keeps Coming to Town." www.foxsports.com cited 3 November 2018.

"MLB's Most Valuable Television Deals." www.forbes.com cited 3 November 2018.

"MLBPA, MLB Announce Pace-of-Game Initiatives, Replay Modifications." www.mlb.com cited 18 October 2017.

"Montreal Expos." www.baseballalmanac.com cited 21 September 2017.

"Montreal Expos." www.mlb.com cited 10 September 2017.

"Montreal Expos: Team History." www.baseball-reference.com cited 6 October 2017.

"National Baseball Hall of Fame and Museum." www.wikipedia.org cited 30 November 2012.

"National League Ballparks." www.ballparksofbaseball.com cited 24 September 2018.

"National League Gold Glove Award Winners." www.baseball-reference.com cited 23 December 2012.

"New York Yankees." www.baseball-reference.com cited 6 October 2017.

"New York Yankees." www.mlb.com cited 6 October 2017.

Newman, Mark. "MLBAM Introduces New Way to Analyze Every Play." www.m.mlb.com cited 27 July 2017.

Nomandin, Marc. "50 Years Ago, Marvin Miller and the MLBPA Changed Sports Forever." www.sbnation.com cited 21 August 2018.

"Opening Day Rosters Feature Record 259 Players Born Outside the U.S." www.mlb.com cited 9 August 2017.

Ozanian, Michael. "Are MLB Fans Getting a Raw Deal From Revenue Sharing?" www.forbes.com cited 29 August 2017.

"Performance-Enhancing Drugs in Baseball: A Timeline." www.cleveland.com cited 15 November 2018.

Perry, Dan. "MLB Seems to Think Its Broadcast Audience is More Important Than Fans at the Ballpark." www.cbssports.com cited 3 November 2018.

Pincince, Zach. "Understanding Advanced Baseball Stats: Hitting." www.baseballessential.com cited 27 July 2017.

"Players Protective Association." www.baseball-reference.com cited 16 August 2017.

"Population of the 100 Largest Urban Areas: 1870–1900." www.census.gov cited 15 September 2017.

Randall, Dakota. "MILB President Thinks MLB 'Will Happen' But 'Not Imminent'." www.nesn.com cited 1 November 2018.

"Ranking All 30 MLB Ballparks." www.nbcsports.com cited 13 October 2017.

"Rawlings Gold Glove Award." www.wikipedia.org cited 23 December 2012.

"Recommendations From the Mitchell Commission Report." www.espn.com cited 9 November 2018.

"Report: Manny, Ortiz Tested Positive." www.espn.com cited 17 October 2017.

"Revenue Sharing." www.fangraphs.com cited 29 August 2017.

Ringolsby, Tracy. "Expansion Could Trigger Realignment, Longer Postseason." www.baseballamerica.com cited 22 November 2018.

Rismondo, Rene. "May 19, 1970: Flood v. Kuhn Begins in Federal Court." www.mlbplayers.com cited 22 August 2018.

"Rodney Fort's Sports Business Data." www.umich.app.box.com cited 6 October 2017.

"Rolaids Relief Award." www.baseball-reference.com cited 21 November 2018.

"San Diego Padres." www.mlb.com cited 22 September 2017.

"San Francisco Giants." www.mlb.com cited 6 September 2017.

Schell, Richard. "SABR, Baseball Statistics, and Computing: The Last Forty Years." www.sabr.org cited 4 August 2017.

Schmidt, Michael. "Ortiz and Ramirez Said to be on '03 Doping List." www.nytimes.com cited 17 October 2017.

Schwartz, Alan. "A Numbers Revolution." www.espn.com cited 27 July 2017.

Schwartz, Alan. "Baseball Statistics and Analysis." www.fangraphs.com cited 4 August 2017.

"Seattle Mariners." www.baseball-reference.com cited 19 September 2017.

Shaheen, Mansur. "Major League Baseball Unveils Official Rule Changes for 2017 Season." www.sbnation.com cited 18 October 2017.

Sheinin, David, and Mark Asher. "Baseball Owners Vote to Eliminate Two Teams." www.washingtonpost.com cited 22 August 2017.

"The Silver Slugger Award." www.baseball-reference.com cited 1 March 2013.

"Silver Slugger Award." www.wikipedia.org cited 23 December 2012.

"Silver Slugger Award Winners—American League." www.baseball-reference.com cited 17 December 2012.

"Silver Slugger Award Winners—National League." www.baseball-reference.com cited 23 December 2012.

Snyder, Matt. "Watch: Clemens Goes Hard After the Mitchell Report, Makes Strong Accusations." www.espn.com cited 10 November 2018.

"Sports and Drugs." www.sfgate.com cited 8 November 2018.

"Sports Biographies." www.hickoksports.com cited 1 December 2012.

"St. Louis Browns." www.baseballlibrary.com cited 1 September 2017.

"Tampa Bay Rays." www.mlb.com cited 20 September 2017.

"Teams." www.mlb.com cited 8 September 2017.

"Tip O'Neill Award." www.baseball-reference.com cited 1 March 2013.

"Toronto Blue Jays." www.baseball-reference.com cited 19 September 2017.

"Toronto Blue Jays." www.mlb.com cited 6 October 2017.

"Toronto Blue Jays Team History and Encyclopedia." www.baseball-reference.com cited 6 October 2017.

"Trevor Hoffman Award." www.baseball-reference.com cited 13 November 2018.

"Ulnar Collateral Ligament Reconstruction (Tommy John Surgery) in the Throwing Athlete." www.orlandoortho.com cited 19 November 2017.

Verducci, Tom. "The Numbers—and the Truth—About Baseball's PED Problems and Why it May Never go Away." www.si.com cited 17 October 2017.

Voort, Bart van der. "Measuring Balance of American Leagues." www.competitive-balance.blogspot.com.

"Washington Nationals." www.wikipedia.com cited 10 September 2017.

"Washington Senators." www.baseball-reference.com cited 19 September 2017.

Weiner, Evan. "Lou Perini Should be in Baseball's Hall of Fame With Walter O'Malley." www.mcnsports.com cited 7 September 2017.

Weiner, Evan. "MLB Expansion is on the Table." www.thesportdigest.com cited 1 November 2018.

Wells, Adam. "Full List of MLB Rule Changes for 2017 Season." www.bleacherreport.com cited 18 October 2017.

"What is the Hardball Times?" www.hardballtimes.com cited 7 August 2017.

Witz, Billy. "Winning Yankees Aren't Faring Nearly as Well at the Box Office." www.nytimes.com cited 8 September 2017.

Womack, Graham. "Tommy John on Baseball Hall of Fame: "I'm Being Held Back." www.sportingnews.com cited 19 October 2017.

"World Series History." www.baseball-almanac.com cited 18 September 2017.

"wRAA." www.fangraphs.com cited 7 August 2017.

Zellner, Ben. "A History and Overview of Tommy John Surgery." www.osmsgb.com cited 19 October 2017.

Zepfel, Evan. "Have MLB's Efforts to Preserve Competitive Balance Done Enough?" www.harvardsportsanalysis.org cited 29 August 2017.

MEDIA GUIDES

Official Major League Baseball Fact Book 2005 Edition (St. Louis, MO: Sporting News, 2005).

INDEX

B

C

D

F

G

H

J

L

M

N

O

P

R

S

T

V

W

Y

ABOUT THE AUTHOR

A former college and semiprofessional athlete with an undergraduate degree in accounting, masters' degrees in business administration and economics, and a doctorate in economics, **Frank P. Jozsa Jr.** is the author of several books on team sports in professional baseball, basketball, and football, and others on intercollegiate sports programs and the role and progress of male and female student athletes on campuses of American colleges and universities. His memoir, *A Hoosier's Journey: Athlete, Student, Teacher, and Author* was published by Dog Ear Publishing in 2011.

Besides books, Jozsa has published several articles in journals, magazines, and newspapers. His dissertation, "An Economic Analysis of Franchise Relocation and League Expansion in Professional Team Sports, 1950–1975," was completed in 1977 at Georgia State University in Atlanta, Georgia. After teaching undergraduate and graduate courses in business administration, economics, finance, and statistics for more than three decades, Jozsa retired from Pfeiffer University in 2007.

CREDITS

Cover and interior design: Annika Naas

Layout: Zerosoft

Cover photos:
Left: From the US Library of Congress Prints and Photographs Division, released into the public domain by Cowles Communications, Inc.
Middle: From the Edison National Historic Site archives, as part of the National Parks Service. No protection is claimed in original U.S. Government works.
Right: © dpa

Graphics: © AdobeStock

Managing editor: Elizabeth Evans

Copyeditor: Anne Rumery

FROM MEYER & MEYER SPORT

JORGENSEN/JORGENSEN

GO, GWEN, GO

A FAMILY'S JOURNEY TO OLYMPIC GOLD

312 p., b/w
24 photos as color insert
Hardcover, 6 x 9"
ISBN: 9781782551911
$24.95 US

Narrated in alternating voices by mother Nancy and sister Elizabeth, Go, Gwen, Go is an inspiring story about Olympian Gwen Jorgensen and her family.

This memoir introduces a young woman of modest athletic achievements who uses desire and discipline to attain the ultimate in sport—the Olympic Gold. You will enter the secret world of Olympic training, professional coaching, international travel, sponsor funding, anti-doping requirements, athlete nutrition, and sports physiotherapy. You will be granted an inside look at the personal life of a professional athlete, complete with family crises and holiday celebrations.

In this inspiring story, Gwen Jorgensen and her family grow together, from average to Olympian.

MEYER & MEYER Sport
Von-Coels-Str. 390
52080 Aachen
Germany

Phone +49 02 41 - 9 58 10 - 13
Fax +49 02 41 - 9 58 10 - 10
E-Mail sales@m-m-sports.com
Website www.thesportspublisher.com